TALENT *and* GENIUS

TALENT
and
GENIUS

The Fictitious Case
of Tausk contra Freud

K. R. EISSLER

QUADRANGLE BOOKS

A NEW YORK TIMES COMPANY

CONTENTS

PREFACE

IF ONE MAY be permitted to sketch highly complicated historical processes in broad strokes, I would venture to outline the development of psychology, which led to a peak in the first half of the present century, in the following way. During the course of the eighteenth century, Western man woke up to the perception, discernment and enjoyment of psychological details of a subtlety and refinement such as the world had not known before. This, I believe, was brought about far more by Mozart's music than by the poetry of that time. The exquisite enlargement of responsiveness to human emotionality and detail that could be implied only in the musical medium became explicit in the great psychological novels of nineteenth-century France and Russia, concomitantly with the new philosophies of Schopenhauer and Nietzsche. One should also think here of the portraits of Goya and the French impressionists.

It could not fail to happen that the new psychological understanding of man that had already imbued music, art, literature and philosophy became the subject as well of scientific psychology. This was the accomplishment of Freud. Such eminence had to be followed, of course, by a decline. With Richard Strauss (1864–

1949) music reflecting the human world vanished. The psychological novel found its last representative in Proust (1871–1922). Heidegger (1889–19) once again turned full face toward pure metaphysics. Auguste Rodin (1840–1917) was the last sculptor of human woes, passions and felicities.

What now dominates music, art and literature is dehumanized abstractions, which are of crushing proportions when they are wielded by a towering mind. At the center lies the alleged discovery that human existence is senseless—something that was already known to ancient Greek tragedians, as well as to Shakespeare and Goethe. Psychoanalysis never did recover from the loss of its founder: discoveries in the fields of the dream and of sex are nowadays made in dehumanized laboratories that conduct investigations.

What the future of psychoanalysis or psychology in general will be is a matter of speculation. Will the felicitous conjunction of *Zeitgeist* and an eminent mind, such as happened during the decades before and after the turn of the century, be repeated? Will psychology once again make a leap forward, as significant as the one that Freud brought about?

At present psychoanalysis is under heavy attack. It is regarded as being outdated, even obsolete, elitist and a hindrance to social progress. However out of place such criticism may be, an optimist could assign to the present fashion a possibly constructive effect —if only it did not lead to a temporary degeneration of psychotherapy. After all, psychoanalysis prevailed for five decades—an unusually long time in the field of science. It may be that the new can arise only when the old—rightly or wrongly—has been debased and defamed. Yet, challenging as it would be to make the broad range of present-day arguments against psychoanalysis the center of an inquiry and to discuss their meaning historically, sociologically and psychologically, this book is devoted to one of the more subordinate avenues of attack. It has become fashionable these days to question Freud's character and personality. Western tradition has in general dealt with the phenomenon of genius in two contradictory ways. One has met genius with mistrust, equating it almost with psychopathology; the other has idealized genius, declaring it to be free from any form of psychopathology. It seems difficult to conceptualize genius as sharing human weaknesses with all other mortals and nevertheless as being essentially different from them. This lack of subtlety in the understanding of genius, however, must be viewed in the light of the general decline of psychology, which manifests itself with increasing explicitness as the century approaches its end.

The defamation of Freud's personality is not a new approach toward psychoanalysis, but I have the impression that it has been gaining in momentum. Whereas this had previously been a matter of mere mud-slinging, now it is done with the added pretense of using "documentary evidence." Moreover, in earlier years the defamation of Freud was always combined with the complete rejection of psychoanalysis proper; now it is fashionable to stress Freud's genius, only in order to hit him all the harder. Another variant is to concede at least some single area of originality, a concession that makes the intimation of plagiarism all the more effective. The now oft-repeated criticism of plagiarism must be all the more surprising for those who for decades have been hearing that psychoanalysis is a composite of the fantasies of Freud and his adherents—and nothing more.

In view of the numerous errors and inaccuracies that are usually to be discovered in such efforts, one may conjecture that here one is dealing with a resistance against psychoanalysis. No doubt a person who would accept as valid such descriptions of Freud's personality as are now current in some quarters, would also evolve doubts about the validity of Freud's discoveries. Although there is in fact no correlation between the type and severity of a genius's psychopathology and the quality of his achievement, most people react like the critic who recently said that, after learning the background of Richard Wagner's relationship to Mathilde Wesendonk, he was no longer able to enjoy the five songs that the master had composed for her poems, and that he was certain this would happen to anyone else. I conjecture that in the same way a good many of the attacks against Freud's personality are aimed at discrediting psychoanalysis itself.

Whenever I read such a biographical attempt, I am over and over again reminded of a saying that is attributed to Johann Nestroy (1801–1862), an Austrian writer of charming comedies: "I think the worst of every human, even of myself—and I have rarely been deceived by doing so." It is delightful to encounter this anticipation of what is, to a certain extent, one aspect of psychoanalysis, presented in this witty, even though vulgarized form.

Some of Freud's would-be biographers do not hesitate to apply the first part of Nestroy's principle to their subject but, of course, they never heed the second. They take it for granted that any incident meant just what the new "psychoanalytic common sense," brought about by the popularization of Freud's findings, would seem to suggest. Sometimes they even go beyond that. Moreover, Nestroy did not let us know whether he thought of the "worst" in terms of actions or of motives. After all—and this is rather readily forgotten—psychoanalysis has never doubted the existence of heroism or charitableness, wisdom or altruism. Motives, meanings and origins—that is just the area into which psychoanalysis has brought new light. Yet, in some instances that I shall discuss, the biographer in question did not even limit himself to deducing, without documentation, that a slip or something like it reflected a certain unconscious process; he expressed the certainty that it was a sign of corresponding action. Indeed, such biographical attempts —if they deserve to be called biographical at all—reveal more about the author than they do about the subject to whom they are ostensibly devoted.

What gives away their intent is the frequency of their mistakes when they quote from Freud's writings—mistakes that cannot possibly be ascribed to the unavoidable inadvertence that victimizes even the most scrupulous scholars. Prof. Percival Bailey, a fierce opponent of Freud, asserted (1956, p. 392) that "Freud tells us, in one of his letters to Fliess, that he stopped reading because he found his own ideas expressed better than he could." No such letter was to be found, of course, but five years later Prof. Bailey (1961, p. 216) published his "proof." Unbelievable as it may sound, that proof was fabricated by putting into direct sequence two sentences that were drawn from two letters separated in the sequence of their writing by over two and a half years and by 136 pages in the publication. The contexts in which the separate sentences stood did not provide any evidence for Prof. Bailey's claim.

In the same way, Prof. Roazen in his book, the disproof of

which will fill a good many pages of what follows, made himself guilty of unconscionable breaches of basic rules of quoting, culminating at least once in his "quoting" the very opposite of what Freud had actually said.

There is honor even among thieves, as a man from whom I had expected a particularly dastardly transgression assured me. The reader who is not expert is at the mercy of the author, when the latter puts a sentence into quotation marks. Honor requires a maximal scrupulousness: once the reader cannot rely on quotations, the whole transaction is bound to go into bankruptcy. Yet it is not without interest that even "expert readers," as can be seen from some of the reviews I shall have to quote, were deceived by what I would like to call "the charisma of the quotation mark."

Another observation has impressed me greatly about the book in question. Prof. Roazen occasionally seems to have drawn a winning card in his game of derogating Freud, when he appears to prove a proposition by quoting the correct sequence of words, as they are printed in the *Standard Edition* of Freud's psychological writings. In almost all instances of this sort, this was possible because Mr. Strachey had been imprecise in his translation. The original text does not, however, support Prof. Roazen's proposition. What does it mean when Prof. Roazen's construction of a Freud-image is based on a selection of precisely those passages that were imprecisely translated? This alone seems to me to prove that he was essentially on the wrong track.

A historical process takes its relentless course and the average man is unable to give its drift a different direction; at best, he can merely slow down its speed. It is not probable that the present book will reach all those who have already accepted the content of Prof. Roazen's book as fairly accurate; but if it does succeed in reaching at least a few of them, I make bold to believe that the speed of the present decline of psychoanalysis's prestige may be abated—even though that slowing down may be perceptible only in an almost imperceptible compass.

All the more I am indebted to Mr. Herbert Nagourney for having readily accepted my manuscript for publication.

I further owe greatest thanks to Harold Collins for his faithful devotion to and great effort in editing the manuscript. Most of the translations which appear in the text as the author's, I owe to his great literary skills;

To Herbert F. Fuerst for having searched in Viennese and other newspapers for material pertinent to the subject-matter of this book;

To Lottie Newman for an important suggestion regarding the title;

To the late Dr. Herman Nunberg and to Mr. Ernst Federn for having given me permission to read the unpublished parts of the *Minutes of the Vienna Psychoanalytic Society*, which contain references to Victor Tausk;

To Dr. Thomas Menaker for valuable suggestions, after having read part of the manuscript;

To Miss Liselotte Bendix (Mrs. Max Stern) for her help in providing badly needed books;

To Mrs. Phyllis Rubinton for excellent bibliographical advice;

To Dr. Mary O'Neil Hawkins for her great patience in listening to the major part of the manuscript and giving substantive advice;

To Ronald Hudson, who was kind enough to comb the manuscript for those unavoidable inaccuracies and oversights that are the perennial headache of every author.

Others from whose assistance I have benefited will be gratefully mentioned in the text.

K. R. E.

New York City

December 24, 1970

All translations of texts that refer to the meetings of the Vienna Psychoanalytic Society dated later than June 1910 are my own. References in the text to the two volumes, *Minutes of the Vienna Psychoanalytic Society*, ed. by Herman Nunberg and Ernst Federn, are abbreviated as *Minutes 1* or *Minutes 2*.

References to Jones' biography of Freud do not contain the year of publication. Thus Jones (1, p. 15) refers to the first volume of that biography.

INTRODUCTION

THE BOOK *Brother Animal,* by Paul Roazen, a professor at Harvard, published in 1969 by Alfred A. Knopf, a distinguished publisher, and favorably reviewed by such persons as Arthur Koestler and Maxwell Geismar, both outsiders to psychoanalysis, compels me to enter into a polemic against it. The late Dr. Max Schur, who was Freud's personal physician and who had finished a carefully detailed study of one critical phase in Freud's life, the Fliess period, was ready to write a critical review of this book when death cruelly annulled his intention. He would have been far better prepared for that task than I am. I never met Freud and I know little more about his life than does any reader who has studied the pertinent literature.

How this happens to be the case, although I have been the secretary of the Sigmund Freud Archives since their inception, I shall not go into here. Since the Archives are supported financially by the contributions of many psychoanalysts, however, it was suggested, after Dr. Schur's death, that I look into what is true and what is untrue in Roazen's book.

I carry out with reluctance what some consider to be my duty, because I am convinced of the futility of the undertaking.

To write positively about Freud in our times is to incur more often than not the comment that a positive transference—and, in my particular instance, perhaps an inner necessity to glorify genius —has made many of one's conclusions *prima facie* untrustworthy. No heed will probably be taken of the extensive documentation I have offered—which, if anything, is likely to strike the reader as being merely tiresome. On the other hand, an *aperçu* by the late Ernst Kris seems still to harbor some truth. As he suggested, if someone wants to become well known these days and to obtain a quick success, he has only to write against Freud.

The central theme of Roazen's book is Freud's relationship to Victor Tausk (1879–1919), who met Freud in 1908, became a successful psychoanalyst, and committed suicide in 1919, at the age of 40. Roazen's central thesis is that it was Freud who was ultimately responsible for Tausk's untimely death.

If my assignment had been to comment only on what is true in Roazen's book, a short essay would have sufficed. The improbable and undocumented conclusions Roazen has drawn, the misrepresentation of information allegedly given to him, the distortion by way of omissions in quotations, the outright wrong quotations—any of these alone, and certainly all of them taken together, make this a painful book to read. It is, indeed, a book that one wishes one had not ever had to read.

The only compensation I find in the ugly and wearisome necessity of having to occupy myself with it is that I have been able to place my repellent task into a broader context, which will give me the opportunity to discuss a few problems having to do with the differences between talent and genius.

I face a difficult problem in deciding how far to go in carrying out the critical portion of my exposition. Roazen's denigration of Freud culminates in an implication that, if correct, would make Freud not only unworthy of respect, but guilty of having neglected his duty and abused his standing as a physician and psychoanalyst—and this for selfish, petty and vengeful reasons. As will be seen, there is indisputable evidence—accessible without great difficulty to Roazen—that *prima facie* shatters the wild construction that he presents.

That alone should dispel any trust the reader might otherwise have in the author's reliability and objectivity, with regard to the many traits and features that he ascribes to Freud. Yet the Romans knew all too well what they meant with their *semper aliquid haeret*; and many a reader of Roazen's book may feel that, even if the author was indeed wrong in his major point, and no matter how grievous his error may have been in that regard, there must be some truth to the many negative traits in Freud's character that he ostensibly documents by the use of Freud's own works and letters, as well as by some quotations from Fritz Wittels' book (1923).

It is particularly the latter who would seem to confirm wide areas of the author's position, since Wittels was a close collaborator of Freud during the early years. Yet it is precisely here that one is able to observe Roazen's negligence, for he ignores the fact —thereby leaving the unwary reader altogether at his mercy— that Wittels (1933) *corrected* the "errors and misrepresentations" in his book (1923), in a long article that has been published twice in this country. He himself called "the tone of the book throughout a striking example of ambivalence," and recognized that his book would be "welcome to all who seek rationalization for their own ambivalent attitude toward psychoanalysis"— and toward Freud, I daresay.

Furthermore, the reader of a book written by a Harvard professor and published by a first-rate publisher would probably never suspect the extent of Roazen's irresponsible documentation. I therefore have no choice but to take up at least some of the worst literary felonies he has committed.

I am fully aware of the weakness that is inherent in a book of this kind. I can only agree with one publisher, who wrote me after reading part of the manuscript: "I can imagine some book reviewer suggesting that the Roazen book was not good enough, to begin with, for such a serious and passionate rebuttal in book-length form. . . . It might be said that you have stacked your argument for Freud, as it is now, against a poor adversary. In contrast, Freud seems overdefended."

Correct as this comment may be, in this instance I believe that it is desirable to write a rebuttal that centers on this one book, for even some reviewers whose names are to be found in the roster of the International Psychoanalytic Association have taken a stand in favor of Roazen's book.[1] This was assuredly due not only to their ignorance of the facts in the case, but also to the reader's tendency to trust the writer who makes use of "documents" in his text.

A curious incident of this sort illustrates the stultifying effect that the sham use of documentary evidence may have on readers. The Gicklhorns published (1960) an important volume of documents regarding Freud's academic career. As is by now well known, Freud had to wait for an unusually long period before receiving the title of professor, even though the number and quality of his publications would have entitled him to this academic advancement much earlier. In the Introduction to their collection of documents the authors adduced, among many reasons intended to justify the tardiness of the University and Government, the "fact" that Freud was desirous of obtaining the title —which at that time almost guaranteed an adequate practice— for the purpose of increasing his income, diminished by the fearfully dwindling number of his patients. The Ministry was not interested, the authors asserted, in assigning a professorship to someone who wanted it primarily for "the purpose of collecting higher fees from patients" (Gicklhorn and Gicklhorn 1960, p. 28. My own translation). Sherwood (1962), who reviewed Gicklhorn's book, was apparently so overwhelmed by the quasi-hypnotic effect of documents that he agreed with the authors on this point and even spoke of Freud's "intent to concentrate on private practice admittedly for the sake of lucre" (p. 236).

I do not cite this passage in order to demonstrate the sort of vulgarity to which Freud's name is still occasionally exposed, but to expose the inefficiency of the reviewer, for he did not notice that Freud's alleged "love of lucre" is "known" only from his letters to his friend Wilhelm Fliess. Since censorship of letters was not practiced even in the reactionary Monarchy, it would have been impossible for anyone in the government, or the University hierarchy, to have known of Freud's urgent need of the

---

[1] The harsh words I use throughout the book to criticize many of the psychoanalytic reviews that came to my attention do not apply to the excellent review by Dr. William Niederland (*J. Hist. Behav. Science*, 7:100–105, 1971), which reached me after I had completed the manuscript.

title for the sake of economic survival. Thus, Freud's need of the title for economic reasons cannot have had the slightest bearing on the delay.

I could not help thinking of the temporary diminution of the powers of ratiocination that Sherwood suffered under the impact of documents, when I read a review of Roazen's book by Peter Lomas, who informed the readers of *The New York Times Book Review* on October 12, 1969 that Roazen's reconstruction was based on the "detailed scrutiny of innumerable documents." This is exactly the impression Roazen creates—and not only among psychoanalytically-trained reviewers. At this point, I shall only state that the material Roazen published that was previously unavailable to the general reader covered no more than the following: two letters that Tausk wrote to Freud; Tausk's last will; one letter that Freud wrote to Silberer, another of his pupils; a letter from the late Dr. Paul Federn to his wife, and one sentence from another letter. Excerpts from ten letters of Tausk (nine of which antedate Tausk's acquaintance with Freud) are not really relevant to Roazen's main construction, although one day, when published *in extenso* and in their original language, they may facilitate the exact diagnosis of the disorder from which Tausk suffered during his stay in Berlin (see below).

Thus even an experienced reviewer was led astray by Roazen's creating an illusion of honest and serious research, which seemed to draw on a huge number of documents, but which actually *concealed* the facts. The reviewers were unaware that Roazen had ignored many published documents that were most pertinent to the explanation of Tausk's suicide (to these I shall refer extensively). In addition, Roazen missed the boat inasmuch as he did not succeed in discovering the true reason that at least triggered, probably even caused, Tausk's suicide, which I shall discuss at its proper place. Yet, when even psychoanalysts who present themselves to the reading public as experts in psychoanalytic theory, practice, and history, let themselves be misled by Roazen's apparently convincing way of presenting his many errors and wrong inferences, what is to be expected of the general reader? Will he not be all the more likely to close Roazen's book with the conviction that what he has read has been proven by well-documented evidence?

It was precisely the fact that an unsuspecting reader would hardly be able to escape feeling certain that Roazen has "proven" his point—any more than the general reader of the book by the Gicklhorns could ever guess the extent of their misrepresentations—that made me think that those few readers who are less interested in the sensational than in historical truth ought to have an opportunity to correct errors that have been imposed upon them by a combination of a negligent author and ignorant reviewers.

Right at the beginning, however, I wish to set forth the essential point I have in mind. Except for one paragraph, the book ascribes to Freud a kind of psychopathology most of which might have been expected in a genius like Freud, or perhaps in anyone who lived under his life circumstances. His genius was sufficiently great for one to expect from him severe psychopathology in the area of possible plagiarism. After all, did not Newton spend half his life in just such a fight? Would one not also have the right to expect Freud to tyrannize the early group that surrounded him and to expect total surrender of their mental autonomy, as Newton did when he was president of the Royal Society? The puzzling aspect of Freud's life is that he did *not* show the psychopathology that is to be observed, more frequently than not, in men of his creative stature.

By ignoring what was truly the problem in Freud's life history, Roazen has not only lured his readers, as well as future biographers of Freud, onto the wrong track, but he has also desecrated Freud's memory. Freud was a man who, despite formidable and at times even unruly passions, learned in his earlier years to establish in himself such discipline and mastery that he was able to harness his unique creativity to the service of mankind, and to cause only that minimal damage and pain to others without which human existence is impossible.

I

QUESTIONABLE

BIOGRAPHICAL TECHNIQUES

IF SOMEONE at present—as had happened not too infrequently in the past—were to describe Freud in consistently abject terms, he would not arouse much interest thereby. Since his death, Freud has gained enormously in stature and respect, and such a description would be regarded as reactionary and biased in the sophisticated circles from which the majority of the readers of such books derive. If, however, Freud's achievements are presented as those of a genius, and the starting point of the presentation contains positive statements, then there is an excellent chance that the general reader may not object if negative terms are gradually slipped into the profile, even if these should finally destroy all the preceding positive statements. One cannot deny Roazen's brilliance in gaining the reader's confidence and leading him by small steps to the abyss. He creates in his book a "new look" of Freud's personality. I shall critically discuss in the following some of the methods he uses to accomplish this.

One of the techniques used by him, for example, is the innuendo. Lou Andreas-Salomé described her meeting Freud in 1912 as the turning point of her life. Twenty-three years later, Freud made the remark that he wrote *Totem and Taboo* in 1912,

when he was (my own translation) "already in the midst of the
plateau in my psychoanalytic work" ("*Bereits mitten auf der
Höhe der psychoanalytischen Arbeit*," literally "already amidst
the height of the psychoanalytic work"). What can the author
(p. 33) make out of this obviously neutral statement? It clearly
has nothing to do with the "climax" of Strachey's incorrect translation (Freud 1935, p. 72). Yet Roazen writes: "Perhaps not entirely by chance, Freud also later wrote that 1912 had been 'the
very climax of my psychoanalytic work.'" Since nothing happens
"entirely by chance," one cannot object to such statements.

One could perhaps say that an author is not to be held responsible when he is the victim of a wrong translation. But the
context of the passage, in which Freud (1935, p. 72) describes "a
regressive development"—which took him as an analyst back to
youthful interests—makes it clear that he cannot possibly have
meant a "climax." Furthermore, in a footnote (p. 210, n. 18)
Roazen adds: "1912 was also a critical year in Freud's falling out
with Jung." If the author had not limited himself to making an
innuendo—such as "perhaps not by chance"—but had instead
taken a position that would have necessitated documentation, it
would quickly have become evident that the three events had no
meaningful connection whatsoever. By keeping the matter on the
level of innuendo, however, he succeeds in producing subliminal
associations in the reader's mind, such as: the climax of Freud's
productivity was caused by his heightened feeling for a woman,
which also forced him to start a quarrel with a rival—all of which
is a splendid preparation for the author's "final kill."

I want to present one instance of how, by making a "slight"
change in the original, innocuous as it may appear, Roazen brings
the reader closer to accepting the false image he has formed of
Freud. He asserts (p. 36) "that Freud saw it as his task to 'disturb
the peace of the world'" (emphasis added). What sort of person
sets it as his task to carry unrest into the world? It is usually the
psychopath or sociopath (as one calls him nowadays)—someone
who feels frustrated in a smoothly-running, well-regulated world.

Freud, in his published works, twice brought up the matter to
which Roazen refers. The first time was in a historical paper
(1914a, p. 21), wherein he spoke of the community's reaction to
his discoveries, which he "treated . . . as ordinary contributions

to science and hoped they would be received in the same spirit." Yet from the reactions that actually did emerge, Freud was forced to recognize that he had become "one of those who have 'disturbed the sleep of the world.'"

Three years later, toward the end of his eighteenth "Introductory Lecture," Freud (1916–1917, p. 285) explained "the general revolt against our science" as a consequence of the "wounding blow" that "human megalomania" had suffered from the proof that "the ego is not even master in its own house." But soon he would have to discuss with his audience an even greater "offense" (his discoveries about man's sexual life), and for that he wanted to prepare his listeners; he therefore closed that lecture as follows: "And beyond all this we have yet to disturb the peace of this world in still another way, as you will shortly hear." [1]

It is evident from this that Freud never expressed the idea that it was his task to *offend* the world—a view that would undoubtedly justify serious doubts about the objectivity of his conclusions. Most painfully, and to his surprise, he had to learn that, even in modern times, scientific inquiries may incur the anger and even the wrath of society, if their results do not fall into traditional patterns but rather have the effect of upsetting them.

Another of Roazen's *modi operandi* is to add to statements that might otherwise evoke in the reader a sympathetic view of Freud a negative qualifying term which is not documented and may even strike the reader as requiring no documentation, since it occurs within a factual framework. When Roazen reports, for example, that Freud was generous with money, "always living quite modestly himself" (p. 26), he then calls the money that Freud gave to at least five pupils "loans," although I do not recall having read anywhere that such sums were ever paid back. At least, as the author himself reports, the money given to Tausk was not repaid, and Freud even refused to be reimbursed by Tausk's son, at a time when he was himself in dire need of financial support. Furthermore, Roazen adds: "Freud used money impersonally, for the sake of the cause" (p. 26)—a seemingly unim-

---

[1] Mr. Collins called my attention to a letter (Binswanger 1956, p. 35) where this is stated earlier and with greater forcefulness. Freud wrote in 1911 to Binswanger: "It has become my *fate* to 'disturb the peace of the world'" (emphasis added). (The phrase was Hebbel's.)

portant little pinprick, but once again preparation for the final picture of Freud that he leaves with the reader, of a narcissistic personality, devoid of charity for and empathy with others.

Yet the literature contains examples of Freud's spontaneous gifts, not loans, quite personal and divorced from any "cause." One instance is noted in Jones's biography (3, p. 88). It occurred in 1922—that is to say, at an age at which, the author maintains, Freud's humanity had been greatly reduced. The son of an old servant had shot his father. Although Freud did not know the youth, he engaged a lawyer and paid all the legal expenses. It may interest the reader that such disbursements were not tax-deductible. Another instance, mentioned in an English publication, was reported by the recipient himself almost half a century after the event (Goetz 1952). In these reminiscences, Goetz recalls how, as a young, impecunious student, he came to consult Freud because of headaches, and how Freud slipped into his hand, before he left, an envelope containing 200 Kronen which apparently amounted to Freud's full day's earnings. This, however, occurred during the first decade of the century, a time at which the author would perhaps concede that Freud was still in full possession of humane feelings.

Be that as it may, it belies the author's malicious remark (p. 105) that, in 1919, when foreigners came to Freud for analysis: "With foreign currency Freud could now afford to be Zeus" (Roazen maintains that Freud had, before the war, already identified with the Greek god, and he therefore gives one chapter the title of "Zeus").

The two instances of Freud's spontaneous charity that I have mentioned were rescued from oblivion only by chance. Apparently Freud was not given to making much ado about his "good" deeds, and some of his previous biographers, such as Fromm, did not painstakingly comb the literature for testimony in that regard. It is true, of course, that testimony directed against Freud arouses more attention; yet it is reasonable to ask how often Freud might have been charitable to people, independently of "the cause." Was Bruno Goetz the one single instance among all of Freud's patients?

We know for sure that Freud derived an exquisite pleasure from the giving of gifts. When he wrote to his lifelong friend, Rie:

"To many I have been, apart from you, permitted to give some-thing; from you fate has let me only take" (my own translation),[2] I believe he described correctly his life's balance between giving and receiving.

Quite generally, Roazen takes it for granted that Freud was hardly able to have a naturally kindly, friendly emotion, or any other than a narcissistic impulse to help others. When Freud helped Felix and Helene Deutsch during their grievous years of starvation, by getting the late Dr. Felix Deutsch a job with the English authority in Austria, he did it, says Roazen, "as part of his effort to woo them both" (p. 76); he "went out of his way to win . . . favor" with Dr. Deutsch (p. 94f). The same line of derogation is pursued when he writes (p. 74): "Freud was ex-tremely flattered by every outsider who came to him." I have lost count of just how often Freud felt "flattered" in the author's account, but he uses the word profusely. Not once, however, does he find it necessary to document such allegations as "wooing" and "flattering."

Another trait the author attributes to Freud is vanity, even though he asserts (p. 38) that Freud was "able to transpose his vanity onto the movement he led." When he introduces Freud, Roazen mentions that Freud was of medium height, and gives the exact number of feet and inches. This may at first strike the reader as a superfluous detail, in a story of which the central issue is the tragic fate of one of Freud's pupils. But later on we are told (p. 165) that Jung and Tausk were "extremely tall," "much larger than Freud". This appears in a context that once again, by in-nuendo, must give the reader the impression that vanity had its share in Freud's dealing with Jung as well, since the next para-graph maintains that "the same issue of priority" (as with Tausk) played its part in Freud's break with Jung.

To be sure, from Socrates to Churchill, geniuses have been,

---

[2] Here Freud presents his good deeds not as an asset of his character, but rather touchingly as a sign of fate's grace. Simon (1957, p. 281) sees in the evaluation of charity as a *privilege for the giver* a typical element of Jewish tradi-tion. A similar attitude was expressed by Goethe in a letter to Krafft who felt scruples about being the recipient of Goethe's extensive charity over many years: "It is rather a charity of God when for once He bids us relieve someone truly miserable, since one can so rarely help" (November 23, 1778).

statistically, of medium height; and one could even say, perhaps, that the taller the man, the less his prospects of becoming a genius—an observation for which both Jung and Tausk might well serve as examples. Yet the way in which the author tries to prove that "Freud was sensitive about his height" is noteworthy. He not only cites the group photograph taken at the Psychoanalytic Congress at Weimar in 1911, but emphasizes it by reproducing one portion of the photograph with the explanation: "Jung can be seen crouching forward next to Freud. Mounted on a box, the master stands out as the leader of his group" (p. 165). The insinuations of this sentence do not need to be spelled out: one can imagine Freud scurrying around in Weimar, shouting: "A box! A box! My kingdom for a box!"

At least the author should have had the courtesy to let us know what stimulated Freud's sensitivity precisely in 1911, for two years earlier, in Worcester, he had permitted a photograph, in which—incredibly—he stood between Jung and Stanley Hall, who was at least as tall as Jung. Also, five years later, he permitted himself to be photographed with his two sons, both of whom were taller than he, both of them in uniform, with Martin sitting erect on the arm of Freud's chair, and really dwarfing him.[3]

Would it not be simpler to assume that Jung, the already declared successor of Freud, was told to stand close to him, and that the photographer insisted he crouch, for otherwise poor Dr. Stegman's face, right above him, would have been blocked off? Of course, it was taken for granted by all present that Freud would stand in the center of the group; and, knowing the fussiness of photographers on such occasions, he was told, not to stand on a box (I cannot imagine anyone in his right mind being so tactless), but to take a step up on the staircase on which the group was evidently gathered.[4]

---

[3] This photograph is, curiously enough, reproduced in Roazen's book.

[4] Through the courtesy of the late Ernst Freud, I have been able to examine an unpublished photograph of Freud and the analyst H. W. Frink (1883–1936). It must date from around 1922, when Frink was in Vienna. Frink must have been a very tall man; at least, on the photograph, he appears to be one third taller than Freud. I do not see any reason why Freud would not have avoided being part of photographs of this kind, if there were any merit to Roazen's claim.

But Roazen's masterstroke, which he achieved by the use of a highly questionable technique, was undoubtedly when he succeeded in building a case where there was none.

Roazen calls his preparatory steps in the writing of his book "detective work" (p. xix) and, true to the role of a sleuth that he wished to enact, he follows the traditional technique of a certain branch of popular literature. In the movies, on television, or in print, all of us have enjoyed watching the professional sleuth— or, better still, a non-professional person—taking an unsuspecting walk on a lovely summer day and stumbling upon a clue that then leads him, against all odds and to the disbelief of the hitherto ineffective police, to the uncovering of a crime and the capture of the culprits.

According to Roazen's account, he found the clue while innocently interviewing, for the purpose of his Freud studies, all the people who had known Freud. It was at that time, he says, that he was told (p. xviii): " 'No one will tell you about Tausk.' That was all the tip-off I needed." Although, as we shall see, the book is filled with instances of lack of discretion, here the author is discreet enough: he does not publicly thank the person to whom he owes the "tip-off." Furthermore, the author does not let the reader know—to do so might have cooled off the tension he had just aroused by reporting the "tip-off"—whether he ever did meet anyone who was not ready to "tell him about" Tausk.

From his book, it seems that three analysts did give him pertinent details with which he then proceeded to write a "mystery story": Drs. Nunberg, Helene Deutsch and Edoardo Weiss. I shall speak about Dr. Weiss's contribution; Dr. Nunberg told him how Freud felt about Tausk, and why he refused to take him into analysis; and Dr. Deutsch gave him all the details she could recall, when Roazen sought to find out about her experiences with Tausk before she took him into analysis and during his analysis.[5]

---

[5] Helene Deutsch devoted a great many hours to conveying all she knew and thought about Freud to a person whom she judged to be a competent sociologist-historian. In so doing, she fulfilled a duty that rests on all who had the signal privilege of having met Freud, since nothing that can be known about a person as unique and eminent as he was should be lost to posterity. However, as will be seen, her sense of responsibility was not rewarded in kind. Regrettably, the in-

Dr. Nunberg, when he granted me an interview for the Archives, told me the same story; I have also heard him tell it to others. Dr. Deutsch told me (I interviewed her only once, in 1954, before the author's book was published) a few of the things she told Roazen —except for one decisive detail, which he, curiously enough (see later), reports quite differently. I also know of several people to whom Dr. Deutsch spoke freely about the same items she reported to the author. Dr. Weiss, whose information Roazen— as will be seen—reported incorrectly, did not tell him anything he would not have told anyone who had asked him.

When I myself met Roazen, I expressed satisfaction and gratitude for his interest in Tausk[6] and begged him to deposit with the Library of Congress all the material he had collected, including whatever he might not be able to publish now for reasons of discretion. Why then does he assert—in the face of his own evidence—that he uncovered "the suppressed account of Victor Tausk's life and death" (p. xviii)? Who are the people who have "repressed out of loyalty to the master . . . Tausk's struggle with Freud" (p. xx)?

Is it all because some unnamed person allegedly said: "No one will tell you about Tausk"—a prediction that, according to the author himself, never did come true? [7] Is it because of that one

---

valuable knowledge that she had imparted to Roazen was often reproduced in such mutilated fashion and so misinterpreted that she herself was not always able to identify it.

[6] In my capacity as secretary of the Archives, I had, of course, tried to obtain biographical material about Tausk but had failed to find more than what Drs. Nunberg and Helene Deutsch had previously told me.

[7] "Each informant had something to teach" (p. xvii) and "to all of them I am indebted for their cooperation" (p. xvi), writes Roazen. This statement must include also the three analysts who were the only ones who knew anything about Tausk, among the many interviewees whose names he enumerates—quite needlessly, since many of them had never met Freud, and none of them with the exception of the three mentioned knew Tausk. Of all the reviewers, if I am not mistaken, it was only Lucille B. Ritvo (1970) who brought this contradiction to attention, although it demonstrates that Roazen's primary assumption of a conspiracy of silence cannot be correct. Enumerating interviewees who had no connection with the main characters in a book seems to have become something of a fashion. Pfeiffer (1965, p. 118), in an essay on the book by Peterson (1962), who used a similar device, has the following to say: "The sight of such a phalanx makes the reader inclined from the very beginning to regard the text as particularly reliable [gesichert]" (my own translation).

wrong prediction that he now feels entitled to cast aspersions on Freud and his group? [8]

We shall soon have an opportunity to observe the author's frequent adherence to the Biblical injunction—the only one, by the way, that he seems to obey in his book—not to let his right hand know what his left hand is doing. At the very start of his book he indulges in a plain contradiction, when he writes (p. 7), only a few pages after his earlier statement: "No one in particular has been actively responsible for suppressing a full account of the difficulties between Freud and Tausk." Thus, it was suppressed, yet no one was responsible for the suppression. Would one be wrong in deducing from this that such suppression might very well not have taken place at all? According to another of the author's versions, it was clearly impossible for the suppression to have taken place, if only because "Tausk's struggle with Freud was misunderstood at the time" (p. xx)—that is to say, the truth about it could not even have been known by those who allegedly did the suppressing.

Roazen and some of his reviewers have singled out Anna Freud as the main instigator of what is now called "a conspiracy of silence" (cf. Rycroft 1970; Storr 1970), and he does not hesitate to assert that she "has always maintained a secretive hold on everything connected with Freud's life, even censoring his letters for publication" (p. xvii). On the other hand, when he reports that Anna Freud "had commissioned Ernest Jones to write an authorized biography of her father" (p. xvii), it remains one of the

---

[8] Sabshin (1970), a reviewer of Roazen's book, apparently shares Roazen's myth about an "information barrier" of some sort; he writes, "Roazen's excitement as he began to penetrate obstacles standing in the way of gaining information about Tausk," evidently having failed to take note of the fact that Roazen did not cite one single instance of an obstacle. In anticipation of some of the criticisms of Roazen's undertaking that I shall present at some length later in this book, I want to emphasize at this point that Sabshin does not refer to even a single one of the many misquotations of Freud of which Roazen made himself guilty, neither does he correct a single one of Roazen's many errors. The only objections to the book that this review contains are that Roazen "does not provide a clear picture of Tausk as a human being," that much in the book "seems" superficial, and that "Tausk remains an enigma." The fact that it was even possible for such a review to be published in a quarterly that pretends to represent psychoanalysis in the United States demonstrates that ignorance of Freud's works and of the history of psychoanalysis is no longer a trait of only a handful of analysts.

many puzzles that Roazen creates (without solving them) why a daughter who is *holding on to everything* that is connected with her father's life should *commission* an author to write her father's biography at all.

When Roazen continues (p. xvii): "She [Anna Freud] scrutinized Jones's work line by line, while helping him in every way she could," this, of course, evokes the impression that Jones's biography of Freud was also censored by her. Whoever knew Jones, knows, of course, that he was an independent, self-willed person, who would never have brooked interference from any source whatsoever.

Is it possible that Roazen's erroneous inference was caused by the fact that he had read only Miss Freud's numerous letters to Jones, deposited in the London Archives carrying his name, but not Jones's letters to Miss Freud? If he had taken cognizance of both, he would have become aware that Miss Freud had not been given an opportunity "to scrutinize," but that she had answered specific questions that Jones had asked her.[9]

The truth is that the Freud family had been shocked by the products of Freud's self-appointed biographers and had therefore become quite averse to endeavors of that sort. However, when Jones approached the family with the suggestion that *he* write a biography, the family thought that, in view of his knowledge and his prominence in the field of psychoanalysis, he should be *authorized* to do so. *All* letters and other documents in their possession were, of course, put at his disposal, without imposing any limitations on their use.

In order to adduce at least some semblance of justification for "a conspiracy of silence," Roazen points out that the last four sentences were omitted in the publication of the letter written by Freud to Lou Andreas-Salomé, in which he informed her of Tausk's suicide. The correspondence between Freud and Lou Andreas-Salomé was published in German in 1966 by Ernst Pfeiffer, the owner and able administrator of Andreas-Salomé's

---

[9] The reader will have an opportunity to form his own opinion about Roazen's allegation when that part of the correspondence between Ernest Jones and Anna Freud will have been published.

literary estate. The unabridged text of the letter was published in English by Binion (1968, pp. 402–403).

Part of these four sentences contains Freud's description of his reaction to Tausk's suicide, his inability to mourn his death: "I do not really miss him; I had long taken him to be useless." I will later go into the discussion of Freud's reaction, which has been wrongly interpreted by Roazen, as well as by most reviewers, who have castigated Freud severely on that score.[10]

It was apparently the deletion of these four sentences that caused Roazen and several reviewers to be convinced that Anna Freud was determined to conceal the truth about her father, and which induced Anthony Storr (1970) to make the preposterous statement that he hoped "that the Freud family . . . had not actually destroyed any original documents." Little did he know that, by the decision of Anna Freud, the Freud family, at tremendous financial sacrifice—a postal card with a few typewritten lines, signed by Freud, is offered for sale for $300.00 in this country—has donated all of Freud's letters in their possession (they run into the thousands) to the Library of Congress for the future use of Freud's biographers. Let us hope these biographers will not be a pack of wolves.

In view of the grave inferences that Roazen drew from the omission of these four sentences, I myself became interested in the history of the deletion. It was not altogether easy to trace. Mr. Ernst Pfeiffer, the editor of the letters, did not remember, and in the galleys that he showed me the ominous passage was reproduced in full. As it turned out, it was present even in the page proofs. Had the family, then, overlooked its alleged implications? Finally, a letter was found, written by Anna Freud to the S. Fischer Verlag, which graciously permitted its quotation. In it, however, Anna Freud urgently pleads that they abstain from the publication of her father's critical and negative remarks about Tausk. One of his sons had just written her, and "Evidently," she wrote, "the memory of his father, whom he lost very early, is

---

[10] Only the anonymous reviewer of Roazen's book in the (London) *Times Literary Supplement* of August 7, 1970 seems to have granted Freud the moral right emotionally to respond to a pupil's death in whatever way he might, and to confide that response to a close friend.

of the greatest concern to him. . . . If he read in print such a statement by my father, this would have very bad consequences, which must be avoided under all circumstances." [11]

Thus was found the evidence that no member of the Freud family had ever objected to the publication of that passage on the grounds that it might compromise Freud; otherwise it would make no sense for the passage to be contained in the page proofs. It was consideration for the Tausk family that was the sole reason for that deletion.

I recognized that such tact has since become obsolete. Roazen did not hesitate to publish the letter that the late Paul Federn wrote to his wife after Tausk's suicide. It contains a devastating indictment of Tausk's character, as will be seen. One finds it difficult to understand the cruelty of publishing such a document during the lifetime of Tausk's sons. I assume that the author overruled any scruples in the matter, if he had any, because Federn's letter also contained critical remarks about Freud.

With the deepest regrets and with an apology to Tausk's sons, I have decided not to follow the tradition to which the late Ernst Freud and Anna Freud adhered by scrupulously deleting all passages from their father's letters that might hurt the feelings of others. (I trust that the bleak moment has not yet arisen when Freud's children have found anything in their father's literary estate that would cause them to feel ashamed for him.) Instead, I have chosen to present the full truth about Tausk's personality as it has gradually been revealed to me through reading all published biographical sources, as well as in the course of interviews with informants who were not known to Roazen. As will be seen, Roazen was not only mistaken in his interpretation of important details, but he also overlooked some of the most important ones. A more reliable reconstruction of Tausk's personality than Roazen succeeded in giving throws a new light on the formidable situation that Freud was facing in a talented pupil's severe psychopathology.

---

[11] "*Offenbar ist ihm an dem Andenken des Vaters, den er sehr früh verloren hat, sehr, viel gelegen. . . . Wenn er gedruckt eine solche Äusserun meines Vaters lesen würde, so würde das sehr schlechte Folgen haben, die man unbedingt vermeiden muss.*"

Roazen, however, goes beyond the fantasy of a family conspiracy; he also denounces Jones as an unreliable biographer. To be sure, even under optimal conditions, the production of a biography is a project replete with hazards. If the biographer was a participant in the events he describes, if he was personally acquainted with the subject of his inquiry and has maintained strong emotional ties to him, that in itself will have great advantages as well as disadvantages. On the one hand, he will be able to convey details, recollections, and opinions that are important and valid contributions to the whole picture; on the other hand, he will be bound to be partisan and subjective.

It would not be difficult to outline the areas in which Jones probably erred; yet his three volumes constitute an outstanding achievement, and it would have been a great pity if they had not been written, even though many passages in them will have to be corrected by later biographers. But Roazen does not hesitate to cast aspersions on Jones's character, when he expresses his certainty that Jones "would never have pursued the unsettling details" (p. xix) that Roazen believes he has found. What this amounts to is saying that Jones would not have had the courage to fulfill his obligations as a biographer. The ease and unconcern with which Roazen tries to lower the moral standing of anyone, particularly anyone who is dead, are impressive; but the absence of any attempt at documentation when he is denouncing others also leaves him open to criticism.

Since Jones was well versed in the historico-biographical method, he would not have become the victim of errors and misinterpretations, as Roazen did; moreover, the idea that he would suppress evidence in order to protect Freud sounds so unlike Jones to anyone who knew him, that one is tempted to call such a claim malicious.

If anything, it is significant how critical of Freud Jones is at times, and how unhesitatingly he presents what, in his view, were Freud's weaknesses. One reads, off and on, that what Jones wrote was a panegyric of Freud. But such an opinion can be put forward only by someone who has read the three volumes perfunctorily— or, what is more probable, has fallen into the old pattern of equating without further examination whatever any collaborator known for loyalty to Freud has to say about Freud with the testimony of a positive transference. Jones possessed enough "ambivalence" toward Freud to keep his biography remote from a panegyric.

A brief statement ought to be added here about psychoanalytic biographies of geniuses. Such biographies, if they are even halfway complete and undertake to discuss what makes the genius different from the rest of mankind, must be different in at least one respect from what one finds in psychoanalytic case histories. A person is called a genius only when he has realized his potential to an unusual degree. In that one respect he is to be considered fortunate, whatever his pains and anguishes might have been. Since most of what has happened with him, in terms of psychological processes, must have served creativity—or else he could not belong to the category of genius—what is examined in most instances requires a different evaluation than if the same things had happened in the life of an average mortal who undergoes psychoanalytic treatment.

For this reason, one may be critical of the biographical study that the Sterbas (1954) wrote about Beethoven's relationship to his nephew. As far as I recall, nowhere is the question raised in that book as to whether (or in what way) the frightful psychopathology, so superbly documented by the authors, is connected with, or perhaps is a prerequisite, or even a manifestation of, the creative process. It might, after all, have been an indispensable step toward the creation of the *Missa Solemnis*. Be that as it may, such a point of view cannot be applied to what Roazen gives out as discoveries of new biographical material about Freud, because closer scrutiny demonstrates the untenability of Roazen's unwarranted deductions, which he puts forth as facts.

But let us return to Roazen's procedure in building up a case. His theory of clandestinity and collusion, which is required in order to give this story the necessary momentum, seems threatened by the fact that in 1934 a paper by Tausk was published in the *Almanach der Psychoanalyse*. In it there is a footnote in which, as Roazen acknowledges, Tausk's morbidity comes out with penetrating clarity (see later). It obviously goes against Roazen's pet assumptions; how then does he resolve this embarrassment? By writing: "It was all so unknown that the publishers had no idea what the footnote referred to" (p. 197). How the author came into possession of that piece of knowledge, however, remains a mystery.

To have an article printed in the *Almanach* was quite an honor in those days, comparable to being selected for publication in the now defunct *Yearbook of Psychoanalysis* (Lorand et al., 1945–1954). Since the majority of the papers published in the *Almanach* were selected from previous publications, particularly from the two leading psychoanalytic journals, and since no editor is mentioned in the *Almanach* of 1934, it is rather plain that the editors of the *Internationale psychoanalytische Zeitschrift* and the *Imago* collaborated in the publication of that volume. Paul Federn was one of the editors. It is therefore beyond any question that Federn must have read the article before it was published, particularly since he had been close to Tausk. Now, if Roazen's deduction were correct, it would mean that Federn, a representative member of the old guard and quite familiar with Tausk, did not understand the meaning of this revealing footnote. What then did the old guard know? And what did it have to conceal? For my part, I am quite certain that Federn knew exactly what the footnote meant, and that the fact that the article was published proves that Freud's collaborators had nothing to conceal.

To justify his claim that a secret had to be guarded, the author reports that "the oldest analysts were incredulous that so little was known about Tausk's significance, and some younger ones were convinced that a secret surrounded him" (p. xviii). *Why* the younger ones thought so, the author apparently forgot to find out from them. At any rate, even "some younger ones" felt baffled by Tausk, and "from many I sensed an air of mystery about Tausk" (p. VIII). The author contradicts himself anew when he asserts, three pages later, that Tausk "has . . . been completely forgotten" (p. 3). However, "the older psychoanalysts, who were already intimate with Freud at the time of Tausk's suicide," cannot understand at all "how he has been forgotten today" (p. 5f.).

All this makes these analysts out to be as confused and contradictory as the author. First they suppress Tausk's story out of loyalty to Freud, and then they feel puzzled that Tausk has been forgotten. But *has* Tausk been forgotten? And, if so, whose fault is it? The answers to these questions are intimated by the author himself—quite inadvertently, as will be seen.

It was in 1964 that Roazen started to interview all the people who had known Freud, after "I had already spent several years in the company of Freud's ideas while preparing a manuscript on the moral and political implications of his work" (p. xiii). Yet he lets us know that, as soon as he had received his "tip-off," he started to ask regularly "if or what they [informants] knew of Tausk, *a figure previously unknown to me*" (p. xviii, emphasis added). Well, if Tausk was unknown to the author in 1964, after "several years" of preparing his manuscript on Freud's sociological ideas, this can only mean that he had not read Freud's *The Interpretation of Dreams*, where Tausk is quoted three times; neither had he read the *Psychopathology of Everyday Life*, where two parapraxes published by Tausk are quoted in full, and a long footnote is devoted to a paper of his that Freud called excellent; nor had he read Freud's metapsychological papers, in one of which Tausk is quoted extensively at a very decisive turn of Freud's discourse. He had not yet perused the seventeenth volume of the *Standard Edition*, which was published in 1955 with Mr. Strachey's indispensable editorial remarks, or else he would surely have found Freud's obituary on Tausk, which is contained in that same volume.

Further, he cannot possibly have read Otto Fenichel's basic text on *The Psychoanalytic Theory of Neurosis*, with its ten references to Tausk; nor the *Psychoanalytic Quarterly* of 1933, where Tausk's most important paper was printed in English; nor the *Psychoanalytic Reader* of 1948, which reprints the same paper; nor the *International Journal of Psycho-Analysis* of 1924, nor *The Psychoanalytic Study of the Child* of 1951, nor the *Quarterly* of 1934, in all of which papers by Tausk were published; nor, probably, has he gone through the various volumes of the *Journal of the American Psychoanalytic Association*, with their numerous references to Tausk. What on earth *did* the author read, "while preparing" his previous manuscript?

Here we may have the answer to the question of why Tausk had been "forgotten"—if he was indeed forgotten. It is as simple as this: the practice of reading professional literature has greatly declined, and that is why so few people knew about Tausk when the author interrogated them. Had he asked them about Hercule Poirot or Nero Wolfe, they would have responded positively, as they probably will in the future about Tausk, as the consequence of the author's own mystery story. But the idea of conspiracy and collusion, as put forward by Roazen, is not based on historical facts; it is based solely on the necessity for constructing a background to his detective story. He would have obtained negative responses, and even more frequently, if he had inquired about Hermann, Stärcke, Sadger, Hollos, Harnik—all of whom made outstanding contributions to psychoanalysis. I could extend the list by at least a dozen names. If anything, it is surprising how often Tausk is still quoted. The mere fact that, in 1965, a paper with the title "Tausk's 'Influencing Machine' and Kafka's 'In the Penal Colony'" (Globus and Pillard 1966) was read at a meeting of the American Psychoanalytic Association should have demonstrated to Roazen that a psychoanalytic author in this country could take it for granted that the name of Tausk was known to the psychoanalytic community.

Most researchers are not historically minded. I would guess that even a name like that of Jelliffe, who held such an eminent place in the history of psychoanalysis in this country, will hardly be known to many analysts who are now under fifty. The author must surely be aware of the rapidity with which the names of those who are renowned in their lifetime are forgotten. As a counterpoise to this common occurrence, he had to elevate Tausk to undeserved heights, calling him a "towering mind" (which he definitely was not, despite his great talents), and intimating at times that he even possessed, potentially, Freud's greatness.

II

THE TAUSK EPISODE

I SHALL present in this chapter the Tausk episode used by Roazen to launch a devastating attack against Freud. I shall first familiarize the reader with Tausk's image, gained from various literary sources; I shall then try to reconstruct Tausk's case history and will follow it by a discussion of Freud's behavior in the matter. An examination of Tausk's suicide will conclude the chapter.

IMAGES OF TAUSK

The Image of Tausk in Lou Andreas-Salomé's Journal

SINCE ROAZEN's attack is based in part on notes in Lou Andreas-Salomé's (1958) diary, we have to turn first to that extraordinary woman.

Lou Andreas-Salomé (1861–1937) was probably, in the prime of her life, the most distinguished woman in Central Europe. Even now, her name still appears in the highly abbreviated *Knaurs Lexikon*, which records her as: "author (*Schriftstellerin*), friend of Nietzsche and Rilke." Her literary, scientific, and philosophical output was prodigious: she published 17 books and 119 articles, covering an incredibly wide range of topics.[1] Peters (1962) was the first to publish a full-length biography, and Binion recently (1968) devoted a work of 587 pages to her life, her personality and her work, but one may doubt whether either attempt has done justice to this formidable personality.

Lou Andreas-Salomé possessed a most remarkable mind. When she was twenty-one years old, Nietzsche said of her that she was "sagacious as an eagle and courageous as a lion" [scharfsinnig wie ein Adler und mutig wie ein Löwe]. For at least five months she succeeded in holding spellbound this most complex of all minds, something no woman either before or after was ever able to achieve. Of a poem of hers, Nietzsche averred: "It is among those things that have total power over me: I have yet to be able to read it without weeping; it sounds like a voice for which I have waited, waited since childhood" (Binion 1968, p. 56). He set her "Life Prayer" to music, and chose her as the one "to inherit and carry on my thinking" (Ibid., p. 69). This may suffice to give some idea of what an extraordinary mind this woman must have possessed, even as a young girl.

Endowed with the most subtle empathy for the finest qualities of the human race, she became acquainted and, in most instances, made friends with a huge number of the members of the Central European intelligentsia. Rilke was a close friend of hers for years and, although she deserted him, he was still longing for her on his deathbed. Gerhart Hauptmann, Beer-Hofmann, Schnitzler and Wedekind were close to her, as were outstanding women of that period, who were also taken by her unusual intelligence and her fascinating personality.

Of course, a young, unmarried woman who despises hypocrisy, and is able to share lodgings with a man for years, arouses contempt and scorn—even though, as is now known, she abstained from intercourse with him. Thus, the contemporary literature contains the severest castigations of her.[2]

---

[1] Since her death, Ernst Pfeiffer has published four more books, with excerpts from diaries, autobiographical papers and letters. The publication of all the papers contained in her literary estate will one day be an event of extraordinary importance.

[2] Nietzsche's sister, jealous of the passion Lou Andreas-Salomé had aroused in

From 1912 on Freud was her hero—probably the only man whose path she crossed who was never afraid of her and who did not ever fall in love with her. He also seems to have been the only man who never wrote or said a bad word about her. For curiously enough, no one—neither man nor woman—who becomes familiar with her life story seems to have a good word for her; almost everyone reproaches her, sometimes with a mild rebuke, more frequently with harsh words. It seems to me that no one is ready to forgive her for the fact that she succeeded in doing what women so rarely succeed in—namely, achieving a synthesis of a free, profound, indeed almost uninhibited sexual life (without submitting to the required concealments of the Victorian period) and high intellectual productivity.

Her sexual impulsiveness, her unusual capacity for experiencing the joys of life to their very depths, never cast any shadow on her eminent rank as a human being capable of creating cultural values of high, if not the highest, order. This seems to be, in the minds of most, a man's privilege, and when a woman's life overleaps what mankind in general is able either to experience or to produce, then envy must needs castigate such brilliant "independence." To be sure, she was not squeamish and she did not torment herself with repentance when a deserted lover suffered a breakdown. In Freud she found the man strong enough to cope with her, and a conflict-free relationship covered the period from their first meeting in 1912 up to her death in 1937.

Before speaking further about Lou Andreas-Salomé's personality and her relationship to Freud, I should first like to go step by step through Roazen's line of thought. With the greatest of skill, he lays the groundwork for the final blow that he will direct at Freud—namely, the accusation that Freud was motivated by petty revengefulness to humiliate Tausk and even to annihilate him. Yet we are still, at this point, far away from this final step. The first step in this sequence is to prove that Freud was in love with Lou Andreas-Salomé. In accordance with the famous principle of *cherchez la femme*, Roazen asserts that "Lou succeeded in making Freud fall in love with her, though in a sublimated

---

her brother, almost succeeded in having her expelled from Germany (she was born in Russia).

way" (p. 43). I shall have more to say later about how mistaken the author was in his judgment of Lou Andreas-Salomé's personality. Here I wish to say only that such a woman had no need to make an effort to arouse positive responses in any person she met —unless that person happened to be jealous, invidious and reactionary, like Nietzsche's sister. Any man, as profoundly devoted to human values and as eager to study humanity in all its variations as Freud was, must have been quickly fascinated by a mind that was so serious and inquisitive, so honest and so passionate in its quest for knowledge. Only an utterly dull-witted person could have missed feeling that in Lou Andreas-Salomé he had met someone unique, such as he would never in his life meet again.

It is noteworthy how the author tries to prove that Lou had succeeded "in making Freud fall in love with her." In ignorance of Viennese customs prevailing before World War I and frequently even afterwards, he "proves" his assumption by referring to Freud's sending Lou Andreas-Salomé flowers and accompanying her home at 2:30 a.m. "These attentions are all the more noteworthy from a man who jealously husbanded his time," the author adds, gradually preparing the reader for worse to come. How he knows that Freud was so jealous of time, he does not tell us. He is here relying, apparently, on common-sense psychology. In reality, Freud was known, like most truly great men, for rarely feeling pressed for time; he was always ready—at least until oppressed by painful and fatal illness—to give his time to whoever asked for it.[3] I do not recall in any of Freud's letters so far published a single reference to his being pressed for time. The most one can refer to can be found in a letter to Lou Andreas-Salomé of November 10, 1912, in which he replied to her request for her first personal meeting with him (*Journal*, p. 44): "I have no free

---

[3] The feeling of an abundance of time is one of the surprising earmarks of genius. Study of the lives of men like Mozart and Goethe (and many others as well) demonstrates that they never felt pressed for time. The feeling that time is running short, that time is lacking for accomplishments, is characteristic of the talented only, but seldom of the genius, and never of Freud. Someone has figured how long it would take for a scribe simply to copy Mozart's scores; the number of years required is incredible. If one considers all that Goethe wrote (and only a part is preserved), it is incomprehensible how all his other pursuits, which would take at least a page to enumerate, could have been compressed into one lifetime.

time earlier than that [ten o'clock at night]. If you will do me the
honor of a visit at such a late hour, I shall gladly engage to see
you safely home."

By ignoring the fact that in 1912 Freud was far from well
known outside Vienna, not to say famous anywhere, but that Lou
Andreas-Salomé was already a famous person, the author fails to
consider what tremendous importance her appearance in Vienna
and her serious intention of studying psychoanalysis must have
had for Freud. There were, as far as I can see, three events during
the grievous years of consistent rejection and ridicule that gave
Freud some hope with regard to the future of psychoanalysis. The
first (1906) was the interest of the Swiss group in psychoanalysis;
the second, the invitation to the United States in 1909; and the
third, the decision of contemporary Germany's best-known woman
author in favor of psychoanalysis. It goes without saying that Freud
must have hoped that such a turn of events, which would necessarily have had to become known after a while in the intellectual
circles of Central Europe, would at last free psychoanalysis from
public ridicule. Consequently, it is surprising that Lou Andreas-
Salomé's *Journal* records only few private sessions during the approximately six months of her stay in Vienna. Binion makes it
almost certain that on these occasions something like the rudi-
ments of an analysis took place. One may suggest that Freud
feared lest resistance would, shortly after her departure, undo the
strides that the newcomer had made.

Yet let us return to Roazen's view of events. When Roazen
writes (p. 43) of Freud's sublimated love for Lou Andreas-Salomé,
no one can object—in view of their deep friendship—to a term
that covers everything from the liking of a pet to the adoration of
God. By introducing the love theme, however, Roazen has laid
the groundwork for further "deductions." Since it has been generally assumed that Lou Andreas-Salomé and Tausk had a sexual
affair (Peters 1962, p. 279; Binion 1968, p. 208),[4] Roazen now
feels entitled to assert with documentation that "Freud was jealous

---

[4] It was only after having completed the manuscript of this book that I was
informed by Mr. Ernst Pfeiffer, owner and administrator of Lou Andreas-Salomé's
literary estate, that he believes he has found evidence which proves that she did
not have a physical relationship with Tausk. Roazen, to whom Mr. Pfeiffer—as
he later informed me—gave the same information, does not mention it in his book.

of Tausk's opportunity to have 'an affair with Lou' " (p. 45); and suddenly there is a "triangle" situation between the three, which later (p. 53) becomes "a spiritual *ménage à trois*" arrangement, with all the innuendoes and implications involved in the use of such a term. Freud's "jealousy" will become in the end a crucial foundation for his supposed annihilation of his disciple. The trusting reader, however, will have forgotten by then that, initially, the author had claimed nothing but a sublimated love on Freud's part.

Since there is no evidence obtainable for the presence of jealousy in Freud (he had written Arnold Zweig after Lou Andreas-Salomé's death of his fondness of her, "curiously enough without a trace of sexual attraction," Jones, 3, p. 213), common-sense psychology has to be applied again.

Thus, Tausk's physical points of excellence are compared with Freud's appearance and, in order to eliminate any doubt about the correctness of the assumption of jealousy, the author adds (p. 46): "When Freud stared spellbound at Lou's vacant chair, she may well have been with Tausk" (she was not, as will be seen presently). The suggestive remark refers to the following: Freud, in a letter to Lou Andreas-Salomé (*Journal*, p. 44), made mention of his "bad habit of directing my lecture to a particular person in the audience" (a personal peculiarity which he may have used constructively to give his lectures their absolutely convincing form). Evidently, he had selected Lou Andreas-Salomé as the "particular person," for he continued: "Yesteday I stared as if spellbound at the vacant chair reserved for you." [5]

First, I want to show how a view that has been born out of prejudice just does not "click." Freud's letter was written two weeks after Lou Andreas-Salomé's arrival in Vienna and ten days after she had met Tausk for the first time (*Journal*, p. 37). I have

---

[5] The German *wie gebannt*, which is weaker than the English "as if spellbound," implies Freud's inability to find quickly a substitute for her as a representative of the audience—that is to say, his eye returned repeatedly to the vacant chair. When she missed a lecture four months later, Freud referred to the same habit and wrote that he had been deprived of his "fixation sign" (*Fixationszeichen*) and had therefore spoken somewhat falteringly (see *Journal*, p. 106). But when the author suggests a jealous reaction on Freud's part while staring at the vacant chair, he is probably right—except that it was not Tausk of whom Freud was jealous, but somebody else, as it will soon be seen that Freud's letter itself reveals.

no idea, of course, how quickly, at the beginning of the century, a lady over fifty "made out" with a man; be that as it may, however, even in gossipy Vienna gossip could hardly have traveled with such speed as to make Roazen's proposition probable. Furthermore, as Roazen erroneously suggests later in the book, Tausk was Lou Andreas-Salomé's second choice—meaning, of course, that she intended at first to seduce Freud. If he wants to remain true to his own theory, therefore, he has to allow at least one "tryst."

Now Freud's letter proves that, up to that time, he had not yet met the lady alone, for he started his letter of November 10 as follows: "If I understand you rightly, you wish an exchange of ideas by word of mouth [*mündliche Aussprache*]. I would long since have proposed it in definite form, if time had not added to my usual concerns the effort to found a new psychoanalytic journal" (my own translation; cf. *Journal*, p. 44).

Moreover, Roazen ignored the fact that Lou Andreas-Salomé recorded in her diary having spent the evening with Maximilien Harden (1861–1927), a famous literary figure and publisher of a weekly that accepted essays from her pen. Thus she wrote: "Unhappily, I had to miss Freud's seminar,[6] Harden having insisted on my seeing him" (*Journal*, p. 43). Since it is probable that she had not yet started her liaison with Tausk at that time; since, if she had done so, the gossip would not have reached Freud that fast; since she spent the evening with her publisher and not with Tausk, and since it can be almost proven that Tausk attended Freud's lecture, it was impossible for Freud to have thought of Tausk when he noticed her absence. And how can it be almost proven that Tausk did attend Freud's lecture? He was working at the Psychiatric University Clinics at that time, as we learn from a remark in Lou Andreas-Salomé's *Journal*, dated November 2, 1912, which refers to Freud's Saturday lecture previous to the one she had to miss on November 9th. She wrote (p. 39): "Tausk . . . was still in the white doctor's smock he wore coming from the psychiatric clinic." It would have been an act of open rudeness if a medical student who was a member of the Psychoanalytic

---

[6] This was not the Wednesday seminar, as one might think from the translation. *Freud-Kolleg*, as she wrote, meant Freud's semestral lecture at the psychiatric clinic on Saturdays, which is a detail not to be neglected, as will be seen presently.

Society did not attend Freud's lecture, which took place at the same institution at which he was active. Therefore—since documentary evidence proves that Lou Andreas-Salomé and Tausk did not spend the evening together—it is well-nigh inescapable to accept Tausk's presence at Freud's lecture of November 9th.[7]

Nevertheless, Freud was jealous, as he wrote Lou Andreas-Salomé, but it was of Alfred Adler: "I am happy to hear that your absence was not occasioned by a visit to the camp of the masculine protest"—by which he meant, of course, Adler's newly-formed society. In order to understand Freud's fear lest she might have preferred a lecture by Adler to one of his own, one must consider the following:

A remark in her *Lebensrückblick* (1951, p. 209; see also Peters 1962, p. 273) permits the conjecture that initially Freud did not believe in the seriousness of her intention to learn psychoanalysis. Indeed, it was far more probable that the famous woman was here adding only one more interest to the huge repertoire of those she had cultivated already. Yet it must have struck Freud quickly —particularly since Abraham had written, "I have never before met with such deep and subtle understanding of analysis" (Abraham and Freud, p. 115)—that there was more involved than that in her coming to Vienna. Since she announced her intention of dividing her time between the study of his and Alfred Adler's theories, he was anxious lest the great appeal of Adler's individual psychology to commonsense, along with its consistent skirting of resistances, might make her turn her back on his own science— which would have seriously disappointed, indeed even wounded him.[8]

---

[7] Likewise it can be proven that when Lou Andreas-Salomé missed another lecture and Freud spoke "somewhat falteringly," as mentioned before, she was not "playing hookey" with her lover, for she wrote in her diary: "Saturday, the first of March, was the last of Freud's lectures, a beautiful one, perhaps the best of my entire winter here, and being feverish and in bed I had to miss it" (*Journal;* p. 107). (There is no way of knowing how she knew of the character of the lecture she had missed. It could very well have been Tausk who told her, when he visited her the following day "with his two little boys" [see *Journal*, p. 107].) It is evident that only events outside her control were able to keep Lou Andreas-Salomé away from one of Freud's lectures.

[8] It is not easy to determine exactly the time when Lou Andreas-Salomé made her final decision between Freud and Adler. Only on August 12, 1913, did she

Having thus established to his satisfaction first Freud's sub-limated love for Lou Andreas-Salomé, and then (but without any documentation) Freud's sexual jealousy of Tausk and Freud's alleged (paranoid?) fantasies when she was absent from his lectures, Roazen must have hoped that the reader would have forgotten that Tausk was eighteen years younger than his mistress. "To his friends it was strange, if not offensive, to see him involved with a woman so much older" (p. 44). Strange, strange! From all that Roazen presents as fact, one might have expected that Tausk's friends were also in love with Lou Andreas-Salomé (and common sense may conjecture that their love was less "sub-limated" than Freud's); yet they were apparently not jealous, but rather felt offended by what may be called an affair in bad taste.

I would like to add here a personal notion, even though many a reader will probably disagree with it. Freud was fifty-six years old at that time. That men at that age often do feel quite jealous when a man younger than they makes the conquest of a young girl, is well known; but that a husband should feel jealous when a younger man has an affair with a woman exactly his own wife's age strikes me as highly improbable—particularly if Roazen's assertion should be true that "on Tausk's part his love for Lou ended in physical revulsion and distaste" (p. 45). Thus the author, in all seriousness, expects us to believe that an aging man is jealous of the sexual affair of a younger man with an older woman, about whom the lover himself feels revulsion, with the liaison also arousing feelings of offense even in the lover's contemporaries! [9] Yet after having postulated Freud's jealousy, Roazen then attempts to make his theory more plausible by asserting that Freud welcomed such a triangular situation, since Lou "could give Freud information about Tausk. She could help keep this potentially troublesome student under control" (p. 46).

A masterly intrigue, indeed—but it would have been possible only in the mind of a man who had lost his memory and forgotten

communicate to Adler, in a lengthy letter, a full exposition of her disagreement with his theories (*Lebensrückblick*, 1951, pp. 362-364).

[9] I go into these details not because I would find it objectionable if Freud had been jealous, but only in order to demonstrate the arbitrariness of the author's claims, which he needs in order to provide his final coup with at least some semblance of probability.

that Lou Andreas-Salomé was married, a resident of Göttingen, and in Vienna for only a short time. And why was Tausk potentially troublesome? Freud "wanted corroborators rather than collaborators"; "originality ended . . . usefulness to Freud" (p. 48); Tausk "was forging ahead of Freud" in a few areas (p. 51); "Tausk's interests were disturbances to Freud" (p. 52). Further, "Tausk's work irritated Freud, and a good part of the problem was Tausk's originality." "Tausk's independence disturbed Freud . . . he needed passive receptacles for his concepts" (p. 53); "Tausk's talents upset Freud's inner harmony." Enough!—even though more quotations of the same sort could be added.[10]

As for the fact that Freud felt irritated by Tausk, of that there seems to be no doubt. Easy as it may be to prove this— partly from documentary evidence, partly from testimony, mainly that of Dr. Deutsch—it may be difficult to say for sure what it was in Tausk that had this irritating effect on Freud. I shall later make some remarks about Freud's affectivity in general. I want to stress here only that the fact that some members of the early (and probably also later) group irritated Freud is per se neither surprising nor puzzling. A great variety of personalities—not just the simple, straightforward type, but rather complex, highly differentiated, conflict-ridden and ambitious ones—gathered around him, as easily happens to the genius innovator. For Freud to have reacted to each of them with understanding, tolerance and the total exclusion of affects would have made of him a rather antiseptic personality, and would have converted the Wednesday meetings into group therapy sessions.

If anything, Freud was most receptive to originality, even when it did not deserve his approval, as one can see amply in his dealings with Adler and Jung (see Chapter IV). Certainly, personal irritation never prevented him from acknowledging originality. Without difficulty he admitted to Jung that "he had often contradicted Stekel's interpretation of a given symbol, only to find on further study that Stekel had been right the first time" (Jones,

---

[10] Indeed, one can scarcely avoid the impression that the author tries to use repetition of the same assertion as a cover for the absence of proof. I must postpone the presentation of the documentary evidence which disproves these allegations to the time when the details of Freud's actual relationship to Tausk will be presented.

2, p. 134).[11] Originality was never an irritant for Freud. We shall have occasion later to investigate how original Tausk really was.

There are about ten passages in Lou Andreas-Salomé's *Journal* that are used by the author to prove his point. It is interesting that, whenever he does find documentation that fits his purpose, he accepts it without evaluation as to the likelihood of its correctness. The bulk of the passages he adduces are her interpretations which never exclude the possibility of error or one-sidedness—except for the few that refer to straight facts. Curiously, it is just in relation to one of this sort that the author makes a grave omission (see p. 85).

Lou Andreas-Salomé was an extremely intuitive and sensitive person, and I would never take any interpretation of hers lightly. I am convinced that she did feel—and correctly—some sort of tension between Freud and Tausk. But what Roazen ignores is that her own disposition might well have made her emphasize single aspects and exaggerate intensities. A strong positive Oedipal tie to her father, and the fact that she grew up with three brothers (two had died in their early years), whom she recalled as "good" and frequently called so, led her, at times in her life, to a division of allegiance—a strong attachment of respect and admiration for the father substitute, and an outright erotic or strongly erotically-colored attachment to the brother substitute. At least in the famous instance of her relation to Nietzsche and Paul Rée,[12] this served to create enmity between the two. In the Freud-Tausk episode, however, the tension between those who apparently quickly became father- and brother-substitutes for her was already present at the time of her arrival, and did not need to be created by her. If her report can be trusted in this respect (and I do not see

----

[11] In the so far unpublished portion of the *Minutes*, I found two incidents that occurred in 1913 and speak strongly for Freud's scrupulousness in giving authors their due credit. On one occasion, he wished to apologize (the German *Abbitte leisten* is much stronger than that) for having done Stekel an injustice in the discussion of a controversial issue; in the other instance, he presented a communication that "confirmed in a splendid way an assertion by Stekel that had seemed arbitrary." (Here and subsequently, translations of excerpts from so far unpublished *Minutes* are my own.)

[12] Paul Rée (1849–1901), moral philosopher and author of *Origin of Moral Sentiments* (1875), *Psychological Observations* (1875), *Origin of Conscience* (1885) and other works. He was, for a while, an intimate friend of Nietzsche.

why it should not be), she not only tried to reduce the tensions that existed between Freud and Tausk, but also found a willing ear in the former. She was even successful in making Freud more patient with Tausk, who was, as will be seen, an irritating and provocative person, to say the least.

One of her observations was that Freud had criticized a lecture by Tausk "more severely than usual" (*Journal*, p. 57). Unfortunately, the *Minutes of the Vienna Psychoanalytic Society* do not contain a record of the discussion of that evening, so that we have to rely entirely on her impressions. All that is given about the lecture is its title, "Two Contributions to the Psychoanalysis of the Inhibition of Artistic Creativity" (*Zwei Beiträge zur Psychoanalyse der künstlerischen Produktionshemmung*), and Tausk's abstract.[13] She reports that Freud felt on that occasion that "with the persistent calumny of our whole movement on the part of official science, we should not dare to move so boldly into new territory" (*Journal*, p. 57f).

This elicits from Roazen the truly astonishing comment that Tausk was "forging ahead of Freud" in his desire "to extend psychoanalytic thinking to the psychology of the artist . . . focusing on the role of inhibitions in artistic creativity. This would one day be considered a perfectly legitimate subject among analysts" (p. 51). Was Tausk "forging ahead of" Freud in 1912, by seeking to "extend" psychoanalytic thinking to the psychology of the artist and artistic inhibitions and would this one day be a legitimate psychoanalytic subject? Why, has the author not even heard of, much less read, Freud's famous essay (1910b) on Leonardo da Vinci, which aroused unending controversy? Does he really not know that the center of it was the role of artistic inhibition, and that it was published two years *before* Tausk's presentation? Even a person with only a smattering of knowledge about the history of psychoanalysis would be taken aback by this howler.[14] To show

---

[13] I owe thanks to the late Dr. Herman Nunberg and Mr. Ernst Federn for having provided relevant material from the as yet unpublished third volume of the *Minutes*.

[14] The frequency and extent of psychoanalytic inquiry into the subject of art, prior to Tausk's paper, can be learned from Rank's (1912) report on psychoanalytic literature. It shows eleven titles under the heading "Biography," and eighteen titles under the subgroup "Aesthetics." It should be noted further that, a week after Tausk's paper, Rank gave a case presentation entitled: "On the

how Freud reacted when young talent was forging ahead, I want to remind the reader that, when Rank introduced himself to Freud in 1906 with a copy of his manuscript, *Art and Artist* [15] (Jones 2, p. 8), "we persuaded him to go through the *Gymnasium* and the University, and to devote himself to the non-medical side of psychoanalysis" (Freud 1914a, p. 25).

If Lou Andreas-Salomé's recollection is at all correct (the initial remark: "but the rest is gone, not having been noted down" [*Journal*, p. 57] indicates that the entry was made at a later date, which may help explain its lack of preciseness), Freud's warning can only have referred to Tausk's conclusions (as noted in the *Minutes*) "regarding certain conditions of artistic production" [*auf gewisse Bedingungen der künstlerischen Produktion*]—that is, to his attempt to explain the psychology of creativity rather than artistic inhibition. That problem, Freud maintained throughout his life—possibly correctly—lay outside of the realm of psychoanalysis. It would be uncalled for to find a sign of jealousy or rivalry in Freud's outlining what he thought the strategy of psychoanalytic research should be. In 1910 or 1911, he begged Jung, as well as Jones, not to go into the field of mythology too extensively and "to return in good time to the neuroses"—advice that neither of them necessarily accepted, without arousing in Freud any untoward reaction.

Thus Roazen's interpretation of the only event (among the many he construed) that may look to a person not familiar with the chronology of Freud's publications to have been proven by well-documented evidence of Freud's jealousy of Tausk bursts like a bubble when looked at in the light of incontrovertible facts. Oddly enough, not a single review, among the many written by psychoanalysts that have come to my attention, contains any reference to Roazen's howler, which makes me think that Roazen shares with a substantial part of the English-speaking psychoanalytic community what I can describe only by applying a term coined by Hanns Sachs—*gemeinsame Tagträume* ("daydreams in common")—with regard to Freud's personality.

---

inhibition of artistic production," which indicates that the problem of artistic inhibition had become quite popular after Freud's publication on Leonardo.

[15] This must have been the book, *Der Künstler*, which was published the following year (Rank, 1907).

To be sure, Lou Andreas-Salomé added to her entry a conjecture about Freud's "conflict with independent, or temperamental, characters" (*Journal*, p. 58). This theme reappears two and a half months later, with some important remarks added. After a personal talk with Freud, she arrived at the conclusion that "Freud acts with complete conviction when he proceeds so sharply against Tausk" (*Journal*, p. 97). A somewhat unclear remark refers to Tausk's "original neurotic disposition."

Apparently Freud had conveyed to Lou Andreas-Salomé what it was in Tausk's behavior that irritated him. "It is . . . clear that any independence around Freud, especially when it is marked by aggression and display of temperament" [the German *aggressiv temperamentvoll* might be better conveyed by "aggressively impulsive"] "worries and wounds him" (*ibid.*). Rightly she adds that only the future will decide the value to psychoanalysis of an independent mind, and further that fights [*Kämpfe*; these are not "battles," as the translator puts it] are unavoidable. Thus a type like Rank who, at that time at least, was acting the seemingly unambivalent role of a son, was preferred by Freud, as he himself averred to her.

With this observation, Lou Andreas-Salomé came right to the heart of the matter: what are the optimal conditions under which a genius is able to create maximal values (his main, if not his only function)? What sort of environment does he need? In studying the lives of the great, one observes in general that the genius finds or creates the habitat he needs.[16] This was true of Freud as well. His rejection by the University, his exile into the solitude of his office—these were the conditions that were optimal for the evolvement of psychoanalysis.

If one looks at the situation of 1912–1913 from the historical viewpoint, one can see that the small group that had gathered around Freud had one chief contribution to make. It can be stated without exaggeration, when viewed retrospectively, that its historical function was to provide Freud with that background of participation, discussion, and stimulation that he needed in order

---

[16] The first to introduce this thought into psychoanalytic literature was Tausk (*Minutes*, 2, p. 332): "The most perfect adaptation is that which we find in the genius, in that he himself creates his own milieu."

to maintain his creativity at its maximal pace. For the group to perform this function, tact was an essential prerequisite.

Lou Andreas-Salomé guessed correctly that Tausk's "neurotic disposition" and his aggressive impulsivity expressed tendencies that were not only capable of annoying and irritating Freud, but also contained a self-destructive element, as will be seen later.

The next relevant episode involving Lou Andreas-Salomé's diary has to do with a complex event, which occurred around the middle of March, 1913. This was two months before Freud finished the last of the four essays that make up *Totem and Taboo* (1913), on the composition of which he had been spending, intermittently, the previous three years (see Jones 2, pp. 350–354). He had already presented three essays to the Society and was at that time in process of writing the last and most important one, in which he would set forth the overwhelming effect of the son-father conflict upon the development of civilization and culture. This may well have been Freud's most daring construction—one that penetrated to the earliest phase of cultural development and that would, if correct, reveal an entirely new aspect of mankind's history.

Freud must have been quite cognizant of the fact that he was absorbed in a momentous creative process. It was at just that time that Tausk gave a lecture to the Society, with a title that reflected the identical subject matter that was absorbing Freud's central interests: "The Father Problem." Lou Andreas-Salomé met Freud before the lecture, and later reported (*Journal*, p. 114) that Freud was restless, "on account of the closeness of the ideas to his own." By this, she may or may not have meant that what disquieted Freud was the possibility that the theory he was in process of evolving might be anticipated by his pupil. It is altogether regrettable that it cannot be learned from her whether this was her own supposition and interpretation, or the substance of Freud's communication to her.

Nothing is known from Tausk's pen, either before or thereafter, that would indicate an ability on his part to give birth to anything that might come even close to the profundity of the presentation Freud gave to the world in that essay. As the reader will later see, Tausk's paper went in a different direction and was of minor quality. But it was precisely because of the momentous-ness of his own developing theory that Freud must have been under great inner pressure. On such an occasion as that, he would not have been essentially different from other geniuses who, curiously enough, are often worried, just when they are in process of creating their very best, lest some external event interfere with the final steps of their great accomplishment. Understandably, the announcement of a lecture that, strangely, referred to the identical subject to which Freud was then in process of putting the final touches, would have displeased him, whoever the speaker might have been.

It is interesting to see what Roazen makes out of that incident. He first quotes (incompletely, as we shall presently see) Lou Andreas-Salomé, who reports that Freud "questioned me during the lecture, passing a note to me: 'Does he know all about it already?' " Roazen continues: "Here lay the center of Freud's difficulties with Tausk; and Freud's distress that Tausk might steal some of his ideas before he had quite finished with them also helps explain why Lou could be useful to Freud in keeping an eye on Tausk" (p. 55).

Here, if Roazen were right, Freud would actually appear to have been haunted by paranoid fears, and capable of debasing himself to the point of attempting to use Lou Andreas-Salomé as a spy. If only Roazen had taken the trouble to let the reader in on the next one and a half lines of her diary! For there she defined, as Roazen does not, the "it" in Freud's question (*Journal*, p. 114): "I wrote back: 'Of course not, nothing at all!' *referring to Freud's remarks to me*" (emphasis added). Thus it is evident that Freud was not curious at that moment about Tausk's theories, his researches and what not, but about whether or not *Lou Andreas-Salomé had told Tausk* something that had been previously the subject of conversation between Freud and her.

A careful study of Lou Andreas-Salomé's diary, which Roazen, by the way, recommends because it "repays closest attention" (p. 49), would have informed him also of what that subject was. She had last met Freud about two weeks prior to Tausk's lecture, and on that occasion Freud "told me a 'fantasy' . . . about the meaning of parricide for the development of civilization from its beginning until now. He has never before worked out anything quite so ingenious—almost more ingenious than he usually permits himself to be" (*Journal*, p. 104). Evidently it had suddenly struck Freud how embarrassing it might be if Lou Andreas-Salomé had communicated to Tausk the theory that he was in process of putting to paper, for Tausk, whose "penchant" for repeating material from Freud's lectures without naming their originator was well known, almost certainly would have made use of her indiscretion, if she had indeed been indiscreet. Since Tausk was already complaining wherever he could that Freud was "assimilating his ideas" (p. 87 n), a distressing situation might easily have arisen.

Here Roazen has made himself guilty of three faults. First, he withholds from the reader the very specific coincidence involved —namely, that Tausk had on that occasion chosen a topic that happened to be identical with Freud's peak interest at the time. Second, Roazen omits precisely that brief part of a quotation that refutes the image he is building up, the image of a childish and paranoid Freud—which the reader is thus invited at this point to accept as proven, on the strength of a half-quoted entry in the diary of an eyewitness. Third, he ignores altogether that it was Freud who had told Lou Andreas-Salomé all he knew about the "father problem," and who therefore had ample reason to consider the possibility that she might have acted, inadvertently if anything, as a "spy" for Tausk. The combination of omission, distortion, and failure to study the sources is in this case so breathtaking that, if I were not convinced of Roazen's ineptitude, I would have to question his good faith in view of so many errors.[17]

During the rest of her stay, those of Lou Andreas-Salomé's entries that are of interest in this context changed their drift, and Tausk's psychopathology, of which she was never unaware, now

---

[17] It will be significant to the future historian that one or the other professional psychoanalyst is as ignorant of Freud's personality as Roazen has shown himself to be. Any analyst who has read *The Interpretation of Dreams* (1900) or the *Autobiographical Study* (1925b) would know that it would have been impossible for one and the same person to have written either of these texts, which I have selected at random, and the note to Lou Andreas-Salomé, as it is mutilated and then evaluated by Roazen. Anyone with a minimum of sensitivity and knowledge would immediately know that someone must have made a mistake somewhere. Nevertheless, in his review of Roazen's book, Peter Lomas (1969), a member of the British Psycho-Analytical Society, repeated Roazen's error in quoting, without adding even so much as a doubt, no less a refutation, but instead accepting it as proof of Roazen's principal theory.

moved into the center. In the end, she was already recognizing that this man was irreconcilably divided in himself and destined for doom. She discovered that, even in his thinking processes, he was entangled in an insoluble conflict about Freud. "His position with regard to psychoanalysis is at once too uncritical and (through resistance) excessively critical. This is then laid at Freud's door" (*Journal*, p. 116). She perceived "the whole tragedy of Tausk's relation with Freud: that is, I realize now that he will always tackle the same problem, the same attempts at solution, that Freud is engaged in." [18]

She recognized the inner compulsion, so to speak, in Tausk, "his 'making himself a son' as violently as he 'hates the father for it'" (*Journal*, p. 166). She acknowledged his difficult present situation, his preparation for medical examinations and "his domestic conflicts" [19] (*Journal*, p. 167), which "leave him no time to read, to orient himself in the publications pertinent to his problems"; but she recognized that what seemed a response to reality factors covered up Tausk's personal psychopathology, for she continued: "Still, working with him, I feel clearly now that there are personal reasons for this also." [20] That Tausk's dangerously excessive narcissism was the core of the whole problem becomes apparent when she observes: "What he *wants* is his blind and dumb self-expression alone, suffering so greatly as he does under the burden of himself" (*Journal*, p. 167; author's emphasis). This final analysis of Tausk was part of her written farewell address, since she knew at the time—what Tausk did not yet know—that their affair was ended.

The two and a half pages (pp. 187–189 in the German edition) are beautifully written and deeply moving; unfortunately, they do

---

[18] As a matter of fact, it took Tausk's physical separation from his father-*imago*, enforced through his military service, to enable him to acquire, at least temporarily, a minimum of autonomy, as Roazen correctly observed.

[19] When Roazen replaces Tausk's "domestic conflicts" with "his responsibilities toward his sons" (p. 57), I would cite this as a minor example of what may be called his attempts to "bribe" the reader. It is highly improbable that a responsibility would be called a conflict by Lou Andreas-Salomé.

[20] Her psychological astuteness made her recognize, perhaps even before it became part of psychoanalytic theory, that the acting-out person uses reality factors to discharge conflicts against which he has built no adequate defense mechanisms.

not come out as impressively in the English translation. Tenderly, she records Tausk's great potentials and then, with grief, notes the barriers in him that will cut them off from flourishing. "It is all so painful to behold that one would like to look the other way and run away" (*Journal*, p. 167f.).[21]

With charming sensitivity, she acknowledges that it was precisely the struggle in Tausk (between his unmastered aggressivity, his "beast-of-prey" nature and his over-sensitivity, threatening self-dissolution) that had "most deeply moved me," and that is: *Der Kampf der menschlichen Kreatur. Brudertier, Du.* "The struggle of the human creature. Brother-animal. You." [22] It is one part of this final phrase that the author used as the title of his book, thereby transforming a beautiful, superbly-touching epilogue into something offensively coarse, if not downright vulgar. What he has done is to tear these final words out of context and use the English translation, which implies the very opposite of the German original, thus converting a poetic expression of the greatest feeling of closeness between a man and a woman into a repellent epithet, which he then employs to characterize a nonexistent rivalry between two men.

Toward the end of her affair with Tausk, Lou Andreas-Salomé made a remark that must not be ignored, if other entries in her *Journal* are to be interpreted correctly. In referring to Tausk's self-defeating behavior, she wrote (*Journal*, p. 167): "That *seemed* to depend so much on the *situation*, but ultimately it is *his* own *doing*." (First emphasis the author's; second and third added.) Thus she recognized, or at least thought she had recognized, that what had initially appeared to be, in Tausk's behavior, a reaction to external circumstances was in the end revealed to be a sign of his innate psychopathology.

This change in her evaluation of Tausk's relation to Freud—from one in which emphasis was placed on external circumstances, to one in which it was the structure of Tausk's personality that

---

[21] Literally translated, it says, "All that is so aching to behold that one turns one's head—[one] wishes [to be] away." [*All das ist so weh anzusehen, dass man den Kopf wendet—hinweg möchte.*]

[22] The change in punctuation between "brother-animal" and "you" from comma to period makes it even more difficult for the reader to grasp the depth and beauty of this passage.

was regarded as the ultimate operating agent—can, of course, be interpreted in two different ways. One could say that Lou Andreas-Salomé fell more and more under Freud's influence and for that reason came to deny Freud's role in the situation; further, that the cooling off of her previous passionate feelings toward Tausk may have prejudiced her against him. But the last words of her unspoken farewell, which carry a statement of intense emotional closeness to the love object she is in process of losing—almost one of deep regret—make this eventuality an improbable one.

I would suggest instead the consideration of two factors. On the one hand, her initial passionate falling in love with Tausk had prevented her from discovering the true depth of Tausk's psychopathology; on the other hand, her early and rapid acquaintance with Freud may easily have made her underestimate the true greatness of the latter's personality. It is my impression that Freud was not the type of person who tried to ingratiate himself with people, or to impress others by his personality, and that this was in contrast to Tausk, who seemed almost habitually to try to impress people, particularly women, and particularly at the beginning of his acquaintance with them. Freud cared tremendously about what people with whom he maintained professional relations thought of psychoanalysis; he cared far less about what they thought of him personally.

How easily Freud's personality may be misjudged can be seen from Wittels' (1923) book. Originally, it contained a commentary on Freud's personality, portions of which were devastating; yet, on closer acquaintance, Wittels had to revoke all his bitter observations and to replace them with their opposites.

What is so striking in Roazen's conception of what he calls the "triangle" is his misconception of Lou Andreas-Salomé's personality, and the truly embarrassing emptiness of his psychological understanding. With his penchant for the commonplace and the trivial, he really believes that she had "a knack for collecting great men" (p. 33),[23] like Alma Mahler-Werfel (1879–1964) and

---

[23] Peters (1962, p. 13) discusses the opinion of Lou Andreas-Salomé's "detractors," who "said that she collected famous men, as others collect paintings." He believes that this criticism came mainly from "women who feared her as a rival." I think this is a correct observation. In men who are critical of her, it seems to be their castration fear that is the motive for their belittling her. A

Madame de Staël (1766–1817). He ignores the fact that Alma Mahler-Werfel attracted famous men without being particularly creative herself, and that Madame de Staël became famous for her interest in men once they had become famous.

Was Nietzsche famous, when Lou Andreas-Salomé spent time with him? Not even his friends were at that time sure of his greatness. She preferred to spend years with his former friend Rée, even though she was aware that he was not to be compared with Nietzsche. Was Rilke famous when Lou Andreas-Salomé fell in love with him? He was unknown. And during her early stay in Vienna, in the eighteen-nineties, she felt most strongly attracted to, and probably loved most intensely, Richard Beer-Hofmann (1866–1945), who was less famous at that time than the rest of the Vienna circle of poets and so remained, although he was probably the truest poet of them all. Precisely the fact that her choice fell on Beer-Hofmann proves that it was the quality of personality that attracted her irresistibly and *not* the person's fame.

The fact that so many of those to whom she was close were not known, or little known, or rejected, but later rose to extraordinary fame—that very fact is proof of her uncanny intuition and knowledge about man, which served her in her unfailing recognition of true values. That this woman, whose mind was equal to that of the greatest of her times, found gratification and pleasure mainly in the company of extraordinary minds was not a result of snobbishness, or arrogance, or of a rage for "name-dropping," but rather a necessity—unless one thinks that she should have been content with the boredom generated by mediocrities.

It is incomprehensible how any author who has read Lou Andreas-Salomé's biography—if indeed he has read it—could ever write: "Lou fit perfectly into such a passive role," as Freud, who

noted psychoanalyst has raised the question of whether she was carrying out an obligation imposed upon her by her Biblical namesake (cf. Stekel 1911b, 1914). Leavy (1964, pp. 569–571) suggests that Jung actually dreamed of her as the Biblical Salomé, and Peters (1962, p. 25) starts his biography with references to the Bibilical Salomés, the grandniece of Herod Antipas and the one who was present at the cross and tomb. Huge is the number of women who have been destructively consumed in the process of making possible the realization of creativity in men. It seems to arouse bitterness, however, when that process is reversed. Also in the subtitle of Binion's (1968) book on Lou Andreas-Salomé ("Nietzsche's Wayward Disciple"), in my opinion, a condescending, covertly ironic attitude is betrayed, which she did not deserve.

"wanted corroborators rather than collaborators" (p. 48), desired. And further: "She could flatter him, while believing everything she said . . . . A woman can more easily dissociate her
sense of self from her professional work, so to give Freud what he
wanted in no way compromised her integrity" (p. 48). "A
woman," perhaps; but Lou Andreas-Salomé? Will the reader recognize in this description the woman to whom the world owes
the first part of *Thus Spake Zarathustra*, the woman who wrote a
story that Gerhart Hauptmann, the celebrated playwright, used
as a plot of one of his dramas? If he does not, then Roazen has
erred.

The author's flights of fancy have nothing to do with the Lou
Andreas-Salomé who in her early years lost her faith in God, and
suffered all her life as a result of that loss; who resisted both the
lure of the luxury and pomp of the Czarist Court, and equally the
cheap escape into political sloganizing; who had the willpower to
live door-to-door with a man for years and all that time to resist
the passionate desires of her youthful years; who studied and
worked hard as a student, never falling for sham arguments,
rhetoric and slogans, but being instead irresistibly driven to get
to the root and essence of things; a woman whose library even the
Nazis dared confiscate only after her death.

And Freud? Among his pupils there were, of course, women
who were of the passivity that Roazen conjectures to have been
present in Lou Andreas-Salomé; but no friendship ever developed
between Freud and them. They were put up with, but they were
not welcome. Deep friendships evolved only with Marie Bonaparte and Lou Andreas-Salomé. The former was, right up to old
age, mentally and physically inimitably active and resolute;[24] and
it was, after all, Lou Andreas-Salomé's independence of mind, and
resoluteness in not being overwhelmed by the greatness of his
mind, that made the young girl so irresistibly attractive to Nietzsche.

Lou Andreas-Salomé's unswerving relationship to Freud, that
mutual constancy of deepest friendship, was unique among the

---

[24] In order to characterize the superb qualities of Marie Bonaparte, I cannot
forgo quoting the witty remark I heard about her: "In watching her, one can
hardly grasp how Wellington was able to defeat her famous great-great-uncle at
Waterloo."

many friendships of her life. All others, as far as I know, either lost their initial intensity or else reached a peak from which there followed an admixture of disappointment or disillusionment. Only the friendship with Freud preserved its momentum and was free of ambivalence, as far as this is humanly possible. To be sure, the age factor must be considered. When they met, she was 51 and he 56—that is to say, they were at the age when the irrational demon has gradually given way to the acceptance of reality. Yet it would be an error to limit the reasons for the uniqueness of this relationship solely to the maturation brought about by age.

One of Roazen's informants was apparently sure that Lou Andreas-Salomé came to Vienna with the intention of seducing Freud, but, discovering that she would not succeed, displaced onto Tausk what had seemed a certainty.[25] According to my reconstruction, this is wrong. Lou Andreas-Salomé never in her life seduced anyone. Ever since the minister of the Dutch Reformed Church in St. Petersburg, Hendrik Gillot (1836–1916), the man who was the first to train her mind and indeed subjected her to a rigorous education, the man under whose guidance she had expected to find a solution for her religious scruples, so that she could accept confirmation in her Church without hypocrisy—ever since that man, who was married and the father of two daughters, tried to seduce her, she never formed any intention of seducing a man, although she seems to have taken it for granted that every man who met her would eventually try to seduce her, or would at least be afraid that he might not be able to resist his impulse to do so.

But in Freud, according to my reconstruction, she met, for the first time, a man who turned toward her with full appreciation and acknowledgment of what she was as a person, who was capable of grasping the depth of her personality, yet without becoming involved in her, even for a moment, as a sexual being. And this despite the fact that he turned toward her with his whole person.

---

[25] Roazen, with his usual legerdemain, follows two versions. On page 33 we read: "She [Lou Andreas-Salomé] came with the intention of eliciting Freud's *interest* in her, and succeeded completely in her aim" (emphasis added). Yet after Tausk's suicide another version became more suitable, and we read on page 145: "She [Lou Andreas-Salomé] had taken Tausk as a *lover* as second best" (emphasis added)—implying that her primary aim in that regard had been to have Freud as her lover.

There is no doubt that he was deeply impressed by a personality that one may call, without exaggeration, one of the rarest specimens of womanhood there has been. To meet a man who was entirely submerged in creativity without losing in any way the full elasticity of his humaneness, and who was able to establish a full object-relationship with her without any indication of expecting or wanting gratification of a wish that in the last analysis would have been the effect of selfishness—this experience at last brought to pass what she had looked for, as a young woman, in Gillot. An early dream, I surmise, had become the most stunning reality—in the person of Freud.

And with that we are back to Tausk. Lou Andreas-Salomé had a very subtle ear, and if Freud had been jealous of Tausk, or if he had sought to debase her to the role of a "secret agent," she would surely have responded to such baseness of character with contempt and turned away from him, as she had from so many before him.

Roazen describes Tausk as "a man bright enough even to anticipate some of his [Freud's] own concepts. Freud did not like the uncertainty lest Tausk have an idea before he did" (p. 55). By contrast, he says, "As a woman, Lou would arouse none of Freud's feelings of rivalry. For such an old-fashioned man women simply did not exist as competitors" (p. 48). Once again, Roazen is tripped by the stale common sense that would reduce the superb, the unique human event to the triteness of wholly unrelated and perimetric circumstances. Freud's mind was rich and constantly engaged in the search for the new, and he gave freely to everyone who desired to listen, man or woman.[26]

Anticipating some of the implications that lay dormant in the richness of Freud's ideas was, however, not unique to Tausk. When, therefore, the author says that Tausk was "bright enough even to anticipate," (emphasis added) he exaggerates, for this must have been a frequent occurrence in the small, tightly knit group of which Freud was the center.[27] Freud admired Lou

---

[26] I shall later present documentary evidence culled from the *Minutes* and Freud's correspondence as proof of his freely sharing his ideas with others.

[27] I shall later have the opportunity to present an example in which Hanns Sachs anticipated Freud's theory at a crucial point, whereas Tausk's ambitious attempt to do so went astray. It is not known that Sachs's prior realization caused any difficulty in his relationship with Freud.

Andreas-Salomé for her ability to continue where he had left off.[28] Thus "anticipation" cannot have been the irritant, with regard to Tausk. When, however, someone makes a hobby of it—in effect, as I would imagine it, staring at the speaker's face as one waits for the prey one will carry away—then that person may become a nuisance to the speaker. Not without reason did Freud compare Tausk with "a beast of prey" (*Journal*, p. 167).

When Roazen writes: "Tausk could repeat Freud word for word" (p. 50), he is not presenting a complete report of the facts. Two informants testified that Tausk actually did so, that they attended lectures by him in which he repeated (apparently almost verbatim) what he had heard from Freud the previous day, while giving himself the appearance of being original. He thus did not "ape Freud," as the author calls it (p. 50), but rather arrogated to himself what he had picked up from Freud, all the while insisting that these gleanings were his own. Such aggressive behavior must necessarily get on one's nerves, especially when the rapacious party starts asserting that *he* has been robbed. Later on, Tausk's case history will be discussed, and it will become apparent that this trait may not have been the worst one that gave Freud reason to feel irritated by this member of the group—even though he was indeed very talented.

The Image of Tausk in the Minutes of the Vienna Psychoanalytic Society

FREUD'S POSITION in the early Viennese group might be compared by some with that of the chief of a clinic, or the head of a university department. This comparison would not be correct, however, because Freud had no power over the members of the Society, as a chief has over those who work for him. The charismatic power of Freud in that group may be regarded as the "unofficial" equivalent of that power that is assured a department head by law, statute and custom. Therefore, a reader might feel inclined to draw the following parallel to the way in which Tausk

---

[28] He wrote her (July 13, 1917; cf. Freud 1960, p. 318f.): "It is quite unmistakable how each time you rush beyond me and round me out [ergänzen]; how like a sybil you keep on striving to round out my fragments into an edifice" (Mr. Collins' translation).

felt himself to be treated by Freud: A talented young man feels unhappy with his teacher; he gains the impression that his own contributions are not sufficiently appreciated, or that his services are being exploited for the advantage of the department. That sort of event is more frequent than not in academic reality. One hears of assistants who do research for their chiefs and are happy if their names appear at all, even if in second or third place. The history of any institute is replete with tales of intrigue, unjust pre-ferments and long delays of well-deserved careers; outright plagiarism, or outright theft of ideas, is less frequent, yet it occurs often enough to be familiar to anyone who has ever worked in a group situation.

When the biography is written of some unfortunate assistant who has fallen into disfavor with his chief, the actual damage he has suffered will necessarily show up in the chapter devoted to his academic career. There will be a long list of papers in which his name appears in second or last place; or there may be a break in the chief's publications, after the assistant has left; or the assistant may lag in academic advancement, when his status is compared with that of his peers. But some objective documentation will surely be found under such circumstances.

Let us therefore turn to Tausk's career as a psychoanalyst and see what were the practical consequences of his alleged difficulties with Freud. Did he lose membership in the Society? was he boy-cotted? did Freud stop sending him patients? was there opposi-tion to his researches, or delay in the publication of his papers? Was he prevented from lecturing? After all, something of that sort at least is to be expected, to judge from Roazen's tale. Freud is described by Roazen as having been "almighty" in his group, surrounded by servile disciples who only waited for the master's signal to carry out any whim, and who, one might expect, in their servility, would not even wait for the expression of a wish on Freud's part, but instead hurry to spare the adored leader even the necessity of verbalizing an unseemly wish. It is Roazen, after all, who asserts: "If Freud reigned as God, it was his students who made his word law" (p. 47); and he agrees with likening "Freud and his circle to a reigning monarch with a court. . . . His pupils were his subjects, owing fealty to him alone" (p. 48).

Now, how did the reigning monarch treat this particular rebel, whom he "feared" and of whom he was "jealous"? In order to facilitate his becoming a recognized psychoanalyst, Freud and a few of his collaborators gave Tausk money, so that he could go through medical school; as far as is known, neither Freud nor the others ever asked Tausk to repay that debt. In May, 1911 Tausk started a cycle of twelve lectures for medical men (*Mediziner*),[29] a singular honor, I would assume, since Tausk had not yet been graduated from medical school. In November, 1912, when the tension between Freud and Tausk had already reached a noticeable degree, as we know from Lou Andreas-Salomé's diary, Tausk was giving regular lectures to the lay public (*Journal*, p. 238)— the first instance of its kind, I believe, in Vienna. The November issue of the first volume of the *Internationale Zeitschrift* (1913) reports that Tausk is teaching a two-hour semestral course. The as yet unpublished *Minutes* of a meeting of January 14, 1914 report Tausk's motion that his courses be declared as officially arranged by the Vienna Psychoanalytic Association. The members voted unanimously in favor of the organization of official training courses and charged Tausk with conducting them for one year. In the September issue of the second volume of the *Zeitschrift* (1914), two semestral courses are announced (supplementary to Freud's lectures at the University); they are to be taught by Tausk.

Also in 1912, Freud fought with Stekel, who was at that time editor of the *Zentralblatt*, to let Tausk supervise the reviewing department of that journal (Jones, 2, p. 136). In 1913, we hear, he sent Tausk an important patient, coming from London, for a short analysis (Jones, 2, p. 98). Rank, as Jones (3, p. 412) reports, once jokingly remarked that "Freud distributed references to other analysts' writings on the same principle as the Emperor distributed decorations, according to the mood and fancy of the moment." Well, Tausk seems to have received no small share of "decorations," as we shall see presently.

In the fourth edition (1914) of Freud's *The Interpretation of Dreams*, Tausk's name appears in three places; in one instance, a full paragraph is devoted to three dreams he had published previously. In the sixth edition of his *Psychopathology of Every-*

---

[29] The *Korrespondenzblatt* of the International Psychoanalytic Association of April, 1911.

day Life (1919), Freud added two full-length samples (a slip and an error) that had been published by Tausk, and it is worthwhile recording that, even though this happened after Tausk's death, in the tenth edition (1924) Freud added a footnote that referred to "an excellent paper by Tausk (1913)." In the first volume of the *Internationale Zeitschrift*, there was an article devoted to "Observations and Examples from Analytic Practice"; one illustration in it was Tausk's and it was published alongside those of Freud and Ferenczi. In his famous paper on "Mourning and Melancholia," written in 1915 and published in 1917, Freud singled out a paper by Tausk (1913a), in order to point to it "as an exception" to the little attention that the economic point of view had so far received.

In his third metapsychological paper, "The Unconscious" (1915b), Freud incorporated observations that "Dr. Victor Tausk of Vienna has placed at my disposal." Evidently, in order to avoid any unclarity about Tausk's contribution, Freud did not limit himself to recording the source of the clinical observation, but continued two paragraphs later: "I agree with Tausk in stressing . . ." Again, two paragraphs later, he quotes a remark by Tausk verbatim. Two pages later Freud summarized "the case of a young patient reported by Tausk some years ago to the Vienna Psycho-Analytical Society," although this case was apparently never published and Freud might very well have possessed observations of his own with which to prove his point. In view of the sinister motives Roazen ascribes to Freud, one would expect him to have gladly omitted the feared rival's clinical material, or to have become forgetful of the true source of the clinical illustration. That Freud was occasionally a victim of such errors, along with the rest of humanity, can be learned from Jones (3, p. 412), who maintains that Freud, at a time when "I was out of favor," attributed "an important conclusion of mine in a book he had read to the reviewer of the book."

There is historical evidence that Freud made such an error at least once, with regard to Tausk. Lou Andreas-Salomé reports (*Journal*, p. 88) that Freud commented favorably in a discussion upon "a clarifying observation" that Tausk had made, but mistakenly referred it to another person. "He [Freud] then smilingly apologized for his error." What does Roazen make out of this incident? "Freud could smile at Tausk's suggestions getting under-foot and at his own unwillingness to give Tausk due credit. The situation never got beyond Freud's control. Ultimately, Freud could afford to brush Tausk aside completely" (p. 55f).

There is a myth that the Gods punish those who are seekers after the truth. I do not know which it is worse to have to endure: the daily hacking-out of one's self-regenerating liver by an eagle, or repeated character defamation. It was Freud who discovered the meaning of slips of the tongue and the Gods have taken their revenge by seeing to it that his own parapraxes are analyzed.[30] Roazen repeats here what many have tried before him, but he does so with a particular lack of caution. Did he investigate what discussion remark Tausk had made? From what source did he learn that this or any other discussion remark, for that matter, had ever gotten "underfoot" at all? After all, such an error as Freud made might have been precipitated by a number of variables, as I will have an opportunity to show later on.

I suggest that the reader consider—tedious as this may be—an abstract of what can be learned from the *Minutes of the Vienna Psychoanalytic Society*, in which, after all, a large number of discussions were reported that reflected Freud's relationship with Tausk. The two volumes of *Minutes* published so far, and the material from the third volume so kindly lent to me by the late Dr. Nunberg and by Mr. Federn, cover, as far as Tausk is concerned, eight papers, a number of shorter communications, and 109 discussion remarks.[31]

It was only one month after Tausk became a member (Novem-

---

[30] The worst revenge to which the Gods seem so far to have felt provoked by Freud's unveiling of the secret of parapraxes is undoubtedly contained in Dr. Rado's psychoanalytic writings. We learn from Alexander (1966, p. 243) that, as a young analyst, Rado attended a lecture by Freud. "He [Freud] spoke for two hours without a note. In content, organization and form, the lecture was fit to be printed without change. However, *Freud made at least a dozen slips of the tongue* [emphasis added] during the lecture and played almost incessantly with one of the rings he wore. . . . 'Voilà!' Rado thought, 'The knowledge of mental mechanisms does not protect the knower from being victimized by them'" (and —let me suggest—*voici pourquoi* he instantly fabricated his adaptational psychodynamics!)

[31] The material covers pretty regularly the time from Tausk's joining the group in October, 1909 to the end of 1913. There are eleven discussion remarks by Tausk in 1914, only four in 1915, and one in 1918. I shall concentrate on those

ber 24, 1909) that he presented a paper to the Society on a very difficult subject: "Theory of Knowledge and Psychoanalysis." At that time, however, Tausk felt acutely indisposed; he had had only a short time for preparation, and he had to stop before completing the presentation of the paper.[32] Freud, in his discussion remark, first corrected a historical mistake Tausk had made. Then he went on to say (*Minutes* 2, p. 335), "Personally, he [Freud] has particular difficulty grasping such abstract ideas as were presented in the lecture, ideas that should have been presented in a much more elementary manner." Freud was not able to judge whether the time was yet ripe for Tausk's subject; but "the speaker, however, seems to be the right man for that undertaking . . . It would be desirable if, despite today's misfire, Tausk would make it his task from time to time to present to us single parts of this broad constellation in a clear, detailed and elementary fashion." [33] One gets the impression from this remark that Freud hoped to find in Tausk a psychoanalyst who would follow up and specialize in a subject that had until then been neglected by the group—apparently because no member had developed interest in the subject, or possessed the ability to pursue it.

Tausk's next full-length paper was "A Contribution to the Psychology of Masochism." It was a brilliant clinical presentation, and was followed by a long discussion, during which Freud made a comment on one remark by a discussant.

In 1911 Tausk presented a paper on the teaching of psychoanalysis. In it he made some suggestions as to how one could teach psychoanalysis without stipulating any premises—that is to say, how it was possible to base the teaching on purely empirical material. Freud thought that Tausk's efforts were interesting and deserved thanks.

---

portions of the *Minutes* that may be relevant to the mutual relationship of Freud and Tausk and to Tausk's personality.

[32] Stekel (1950, p. 132f) maintains that after Tausk "had started off excellently," he became "confused" in the middle of the speech, and Stekel "continued the lecture extemporaneously." Stekel surmised that this may have been the reason why Tausk was later so antagonistic to him.

[33] Roazen calls it "a backhanded compliment" (p. 142) when Freud expresses in his obituary of Tausk his high regard for Tausk's philosophical and epistemological interests. The *Minutes* leave no doubt that Roazen is wrong in this comment.

The next lecture was on "Sexuality and Ego," to which I shall come back later. In it Tausk presented the differences and the interplay between sexual and ego drives, and Freud discussed a few differences that Tausk had not mentioned. The lecture on artistic inhibition I have already discussed earlier.

I now come to that lecture by Tausk on "The Father Problem", during the course of which Freud passed the note that Roazen has recorded so incompletely. Tausk first spoke of the institution of the matriarchate—the opposite of the patriarchate, as Tausk demonstrated in its Roman form, in which the father's power was restricted by the prohibition of incest with his own daughter. Once upon a time, the father, who had access to all women, must have voluntarily renounced the daughter; incest is destructive to the species. Society being founded on the existence of the father, patricide was forbidden, whereas the killing of the son was permitted, as a way of protecting paternal prerogatives. Later, the killing of the son was limited to castration and circumcision.

Then Tausk offered a review of the conflicts of the son in his relation to the father. In the last part, pathways of solutions were outlined: "A great man is he who has overcome his father. . . . The liberation of the son starts with a successful identification with the father." [34]

The lecture was in general unfavorably received by the discussants. Sachs spoke against Tausk's using, in this context, the matriarchate and the Roman patriarchate. A voluntary renunciation of incest is very improbable; it is also questionable whether race is harmed by incest. Freud agreed with the discussants more than he did with Tausk. Tausk, he said, did not show "how the neurosis is based on the father complex, and how the neurosis that developed in that way then has an effect on society." [35] The biological explanation Freud found untenable. "About the relationship of totemism to incest and father, he himself will soon give a lecture."

---

[34] *Ein grosser Mann ist der, der den Vater überwunden hat. . . . Die Befreiung des Sohnes geht von einer gelungenen Identifizierung mit dem Vater aus.*

[35] It seems that there was at that time a series of papers presented to the Society around the problem of society and neurosis.

Indeed, Tausk's presentation was a poor one. There is little to be found in it that can be regarded as original. Principal processes are left unexplained, though attributed to voluntary decisions or teleological goals. There is a clue, however, to Tausk's relative failure. Not much more than a year earlier, Tausk had said in a discussion that the matriarchate "is something hypothetical." Freud began his conclusion that evening with a reference to Tausk's remark, pointing out that "the matriarchate is not a hypothesis, but [its historical existence] is as much as proved by historical material; it is not a political but a social system." Is it not strange that someone who still believed a year or so previously that the matriarchate is nothing but a hypothesis should now make it the starting-point of a lecture on the Father problem?

From the discussion remarks, and from an entry in Lou Andreas-Salomé's diary (*Journal*, p. 114), one receives the impression that Tausk's elaboration on the matriarchate took up a far larger portion than one would guess from the *Minutes*. It was Freud's vigorous remark about the matriarchate of a year earlier —I surmise—that incited Tausk and may have made him believe that Freud was looking at the matriarchate as the first great step in the evolvement of civilization. If my hypothesis is correct, it would illustrate how Tausk picked up any clue he could gather, in order to steal a march upon Freud. In this instance, he was seeking to rival Freud in a matter that was evidently quite important to Freud and very close to his heart. Yet he went completely astray in his anticipation of Freud's viewpoint, even though Freud had already given three lectures that were signposts on his way toward the brilliant conclusion in the form of the last essay of *Totem and Taboo* (Freud 1913, pp. 100–161).

Hanns Sachs, who was far less rivalrous with Freud than Tausk was, and who therefore preserved a higher degree of autonomy in his writing, actually came far closer that evening to Freud's ideas, for he remarked that "the weak, old father was killed by the sons," and that that might have been the reason why the father renounced the daughters. Roazen attributes to Tausk a particular brilliance that made him superior to his colleagues in anticipating Freud's ideas. While he never documents that claim, here is at least some evidence of the opposite.

Two more lectures by Tausk have to be mentioned: "Contributions to a Psychoanalytic Exposition of Melancholia" in 1914, and "On the Psychology of the Alcoholic Occupational Delirium" (1915). About the first, Freud said that he "found in the lecture a few things new and a few not new at all." He then proceeded to present his own views. About the latter, Freud commented that Tausk had "correctly taken the essential point in his explanation."

As far as one can see from the *Minutes*, therefore, Freud's reaction to Tausk's eight full-length papers was in general positive. There is no visible indication that he behaved differently on these occasions from the way he behaved when he was discussing the lectures of other speakers.

The only unusual incident occurred when Tausk was reviewing the papers of two outstanding colleagues. In February, 1913, Tausk was the first speaker at a meeting devoted to "Reviews and Communications." His topic was a "Discussion of Papers by Ferenczi and Putnam about Philosophy and Psychoanalysis." It is regrettable that the *Minutes* do not contain anything but the agenda of that evening. Something must have gone wrong, because "Freud took the floor from Tausk," as Lou Andreas-Salomé recorded (*Journal*, p. 97). It is not clear from her diary what may have forced Freud's hand. I conjecture that Tausk's critique might have become excessive, for she reports: "The critique of Putnam burst out with the sound of drums and trumpets." The few remarks we find in her diary, however, do not sound as if this incident had had any particular consequences. It may have centered on a quarrel with Tausk's colleague, Paul Federn, whom "he [Tausk] gave a piece of his mind," as she informs us. In the English edition of her diary, Lou Andreas-Salomé's remark that Freud rejected Tausk's critique is omitted. It is the only instance of an outright rejection by Freud of a presentation by Tausk.

James Jackson Putnam (1846–1918) was Professor of Neurology at Harvard. Initially he had rejected psychoanalysis, but he became a follower of Freud. He was a founder of the American Psychoanalytic Association. Freud wrote him some letters that belong among the best he ever wrote. It would take the reader too far (and it is not really necessary) to go into the reasons why

Putnam was, for Freud, a person for whom he felt the highest respect, admiration and gratitude (see Freud 1919a, 1921).[36]

It seems that there is no other instance recorded of Freud's taking the floor away from somebody. I cannot therefore escape the impression that Tausk's rhetorical violence made Freud fear that Putnam, upon being informed of that meeting, might feel seriously offended. Be that as it may, the incident has nothing directly to do with the problem under discussion here. It is not related primarily to Tausk's creativity or to his originality. Whether Freud would have responded with greater composure if another speaker had attacked Putnam, no one can know. Freud's reaction, of course, might have been caused not solely by his obligation toward Putnam, but also by his irritation about Tausk.

I do not dare burden the reader's patience with a report on the subjects of Tausk's shorter communications and Freud's responses to them. As far as I can judge, nothing significant would be revealed thereby. It is a quite different matter, however, when Tausk's discussion remarks are considered. Here we may get closer to the heart of the problem. What comes quickly to one's attention is the frequency with which Tausk's comments were offensively aggressive. This aggressiveness was directed not at Freud, however, but at his colleagues.

Tausk had been attending the meetings for barely three months when the *Minutes* report that he made the following remark after Edward Hitschmann (1871–1958) gave a paper on obsessional neurosis: 'Tausk has the feeling that everything Hitschmann presented is already known and solved. He is surprised that all of this has been brought forward as a new problem" (*Minutes* 2, p. 411). The last paper before the summer vacation was J. Sadger's (1910b) presentation "On Urethral Erotism." The *Minutes* (2, p. 578) report: "The only thing Tausk learned from the paper was that the genital apparatus is involved in micturation." As a matter of fact, the paper brought many new insights. One finds in it what was probably the first psychoanalytic references to the connection between urethral erotism and premature ejaculation. Here Sadger actually forged ahead of Freud, and we see Tausk responding in

---

[36] For the problems that were the center of discussion, see Putnam (1912ab), Ferenczi (1912).

the way that Roazen consistently ascribes to Freud. Hitschmann, along with Sadger, was a member of several years' standing, and Tausk's abrasive manner must have been particularly provocative in these instances. Quite a few more discussion remarks of this sort could be cited.[37]

Another question of interest, of course, is whether or not Tausk's discussion remarks reveal significant originality. Can one learn from them that he was *ahead* of Freud or the others in the group, or perhaps on the verge of achieving what one might call a *breakthrough?* As far as I can judge—and how easily one may become a victim of misjudgment in dealing with such a comprehensive question, I do not need to spell out—there is only one such instance, aside from the one cited earlier. In 1911, discussing a paper by Hanns Sachs "About the Applicability of Psychoanalysis to Works of Poetic Art," Tausk asserted that certain resistances against the interpretation of literary works come from the subject's unwillingness to let complexes go, "because we need them as motors of psychic life and perhaps justifiedly fear that we could deprive them of their powers in this way." This is, I believe, original with Tausk and a rather pregnant idea.

It seems typical of Tausk. He apparently had productive flashes on the spur of the moment; yet he did not carry them through to a fruitful end. Following a remark of the same character that Stekel had made, he once spoke against the analysts' procedure of simply uncovering repressed processes in poets and artists, and demanded instead "a psychology of creativity." Yet I do not recall his having devoted much effort toward evolving such a psychology; at best, there are striking, well-turned statements, sometimes in epigrammatic form, such as that "the allegory is the interpretation of an interpretation."

Since the concept of identity is usually connected with Tausk, it is of interest that, already in the spring of 1913, he made the remark that narcissism is the "identity formula" (*Identitäts-*

---

[37] Stekel (1950, p. 133) complained that Tausk "decried my new book [Stekel 1911a], and spoke at length about the mistakes in grammar in the preface." Even though the recorded *Minutes* do not contain any reference to this particular criticism, they make it clear that Tausk rejected Stekel's book *in toto*, whereas other discussants seem to have managed to find reasons for saying something commendatory about it.

formel), by means of which the individual identifies with the sexuality of the species. The statement is somewhat obscure, as are many passages in the *Minutes*, the purpose of which of course was merely to preserve an abstract; but the originality of the remark is somewhat reduced when it is found that Freud had already asserted, at a meeting in November, 1911, that certain symbols express the dreamer's "identity with the other sex."

Occasionally, we find weighty remarks, such as the one following Reik's presentation on "Death and Sexuality," in the fall of 1911. One cannot say that these remarks were without historical precursors, but they do strike the reader as manifestations of Tausk's quick and correct understanding of what the speaker had in mind. When he says that every anxiety is fear of death, he is following an idea that Stekel had formulated before, and that was original with Fliess, as Freud pointed out that evening. When he says that every instinctual damming-up elicits anxiety, however, he remains within the framework of Freud's thinking.

It is different when he asserts that a full absorption (*Aufgehen*) in sexual pleasure is "perhaps never completely possible," that part of the libido goes over into anxiety. "Orgasm turns against itself; therefore, death. From this point of view, Christianity is nothing but a manifestation of anxiety supplied with an object." It would be worthwhile, if space permitted, to reproduce Freud's lengthy discussion remark on that occasion, his concise delineation of the variety of problems involved, and his precise statement regarding the areas that need further psychoanalytic investigation. It was perhaps typical of Tausk to speak once again after Freud, in order to add: "It is a matter of the conflict between species and individual. The primary function of the (sexual) drive, to serve the species, gets into conflict with the secondary, to serve individual pleasure, which therefore can never be fully satisfied." This seems to have been Tausk's favorite idea at that time. In the way in which it was formulated by him, it is incorrect, even though the idea does contain a kernel of truth.

It is of interest to watch Tausk grasping the essential new elements in a presentation, as he did after Sabine Spielrein's paper ("On Transformation") (cf. Spielrein 1912a, 1912b) in November, 1911, whereas Freud was on that occasion diverted to a peripheral issue. Only eight years later did Freud (1920a, p. 55 n.)

acknowledge the depth of her thinking. Looking back, one must say that Spielrein was forging ahead of Freud, yet he showed no sign of perturbation or intolerance.

At one session Tausk was clearly the conservative, as compared with Freud, even though he was in all probability correct in his objection. Presenting the results of his analysis of the Wolf-Man which was published in 1918, Freud put forth the idea of the existence of some inborn "primordial fantasies" (*Urphantasien*). Tausk objected to the assumption of inheritance at this point; the assumption of the inheritance of a capacity to react in a certain way was, in his opinion, sufficient. Freud countered that, even though Tausk defended the position that psychoanalysis had taken up to then, "he was fighting for a lost cause." Tausk, however, was right, and the modern geneticist would agree with him, that it is a matter of inherited capacity to react. Even though Freud was wrong, he was here pursuing a new line of approach, and it was Tausk who was trying to defend the traditional viewpoint.

On another occasion, however, Freud took sides with Tausk and—looking back—one has to say that Tausk was in the wrong. This happened after Tausk's paper on alcoholic delirium, when Federn, anticipating psychoanalytic insight by two decades, spoke of "the general anxiety of the manic defense mechanism." Tausk "determinedly disputes" (*bestreitet entschieden*) the notion that "mania has anxiety," and Freud remarks that in mania anxiety has no place. Here Federn was definitely far ahead of both Freud and Tausk. Are we to assume that it was because Freud was jealous of Federn and felt threatened by him that he rejected Federn's very astute proposition? I would say rather that it is Tausk's "determined" objection that sounds suspicious. We shall presently observe his rivalry with Federn.

In reviewing Freud's discussion remarks, one observes just the opposite of what Roazen's propositions would lead one to expect. There are many instances when Freud, in his discussion comments, which usually concluded the debate, singled out Tausk's remarks in a commendatory way. I could cite at least ten such instances, but I shall cite only one, because it occurred in the spring of 1913—that is to say, at a time when Freud was allegedly seriously involved with his rivalry with Tausk, and because it occurred, at least, according to the *Minutes*, at a prominent place —namely, at the very end of Freud's discussion remark. Theodor Reik had given a paper on Arthur Schnitzler, and Freud concluded his discussion of it with the remark that Tausk had "correctly emphasized" a point that had referred to female sexuality. Curiously, it had to do with a point that came very close to a subject of interest to Freud at that time—namely, the function of female narcissism in the relation of the sexes—and which he took up soon thereafter.

I can now disprove the validity of the comment Roazen made (p. 55f.) upon Lou Andreas-Salomé's report of Freud's error in ascribing Tausk's discussion remark to another speaker (*Journal*, p. 88). If Roazen had informed the reader what remark Tausk had made on that occasion, it would have come out that it was one of no interest to Freud at that time. Following Sadger's paper "On the Necessity to Differentiate the Erotism of the Posterior from Anal Erotism" (see Sadger 1913), Tausk, in his usual opposition to Sadger, pointed out the speaker's "methodological mistake" (*prinzipieller Fehler*), and went on to say that Sadger had described the posterior as an object of erotic excitation, but that sexual objects can never bring about erotism. It is impossible to find in this remark anything that could "get underfoot" with Freud, who had already discussed such questions in his *Three Essays* (1905a). His interest was going at that time in an entirely different direction.

By the way, the *Minutes* do not report any discussion remark by Freud on that occasion. Lou Andreas-Salomé does not say to whom Freud erroneously ascribed Tausk's remark. If it was to Federn, who had spoken after Tausk and had also raised an objection, that would have to be considered as a proximate cause of Freud's error. A comparison with Freud's response to Tausk's remark after Reik's presentation proves that Roazen's acid interpretation of Freud's error is unwarranted.

However, a review of the discussion remarks does reveal some aspects of Tausk's character that almost undermine the entire edifice of Roazen's philippic against Freud. The reader will not mind if I go into details on this occasion. Already in the fall of 1910, Tausk asserted that a certain report, published in an article by the German sexologist, Erich Wulffen, had come from him.

No particular reason can be seen why Tausk should have brought this to the attention of the group.

More important—indeed, quite decisive for the future—is an event that occurred after Freud's presentation, on October 26, 1910, of "The Two Principles of Psychic Functioning." I shall come back to that memorable meeting, which historically served to introduce Freud's turn toward ego-psychology (see Chapter VII).

Tausk was the first one to discuss the paper. His remark is not quite exactly recorded; but evidently he asserted that he had evolved "a few [comparable (?)] small theses on quite different pathways"—even though they did not contain "the genesis of the mechanism," which Freud presented.[38] Whether Tausk meant that he had published something of that sort, or that he had had comparable thoughts, we do not know. He spoke occasionally as if he had published articles before he became an analyst; yet Roazen apparently was not able to discover more than one such.

Be that as it may, here was Freud presenting thoughts that are regarded in the history of analysis as being of the highest originality, and yet they precipitate a remark from Tausk in which one hears at least overtones of an implication of something approaching a claim of priority. No one seems to have asked Tausk where he had published his small theses, and Freud did not respond to Tausk's remark. Tausk did have a good ear for the significant, and apparently, by contrast with the rest in this case, he was aware that, at that moment, Freud had initiated something entirely new. That he did not grasp its actual meaning, however, can be observed in his later paper on "Sexuality and Ego"; but I shall come back to that in due time.

I attribute paramount importance to this incident. It occurred one year after Tausk had joined the group, and probably less than two years after he had started to familiarize himself with psychoanalysis. It is utterly impossible for Freud, in this instance, to have inadvertently used anything Tausk had told him; and yet Tausk did put in a claim of his own, subtle as it may have been, being somehow unable to tolerate the fact that Freud was (without his

---

[38] . . . dass er seinerzeit auf ganz anderen Wegen zu einigen kleinen Thesen gekommen sei, denen jedoch das Substrat, die Genese des Mechanismus wie wir sie heute gehört haben, fehlte.

participation) in process of initiating a new channel of psycho-analytic research.

It soon becomes apparent that Tausk was preoccupied with questions of priority; I would surmise that that preoccupation was stronger in him than it was in others.[39] In 1911, he made a special point. After Sachs's (1912) paper, he said that he wished to demand priority for the thought that the sexual drive is not always able to provide complete gratification, "as far as Prof. Freud does not demand it for himself." It seems that Tausk's idea was not recorded correctly. He evidently meant—as has been mentioned before—that there is something in the sexual drive that resists complete gratification. Hitschmann, who was considerably less romantic than Tausk, remarked that this occurs only in cases of perversion or neurosis.

Be that as it may, one must admit that Tausk's behavior, was, to say the least, strange. Whatever may be the correct formulation of the idea for which he claimed priority, it was not original with him and, besides, it appears to be rather trivial. Only someone who overestimates his own thoughts and who is, in addition, excessively fearful of being cheated, could have proceeded in that way. His added reference to Freud sounds like a paranoid provocation; it is as if he were saying "Here, of course, one must first get Freud's permission to be original." Little did he know, apparently, that Freud had renounced any claim to priority with regard to discussion remarks, long before Tausk had joined the group (cf. Chapter IV).

There is another of Tausk's discussion remarks that appears to be in keeping with such behavior. When Ferenczi, who made a special trip from Budapest to Vienna in order to contribute his

---

[39] Lou Andreas-Salomé recorded that Alfred Winterstein's (1913) paper was "excessively praised" because, she thought, it did not trespass on someone else's domain, which "the lecturers usually do to each other, [carrying this] up to the complete confusion of the priority question, because all [of them] reach into the same cornucopia" [Füllkorb meaning, of course, Freud] (my own literal translation; cf. Journal, p. 69). The so far unpublished Minutes that I have had the occasion to peruse, however, do not convey this impression. It may have been that Tausk was more vehement than others in questions of priority, or more insistent on keeping his own remarks on that question on record, for the remarks relating directly or indirectly to priority that can be found in the Minutes are generally his. This does not disprove, however, that disagreements about priority were frequent among the early analysts (see e.g., Freud 1914, p. 25).

share to the discussion on masturbation that was going on there (Jones, 2, p. 301), presented his ideas, Tausk made a point of their similarity with his own (*die Ähnlichkeit mit seinen Ausführungen*).

From some of Freud's discussion remarks, one may deduce that he actually felt provoked by Tausk at times. A few remarks that may fall into that category are recorded as having been exchanged between Tausk and Freud, following Schrötter's (1912) famous paper on experimental dreams. Freud expressed the opinion that even Schrötter's dream experiments, which had impressively proven the correctness of one of Freud's theories about dreams, would not convince those "who do not want to let themselves be convinced" (a prediction that proved to be true). Tausk contradicted Freud on this. He added that the fact that the censor also remains strongly active in hypnosis and leads to symbolization "throws *new* light on the essence of hypnosis" (emphasis added). Now Tausk should have known from Freud's writings that Freud (1910a, p. 26) had described exactly that state of affairs. Freud replied that he had known this ever since his first attempts at influencing patients by hypnosis. Later in the discussion, Tausk suggested that one might order the hypnotized subject, after he had related the dream, to reproduce its infantile roots. Freud doubted the success of that experiment. Here Freud may have made a mistake: Tausk may have had a promising idea. Whether Freud still felt irritated by Tausk's previous provocation and answered brusquely is not, of course, recognizable from the record.

If Roazen were to cite such an instance, when he makes statements about Freud's detrimental effect on Tausk's creativity, one would have to shrug one's shoulders. Why did Tausk not follow up his idea? Freud had relinquished the hypnotic method after a period of doubt, perhaps even of crisis; it was out of the question for him to return to that method. For him, that would have been a regressive step. Tausk, on the other hand, might have been able to make some highly interesting discoveries. If the reason why he did not follow up his idea was that he felt discouraged by Freud, responsibility must be laid at Tausk's doorstep. Later, he worked in a hospital clinic, where he had all sorts of opportunities to carry out the experiment he had suggested.

On another occasion, Freud did sound irritated by Tausk. Freud had presented a case of foot fetishism (Jones 2, p. 306). Tausk, the first speaker, complemented Freud's analysis by demonstrating that "the homosexual seeks himself [in the object] quite directly." In his concluding remark, Freud observed that Sadger and he had described the homosexual's amorousness toward himself. While he agreed that his own interpretation of the case had been complemented by Tausk's remark, he objected to a conception that made it seem as if the patient were only incidentally (nebenbei) identifying with the woman.

The remark does not sound like part of a discussion about priorities. Rather, it appears to have been intended to remind Tausk that he was presenting something that was already quite well known in the group, as if it were quite new and original with him. (I do not know to what extent Freud felt compelled to protect Sadger, since he put Sadger's name before his own.) Furthermore, a tendency toward oversimplification in Tausk's thinking can be noted in his reduction of the homosexual problem to a one-dimensional one, through the exclusion of intervening mechanisms.

Again, contrary to the expectations that may be aroused by Roazen's book, one never observes Freud being irritated by Tausk when the latter has something new and original to say; remarks into which one might read an implication of irritation on Freud's part occurred only when Tausk foolishly claimed originality where there was none. One can easily imagine that such behavior got under Freud's skin. I want to close my abstract of the Minutes with the one incident that in my opinion offers definite proof that Roazen was utterly misled in suggesting that Freud had contributed his own share to an issue of priority that supposedly existed between him and Tausk.

Federn (January 14, 1914) presented, as a supplement to a previous paper, further observations about dreams of inhibition (see Federn 1914). He also reported an analogy between certain dreams and the psychotic state of catatonia. Freud "sees in the reference to the analogy with schizophrenia an important novum," reports the Minutes. The next speaker was Tausk, who "lays claim to the priority of this [Federn's] assertion on the basis of a statement that he himself made in Dr. Pötzl's course,[40] the value of which for claiming a right to priority Federn disputes." Here we observe Tausk attacking a colleague in exactly the same manner as he had attacked Freud. His pathological behavior goes so far that he publicly claims priority, even when it has to do only with a discussion remark.

I will point out in Chapter IV through what mental contortions Roazen had to go in order to prove that there existed an issue of plagiarism in Freud's life—how many objective sources of information he had to ignore; how many statements of Freud he had to misinterpret. The documentation of Tausk's preoccupation with priority is plain, neither do the documents require interpretation; they speak openly and concisely. Was it Freud who felt threatened when Federn discovered something new about schizophrenia? Did he not instead praise him for his astuteness? Did not Tausk reveal himself here as a querulous person who did indeed feel threatened by a gifted colleague? And if the reader had found this little incident in Roazen's book, would he not have had the right to regard it as proof that Tausk was suffering from a pathological urge, if not a compulsion, to quarrel about questions of priority or its like?

The *Minutes* do not contain a single instance that would suggest Freud's "unwillingness to give Tausk due credit," as Roazen falsely claims, without presenting a shred of historical evidence.[41]

It must be plain by now that Roazen's assertion that "Freud's mode of thinking was bound to elicit Tausk's resentment, because it prevented him from ever gaining credit for asserting himself in an original manner" (p. 87) is untenable. How little Freud was averse to acknowledging the contributions of others to psychoanalysis, even if they were opponents, can be learned from his *History of the Psychoanalytic Movement* (Freud 1914a). There, he scrupulously and painstakingly referred to whatever accretion of knowledge psychoanalysis still owed to Adler and Jung; what, in other words, their *original* contributions had been, and this even

---

[40] Otto Pötzl (1877–1962) was assistant at Wagner-Jauregg's University Clinic. He later became a full professor of psychiatry and neurology at the University of Vienna.

[41] For a discussion of Roazen's criticism of Freud (p. 192) for not having cited Tausk in his paper on Melancholia (1917a), see Chapter V.

in a polemical treatise. However, it is reasonable to ask what it means when a professional person is driven by an incessant concern about whether or not he is receiving sufficient credit. This had apparently become an *idée fixe* in Tausk's mind.

What more should Freud have done for Tausk than to quote his papers, send him patients and favor his public career, as well as discuss his papers and frequently commend his discussion remarks? One wonders what Tausk did expect of Freud. The only thing left for Freud to do would have been for him to retire and surrender his position and standing in the psychoanalytic movement to his ambitious follower. Is Roazen suggesting that *this* was what should have taken place?

THE CASE HISTORY OF TAUSK

LET US RETURN to the subject at hand. Before going into a clinical consideration of Tausk's personality, I prefer to present briefly the salient point of Roazen's book.

Tausk had gone into Army service, and when he returned to Vienna was facing many difficult problems. The proximate reason for his seeking treatment with Freud is not known. At any rate, Freud refused to treat him. He sent him to Dr. Deutsch, who was at that time in training analysis with Freud himself. As soon as Dr. Deutsch started to analyze Tausk, she filled her own analytic sessions with reports about Tausk; after three months, Freud confronted her with the choice of discontinuing either Tausk's analysis or her own. She chose the former. A few months later, Tausk committed suicide.

This is the external frame on which the author has hung a terrible accusation against Freud. As we shall see later, it can be proven wrong. At this point, in order to understand the insoluble dilemma Freud was facing in dealing with Tausk, I shall outline briefly the patient's history.[42]

---

[42] For the following reconstruction of Tausk's case history, I have used, aside from the biographical data that Roazen has presented in his book, biographical material culled from Tausk's publications, from Lou Andreas-Salomé's *Journal*, and from the *Minutes*. As will be seen, Roazen ignored decisive passages in these three sources. In addition, Mr. H. F. Fuerst found a newspaper article that is of

Tausk's family background was not favorable, inasmuch as the father, an internationally known journalist, was authoritarian and attempted to impose a hypermorality on his children, whereas he arrogated to himself the privilege of being unfaithful to his wife and was a poor provider to boot. He was restless, frequently changing his domicile and finding himself "sometimes in need of a journey to quiet his spirits" (p. 9). Tausk was antagonistic to his father. "He was forever embarrassed to be called by his father's name" (p. 10). He led the opposition not only at home against the father, but also at school, where he organized a strike over a religious matter (he came from a nonpracticing Jewish family).

He was brought up in a province of the Austro-Hungarian monarchy; at the age of eighteen, he went to Vienna to study law. Three years later he married a girl who had become pregnant by him. Before the marriage he was baptized; but he concealed this whenever it was possible to do so. He and his father-in-law hated each other. After starting a promising law practice in his home province, he decided to change his profession. Thereupon, Tausk and his wife separated—she, with their two sons, going to live and work in Vienna, and Tausk going to Berlin.

The report of Tausk's suicide in the *Neues Wiener Journal* (July 4, 1919, p. 7) contains a few details of the kind that should have been found in Roazen's book. Tausk left his assignment as *Gerichtsadjunkt* (assistant to the court) because of a conflict with the court authority. When a death verdict was passed in a trial in which he had been active, he refused to sign the judgment. This is an important detail, because it reveals that his discontinuance of his original profession was not only prompted by inner restlessness, but also based on a professional objection. The report continues: "The highly talented, educated young man turned thereupon to journalism, to which he devoted himself in Vienna. For a while he was a member of the editorial staff of the *Neues Wiener Journal*. In this profession, too, in which he distinguished

---

interest. Furthermore, I obtained important evidence, which I have included, from a source that was unknown to Roazen; however, I did not get permission to publish the information I received from one of Tausk's former lovers. The ensuing loss is hardly of consequence, since this information would only have confirmed the general picture obtained from the other sources.

himself through his brilliant abilities, he did not permit himself to remain long" (my own translation).

In Berlin, Tausk started a new career, "wrote poetry, practiced his violin, drew charcoal sketches, and directed plays" (Roazen, p. 15). A letter is recorded in which he defends himself against a friend's charge that he had no right "to act the way I do," instead of providing for his children. Yet he did not neglect his children entirely, but sent money for them whenever possible and showed an interest in their welfare.

We note here for the first time (possibly out of identification with his father, who was also a poor provider) a tendency to shirk responsibility and to let other people—in this case, his wife—shoulder the duties that were his. "I have not really tried anything in my life. I have immediately been pressed into a mold. I am vacillating between desire and duty," he wrote (p. 13). Apparently, he was going through the kind of crisis that almost every well-endowed young man with intellectual interests goes through, but it was somewhat delayed (he was 26 years old) and, when it did come, it was at the expense of his progeny.

The crisis was not a constructive one, however, and, at the age of 28, Tausk was hospitalized in a sanatorium for 25 days. His condition was diagnosed variedly as "mental-physical exhaustion," "hereditary inclination towards the psychopathological side" (by which was meant, I would assume, what is called "sociopathy" today). He himself called it "neurasthenia." He described the plight of the crisis movingly as, "one can be more alone than alone" (p. 20). "He was searching for 'salvation'" (p. 20). "I am incurably ill in my soul. My whole past appears to me to be nothing but a preparation for this terrible collapse of my personality. . . . Hereditary unfitness for life" (pp. 20–21).

It is not easy to make a reliable diagnosis of the condition from which he was suffering at that time. When he records "I am trying again to feel nature. In those last twenty months in Berlin, there have been strange changes in me, I have lost the feeling for nature" (p. 20); or, later, "Only the doctors have intelligent faces. The patients all look like poisoned rats and mules" (p. 21), and "obsessional ideas, heavy depressions, pressures in my head, and tired, tired" (p. 22)—one is not inclined to think of "a classic depression" (p. 22), as Roazen does, but rather of a schizophrenic phase that ended in remission. Particularly when he wrote: "Life has not shaped me, it has crushed me. I'm an ugly powerless mass, deadly tired, and I have had enough of this life" (p. 23), he was describing a mode of experiencing existence that is frequently heard from schizophrenics. Evidently the feeling about self had deteriorated, and the inner tonus and feeling of activity had come close to zero—two ominous indications of a far more severe disorder than classic depression, although they do not exclude it.

Tausk's rather rash decisions, his restlessness, his lack of any sense of responsibility, as shown by his premorbid history, however, would not speak against the diagnosis of schizophrenia. Persons who are inclined toward "classic depressions" are usually dominated by a strong sense of duty; in psychoanalytic parlance, their superego is too demanding. This was definitely not the case with Tausk.

There is another circumstance that speaks strongly against the diagnosis of classic depression. While he was in Berlin, Tausk had "a very happy love affair" (p. 18) with an actress who apparently felt crushed when he later abandoned her. His happiness, according to Roazen, was never mentioned in his letters. "If he appeared to his wife as a miserable wretch, then he had never denied her anything he was capable of giving" (ibid.). Such duplicity is almost incompatible with the author's diagnosis, but it does occur in the depressions of sociopaths and preschizophrenics.

The mechanism of producing feelings of guilt in others by exhibiting one's own sufferings and at the same time concealing one's joys, in order to make the other person feel miserable, was perhaps a leading mechanism in Tausk. In reality, Tausk owed his wife a debt of gratitude. She evidently took excellent care of his sons, even though her husband's contributions to the family's support must have been minimal. Despite the way she was treated by Tausk, "she never turned her sons against their father" (p. 16). By the fall of 1908, he had recovered to the extent of being able to make a trip to Italy. He wrote Freud a letter, the contents of which are not known, but Freud was sufficiently impressed by it to think that the writer was a medical doctor and to invite him to come to Vienna to study psychoanalysis (p. 24).

It seems to me that Tausk could not have asked for more than he got, once he decided to become an analyst. His great talents were acknowledged from the beginning, and the little group that had gathered around Freud received him with open arms. Roazen erred in his evaluation of Tausk's joining the group in Vienna. He asserts (p. 27): "Tausk was not the only pupil of Freud's to abandon his previous profession to become an analyst. That whole early generation of psychoanalysts typically came to Freud with the bravado of a frustrated or failed career." This is an unfounded assertion: Hitschmann relinquished a prosperous medical practice, and did so against Josef Breuer's advice; Federn, whose father was a noted physician, gave up a most promising career in the field of internal medicine; and Hanns Sachs, who came from a prosperous family, could easily have continued his law practice, if he had wished to do so. Also, Adler and Jung were already respected in their professions at the time when they became interested in psychoanalysis. In most of Freud's early followers who joined psychoanalysis for good, the signs of sacrifice and idealism are clearly visible; as far as I know, Tausk was the only one who was foundering professionally before he decided upon a psychoanalytic career.

When Tausk came from Berlin, he was without roots, without purpose, without profession. Psychoanalysis gave him a field of study, research, and professional activity—all of which was a blessing to him. Evidently, until then his temperament did not permit him to remain long enough engaged in an activity to have given him the prestige he needed or to have enabled him to feel at ease. In Vienna he found not only a well-organized group to which he could belong, but also an ideal leader. He had expressed, during his crisis in Berlin, the need "of some 'mentally normal . . . wise and good human being' " and he had written on another occasion: "One needs a guide" (p. 20f.).

Tausk's psychoanalytic career was a particularly quick one. His publications were numerous and apparently well received. He participated vigorously in the inner struggles of the Society, siding with Freud against Adler and Jung. His differences with Stekel have already been mentioned; here Freud, in turn, sided with Tausk. Once he decided in favor of a medical career, Freud and some members of the group supported him financially for several years.[43]

However, despite this conspicuous turn for the better, the signs of psychopathology did not subside completely in Tausk. I have mentioned earlier the necessity of his ending his first lecture prematurely. Federn may have been correct in suggesting the unconscious reason for Tausk's failure, when he said "that the weariness of the speaker when he was proceeding from Kant to Freud, and declared that he could not go on, was more deeply determined" (*Minutes 2*, p. 336). At the Psychoanalytic Congress in Budapest (1918), it became evident that some acute condition was in the making.

There is a noteworthy entry in Lou Andreas-Salomé's diary, referring to a description Tausk gave her of an experience that he apparently had with some frequency after "strong intellectual productivity, forcibly terminated by outer and inner distractions" (*Journal*, p. 119f.).

> He would spontaneously develop an oversensitivity to certain forms and lines. He could stare at the movement of a horse on the street or interpret an S-shaped ornament on the table leg as if they suggested a whole world of inner relationships; it was as if he were experiencing at one and the same time all the steps that led to these formal phenomena of existence and that had been poured into them, finding in them total and boundless fulfillment.

Was the severe acute spell of five years earlier continuing subterraneously? It is hardly possible to arrive at a decision on the basis of such scant data, particularly since experiences of this type are often reported by artists. But the possibility should not be dismissed lightly. Questionable as a correct evaluation may be in this instance, the full measure of Tausk's psychopathology, which ultimately resulted in his downfall, can be observed in his relationships with women.

Tausk's love affair in Berlin has been mentioned. The author records that the woman "was in a terrible depression after Victor broke the engagement; for some time thereafter it seemed to have

---

[43] The author is probably in error when he implies that before World War I Freud took it for granted that analysts would be physicians.

crushed her life. Almost exactly the same problem arose with another woman in Tausk's life" (p. 107f.). I read into this passage the intimation of possible suicide. I was able to trace both women. The latter, I found, died in 1936; and the former, I found, is still living. But I do not doubt that Tausk had murderous impulses against women; this can be substantiated from his childhood history, as will be seen presently.

During the war, while he was in Belgrade, Tausk rescued a woman who had been arrested by the Austrians. An affair evolved; he lived with her and even became engaged to her. After the war, he had the opportunity to marry her and to obtain a professorship in the capital of the newly-established Yugoslavia; instead, he broke the engagement. Earlier during the war, he had become engaged to another woman (the only one whose name the author does not reveal—out of discretion or from ignorance?), who was unfaithful to him and consorted with one of his patients. Tausk then became seriously depressed. At this point, I shall stop discussing Tausk's love life.

It sounds rather heartless when Roazen in all seriousness asserts: "While a man of tremendous and primitive passions, it was only at the end that they decisively worked against him" (p. 134). The author even dares to give Tausk credit for the fact that "he had won the love of many women," instead of recognizing that it was in this connection that Tausk's fundamental sadism against women came to the fore. By his charm he drew them closely to himself, only to hurt them so deeply that some might not have recovered from the injury. After all, had he been a responsible person, he might have taken note of the fact that he was indeed dangerous to women and tried to restrain his urge rather than to make women helplessly dependent on him.

Be that as it may, the author reports an incident that permits the making of certain far-reaching inferences. At the clinic, "Tausk once stimulated a woman's genitals with a galvanic rod after her ovaries had been removed, to see whether they retained their erotogenicity" (p. 118 n.). Such an experiment would not now be permitted, at least not in a hospital of good repute—even in the age of Masters and Johnson. It would lead, I think, to the psychiatrist's immediate dismissal. Furthermore, it is quite strange to hear that a psychoanalyst needs any such method in order to ascertain the continuing erotogenicity of an organ; this surely indicates that Tausk was subject to strong perverse impulses.

I do not hesitate to look at that incident as an abuse of medical authority. Tausk was not able to resist the temptations to which a physician may be exposed when he is practicing medicine. The worst incident of that sort, which ultimately brought about Tausk's downfall, will be reported later. Incidents of abuse of professional authority already occurred at a time when Tausk was still studying medicine. One informant has recalled the following: Tausk held a position of some authority among the students, on the strength of his age and his law degree. He had organized a group among the students, whom he instructed in hypnosis. He asked the female participants, while they were in the hypnotic state, with whom among those present she would like to cohabit. If *he* was named, he subsequently dated the girl, with obvious intentions, and was said to have succeeded in most instances.

Further, it is not without reflection on Tausk that one of his fiancées cohabited with a patient of his. Such incidents can occur only when a man makes pathological object choices and unconsciously cooperates with the love object's acting out.

Thus, Tausk's clinical history demonstrates a high degree of sociopathy. One of the basic patterns of his pathology was to attract a woman and, once she was firmly tied to him, attempt to destroy her. In the author's account of Tausk's life, there is not one single instance of a relationship with a woman that could have worked toward mutual happiness and growth.

Roazen suggests a large number of possible explanations for Tausk's pathological behavior toward women, as if he were eager to enumerate all the possibilities recorded in the psychoanalytic literature that could relate to this topic. As one of the main reasons why Tausk failed ever to establish an enduring object relationship to a woman, Roazen puts forward his idiosyncrasy against having a woman dependent on him. This must be an error, because his wife showed an ability to be independent that was, if anything, superior to his own. She was a socialist and apparently did not hide it, which was not a matter of ease and comfort in those years; whereas Tausk, as we shall soon see, did not always have the courage to abide by his convictions. She had left her family for her husband's sake, and had gone against the father's will in so doing. She apparently always earned the money necessary for the support of her two sons, and never tried to put any pressure on her husband, either for money or for his return.

Rightly, Roazen says that it would help if more were known about Tausk's relationship to his mother; yet, curiously enough, he ignores the two key passages in Lou Andreas-Salomé's *Journal*, which tells us something about Tausk's need to destroy women. Her diary (*Journal*, p. 107) reports that Tausk, as a child, "helped himself when his mother punished him severely, silently answering her scolding epithets 'That's just what you are, you are!' and how, finally, it came to be an automatic reactive discharge that pacified him, until one day it slipped from his lips like an uncontrolled act and stood there, alien and unintelligible to him" (author's emphasis). Did he not do the same thing all over again with women later on: "It is you, not I"? Whatever they were ready to do for him, apparently nothing was enough.

The decisive episode, however, which must have left a fatal feeling of guilt in him, was the following (*Journal*, p. 107f.): ". . . in an unbridled rage that demanded action, he went to the room where there was a picture of his mother in her youth and pierced it through the heart with a needle—so that for a long time he hardly dared enter the room, as if it were the scene of an actual murder. Later, his mother made mention of the 'scratched' picture and he was astonished until he was able to convince himself that it really was only scratched, the penetrating thrust having been made only mentally." I seriously doubt that last statement. A needle is not a knife; when it pierces a canvas or heavy paper, the mark it makes may look like a scratch.[44]

---

[44] The case history of Tausk is reminiscent of that of Wilhelm Reich (1887–1957). In the lives of both, matricide played a far greater role than one would expect to find in contemporary society. In Reich's instance, it took a terrible turn. When he was 14, the mother committed suicide, following his revelation to the father of a love affair she was having with a tutor. His feelings of guilt on that score must surely have been compounded by the fact that, in consequence, his father wanted to commit suicide. He did not carry out that desire, but he did bring about his death indirectly. After first insuring himself heavily, he then exposed himself to inclement weather until he contracted pneumonia. He died from tuberculosis; but the insurance company refused to pay (Ilse Reich 1969, p. 4). Attitudes of irresponsibility toward women were to be seen in Reich, as they were in Tausk, as well as a relative neglect of his progeny and an overconcern with questions of priority (Ilse Reich 1969, p. 45f). Moreover, Reich's later

Why did Roazen fail to refer to that account, despite the fact that he says that *more* would have to be known about Tausk's relationship to his mother, in order to understand his strange dealings with women? Why does he find it necessary to suspect all kinds of evil consequences arising from the way Jewish mothers in general raise their children, instead of using the overt and explicit clinical material available in the *Journal?* I am not speaking here in contradiction of his speculations about Jewish mothers; I only wish to point out that the little that is known about Tausk's mother is not of the sort that could possibly account for such a severe reaction in the child.

I myself have had two patients whose childhood had been marked by comparable episodes; both of them suffered as adults from circumscribed psychotic episodes, and both were unanalyzable.[45] The fact that, as a boy, Tausk was unable to defend himself against his matricidal impulses by way of the evolvement of anxiety or of a neurotic symptom, but was instead compelled to act them out in the way he did, is of an importance that can hardly be overrated. This is rare behavior in a child; it allows for only a grave prognosis.

We do not know how often that same matricide was re-enacted by the adult, when he found himself impelled to bring the greatest unhappiness into the lives of women who knew him. We observe in the adult Tausk, as well, an ego that is gravely lacking in structuralization, so that it is compelled to deal by action— not by fantasy, creative work or symptom—with an impulse like that of committing matricide. Such impulses, one may argue, are

---

misfortunes have been brought into connection with Freud's refusal to accept him as an analysand (Ilse Reich 1967, p. 14). There is also in Reich's case a question of what is the correct diagnosis of his psychopathology. In the light of the similarity of their psychopathologies, the idea presents itself that, had Tausk lived longer, his further development might have shown even greater similarities with the course taken by Wilhelm Reich's career.

[45] One had tried to poison his younger brother and later suffered from manic spells. During one of these, he declared that peace had started all over the world, and demanded that the Church bells be rung. The other had shot an arrow into her father's portrait, and later suffered from sporadic spells that were indistinguishable from schizophrenia, one of them even resulting in the development of a delusion of an influencing machine. She regularly recovered, and then had long symptom-free intervals.

ubiquitous. Yet they are usually firmly and solidly repressed, if not indeed dissolved, in the overwhelming majority of males.

We are accustomed now to recognizing that there appears to be no limitation to what may become the content of a manifest dream; and yet it is possible that no human being has ever dreamed of killing his mother. That latent dream-thoughts may refer to a matricidal wish is, of course, well known; also, the manifest dream of sexual intercourse with the mother is reported with some frequency. Yet, although I have made inquiries on that score among colleagues, I have never yet heard of a manifest matricidal dream. (It seems that, even in instances of extreme hatred of the mother, man's consciousness would not be able to tolerate an open dream of matricide.) It would be worthwhile investigating whether there are other contents that have never found direct depiction in dreams. I am here stressing the limits of dream formation, because that may serve to bring to the fore the full consequences of Tausk's piercing, as a child, his youthful mother's portrait.

So much at this point about Tausk's psychopathology in his relationship to women. I shall return to the subject once more in connection with Tausk's suicide. There is also evidence that Tausk had an equally intensive, unabated conflict about his father. Roazen reports that Tausk "was forever embarrassed to be called by his father's name" (p. 10). That is an ambiguous statement (did he change his name?); whatever it means, however, it does prove that Tausk's aversion to the father persisted without abatement, and did not undergo the reduction that is natural in any instance in which even half-way adequate maturation has been achieved. This acute remnant of an unresolved father conflict, attached as it was to something as personal as one's name, makes it understandable why Tausk's relationships to men were also turbulent.

When Roazen reports that Tausk tried to seduce the wife of one of his psychoanalytic colleagues—a man who had been most generous to him, to boot, and had supported him financially—I take this less as a symptom of psychopathology in heterosexual relations, and more as the acting out of a homosexual conflict. It was also an attack against Freud. It had been Freud, after all, who had introduced Tausk to the group and who, as his sponsor, bore at least indirect responsibility for Tausk's membership in it. The small group around Freud had at that time a rather solid cohesiveness, despite the internal rivalry and competition. Tausk's unconscionable acting out against a colleague, however, must have harbored the seeds of a serious threat to the cohesiveness that was of such critical importance to the growth of psychoanalysis at that time.

The author reproduces a letter by the late Dr. Paul Federn, written to his wife after Tausk's suicide. In Federn's judgment, Tausk was a man who "always bit the hand that reached out to help him. . . . He . . . insulted me. . . . Whenever I approached him in a friendly way, I found only vanity, envy and lack of interest. . . . He made enemies for himself everywhere and always" (p. 153). What we have here, according to Federn, is the customary make-up of a sociopathic character: ingratitude, vanity and envy, along with arrogance and provocativeness.

There is also evidence that there was a different area in which Tausk suffered from a serious character defect. In 1917, he published a paper, giving the analyses of three parapraxes. As Roazen agrees (p. 209n.), one of these—reported in the first person, but ascribed by Tausk to a Mr. A.—is certainly autobiographical.[46] It has to do with a man who was baptized in order to marry a Christian girl. He had two sons, who were also baptized. He himself always acknowledged the fact that he was a Jew, and only a few of his acquaintances knew of his baptism. His two sons were told of their Jewish background so that they would not fall prey to anti-Semitic views.

The incident that is of relevance here is the following: Once, when Mr. A. (Tausk) was staying with his two sons at a summer resort, the lady of the house, who did not know that her paying guests were of Jewish ancestry, sharply attacked the Jews. "I ought to have made a bold declaration of the facts, in order to set my sons the example of 'having the courage of one's convictions,' but I was afraid of the unpleasant exchanges that usually follow an avowal of that sort." He was also reluctant to face the possibility

---

[46] Freud (1901) incorporated this part of Tausk's paper in his *Psychopathology of Everyday Life* (p. 92f.).

of losing the good lodgings and "of thus spoiling my own and my children's in any case limited holiday period" (Tausk, 1917, p. 158) (My own translation). Fearing that the sons might betray the truth, he sent them into the garden. The slip of the tongue that occurred is of no interest here; but Tausk's comment on it is: "In this way I enabled the 'courage of my conviction' to be expressed in a parapraxis . . . I was obliged to learn the lesson that the 'faith of our fathers' cannot be disavowed with impunity, if one is a son and has sons of one's own."

If any such account—which Roazen has ignored in his analysis of Tausk's psychopathology—could conceivably have been true of Freud, we can be quite certain that we would have had to read, from the pen of the author, some bitter words about the duplicity of concealing one's baptism when with Jews and concealing one's Jewish ancestry when with Christians, not to speak of strong comment about the cowardice (and its rationalization) involved in pretending to worry about the sons' welfare and yet denying the very moral corruption to which, as their father, one has exposed them. There might even have been some vivid sentence about the sanctimoniousness of calling it a "punishment," when such cowardice is followed by nothing but a slip of the tongue. It is quite evident that Tausk suffered in this area from a character defect that originated in hatred of the father and resulted in a conflict about his ancestry, yet was never balanced by the courage of his own convictions.

If all the data about Tausk that are now available are gathered together, instead of being scattered throughout the book, as Roazen did, they indeed create a dismal impression. Here would be the history of a person acting out wildly; using women unscrupulously for his own personal advantage and abusing professional opportunities (as is now known, when he hypnotized fellow-students during the period of his medical studies, as well as in the recorded instance of electric stimulation); lacking a sense of responsibility (deserting two sons[47] and letting the mother provide for them), and lacking in the moral fiber and courage that are called for by the conflict about his ancestry. His relation to

---

[47] This description is valid, even though there is evidence that Tausk was touchingly affectionate on those occasions when he did have direct contact with his sons (see *Journal*, p. 107).

men was burdened with excessive rivalry, insatiable ambition, ingratitude—and acting out, so as to humiliate those to whom he
was indebted. In addition, in early manhood, Tausk had gone
through an acute psychogenic illness with a questionable diagnosis.

SHOULD FREUD HAVE TAKEN
TAUSK INTO PSYCHOANALYSIS?

IN CONSIDERING the full panorama of Tausk's psychopathology, as
summarized at the end of the preceding section, one is compelled
to draw the following conclusion: it seems rather clear that such
a person would not be accepted as a candidate at present by any
responsible psychoanalytic institute, whatever the eminence of his
creative and intellectual talents. (More later about this far-reaching aspect of the problem of selection.) Indeed, one has to go a
step further and say that any patient who is unable to contain
his acting-out tendencies to the extent to which such inability was
observable in Tausk, or who shows such a high degree of impair-
ment of judgment and of the reality principle—any such patient
cannot or, better, should not be treated by the technique of
classical psychoanalysis. It is questionable whether even a highly
modified technique of psychoanalytic psychotherapy (this was not
yet at the disposal of psychoanalysis in 1919) should be applied in
such instances. It is, however, not clear how much of Tausk's
psychopathology was known to Freud. We know only Freud's
remark to Lou Andreas-Salomé (p. 140): "I had a chance to cast
a few glances into the substructure on which his proud sublimations rested." This would suggest only a summary consideration
of his difficulties; Freud, of course, did not want to aggravate an
unyielding transference by repeated interviews.

It may sound like an apology for an erroneous initial assessment
of Tausk's personality—it was not at all a flattery, as Roazen thinks
—when Freud continued in his letter: "[I] would long since have
dropped him, had you not so boosted him in my esteem" (emphasis in the text). The reader will recall that, in this regard, Freud
lent Lou Andreas-Salomé, from the beginning, a willing ear. It
is very probable that Freud would have acted quite differently all

along had he not had great respect for Lou Andreas-Salomé's judgment. Whether, in the long run, it would have been better for Tausk if Freud had acted as he had originally thought best, cannot be decided in retrospect.

It now becomes necessary to discuss the author's comments on Freud's decision not to take Tausk into psychoanalysis, but instead to send him to Dr. Deutsch, who was at that time in the third month of her own training analysis with Freud. Tausk had demanded that Freud take him into analysis, and had apparently done so with great insistence; Freud had apparently just as insistently refused to do so. There were many reasons for this. The closeness of professional collaboration, covering years, would make a therapeutic relationship inadvisable, in terms of present-day conceptions of optimal conditions for psychoanalytic treatment. Roazen, in an effort to disprove the bearing of such deliberations upon Freud's decision, enumerates the many instances of Freud's carrying out psychoanalyses under so to speak atypical conditions —conditions theoretically incompatible with classical analysis.

One example cited by Roazen is well known: Freud's analyzing his daughter Anna. Evidently, if the analysis of his daughter is typical of the deviations that he did permit himself, Freud was quite able to judge what the conditions were that made any such deviations propitious, for one has to be deeply indebted to him for having had the courage to carry through such an act. It is obvious that, in Tausk's case, Freud was convinced that the preconditions were *not* propitious for him to carry out an analysis.

First of all, it was very exceptional for Freud to take any member of his group into analysis. Helene Deutsch, after all, was in training analysis; and it was not accidental, I would assume, that it was a woman for whom he made even this exception. So far as I know, Freud took only one male analyst who was a member of the Vienna Society into analysis, and he did so for the explicit purpose of preparing him for the leadership of the psychoanalytic movement; and moreover, at a time when he had retired as an active leader, and had not participated in the meetings of the Society for many years.

It can easily be imagined what the situation would have become if, to all the complex emotional relationships that were unavoidably present in a group structured around a genius whose

mental output cannot be excelled by that of his ambitious collaborators, there had been added the conflicts of transference, engendered by the personal analysis of some group members.[48] As
the author rightly sets forth, it was not an easy matter for those
early analysts to preserve their personal and creative autonomy in
the presence of Freud's overwhelming personality and his un-
ceasing creativity on the highest level.

If, around 1919, when Freud had already passed beyond the
sixth decade of his life, the first signs of declining productivity
had appeared—as happens ordinarily—the tendency toward conflict within the group might have been reduced. But with each
new publication of Freud's it became manifest that his physical
aging was not affecting his creativity, and that the quality and
quantity of his contributions would continue without interruption.

In view of Freud's continuing to maintain a level of originality
that was superior to that of his colleagues—something that may
have surprised Freud himself, in view of his own aging and the
great talents of his collaborators, who were so much younger—
there was certainly no inner need for him to replace a waning
mental superiority with the sense of dominance that is generally
acquired when an analyst becomes the best-known training analyst.
Further, taking Tausk into analysis would have made it impossible
to refuse the same privilege to other members, and the price
that would have had to be paid for this might have been too
great. Yet Freud was certainly a man who would, in any emergency
situation, brush aside considerations of that sort.

Roazen conjectures that "Tausk's unstable and free attitude
toward women . . . would not have endeared him to the puritanical and Victorian Freud" (p. 118), and it is on that occasion that
he reveals Tausk's unacceptable behavior of stimulating a female
patient's genitals. My own feeling is that it would have been

---

[48] Curiously enough, the author expressed the same opinion in a different
context (p. 65); it will be taken up later. In some institutions at the head of
which there is a training analyst, the clinical employment of residents has been
combined with analytic training, the chief of staff functioning in the dual
capacity of training analyst and chief of service. The observations one has an
opportunity to make in connection with such dual relationships would retro-
actively justify Freud's evident reluctance to take members of the Vienna Society
into analysis.

proper of Roazen to indicate that Tausk's way of behaving toward women was objectionable; that it *is* indecent to arouse a patient sexually for experimental purposes. Therefore one may ask whether it was Freud's unfavorable response to Tausk's sociopathy that made him reluctant to start Tausk's treatment.

I have to interpose a general remark here. Every generation believes in the correctness of its own standards of conduct. The Victorian was certain that not *he*, but *it* is right to look upon a woman as an angel, and to insist on virginity as a prerequisite to marriage, just as so many today are certain of the absoluteness of the opposite idea—namely, that *it* is right to be promiscuous and not to restrain one's appetites. To be sure, no one can wholly escape the spirit of his times; but a historian or a biographer ought to be careful not to surrender to contemporary biases. It is now fashionable—and the author follows the fashion—to call Freud puritanical and Victorian whenever he expected moral behavior of others.

To be sure, when a physician has accepted someone as a patient, it is his obligation to keep his own moral biases out of the therapeutic area. But before he accepts that person for treatment, he ought at least to find out, if he can, whether the patient's moral conduct passes beyond the bounds of what is tolerable to him; and it is not only the physician's right, it is in fact his moral obligation as a physician, not to accept for mental treatment a subject whose moral conduct is offensive to him.

To believe that it was Freud's obligation or his function, or that it would have been wise for him, to pay no attention to the morality of his colleagues itself constitutes, in point of fact, an unjustified expectation. Strong as I believe Freud's moral convictions to have been, nevertheless, as far as I know, Stekel was the only colleague of his in relationship to whom questions of moral conduct might have been regarded as relevant.[49]

Tausk had a combination of character traits to which Freud may have responded idiosyncratically, since he occasionally had a negative response to sociopaths, as can be learned from some passages in his writings and letters (Freud 1909, p. 197; Weiss 1970).

---

[49] In general, Stekel's reputation seems in that regard to have been a poor one. The witty Lou Andreas-Salomé was the only one I know of to take note of the delightful pun that his name affords in German: she once wrote his name as St. Ekel. (In German, this means St. Disgust.) (Pfeiffer 1966, p. 62.)

It goes without saying that the first prerequisite of an analysis—
if there is to be any hope of a satisfactory termination—is the
analyst's "feeling at peace" with the analysand. I would not be
surprised if Tausk's tendency to act out in a way that occasionally
went beyond some moral tenets of society may have irritated
Freud. If such were the case, that alone would have made it
Freud's duty, of course, both as an analyst and as a medical man,
to refuse to accept Tausk as a subject for treatment. But there is
no indication or proof of Freud's idiosyncratic reaction to Tausk's
morals and therefore there is no reason to assume that Tausk's
moral conduct was a relevant factor in Freud's decision. There
was a simple clinical reason, as valid in the early phases of the
development of psychoanalysis as now, that made Tausk's analysis
by Freud impossible and Freud's personal reaction, whatever it
might have been, is therefore irrelevant. Tausk, as will be seen,
had formed ideas, fantasies or delusions about Freud—whatever
they may have to be called clinically—that ruled out any possibility of his starting a treatment with him.

Roazen records Dr. Edoardo Weiss as saying (p. 87n.) that,
already in 1913—that is to say, only four years after he had started
to study psychoanalysis—Tausk was complaining that he felt hampered, because his own discoveries were being "assimiliated" by
Freud. Does Roazen accept this information of Dr. Weiss's as
correct? I do not find any reason to assume an error of memory
on the informant's side. But then Tausk must have spoken to
others in the same vein, and it is impossible not to assume that
Freud had been hearing for years that Tausk was openly accusing
him of what amounted to plagiarism. Instead of acknowledging
the fact, however, that Tausk had lost his ego boundaries in his
relationship with Freud, the author asserts: "Tausk was the only
one in the group brilliant enough to be such a rival" (p. 78).

There is a revealing passage in Roazen's book (p. 78), in which
he relates that the late Dr. Sarasin had informed him of Freud's
saying that, if he had taken Tausk into analysis, "he would never
be able to publish another line without Tausk thinking Freud
had stolen it." Indeed, it is almost certain that, if Freud had
acceded to Tausk's request, Tausk would have claimed from
then on, subsequent to each of Freud's publications, that at least
it had been inspired by him—or, even worse, that Freud had

appropriated the bulk of his ideas from what Tausk had told him in his analysis. A veritable pandemonium would have broken out; and Freud would have made himself a defenseless victim of Tausk's psychopathology.

Let us assume for the moment that Tausk was right in his perennial complaint about Freud's latent or manifest plagiarism. What mind that is not diseased would then ask, or even wish, to go into analysis with the very analyst who he thinks has the tendency, perhaps not consciously, to plagiarize his work? We shall see that Tausk had many reasons for leaving Vienna, and it is not clear why he did not do so. But his request to be analyzed by Freud must be regarded as the peak of unreasonableness, in view of his repeated claim that Freud was, so to speak, the thief of his mental goods. The only explanation I can offer for this para- doxical behavior is the well-known fixation of the paranoid to his alleged persecutor. It was, I am forced to conclude, Tausk's paranoid belief of being robbed by Freud that compelled him to seek intimate proximity with Freud (cf. Bak 1946).

It should be easy to understand that a psychoanalysis is im- possible to carry out with a subject who, before the treatment has even started, has lost his ego boundary with regard to the analyst in question and is already accusing him of malfeasance. Thus, it is rather clear for this reason alone that Freud did not even have to weigh the possibility of taking Tausk into analysis.[50] Yet, to understand the inconsistency of Roazen's reasoning, one has only to consider the fact that, according to his reconstruction, Freud was jealous and afraid of Tausk. Whoever heard of a conscientious analyst permitting himself, in terms of psychoanalytic standards, to take a person into analysis toward whom he harbors such feel- ings? The paradoxical situation thus arises wherein Roazen accuses Freud of not having done something that—if Roazen's construc- tion were correct—psychoanalytic standards would have forbidden Freud to do.[51]

It is evident that there are sufficient reasons available to ex-

---

[50] In order not to complicate this matter further, I shall not go into Tausk's directly aggressive behavior, which the late Dr. Nunberg adumbrated in his inter- view with Roazen (p. 71).

[51] It is surprising that such experienced analysts as Rycroft (1970) and Lomas (1969) apparently did not notice this inherent contradiction in Roazen's reasoning.

plain Freud's reluctance to agree to Tausk's request; an auxiliary hypothesis regarding his motives on that score is unnecessary, since plenty of reasons, which are almost self-evident, are already known.

Without denying the bearing of other factors, Roazen nevertheless makes an entirely different set of motives the pivotal issue. The paragraph in which, in my opinion, the essential thesis of his attack against Freud is set forth, must be quoted in its entirety (p. 103):

> In the light of the prior history of Freud and Tausk, it is easy to see even more in this devilish arrangement [of having Tausk analyzed by Dr. Deutsch]. Freud had in a sense enticed Tausk, consciously or not, into another triangular setup, as with Lou. They could be rivals for a woman, they could use her as a bridge between them, yet this time Freud could fully control the situation. Through Helene Deutsch, Freud had his revenge for Tausk's affair with Lou. Now Freud triumphed over Tausk. But before getting rid of him, Freud had wanted to find out what he had to say. Freud could not resist the satisfaction of hearing Tausk out, yet he felt safe only if he could do so at a distance.

The author had better be terribly sure of everything he is saying here, because what he is doing is nothing less than accusing Freud of actions that are abominable, in terms not only of psychoanalytic ethics but of general human standards. Roazen is saying, in effect, that Freud abused his medical profession—in particular, his prerogatives as a psychoanalyst—in order to carry out a personal vendetta, to the detriment of a person who had come to him as a patient and who had trusted to his human as well as professional integrity. Furthermore, what is implied is that Freud abused his standing as a psychoanalyst in order to satisfy his voyeuristic cravings with regard to one of his colleagues.

Here the author does not accuse Freud of an error, neither does he refer to the effects of a deeply repressed archaic impulse such as would give color and vitality to actions. It goes without saying that no one can carry out a psychoanalysis without in some way gratifying an infantile voyeuristic impulse. The author's assertion does not by any means refer to such self-evident, elementary conditions. What he contends is that Freud acted deliberately —in a specific way, in response to a specific situation, and for a specific, base purpose. If the author's assertion is correct, then Freud deserves to lose all respect; he does not deserve to be regarded a great man. The few good things that Roazen has to say about Freud, even in this pasquil, disappear vis-à-vis this terrible accusation. Indeed, if such a thing had become known during Freud's lifetime, it would have sufficed to deprive him of his good standing in the professional organizations to which he belonged.

The reader should be aware, however, that Roazen does not adduce any documentation for his claims. They are the end-product of a process of pure deduction, which started with the observation that Freud had fallen in love with Lou Andreas-Salomé, "though in a sublimated way" (p. 43).

Now, it can be proven that Roazen is wrong in his accusation and that he is either directly or indirectly responsible for being wrong. Dr. Deutsch asserts that Freud tried hard to persuade Tausk to go into analysis with Federn or Hitschmann—senior members of the Society, and with years of psychoanalytic experience—but that Tausk obstinately refused to accept any male colleague of his as his therapist. This report, of course, leads prima vista to the collapse of Roazen's wild construction, which surely could never have come to the mind of anyone who was less than obsessed with the desire to detract from Freud's reputation. Yet, even if Dr. Deutsch had not recalled that decisive detail after fifty years, what would be the intrinsic probability of Roazen's construction?

Could anyone seriously believe that, after the terrible four years of the first World War, at the time when Freud had had to tremble for months for his sons' lives; when he had lost all his savings; when the world in which he had grown up had collapsed in a revolution; when he was filled with the most elementary worries, imposed by an uncertain everyday reality, and, in addition, so preoccupied with a wealth of new scientific ideas that he was distracted from full mourning when his daughter Sophie suddenly died a year later—could anyone seriously believe that, with all this, Freud would still respond to the fact that, seven years earlier, a thirty-three-year-old man had had a sexual affair with a woman eighteen years his senior?

If Freud had been concerned as a rival, would he not have taken that man into analysis himself, and in that way mastered the alleged fear he had of his presumed rival? Would his curiosity have been satisfied after three months of listening to the man's analyst? Finally, if what he wanted was to humiliate his enemy, would he not try to *extend* this situation and so *continue* his revenge?

The whole construction is *prima facie* so incredible that one can only be awe-struck by the credulity of the publisher, the reading public and many reviewers. Dr. Deutsch's recollection of the situation would, of course, give Roazen the appearance of being a calumniator, and therefore counterarguments are to be expected. The first question, to be sure, is whether her present recollection is correct. I could well imagine that, kindhearted as most people are, some will consider this an *ex post facto* recollection, designed to rescue Freud's good name. Why, one wonders, did she not tell Roazen about it during the many, many hours when she was supposedly telling him everything she knew about Freud? *Did* she not tell the author?

The transcript of my interview of February 13, 1954, with Dr. Deutsch and her late husband contains the following passage, which I now quote at her request:

> And Tausk wanted [to go] to Freud. And Freud did not want to take him. This was a very interesting and complicated matter. And Tausk had such a contempt for all his colleagues in the [Vienna Psychoanalytic] Society that it was simply impossible to send him to anyone else. He declared suddenly that he will go to me. I was not yet out of my analysis.[52]

According to this interview, there is the possibility that Dr. Deutsch was not even Freud's choice, that Tausk himself suggested her to Freud, since it was apparently impossible for Tausk to go into analysis with any one of the male colleagues Freud had suggested to him. Four women, besides Dr. Deutsch, were listed among the members of the Vienna group of 1919: Dr. H. von Hug-Hellmuth who, as far as I know, treated mainly

---

[52] *Und Tausk wollte zu Freud. Und Freud wollte ihn nicht nehmen. Das war eine sehr interessante komplizierte Angelegenheit. Und Tausk hatte eine solche Verachtung für alle seine Kollegen in der Vereinigung gehabt, dass es einfach unmöglich war, ihn zu jemanden zu schicken. Er hat plötzlich erklärt, er wird zu mir gehen. Ich war noch nicht aus der Analyse.* (This is the verbatim transcript of a tape.)

children and was not a physician; Mrs. Sokolnicka, who resided in Warsaw; and two others, Drs. Tatjana Rosenthal and S. Spielrein-Scheftel, whose addresses were not known. Dr. Deutsch was the only choice possible, since Tausk had consistently refused to go to a male psychoanalyst.

When I re-interviewed Dr. Deutsch on January 24, 1970, she did not recall her statement of 1954 about Tausk's having chosen her. The most she can say now with certainty is that Freud first suggested Federn and Hitschmann. In view of her 1954 statement and her recent statement, one can be quite certain that either Freud thought of her only as a second choice, after failing to persuade Tausk to go to one of his male colleagues, or that Tausk himself suggested her after he found out that Freud would not accede to his request. Either eventuality proves that the author's construction is untenable,[53] because it was built on the wrong premise to begin with. As I have said before, Roazen carries direct or indirectly responsibility for this egregious and unfounded accusation against Freud. His "In the light of the prior history . . . it is easy to see," in a matter that is not supported by the "prior history" nor easy to see at all, is mere rant and verbiage. Yet Roazen claims (p. 101): "She [Dr. Deutsch] simply assumed that Tausk would go to no one else."

Dr. Deutsch correctly complained to me that Roazen frequently does not make it clear to the reader whether he is recording information that she had actually given him, or is setting down his own interpretation of something she had told him.[54] If Dr. Deutsch's alleged "assumption" is the product solely of Roazen's interpretation, then he has neglected his duty, for it would have been his obligation, prior to voicing such an accusation, to ask

---

[53] It would be, of course, particularly piquant if it turned out that Tausk himself had selected Dr. Deutsch. She was, at the time of her first interview, seventy; at the time of the second one, she was eighty-six. However, much as the earlier date would favor the correctness of her recollection at that time, it should be recorded that the first interview was not held in a formal way but rather at a conversational level. The statement about Tausk was made spontaneously and close to the beginning of the interview. I had not inquired about Tausk; the question of Tausk's analysis with Dr. Deutsch came up when the Deutsches were trying to figure out in what year either of them had met Freud for the first time.

[54] Of course, her criticism does not involve ridiculous statements, such as that Freud wooed her—which is pure invention on Roazen's part.

Dr. Deutsch *why* Freud did not send Tausk to somebody else but chose her—at which point she would have told him that Freud had previously tried to persuade Tausk to accept Hitsch-mann or Federn as his analyst.

Perhaps Roazen may claim that Dr. Deutsch actually did tell him that it was only an assumption on her part. Then the reader will have to decide whether to believe Dr. Deutsch, whose spon-taneously offered assertion of 1954 can still be heard on the tape, or Roazen, who several times quotes Freud misleadingly, who in other parts of the book claims to have received from two informants statements that neither can recall having made, and who has depreciated Freud's character without adducing any evi-dence, and in some instances in the face of existing evidence.

Be that as it may—whether the reader is granting the author the privilege of good faith, or reproving him for having manip-ulated data, and having disregarded historical evidence—the one paragraph that would otherwise amount to the condemnation of Freud as a moral human being and a professional man turns out to be arbitrarily constructed and without any roots in fact.

Before closing this section, I shall express an opinion on a matter which is of some importance to the whole problem of Tausk's analysis, and which I do not see Roazen having taken into consideration. It concerns the question of what really mo-tivated Tausk in requesting analysis with Freud. Was it a serious desire to be analyzed, or did another motive hide behind what was ostensibly a request for treatment? Looking back and considering the full scope of Tausk's behavior with regard to his own analysis, I am forced to doubt the sincerity of his desire to be analyzed. I would tentatively suggest that his request was part and parcel of the acting out that played such a dominant role in his life. What the specific underlying fantasy might have been of his insistence on being analyzed by Freud is, of course, unknown to me; but it may not be difficult to reconstruct the proximate in-tention.

When Dr. Deutsch discontinued the treatment, Tausk did not protest, neither did he raise the question of what there was for him to do now. I have never heard of a patient feeling the need for treatment and then accepting, without any sign of per-turbation, a sudden dismissal by his therapist in the middle of his psychoanalysis. The equanimity with which Tausk took the interruption of his treatment favors the assumption that the real reason for his insistence on treatment by Freud may have been his desire to tell Freud all the grudges he bore against him. Once Freud refused, he could achieve his goal only by being analyzed by Helene Deutsch who, he knew, was in training analysis with Freud. When Dr. Deutsch discontinued Tausk's treatment, any motive for further treatment on his part apparently vanished. What impresses me as his primary desire had been gratified, since Freud had heard from Dr. Deutsch all the reproaches Tausk had so eloquently recited to her for three months.

If he had earnestly wished to be analyzed, an attempt to continue—in view of his prejudice against his Viennese male colleagues—either with Abraham in Berlin or with Ferenczi in Budapest, would have been inescapable. To be sure, a temporary change of residence would not have been easy; but it was certainly not impossible, and many a patient has made greater sacrifices than that, once he has become convinced that he needs to be analyzed. In view of all this, I must doubt that Tausk was really convinced that he was in need of psychoanalytic treatment. It is curious that Roazen nowhere raises the question of how seriously Tausk wished to be analyzed. At one point Roazen makes a remark that renders it almost inescapable to doubt Tausk's sincere motivation. Every patient who goes into psychoanalysis under the pressure of an acute need for treatment forms a transference reaction to the therapist. Roazen, however, observes (p. 83): "Yet no transference was ever established between Tausk and Helene Deutsch, or at least so it seemed on the surface." (The latter alternative Roazen needs for holding the abrupt ending of treatment responsible for Tausk's falling in love with a patient.) Yet if Tausk was using Dr. Deutsch merely as a messenger, then it is very probable that in this instance actually no transference was formed, which is extremely rare. But that fact would provide additional support for doubting the sincerity of Tausk's desire to be analyzed.

There are what I suppose one should describe as "ominous" statements in the book. When Roazen writes: (1) "They [Freud's early followers] made his every wish into command. King Henry is supposed to have breathed with a sigh that Becket be dispatched, so if Freud wanted Tausk dead, it seemed perfectly in order for Tausk to oblige. Freud had such tremendous power over them because they all wanted to have it so" (p. 157); when he further states: (2) "There really was something uncanny in the relationship between Freud and Tausk. For as if in continuation of their tie, at the time Tausk killed himself, Freud was beginning to formulate the concept of a death instinct" (p. 143); and when he finally raises the question: (3) "Could Tausk have been acting out Freud's newest . . . idea?" (p. 143), then I find myself forced to refer the reader to Freud's (1911a) comments on Daniel Paul Schreber's self-revelations.

FREUD'S PERSONAL REACTION
TO TAUSK'S SUICIDE

THERE ARE SOME other issues raised by Roazen that need clarification. The most interesting of these has to do with a passage in a letter that Freud wrote to Lou Andreas-Salomé, in which he informed her of Tausk's suicide. Roazen describes that letter as "shocking," "inhuman," "heartless," and "ruthless" (p. 140). It is not quite clear which passages in the letter evoked that reaction in him; but my conjecture is that it was caused by the following sentence, which is a part of what the editor of the *Briefwechsel* (Pfeiffer 1966) deleted: "I confess I do not really miss him [Tausk]; I had long taken him to be useless, indeed a threat to the future."

In order to derive the full implication of this sentence, it would be necessary to read it within the context of the letter as a whole; yet this much may be stated initially: if Roazen's epithets are to be understood as no more than expressions of his own feelings, then any discussion would prove fruitless. Yet it is more probable that, in saying, "It is scarcely credible that Freud could have uttered such thoughts" (p. 140f.) Roazen is expressing his belief that Freud was inhuman, heartless, and ruthless in writing in such a way about the tragedy that had occurred.

Before entering into a discussion of what Freud's reactions to Tausk's tragedy could possibly have been, and the way in which these various reactions might be interpreted, one has to consider the general evaluation that Roazen puts on Freud's final dealings with Tausk. "Freud had left him [Tausk] with his dilemma about women. Freud had refused to help him by an analysis. Tausk felt ready to become a beloved son of Freud's and then Freud put him off" (p. 133). Did Tausk really try "to become a beloved son"? The fact that Tausk became an analyst, that he wrote excellent psychoanalytic papers, or that he sided with Freud in the controversies with Adler and with Jung—all this should not, I hope, be taken as some sort of gift to Freud, but rather as the expression of Tausk's own convictions.

For six years Tausk had been telling people—not a few of them—that Freud was stealing his ideas. Dr. Deutsch recalls that he filled his treatment hours with constant complaining about Freud's unfair behavior. If someone were trying to become a beloved son, he would be, I should imagine, proud and joyful that the revered father-*imago* is making use of his ideas; if anything, he would keep this, tactfully, a secret. His feelings of affection, respect and admiration for Freud notwithstanding, Tausk was the typically rebellious person, unable to acknowledge without grave conflicts the actual superiority of an authority.

I myself have the impression that Tausk's "dilemma about women" was unanalyzable, because there were too many realistic feelings of guilt attached to it. Since Tausk had already formed a highly aggressive attitude toward Freud, and was moreover convinced that his attitude was justified by reality—as if Freud were really the father whose name he detested—one can easily imagine how far Freud would have been able to get in the analysis of Tausk's "dilemma about women." As the consequence of his refusal to take Tausk into analysis, therefore, Freud cannot possibly have had any reality-based bad conscience or feeling of guilt.

There was scarcely any other analyst (with the exception of Rank, perhaps) who owed Freud so much, and for whom Freud had done so much. He had given Tausk money, had made his medical studies possible, had provided him with the springboard for his profession and his prestige. At the time of his suicide, Tausk was even on the verge of acquiring the prized position of lecturer [*Dozent*] at the University of Vienna—an honor no other among Freud's followers had ever applied for, and which was now possible for Tausk only with Freud's tacit consent. But Tausk's insatiable demands and his moral weakness are traceable to the very beginning of his association with Freud.

One year after his arrival in Vienna, shortly after Freud had sent him the not insignificant sum of 150 kronen, Tausk complained that "it was not enough to finance his planned *vacation*. 'What is going to come now only Freud and God know'" (p. 27, emphasis added). What is one to think of a thirty-year-old man, whose wife is supporting his two sons, and whose teacher is apparently giving him quite freely the money he needs for his upkeep, invoking "Freud and God" because he is not sure whether or not he can go on a vacation?

There are limits to which an adult can expect to be able to obtain gratification of his oral dependence—particularly when he is giving free rein to orally aggressive behavior. Thus Freud was quite justified in drawing a line somewhere with Tausk; and even if it were true that it was specifically Freud's reluctance to accept Tausk as an analysand that triggered Tausk's suicide—what did trigger it off I shall have to report later—that would still not be sufficient to make Freud a guilty person, or someone who had to activate denial in order to evade realistic feelings of guilt. By no stretch of the imagination can one ever refer to an *obligation* on the part of an analyst to accept anyone as a patient.

How profoundly Roazen misunderstood the situation, and therefore how incorrectly he appraised Freud's behavior, comes to the fore when he writes (p. 159): "If someone of his [Freud's] followers got crushed, well, that was too bad. But he could not allow them to become a burden to him. Had Freud chosen, he might well have been able to save Tausk, but taking him into analysis would have been a challenge and a sacrifice."

Freud was at that time sixty-three years old, and he would have had every right to expect that his pupils and collaborators should not burden him or expect sacrifices of him, but should instead try to find out in what way they could lighten the heavy burden he had to carry. It sounds strange, indeed, when a man who is allegedly seeking only affection consistently makes himself a burden. Yet Roazen writes as if the reason why Freud did not accept Tausk as an analysand was that he (Freud) was given to shunning sacrifices and burdens—which would, indeed, have produced a strong feeling of guilt after Tausk's suicide.

I do not doubt that Freud at that stage had the human right—even if it were solely for the reason of avoiding a sacrifice—to refuse to analyze Tausk. Yet there is evidence that Freud was quite willing to carry burdens, whenever it was possible for him to do so. Historically, it can be proved that Freud, at a time when he was considerably advanced in age, conducted two analyses without asking for any fee. Evidently, he was not, in principle, averse to making sacrifices; indeed, I would say that he was far more generous with his time and more indifferent to remuneration than any contemporary analyst I know of. Be that as it may, Freud's conscience must have been justifiedly untroubled and clear, as far as his rational reaction to Tausk's death was concerned. Yet general experience has taught us that the death of a person with whom one is closely involved in one or the other way frequently leaves an irrational trace of guilt, the intensity and extension of which varies with the circumstances of the death and with the idiosyncracies of the survivor.

A careful study of Freud's letter to Lou Andreas-Salomé reveals traces of a reaction quite different from the one that shocked the author. Roazen has rightly called attention to the delay of Freud's letter to Lou Andreas-Salomé—something that is indeed remarkable in a man who was well known for his promptness in writing letters. It was, in fact, twenty-nine days after Tausk's death that Freud informed Lou Andreas-Salomé of it.

The first sentence of Freud's letter is worthy of note. He had delayed answering her letter, which he had received nine days before, because—as he wrote her—he had been waiting to see "whether I might not still come into possession of something to communicate to you" (*ob ich Ihnen nicht noch etwas mitzuteilen bekäme*). Purportedly, what this meant was some professional item; yet Freud actually had something grave to communicate to Lou Andreas-Salomé, something that he apparently hoped she would already have learned from some other source.

One might have expected Freud to start his letter with the message; but it is pointedly put off to the beginning of the third paragraph. This delay introduces an atmosphere of casualness,

which stands in sharp contrast with the phrase: *Der arme Tausk*—
with which Freud introduced the distressing part of his communication. The combination of "poor" with the name of a
deceased person was in common use, but it is important to compare the way Freud employed the word regarding Tausk's death
and the only two other instances I could discover. When he
wrote Pfister a year later about the death of his daughter Sophie,
he called her "our poor Sunday child [*unser armes Sonntagskind*]"
(Freud 1960, p. 327) and around the same time he wrote about
Anton von Freund (1880–1920), a former patient and friend of his,
"Poor or fortunate Toni Freund [*Der arme, oder der glückliche
von Freund*]" (Jones 3, p. 19).[55] Once the term was used by
Freud in reference to a living person. Thus he wrote about the
widowed son-in-law: "the poor man, who has been made lone-
some [*der arme vereinsamte Mann*]" (my own translation; cf.
Freud 1960, p. 366).

It seems to me that in all these instances the full implication
of the word "poor" is softened by an extenuative addition. *Der
arme Tausk* is to my ear a powerful and trenchant expression,
whose tragic implication is lost in the English translation: "Poor
Tausk." It is the equivalent of a compassionate heaving of a sigh
of commiseration for a man whom Freud had long since recognized as being incapable of preventing himself from frustrating his
own capabilities.

Moreover, the wording of *hat seinen Leben . . . auf gründ-
liche Weise ein Ende gemacht* ("put a thorough end to his life")
is perplexing. The word *gründlich* in this context is hardly trans-
latable. Freud may have had in mind Tausk's both shooting and
hanging himself. But Tausk's way of ending his life was not yet
known to Lou Andreas-Salomé. At this point Freud was not em-
pathizing with the recipient of the letter—a rarely occurring
failure on his part, perhaps to be explained here by the great inner
pressure under which he was writing.

It is my impression that in all this what came to the surface
was only the ripple of a severe inner stress. I would guess that
what had actually come to pass in Freud, during the weeks subsequent to the fatal event, was quite different from what he

---

[55] I cannot account for the difference between "Toni Freund" in the English
edition of Jones' biography and the "von Freund" in the German.

demonstrated on the surface. Yet how is one to know what the inner process actually was? Was Freud's defense successful, and did his conscious mind therefore remain quite untroubled? Was his "I do not miss him" a gesture of deliberate concealment, in order to hide what might otherwise have had to be appraised as a weakness?

Roazen tries to explain in his own way what he considers a defect in Freud. He begins by referring to Freud's remarkable letter of September 16, 1893 (Freud 1960, pp. 156–166), written to Martha Bernays on the occasion of the suicide of his colleague, Nathan Weiss (1851–1883).[56] In relation to this, Roazen states: "As a young man, before founding psychoanalysis, Freud would not have been so heartless in the face of human tragedy." But thirty-six years later, as he sees it, Freud was already quite different: "His dedication to the cause of psychoanalysis sanctioned his ruthlessness. As he aged . . . his humanity grew restricted. Psychoanalysis, he later wrote, had 'become my whole life to me.' "

The reader will not be surprised to learn, I assume, that Freud has once again been quoted altogether misleadingly by Roazen. It is true that the words Roazen quotes are to be found in the Standard Edition (Vol. 22, p. 224); yet who could possibly guess from the quotation, as it is used here, that what Freud (1932) said was no more than this: that when he met his older contemporaries, he occasionally felt as though he were being rejected by their lack of comprehension of "what had come to be the content of my life" [was mir zum Lebensinhalt geworden war]— a passage that cannot possibly be understood to imply anything even remotely resembling the interpretation Roazen gives it.

That Freud meant by "content of my life" a main interest of his, to whose service he was devoting all his professional efforts, can be observed in a similar passage in another paper; there he says, of Rank and Sachs, that they are investigators who "have made the application of psychoanalysis to the humanities their life task" [die Anwendung der Psychoanalyse auf die Geisteswissenschaften zu ihrer Lebensaufgabe gemacht haben] (emphasis added, my own translation).[57] "Life task" is, to be sure, somewhat

---

[56] For Nathan Weiss, see Lesky 1965, p. 394.

[57] Mr. Strachey (Freud 1914a, p. 35) has translated that passage as "have taken up the application of psychoanalysis to the mental sciences as their profession in life."

weaker than "content of life"; but it seems probable that Freud took it almost for granted that in this respect he was not very different from most analysts, for he wrote (1933, p. 153): "As a rule psycho-analysis possesses a doctor either *entirely* or *not at all*" (emphasis added).

If, however, Roazen were right in his assertion that Freud's emotionality had changed under the impact of his lifework, then this would mean that while, as a young man, Freud had been sensitive and very much alive in his emotional responses, during the course of his growing into the giant of innovation and science that he did become, his life's mission became the all-embracing mold into which his emotions were cast, to the exclusion of whatever he now saw as less meaningful.[58] The explanation is, as the reader will presently see, quite surprising, coming as it does from an author who has taken a predominantly critical line against Freud, notwithstanding some complimentary statements. It requires a short digression.

The question at issue has general significance. I want to summarize its contents, in order to avoid confusion and misunderstanding. The specific subject under consideration is the absence of mourning on Freud's part after Tausk's suicide. One of the premises of my argument is that, from a rational point of view, Freud had no reason for self-reproach.[59]

Whatever may have been Freud's actual response to Tausk's death, a careful analysis of subtle details makes it highly probable that he did not let Lou Andreas-Salomé know the whole state of affairs, and even that he himself did not know of it. The issue at hand, however, is his description of the conscious state of mind in which Tausk's suicide had left him. Roazen suggests that Freud's personality had undergone a transformation, that his work as scientist and discoverer had taken over so completely that he no longer responded emotionally to events in a human and humane way. He also suggests, as Federn did, that aging had by

---

[58] Rycroft, in his *Observer* review, also seems to be critical of Freud in this respect, although he is not explicit. He quotes the passage from Freud's letter in full and adds only: "This is about a colleague and former protégé he had known for 10 years, etc."—thus implying a negative response.

[59] A remark by Paul Federn that seems to contradict this contention will be discussed later.

that time left its traces. Neither argument—that based on the supposed inroads of superego, nor that based on aging, with regard to the sphere of intimate emotional responses—is valid. Quite surprisingly—that is to say, atypically, by contrast with one's observation about men in general—Freud apparently preserved to the end of his life his full capacity for emotional response—particularly for mourning, a question I shall take up later on. But if Roazen were right in his assertion that the nature of Freud's response to Tausk's death was caused by his having become the embodiment of his superego, so to speak, and at the same time the victim of aging, then his earlier value judgment of "shocking," "ruthless" and their equivalents would be out of place and he would be lacking in any justification in reality.

When a man acts in conformity with his biological state, his behavior may shock us, but it cannot be criticized within the biological frame of reference.[60] Further, if a genius's personality becomes completely engulfed by his superego—that is to say, by his life's mission (which may have occurred in some rare instances, but certainly not in the case of Freud)—then it makes no sense to call the effects of such a transformation "shocking" and "ruthless," for such a transformation is desirable, admirable, and advantageous to the world at large, whose primary interest is not in the genius's psychological processes but rather in his creation of highest possible values. From this one could deduce that the more such a person is engulfed by the creative process, to the point of utter absorption, the more will posterity profit from his mortal days.

Indirectly, I am here entering upon the very complex problem of whether or not exemptions that would not be made for the non-genius are to be extended to the genius—a problem to which I am not able to do justice in this context. At one point (in a so far unpublished manuscript), I have suggested that artists (this is obvious enough and will not be disputed in the case of the genius, but I there extended it also to the talented) should *always*

---

[60] In my limited experience, a reduction of the capacity to mourn occurs with fair regularity in the seventh decade—in men earlier than in women, it seems to me. With greater certainty, however, it can be said that every human being eventually would reach the point, if he lived long enough, at which the ability to mourn would subside.

be exempt from service in the army, whether in peace or war. In my experience, the suffering of men whose lives center on the creation of artistic values—whether their actual products be outstanding or mediocre is of no relevance here—is so excessive, once they are in uniform, that they deserve to be exempted solely on the grounds of the mental pain involved.

Another area that concerns only the genius is typified by Beethoven's behavior toward his nephew. In accordance with certain laws of creativity, some types of genius behave in a way that is destructive to the young ones that live within their orbit. It is up to the community to protect these young ones, for this type of genius cannot be expected to create incomparably great works and at the same time to be reasonable in his dealings with his progeny. This also holds true for many other behavior patterns. Here the community must decide which is more important—highest level creativity, or the assurance of a solid citizenry.

When Shakespeare left Stratford, clearly shirking his responsibility to his wife and his three children, he committed an act that would have been reprehensible in anyone else; yet it certainly was an absolute necessity for him to do so, in terms of the subsequent creation of the plays that he gave the world. To be sure, there are talents who abuse this type of behavior, which is proper for the genius, in order to rationalize their own selfish pleasure-seeking actions. In talents, however, such behavior has a meaning that is essentially different from the one it has in the life of a genius.

It is my contention, and that of other investigators as well, that the key to the explanation of such asocial behavior is conceptually quite different, whether it is used to unlock the life history of a talent or of a genius.[61] But it is also my contention that surprisingly, and quite atypically, one does not find in Freud's life any instances for which one has to plead exception, on the grounds of the subject's excessive creativity, as one has to in the case of Beethoven's destructive behavior toward his nephew and

---

[61] In discussions of this topic, the question is regularly raised of what are the differentiating characteristics of talent and genius. Even though no reliable yardstick has been yet established, I shall attempt to answer that question in the final chapter.

Shakespeare's abandonment of his family—to cite again the two instances I have selected at random.

After this clarification of a significant and so often misunderstood aspect of the social implications of what I have taken to be the psychology of excessively creative persons, I return to the starting point that made this detour necessary—namely, Freud's letter to Lou Andreas-Salomé.

To my great surprise, Roazen writes (p. 140) that "Freud was characteristically honest about his feelings, courageous about some of his worst qualities—which is exactly what has laid him open to criticism." To criticism by whom, may I ask? By people who are insensitive to the subtleties of human life? If so, I am quite convinced that no one ought to hesitate for a moment to be utterly candid about his own feelings and qualities, even though one part of posterity may have lost its sense of humanity, and he may therefore incur its vituperation by so doing.[62]

And what were Freud's "worst qualities"? What in the author's opinion should Freud have concealed in his letters, in order to find himself in good grace with Roazen and Rycroft, as well as with other critics who have taken exception to that letter? After all, one man who knew a few things about the world—even though he may have been mistaken in the statement that he who "filches" a good name is never enriched thereby—seems to have bestowed the highest praise on a good name, when he called it "the immediate jewel of their souls."

It is noteworthy that, in this instance, Freud's good name was "filched" because of a feeling—or the absence of a feeling, as the case may be—not because of an action, as in the instances cited about Beethoven and Shakespeare. Moral indignation about geniuses usually rises in connection with such behavior patterns as Rimbaud's vagabondage, Baudelaire's addiction and Verlaine's

---

[62] Of course, this applies not only to the question of the letter's content, but to the very fact of Freud's having written it. Rycroft (1970) seems to take exception to Freud's having addressed it to an ex-lover of Tausk's, "who must, one presumes, have been fond of him." Lou Andreas-Salomé's answer—in which, by the way, I do not find any trace of her being "taken aback by Freud's cold portrayal of Tausk's death" (Roazen, p. 143)—does not confirm Rycroft's concern. She had internally broken with Tausk a long time previously.

double attempt at murder—if the epithet of genius can be added to their at least illustrious names.

When a genius responds emotionally in a way the excessively "rational" person cannot empathize with—such as Goethe's starting a passionately amorous correspondence with a woman he had never met and whom he never would meet, at exactly the time when he became engaged to his sweetheart—then the critic usually resorts to a vocabulary that falls within the orbit of "lacking balance," "inconsistency," and the like. This is, of course, less hurtful to a genius's "good name" than the sort of moral vituperation to which Roazen and like-minded critics have given vent, in Freud's case. From their writings, it is quite evident that a man who is honest, uncowardly and ready not only to face but also to share with his friend important issues of his emotional life, will not meet with general approval. If any genius were to take Shakespeare's dictum to heart, he would do better not to be honest with his friends.[63]

Be that as it may, Roazen acknowledges that Freud had pity for Tausk; what he misses, evidently, is any trace of mourning. The affect (or process, as it would be better called) of mourning can set in only when one has loved a person, or had an affectionate feeling toward him.[64] Freud had evidently had no affectionate feelings for Tausk, probably for many years before Tausk's death. Tausk had never been his friend, as probably no one of his pupils —in the narrower meaning of the term—had ever been. Yet there is evidence that Freud mourned after Abraham's death, and after that of Anton von Freund (1880–1920), who had been his patient and who died in Vienna of a malignant disease, while still under Freud's care. To be sure, Anton von Freund meant more to Freud than a patient usually does; Freud was deeply attached to him.

---

[63] Freud was evidently fully aware of an invidious world's reaction to truthfulness. He wrote (1935, p. 73), "I have . . . been more open and frank in some of my writings . . . than people usually are who describe their lives for their contemporaries or for posterity. I have had small thanks for it, and from my experience I cannot recommend anyone to follow my example."

[64] I have simplified the matter. I do not take into consideration here the instance when mourning is brought about almost exclusively by conscious or unconscious feelings of guilt. Sometimes the loss of a hated person also evokes intense mourning, but in that case the love, or other affectionate feeling, had been repressed earlier, and shows itself only after the disappearance of the person.

As Jones asserts, on the basis of a letter by Freud to Ferenczi, von Freund's death "was an important factor in his aging" (Jones 3, p. 19). Freud's strong reaction to von Freund's death alone proves how wrong Roazen was when he suggested that Freud had lost any of his humaneness by virtue of his having become a great scientist.[65]

And is there any reason to criticize Freud for not having had affectionate feelings toward Tausk? This question I must leave to the reader to answer; I do not know in what way he will decide. According to the New Testament, man ought to feel only love —even toward his enemies. If this demand is posed as the necessary core of moral behavior, then Freud fell far short of morality, for he seems never to have accepted it as a valid postulate. As much as he took pains not to hurt his fellowman (see Freud 1960, p. 308), he concentrated his personal affection only on those whom he respected (see Freud 1930a, p. 109f).

There seems hardly any doubt that, once he had been seriously disappointed by an individual's personal conduct, it was often difficult for him to forgive. And Tausk must have been for him, over and over again, a source of disappointment. If actions of the sort that Roazen reports in his book, and which Federn mentions in his letter (see p. 246), actually did occur, then I do not see how Freud could have helped deeply regretting that he had ever accepted Tausk into the early group of analysts.[66]

Freud knew what the occasion called for. He wrote a beautiful obituary of Tausk—the longest he ever wrote, Roazen believes.[67] It gave Tausk's name a firmer niche in the history of ideas than any paper he himself wrote, probably firmer than any he might have written, had he lived longer. No shadow of Freud's personal

---

[65] For Freud's observations of what the psychological changes brought about by aging may have been, the reader is referred to his letter to Lou Andreas-Salomé of May 19, 1925 (Freud 1960, p. 360f).

[66] Tausk's contributions to analysis were by no means great enough to have made him indispensable, nor were they of a kind to have given the development of psychoanalysis a direction different from the one that it actually took. That might easily have been true, however, if Adler or Jung had continued to hold a prominent place in the movement.

[67] This is only true when one ignores Freud's magnificent paper on Charcot (1893), which is essentially an obituary, as Strachey rightly calls it in his Editor's Note, and as it is listed in Grinstein's (1956–1966) Index.

experience with Tausk—of the annoyance he had to suffer at
Tausk's hands—found its way into that obituary. It is written
with the beauty of style to which the reader of Freud's works is
accustomed, and it characteristically condenses a breadth of information into a few pages. It is certainly not hypocritical, but
rather commensurate with Tausk as a historical figure, so to speak.

The subjective image that Freud had formed out of his personal contact with Tausk was completely omitted; but this would
have found its logical place, if at all, only in a volume of memoirs,
and certainly not in the pages of the journal to which Tausk had
made his own contributions. I would surmise that the discrepancy
between the objective portrait of Tausk that Freud in his role as
quasi-historian left to posterity and the subjective one that he had
formed out of his personal contacts with the deceased was one of
the reasons why Tausk's obituary was published over the signature
of "editor's office" (Die Redaktion).[68]

Dealing with the question of hypocrisy may throw additional
light on the absence of mourning in Freud. In view of the frequent anger that Freud may have felt toward Tausk, as well as the
absence of any fondness for Tausk over many years, it may be that
Freud's superego would have condemned as internal hypocrisy, so
to speak, the unfolding of grief and mourning.[69]

If some reviewers (by contrast with Storr, 1970) had not sided
with Roazen, as it seems, with regard to the latter's moral indignation, I might not have written a substantial part of that last excur-
sus, but merely cited those passages that demonstrate Roazen's
prejudice in favor of Tausk and against Freud, even in his presen-

---

[68] Roazen believes that this was done by Freud for the purpose of diffusing responsibility for Tausk's suicide. Freud wrote eight obituaries besides the one for
Tausk, seven of which were published in the Zeitschrift: one was signed by "the
editor"; one "the editorial office and editor"; one, "the editor Freud"; one,
"Freud"; and two, "Sigm. Freud."

[69] I feel unable even to guess what specific meaning it may have had for
Freud that Tausk had died by his own hand. Nathan Weiss's suicide elicited
a response that one may call almost excessive; but in 1914 Freud added a remark
in the text of his book on dreams that may imply a moral condemnation of
suicide. Even though Karl Schrötter's dream experiments (1912) strikingly confirmed some of Freud's propositions about the meaning of dreams, Freud nevertheless expressed some uncertainty about their value, because of "the unfortunate
circumstance that Dr. Schrötter committed suicide soon after making them"
(1900, p. 384).

tation of the raw psychological data. That alone would have made it unnecessary to pay any attention to his moral judgments.

Thus Roazen wrote (p. 111): "Tausk's belief that Freud needed to take his ideas *may* have stood all along for devaluation of his teacher" (emphasis added). Yet there can be no doubt that this was an aggression, directed as it was toward a teacher who had single-handed founded a discipline, and who was to continue to write papers of the highest quality throughout the twenty years following that pupil's death.[70] He further writes (p. 85), contrary to all evidence: "Tausk's relations with people were never restricted or impoverished. He was a warm and dynamic person, jolly and sociable, in good human contact."

There is no need to repeat all the clinical evidence that contradicts such a description. Yet all Roazen will say is that Freud "*could* be kind and generous, supportive and encouraging" (p. 168, emphasis added), although one can adduce ample evidence that Freud *was* kind and generous, etc. To cite one more example, for years I have been trying to find a letter by Freud that I am certain I read in my younger days. It was printed in one of the Viennese daily newspapers, and in it he suggested, at the depth of the post-war economic conditions, that every Viennese should daily donate a substantial part of his earnings to the welfare of the city, and expressed his readiness to make a start in that direction.

Should one not call it a prejudice against Freud when an author asserts (p. 217, n. 16) that Freud "admitted" having been "*reluctant* to analyze the negative reactions of his patients" (emphasis added), whereas the reference he gives (Freud 1937, p. 221f.) clearly states that, in the patient in question, "at the time of the analysis, *there was no sign of a negative transference*. But even if he [Freud] *failed to observe* some very faint signs of it . . . [this] was altogether ruled out, considering the limited horizon of analysis in those early days . . ." (emphasis added).

The degree to which Roazen is ready to "debunk" Freud's humaneness is recognizable early, when he writes of Freud that he "collected able people" and "collected students" (p. 47). In

---

[70] However, Roazen may need that "may" here because, on other occasions, he has suggested that Freud may have used Tausk's ideas without quoting him, and he did so, of course, without mentioning a single occasion on which this may have happened.

this context, it is worthwhile to repeat Roazen's allegations of Freud's vanity—such as (p. 74) that "Freud was extremely flattered by every outsider who came to him" (could anyone have joined the group at that time without his *first* having been an "outsider"?); or that he knew "how to woo" Dr. Deutsch and her husband (pp. 76, 98).

When I seem to dispute Roazen's ability to make a reliable evaluation in such a difficult area as moral judgments, I would not like to be misunderstood. Jean-Jacques Rousseau deposited all his children in a foundling home; nevertheless, he wrote perhaps the most penetrating treatise on the raising of children that has ever been written. If a person fails to practice his own theories, that alone does not warrant dismissing those theories. Whatever Roazen's own ethics may be in the reader's eyes, that in itself would indicate nothing about his astuteness in matters of moral judgment.

In order to evaluate the morality of a specific person, however, one has to have at least an approximate idea of the structure of that person's character. That Roazen has put together a portrait of some person, whom he by some regrettable error has called Sigmund Freud, should be clear by now. His moral judgment of that person may be correct, but it cannot be extended to the actual Sigmund Freud, who is so well-known as the founder of psychoanalysis, and with whose life and character Roazen has apparently never become acquainted.

POSTSCRIPT

Some of the foregoing may have to be revised in view of Edoardo Weiss's (1970) recent book, which was published one year after Roazen's. It contains the letters written to him by Freud, some of which had appeared four years earlier in the *Psychoanalytic Forum*. This time Weiss added his recollections of Freud. In writing about Tausk, Weiss showed a striking similarity of approach to Roazen's basic thesis—without, however, permitting himself to be drawn into the absurd.

Thus Weiss writes: "Gradually, he [Freud] lost some of his compassion. For example, when after the first World War Viktor Tausk was destitute and had fallen into a deep depression, Freud could not give his old friend the moral support he badly needed"

(p. 8). How poorly informed Weiss was in this area can be seen from his belief that Tausk was an old friend of Freud's. There is possibly an ambiguity when Weiss (p. 11) writes that he himself was "saddened but not surprised" when apprised of Tausk's suicide. "I realized that he must have felt abandoned by persons close to him and perhaps particularly by Freud" (p. 11).

Why was Weiss not surprised? He reports that he had met Tausk by accident during the first World War, and "was shocked by his state of deep depression" (p. 11). His fiancée had betrayed him. "Other acquaintances of ours, he told me, had been betrayed by their wives." (This sounds almost like a sarcasm, since Tausk had tried to seduce the wife of a colleague, who was also his friend.) But if Weiss had already observed that Tausk was capable of being thrown into "a state of deep depression" because of his having been abandoned by a woman, why did he not anticipate that it was again the conflict about a woman that precipitated Tausk's suicide, instead of speculating about Tausk's having felt abandoned by Freud? Had he stuck to the observation he had already made on Tausk during the war, he might have been on the right track. One can detect a note of duplicity on Tausk's side when Tausk, according to Weiss, spoke of Freud as having "a slight paranoiac trait. He based his diagnosis on the fact that Freud seemed to have a way of becoming strongly attached to a follower and later rejecting him" (p. 10)—referring, no doubt, to Freud's relationships to Adler, Jung and Stekel.

It will be recalled that Tausk had been one of Freud's strongest supporters in the discussions with Jung, and that it was Freud's wish to give Tausk a greater share in the *Zentralblatt*; this had aroused Stekel's anger and contributed to his break with Freud. Then why did Tausk now disparage Freud by gossiping about a "paranoiac trait," in just those matters in which he had earlier ostensibly agreed with Freud?

The similarities between Weiss's recollections and Roazen's book cannot be coincidences. They extend to such points as these: that Federn was able to present his views with clarity only after Freud's death (Roazen, p. 190; Weiss, p. 15); and that Freud lagged in both interest and research in the area of ego psychology (Roazen, p. 185; Weiss, p. 12). Even the fundamental error that Tausk's paper on the influencing machine is significant because it demonstrated the importance of projection in schizophrenia appears in both books (Roazen, p. 193; Weiss, p. 10). Since Roazen cites Weiss sparsely and never on the aforementioned questions, and Weiss never cites Roazen, one cannot be certain who profited from whom. Roazen does refer once (p. 220) to an unpublished manuscript by Weiss: "My Acquaintance with Victor Tausk." This makes it highly probable that he derived far more profit from his interviews with Weiss than he lets the reader know. Future investigations will perhaps reveal whether it is here that the psychological motivation may lie for Roazen's having devoted over 15% of his book to a chapter titled "Plagiarism."

To suspect ambivalence in a writer when he expresses himself negatively about Freud is by now a commonplace among psychoanalysts; and it has become a banality to link an erratum with the author's unconscious. Nevertheless, I wish to report that, in discussing Tausk's resentment toward Freud, Weiss wrote (1970, p. 14): "To demonstrate the *usefulness* of Freud's therapeutic procedure, Tausk dismissed many patients after a short period of treatment" (emphasis added). However, when Weiss wrote about Freud (p. 19) that "he fainted easily at the sight of blood and injuries and so could not have become a physician or surgeon," he exposed himself to criticism and the suspicion of bias. No instance of such fainting has ever been reported. Furthermore, Freud worked for three years in a general hospital as a resident physician, starting for two months with surgery.

Notes on *Paul Federn's Assessment of Tausk's Suicide*

ROAZEN SEEMS to draw on Paul Federn in support of his theory about the deficit in Freud's emotional sphere, at this time of his life. "The motivation" [of the suicide], Federn wrote to his wife (Roazen, p. 153), "was Freud's turning away from him." Then, after giving the devastating character picture of Tausk ("only vanity, envy, and lack of interest"), which I mentioned before, Federn goes on to assert that "If Freud had shown him a human interest, not simply recognition and support, he might have continued to bear longer his martyr-like existence. . . . But he [Tausk] was not *kind*, as little as Freud is kind—i.e., Freud possesses so much love for people that he can be kind, but in his old age he became increasingly harder and this is understandable with Freud because he, too, had to live a life unworthy of his greatness" (emphasis in the text).

It is of interest to note in this connection that, according to Federn, Freud had *not* withdrawn his recognition and support from Tausk. Did Federn have in mind Freud's refusal of Tausk's request for an analysis, when he expressed regret that Freud had not shown "a human interest" in Tausk? That is not likely, since he himself avers in this same letter that, even though he "had forgiven him [Tausk] inwardly" the many insults he had to bear at his hands, he "was no longer fond of him." Now, since Tausk was not particularly discreet in his allegations which amounted to Freud's having appropriated his ideas, Federn must have known that Freud, too, had had to bear at Tausk's hands many "insults" and could hardly therefore be expected to have for him that degree of positive feeling that is, after all, one of the prerequisites for accepting a person into treatment. Thus it is difficult to learn from Federn's letter just what might have been the particulars of Freud's alleged shortcomings.[71]

Toward the end of Federn's letter, there is to be found a point of ambivalence toward psychoanalysis itself. With some justification, he alludes to Tausk's inability to love as one of the reasons for his suicide; but he links this deficit in the ability to love with "the methodological rigor which Freud teaches" which "makes people hard and alienates them from their fellow men" (p. 153). This is quite an attack against Freud; certainly, it is not in keeping with what Federn later taught, even though it is a reproach that one hears raised quite often against psychoanalysis by outsiders.

Federn's letter proves also that Roazen was wrong in his appraisal of the bearing that Tausk's disturbance had on his professional comportment. When reporting that Tausk "had periods of depression in which he was full of despair" (p. 83), Roazen adds pointedly: "Most important, he always functioned in the demanding role of a psychiatrist, with all that means in terms of the day-

---

[71] It is evident from Federn's letter that he had developed—even though unrealistically—a feeling of guilt about Tausk's death. I would conjecture that his reproach against Freud stood in the service of assuaging his own mental pain about the catastrophe. I shall presently have another interpretation to suggest.

to-day bearing of emotional stress" (p. 84). Yet Federn had
written to his wife that "at the end he [Tausk] drove his psychological patients away," and that this was done "apparently in order
to demonstrate the uselessness of the method, out of rancour
against Freud" (p. 153; it is possible that closeness to Freud
elicited in Tausk patterns of acting out that were incompatible
with the practice of psychoanalysis).

Sanctimoniously, Roazen asks (p. 142) what Freud could
have had in mind when he wrote Lou Andreas-Salomé that he
had taken Tausk to be a threat to the future. "Tausk was not yet
in the line of succession," he adds maliciously, as if it were not
plain that the progress of an entire decade, little as it may have
been on the local scene, might be undone by the indiscreet behavior of one member of the Psychoanalytic Society who acted
the way Tausk apparently did: who insulted his colleagues, and
went so far in his attempt to disavow psychoanalysis as to dismiss
his patients. This was especially true in a locality like Vienna,
where, of course, every analyst was known individually to the
medical community.

I wish to conclude with an attempt to reconstruct an unconscious process that, it seems to me, can be deduced from Paul
Federn's letter to his wife. The mood or emotional atmosphere
that pervades that letter provides me with the opportunity to point
to a reaction that occurs frequently in those who have chosen a
great man as a leader. When a misfortune or catastrophe occurs—
particularly when it happens with traumatic suddenness—the very
leader to whom something like superhuman qualities have been
attributed up to then is held responsible, even though he has no
realistic connection whatsoever with the event.

I observed a faint effect of that sort among some psychoanalysts after the occupation of Austria by Germany. Evidently,
the unconscious magic belief existed that Freud's presence in
Vienna would be sufficient to protect the profession (and the
country?) against the victory of brute force. When this belief was
proven wrong by the historical event, one was able to observe in
some analysts a resentful, although short-lived, reaction against
Freud. A consequence of such a reaction can be found in Bruno
Bettelheim's (1960) book on his concentration camp experiences,
and in the bitter criticism he extends there against psychoanalysis.

In his instance, the "symbolic wounds" apparently did not heal. It was, it seems to me, something of a trauma to Federn that anybody who had lived and worked under Freud's shadow for as long a time as Tausk had should have remained unprotected against his own self-destruction.

I have earlier reported the grandiose fantasies that Roazen projected onto Freud—as if he were almighty, and a mere thought or gesture on his part would have been sufficient to make Tausk kill himself. One of the unconscious ideas that lay behind the contents of Federn's letter is the very opposite of Roazen's fantasies—namely, that Tausk's suicide was for Federn a sign of Freud's *weakness*. The spiritual leader's charisma should, of course, be able to keep alive all those who are part of his environment. By asserting that Freud really had had the power to keep Tausk alive, Federn was reinstituting the image of the all-powerful teacher.

The thought of a Freud who was entirely disconnected from the catastrophe—a Freud who, whatever he might have done, would still have been unable to preserve his pupil's life—may have been out of keeping with a truly charismatic image. The assumption that Freud did have the power to keep Tausk alive yet failed to do so, for whatever reason, may have made it easier for Federn to bear the trauma of Tausk's suicide. The reaction of the general public in Vienna was, of course, that Tausk's suicide constituted lasting proof that psychoanalysis in theory and practice was, in the long run, but a capital error—otherwise how could one of Freud's collaborators have done what, according to the imagination of the average person, only someone who was himself mentally aberrant would do?

ON TAUSK'S SUICIDE

ROAZEN'S ATTACK against Freud culminates in the contention that Freud wished Tausk out of the way, and that, although Freud had it in his power to rescue Tausk, he did not do so for selfish and unethical reasons. The explanation Roazen offers of Tausk's suicide, however, is not reduced to the one factor in it that can allegedly be attributed to Freud, but suggests a plurality of reasons. He writes (p. 161): "Each of us is likely to interpret Tausk's life

on the basis of quite personal lessons derived from our own experience." Anyone who adopts this impressionistic approach—
whether writer or reader—would thereby be permitted to interpret
at will the objective facts of Tausk's life. One consequence of this
is succinctly expressed when Roazen calls his final chapter: "Free
Associations."

This time I shall not start out by demonstrating the contradictions in which Roazen becomes hopelessly entangled, but shall
rather set forth a reconstruction of the background of Tausk's
suicide and, if possible, the main inner processes that may have
led up to the final catastrophe. I shall then describe that reality
event that Roazen failed to discover and which Tausk was not
strong enough to cope with. Jones (1924), in his review of
Wittels' book on Freud, did not hesitate to diagnose Tausk as "a
paraphrenic"—that is, as someone who was suffering from schizophrenia. He further stated that "Tausk could come to no other
end." [72]

Whatever the correct diagnosis of Tausk's psychopathology
may be, his posthumous paper is an adequate starting point for a
reconstruction of the psychological background for Tausk's suicide.
It ends with the following footnote:

> [The] relation . . . of a creative individual to the master who
> represents his ideals [literally: of a productive man to a master
> who is his model (vorbildlich)], is patterned after the father
> complex and is cathected with great quantities of libido. . . . In

---

[72] Roazen, who made several disparaging remarks about Jones throughout his
book, ascribes to Jones on this occasion (p. 213, n. 16) the statement "that Tausk
had 'caught' schizophrenia" and adds a sarcastic remark about Jones's alleged view
on schizophrenia. Prof. Penrose, however, whom Roazen cites as informant, as-
sures me that Roazen must be mistaken, that the implication of the word "caught"
was simply that the disease had arisen unexpectedly; in short, the term was a
metaphor, and indicated nothing about what Jones's ideas about schizophrenia
might have been.

This technique of misinterpreting a term, as Roazen did in his interview with
Prof. Penrose, strikes me as being even more significant than his errors with regard
to his interviews with Drs. Edoardo Weiss and Richard Wagner. An informant
uses a term, and then a highly improbable interpretation is attached to it, so that
it becomes suitable for purposes of attack. Without first making sure that the
interpretation is correct, Roazen then proceeds as if there were no room for doubt—
as if the derogatory remark were not the author's own subjective interpretation
but actually did contain a statement of fact.

the life of rivals struggling with their masters, the hatred . . . is derived from the son-father relation. Hence the conflict between master and disciple striving for independence resembles very closely the severest type of conflict between father and son [Tausk 1934, p. 141 n.].

This footnote contains Tausk's posthumous confession of an unresolved hatred against his father, which he displaced upon Freud.[73] Yet one gets the impression that not only the quoted footnote, but the entire article is closely linked to one aspect of Tausk's unresolvable conflicts. This is all the more probable since the article does not deal with a psychoanalytic experience—that is to say, it is not the result of interpretations made during the course of a subject's psychoanalysis—but rather with an incidental observation made in everyday life, the gaps being filled in by Tausk's own assumptions.

The article gives the impression of having been written hurriedly; it is a condensation of many far-reaching thoughts. The topic of the article is the observations Tausk made of an acquaintance, a Mr. B.,[74] who forgot that Henrik Ibsen—whom he greatly admired, and with whose life history he was familiar—had been a pharmacist prior to his literary career; further, he did not recognize Ibsen's sculptured bust the following evening, although he had been quite familiar with it.

About the second parapraxis Tausk wrote: *Freilich er hat allen Grund zu diesem Gedächtnismord,* which Dorian Feigenbaum has translated as follows (Tausk 1934, p. 139): "Indeed, he has every reason for this abolition of memory," thus getting around the

---

[73] Roazen believes that the manuscript, which was published in 1934, "escaped being destroyed with the rest of his papers (p. 197), Tausk having "left instructions in his will for all his papers to be burned unread" (p. 130). An explanatory note in the German publication says that the article stems from Tausk's literary estate (*Nachlass*), but evidently, since Tausk's instruction was carried out by his son, there was no such estate left. Justifiedly, it may be assumed that Tausk had sent the manuscript to the editors of *Imago* or *Zeitschrift*, but that the editors did not publish the article at that time, since it contained Tausk's own self-indictment, and certainly nothing was further from their minds than the desire to hurt Tausk's sons. After fifteen years, however, they evidently thought that memories of the tragedy had receded sufficiently to make possible the publication of the paper without causing embarrassment to anyone.

[74] In the paper discussed earlier (Tausk 1917), Tausk assigned his own parapraxis to a Mr. A.

crucial Gedächtnismord (lit.: "memory murder"), which is a
neologism and therefore not easily translated. Since in the preceding sentence Tausk had written that his acquaintance "had no
choice but to eliminate from memory the . . . idea 'Ibsen,' " [75]
what the neologism means is that the dysfunction of memory was,
in effect, the murder of the revered playwright.

When we hear that Mr. B. had started an affair with a pharmacist's wife; that the cuckold had threatened the adulterer with
physical violence; that in Tausk's estimation both adulterer and
husband were cowards—the former because he wanted to use the
husband's threat for the purpose of putting an end to a relationship of which he had grown weary, and the latter because he made
threats but was actually afraid of taking action—then it becomes
clear that the background of the neologism is an acute and acted
out oedipal situation.

Ibsen, however, was not known personally by the man who
perpetrated this Gedächtnismord, and he had done nothing to
warrant being so brutally treated. If Tausk's last paper can be
understood as reflecting a preconscious insight into his own conflicts, displaced upon a chance observation in an acquaintance,
that would testify to the fact that Freud had done as little to
provoke Tausk in the imbroglio that stands at the center of
Roazen's book, as Ibsen had done to provoke Mr. B., the person
at the center of Tausk's paper. The last sentence, completely unconnected with the paper's subject matter, suddenly puts forth
the idea that here "a piece of paranoiac mechanics becomes
transparent" [76] (author's emphasis)—which, in turn, may also be
interpreted as an unconscious self-diagnosis.

Be that as it may, the paper contains clues that deserve to be
considered in any reconstruction of Tausk's suicide. It is necessary
to say a few words about neologisms in the German language,
which is much less opposed than the English to the formation of
new words, particularly word combinations. But the neologism
must clearly convey the meaning that it is supposed to carry. This
is not true of Gedächtnismord. Feigenbaum caught one possible
interpretation when he translated it as "abolition of memory," in

---

[75] . . . bleibt ihm nichts anderes übrig, als die . . . Vorstellung von Ibsen aus
dem Gedächtnis zu schaffen.

[76] Ein Stück von der paranoischen Mechanik wird hier durchsichtig.

which case it would mean that it was memory that was murdered. But the context permits (or, better, even suggests) the implication: murder (committed by) memory. The formation of a neologism, however, that does not clarify the meaning of a situation unambiguously; that sounds strange; that requires the subject's associations for clarification, and is formed by condensation—all this is reminiscent of those neologisms that occur in dreams with some frequency, and are therefore to be expected in certain types of schizophrenia, where their occurrence has indeed often been observed.[77]

Furthermore, in the footnote that I have quoted before, there is some indication that Tausk was on the verge of switching his point of view. Whereas in the paper Mr. B. displaces his personal conflict onto his own relationship to an ideal model with whom he was not personally acquainted, the footnote first speaks of the hatred that results from the "son attitude" (*Sohneseinstellung*)[78] of those who are rivals of their masters; yet in the very next sentence it speaks of conflicts between "masters and disciples" and "fathers and sons" (the preceding text would have required the opposite sequence of "disciples and masters" and "sons and fathers" respectively).

Even more revealing is the comment that Tausk makes when he asks why Mr. B. had to halt before Ibsen's bust, in a room in which every object had long been familiar to him. The answer he gives (it is not the result of Mr. B.'s psychoanalysis, but solely of Tausk's conjecture or construction) is that the bust had become for Mr. B. estranged (*fremd geworden*). The article closes with the comment that persons from whom the (paranoiac) patient withdraws libido make their appearance once again as "strangers."[79]

Yet it was quite possibly at the time when Tausk was writing this sentence that he felt unable to go ahead with his marriage to a former patient of his—a pianist, sixteen years his junior—with

---

[77] I have consulted Dr. Henry D. von Witzleben, who combines an exceptional literary sense for the German language with equal knowledge of schizophrenic neologisms. According to him, the neologism *Gedächtnismord* cannot be construed as symptomatic of any mental disorder.

[78] Translated by Feigenbaum as "son-father relationship."

[79] *Die Personen, von denen der Kranke die Libido abzieht, erscheinen als "fremde" wieder.*

whom he had fallen in love not long before his suicide. One of
the reasons for his inability to marry may have been an ever-
increasing sense of depersonalization. Further, it cannot possibly
have been without a very personal meaning that Tausk in his
paper compared the incident of Mr. B.'s not recognizing Ibsen's
bust with a parapraxis Freud had reported: a woman did not recognize, the day after her return from the honeymoon, that "a
gentleman on the other side of the street" was her husband. The
marriage came "to a most unhappy end" (Freud 1901, p. 203).

Tausk also reported that, when Mr. B. forgot the fact that
Ibsen had been a pharmacist, he himself had a vague feeling that
he knew something about a relationship between Mr. B. and a
pharmacist, something that he could not recall distinctly. Yet
when Mr. B. did not recognize the bust the following day, the
reason for Mr. B.'s memory difficulties suddenly came to Tausk's
mind. Tausk added that he had not concealed from himself the
explanation of his own forgetfulness of the previous evening, but
that he was concealing these reasons from the reader.

It will be recalled that the fact of which Mr. B. did not wish
to be reminded was his extramarital affair with a pharmacist's wife,
and all the unpleasant consequences attached to it. Now, it
happened that Tausk was still engaged to a young Serbian widow
with whom he had lived in Belgrade during the war, at the time of
his affair with the patient whom he had decided to marry. He
thus was facing, for a while, the same problem as Mr. B.: both had
to desert a lover of whom they had grown weary.

In evaluating Tausk's posthumous paper, one is forced to arrive
at the conclusion that he was on the verge of gaining insight into
his conflict with Freud. He was so keen in suddenly understanding
Mr. B.'s dysfunction, because its interpretation led to the same
conflicts as those that were burdening his own relationship with
an admired teacher. Whether Tausk was actually aware of this at
the time of writing the paper is, of course, unknown. The least
that may be assumed with approximate certainty is that he was on
his way to becoming aware of a content that he had until then
successfully warded off by his insistence that Freud was assimilating his ideas, and holding him down through withholding the
recognition that was due him. One might say that his defenses had
become weakened.

Another set of circumstances must also be considered here. They are known from Lou Andreas-Salomé's answer to Freud's letter, in which he informed her of Tausk's death. As she wrote Freud, Tausk had wanted to visit her three months prior to his death. She had objected and had stopped answering his letters. "He was correct in writing a year or so ago: 'One does not take a seat at the same table with an unhappy one: you too have not done it.' No, I too have not." [80] (Pfeiffer, 1966, p. 109; cf. Binion, p. 403). Is it really true that one refuses to share a table with the unhappy? One does so rather with a person who is guilty.

Lou Andreas-Salomé seems to have been one of the few women who proved to be stronger than Tausk. One pattern of his dealings with women was that he would rescue them, if need be, as he did with the young aristocratic Serbian woman, who had been arrested by the occupying army and was in great danger; another pattern was that he would excite them and attach them inextricably to himself—only to hurt them gravely (by sudden and permanent rejection, I would surmise). Of two such women, as mentioned before, Roazen reports that they suffered for a long time from the fact that he had abandoned them; the Serbian lady came to Vienna once a year to put flowers on his grave (p. 196).[81] From Roazen's book, however, we learn of at least one instance that shows how vulnerable he was to situations in which a woman proved to be stronger than he was. When his bride-to-be, to whom he had been engaged during his army service, betrayed him with his own patient, and he was made the loser, Tausk became depressed; he "expressed very pessimistic ideas about life, and . . . felt he could no longer trust anyone" (p. 108).

Lou Andreas-Salomé was a woman who had left him, had escaped falling into bondage to him. The fact that she did not re-

---

[80] Er hatte Recht vor Jahresfrist zu schreiben: 'man setzt sich nicht mit einem Unglücklichen an denselben Tisch: auch Du hast es ja nicht getan.' Nein, auch ich nicht.

[81] Roazen feels that attachments of that sort go to Tausk's credit. I would feel quite the opposite. There are sociopaths who possess a technique for exploiting feminine masochism, with the result that they force women into an unbreakable bondage (Hörigkeit) to them; for such men, the fact that they are capable of arousing a passionate attachment, which persists even after they have left, provides the highest narcissistic gratification. The strong responses Tausk regularly evoked in women are an indirect sign of his psychopathology.

spond to his attempt to get closer to her at the moment when he was in a crisis must have had a devastating effect on Tausk. Lou Andreas-Salomé, as the result of her fame and her mental superiority, symbolized for him, I surmise, an idealized mother. Her independence meant that she was indestructible; and to be ignored by such a woman must have greatly reduced his feeling of self-value and self-respect. It would be of interest to know whether it was the rebuff by Lou Andreas-Salomé that had such a traumatic effect on Tausk that he felt it necessary to ask for psychoanalytic treatment.

The third set of circumstances that strikes me as being relevant has to do with Tausk's aging. Roazen reports about Tausk (p. 84): "Physically he was getting a little flabby; he gave the impression of being round. Tausk both walked and looked now like a middle-aged man." If this was true, the first signs of aging must have come as a real blow to a man as narcissistic as Tausk was.

Did doubts about his potency arise,[82] as happens at that age, and was he also therefore uncertain about the prospects of a marriage to a woman so much younger than himself? One may assume that it dawned on him, in view of the unhappiness he had, in the past, regularly brought on women, that it was unfair to exploit the acute transference reaction of such a young woman patient. But we shall see that there was a quite different reason for his inability to marry his former patient. At any rate, this time even his older sister, who had apparently condoned all his previous acting out with women, protested (p. 111). The sister's reproaches, one must assume, would strengthen the feelings of shame that are hardly avoidable when a divorced man breaks his third or fourth engagement, in order to remarry. Since, in the letter to his wife, Federn wrote that he was "certain that being destitute and unable to borrow money for enough to eat was but the last push" (p. 153) that caused Tausk's suicide, it would be necessary to consider

---

[82] In one of Tausk's articles (1916a), I find a passage that may support the reconstruction of fear of impotence. Tausk described a type of neurotic deserter who suffered from "typical anxiety at every beginning of an activity and at every change in the situation. . . . My guess was confirmed that the man was suffering from anxiety about sexual impotence" (my own literal translation, cf. 1916a, p. 375).

material want as at least a precipitating factor. Yet evidence proves Federn to have been wrong in this regard. Roazen reports (p. 84) that Tausk had six patients in the spring of 1919.

I have met one of them who was in treatment with Tausk right up to the day of his death. He was sent to Tausk by Freud and paid forty Kronen for each session, which made an income of almost one thousand Kronen a month derived from this patient alone, a considerable amount of money. Mr. H. F. Fuerst has been kind enough to gather from the daily newspapers some data on the purchasing power of the Krone at that time. The following prices may serve as illustrations: the monthly salary of a typist was between 300 and 800 Kronen; room and board for one month in the country for vacationers was between 400 and 750 Kronen; a luncheon cost between three and ten Kronen. Though it is improbable that other patients paid an equally high fee, because this patient came from a rather wealthy family, it is evident from these figures that Tausk did not find himself in a desperate economic condition at the time of his suicide.

For a final diagnosis, the proximate circumstances surrounding the actual suicide are relevant. The afternoon before he committed the deed, Tausk met his 17-year-old son. His parting words were: "Don't worry about me" (p. 124)—the sort of reassurances that a father should hear from the son. If Tausk had really known at that time that this was to be their last encounter, such an assurance, in my opinion, would have been particularly cruel, since it necessarily had to strengthen the feeling of guilt that would be unavoidably engendered in the son after the father's suicide. The same evening he wrote his favorite sister of his impending wedding. Instead of going to the psychoanalytic meeting, he wrote Freud a note, explaining his absence by way of the necessity of "solving the decisive affairs of my life" and the determination not "to be tempted to wish to resort to your help. I shall probably soon be free again to approach you. I intend to appear [make my appearance] with a minimum of neurosis" (p. 122f.).

If one encountered these words in a novel, or on the stage, one would describe them as an instance of poetic irony. It is not known what happened later that night between Tausk and his fiancée. The next morning "He wrote a will, with a lengthy itemization of all his possessions, noting down even the smallest details" (p. 125), along with two letters, one to Freud and one to his fiancée.

As a further complication, it must be recorded that Tausk, according to Roazen's report, was sipping brandy while writing the letters and the will. Yet it seems not to be known at what time Tausk actually started to drink. The determination to go ahead with the suicidal act may have arisen as a reaction to the intake of alcohol.

It is evident that a large number of variables had to conjoin to make Tausk resort to the final act of self-destruction. Nevertheless, it is my impression that he had been doomed, since childhood, to live a miserable and unfortunate life that could all too easily lead to suicide, whatever the particular external circumstances of his later life might have been. When the little boy pierced the heart of his mother's portrait, the adult's own existence may have been thereby doomed. Roazen's explanations—such as (p. 124): "His involvement with Freud had eaten up his emotional energy" (quite aside from the fact that there is no proof or even indication thereof to be found in Roazen's book)—are nothing but verbiage; it merely serves his purpose of making Freud *la bête noire*. When he continues: "he [Tausk] had failed in his search for a solution to this conflict," one can only comment that Tausk was evidently unable to find solutions to several conflicts that had been sapping his energy for many years; but there is no evidence to be found in the data that Roazen presents in his book for any suggestion that Freud stood at the center of Tausk's conflict, at the time when he ended his life.

A fair appraisal of the clinical material that is known almost proves the opposite. If anything, what contributed to Tausk's suicide was apparently the *solution* of the conflict that had played such a decisive role in his relationship with Freud. This becomes evident when Tausk's farewell letter to Freud is scrutinized. After a preamble, in which he asked Freud to give assistance to his fiancée, he stated (p. 127):

> I thank you for all the good which you have done me. It was much and has given meaning to the last ten years of my life. Your work is genuine and great, I shall take leave of this life

knowing that I was one of those who witnessed the triumph of
one of the greatest ideas of mankind.[83]

Why would a man who has had to suffer so much humiliation,
deprivation, indeed oppression, by his teacher, as Roazen claims
throughout his book, take his final leave from his alleged persecutor in such a way? Accusations and curses are, after all, not rare
in the farewell letters of suicides (14 out of 44 in Morgenthaler
and Steinberg's [1945] cases; pleas for forgiveness, apologies and
justifications are more frequent—22 cases [p. 99f.]).[84]

Jellinek (1947), the founder of electropathology, was greatly
interested in the psychology of the dying. From some of his observations, it becomes clear (I was able to confirm this in my own
study of 1955) that not infrequently the dying patient solves, in
his last hours, a problem with which he has been wrestling for a
long time. Even though the conscious content of the conflict may
have arisen during adulthood, it can be safely assumed, in the
light of general experience, that such conflicts of long duration
have their roots in the childhood period. In other words, some
dying patients achieve in their final hours a structural change
that they were unable or unwilling to accomplish, as long as an
extensive future still lay ahead of them.[85]

The remarkable feature of the paragraph from Tausk's last
letter to Freud is its complete correctness. Tausk had ample reason to be grateful to Freud, for no one had ever done so much for
him, or been so generous to him. The fact that Freud had accepted
him a decade previously had rendered that portion of his life
meaningful. Prior to that decade, he had pursued many activities, but had not become rooted in any of them; only being

---

[83] Roazen (p. 128) interprets this suicide note as being "really quite aggressive
toward Freud." The anonymous reviewer for the (London) Times Literary Supplement (August 7, 1970) has this to say about the author's interpretation: "Only by
the most strained interpretation could such an attitude be inferred." I would go a
step further and say that it cannot be inferred at all.

[84] For a survey of the modern literature on suicide notes, see Frederick (1969).
According to one study, "slightly more than half of the notes displayed positive
affects, such as gratitude and affection" (ibid., p. 19). It is also noteworthy that
"individuals who were separated or divorced disclosed more hostility than those
who were single, married or widowed" (ibid.).

[85] I owe thanks to Dr. Paul Kramer for his suggesting and encouraging me to
view Tausk's last hours in this light.

an analyst had given him a permanent niche in the professional world. At last, shortly before his death, he became able to acknowledge Freud's greatness without ambivalence, and to be aware that it had been a rare privilege to contribute his little share to "one of the greatest ideas of mankind." At last he had accepted the fact that that idea would be forever connected with Freud's name, and that he himself would have been not a foot-soldier, but at the least a sergeant, in the unrelenting advance of the march of ideas.

One is here reminded of Freud's statement (1917a, p. 246) with regard to the melancholic patient's self-criticism: "We only wonder why a man has to be ill before he can be accessible to a truth of that kind."

In his will, Tausk also showed insight into the basic conflict that made it impossible for him to establish an enduring relationship to a woman. He wrote (Roazen p. 130): "The recognition that I cannot gladly enter into a new marriage, that I can only keep myself and my beloved fiancée in conflicts and torments, is the true conscious motive of my suicide." Yet this enlargement of the insightful self was brought into being at the price of self-depreciation, as is to be observed in melancholic patients: "My talent is too little to support me" (p. 129f.); "my suicide is the healthiest, most decent deed of my unsuccessful life" (p. 127). In these two statements he certainly took upon himself a guilt that was not really his. He was sufficiently endowed to support both himself and his family, and no one but himself would have called him unsuccessful.

It was no accident that Tausk (1916a) had written a study on the deserter; he himself was a life-long deserter.[86] He had deserted his wife, his children, and every woman with whom he ever fell in love; and now he was indirectly disowning psychoanalysis, for his final deed was to add to the disrepute in which psychoanalysis was then held in Vienna. I myself remember very well that

---

[86] Strangely enough, Roazen has completely overlooked this element in Tausk's life story. He writes (p. 156): "Again like Tausk, Federn had never become a deserter." This is, of course, very true of Federn, even though he, too, ended his own life. But a fatally sick man, who has fulfilled his life's mission and knows that his creative potential has been realized, is not a deserter when he makes that choice.

his suicide was frequently cited as an argument against psychoanalysis (cf. Wittels 1923, p. 57). But the hostility implicit in
that act is, in my opinion, of secondary importance.

There is one sentence in Tausk's last will that is particularly
significant. He writes of his life: "I have systematically disinte-
grated [it] ever since my childhood and [it] has now completely
lost its sense, since I can no longer enjoy it" (p. 129). Degrees of,
or even lack of enjoyment should no longer be decisive in adult
life. Tausk here appeals to the pleasure principle in the way one
encounters in melancholic patients, and yet the two letters do not
sound as though they were written by a man who is suffering from
melancholia. The melancholic patient is usually paralyzed in his
ability to act. We can be certain that Tausk was not paralyzed,
in view of his meeting his son the day before his death, his writing lucid, well-composed letters and going through with a variety
of actions rational in themselves.

If it was not melancholia that drove Tausk to his death, then
it is reasonable to ask what did. The orbit of his insight had
grown, one instance of this being his admission of Freud's greatness without claim to any reason for being angry with him. What
he says about Freud in his farewell leter can easily be confirmed.
Yet he was apparently unable to continue functioning under the
impact of that insight. For it meant that the father-substitute was
greater than Tausk would ever be able to be, and that Tausk had
many reasons for feeling grateful to him.

With this, however, the case of Tausk contra Freud, which
Roazen has so ingeniously built up, is proven never to have existed,
but to be purely fictitious. To be sure, something of the sort Roazen
presents probably did have a temporary place in Tausk's psychic
reality and was reborn in Roazen's psychic reality, from which it
will probably trickle into the minds of poorly instructed and/or
suggestible readers.

Shortly before his death Tausk, however, was able to recognize
the illusionary or delusional nature of the image he had formed
of Freud, and to admit it in a form that strikes me personally as
being marked by what I can only characterize as solemn dignity.[87]

---

[87] It is a pity that Roazen's book does not have an appendix with Tausk's
letters and last will in the original language. So much in interpretation depends

The other insight he had gained concerned his relationship to women. He evidently had become aware of the severe ambivalence that compelled him to separate from them.

Roazen holds Freud responsible for Tausk's falling in love with his young patient. He suggests (p. 110) that Tausk's intended bride "may have been partly a substitute for" Dr. Deutsch, for he had fallen in love only after the termination of his own analysis. "His elation at falling in love may have masked grief and mourning, and it would not be unknown for a patient to act out his emotional conflicts after such a sudden blow."

How did Roazen know that Tausk was ever in love with his fiancée? As we shall presently see, this is highly doubtful. Yet the author's general observation is correct. Some patients, perhaps even many, do act out their conflicts even while they are in analysis, sometimes even after they have been in analysis for many, many years. It seems to me, however, that Roazen has seriously overextended this observation, in order to heap one more accusation on Freud.

Is it not clinically more correct to think here of Tausk's *perennial* acting out with women; his unpreparedness to enter the declining period of man's life at a time when he was not yet even prepared to accept the basic responsibilities of adulthood? The pattern of falling passionately in love with a much younger woman is a far too frequent event in the lives of men between the ages of 40 and 50 for it to figure here primarily as a specific reaction to an adventitious event in Tausk's analysis. To all the earlier narcissistic motives implicit in Tausk's so successfully wooing women had now been added the need to rejuvenate the aging body by the embrace of youth. And if his falling in love was indeed a defense against grief and mourning, he did not after all commit suicide because he loved, but rather because he was *unable to love* —as he lets us know in his last will—and because he knew that the marriage vow would bring a curse on the young woman. His

---

on language. Roazen mentions (p. 116), for example, letters that Tausk wrote to Freud that "include almost childish accounts," etc. Acquaintance with these documents, particularly in the original, would facilitate a diagnosis. One wonders how expert Roazen is in the biographical method *per se*, since he has omitted from the text such significant biographical material as Tausk's early childhood recollection, his published slip of the tongue, and decisive parts of the *Minutes* of the Vienna Society.

inability to love, however, and his knowledge of impending disaster cannot be laid at the doorstep of a traumatic separation from the analyst.

Tausk had incurred reality guilt as the result of his conduct toward women, and no analysis can free a man from such guilt. The power of the psychoanalytic technique ends at the border of neurotic guilt feelings. What lies beyond calls for the power of the priest, who alone can give absolution. In terms of classical psychoanalysis, Tausk was incurable.[88]

When Tausk concluded his will with what may have been the last sentence he ever wrote (p. 130), "I have deceived you all by living a role to which I was not equal," he was making a comprehensive statement that again proved the level of self-recognition that he achieved toward the end of his existence. For he was correct in that confession. He had acted like a great lover—which he was not. His proposition that orgasm cannot give full gratification—a proposition for which he claimed priority—was almost certainly autobiographical. He acted like a great seeker of truth; yet he was not, for his rivalry with Freud was more important to him than questions of truth. Finally, he wore on the surface all the paraphernalia that the common imagination attributes to genius—which he was not.

Doubt may be felt that self-recognition, which Greek culture lauded as the ultimate of wisdom, and which is the principal aim of psychoanalysis, could have such a crushing effect on a man. Only a disease process—one that leads to distorted self-knowl-

---

[88] In groping for a metapsychological model that might fit the dynamics of Tausk's suicide, one may have to consider a remark Freud once made, even though its correctness may be doubted by many. Freud (1924a, p. 186) wrote: "Probably in a psychosis the rejected piece of reality constantly forces itself upon the mind," thus explaining the mental pain so frequently observed in psychoses, which require the continuous mobilization of countercathexis against the correct representation of reality. Even if one is not inclined to assume the presence of a psychosis in Tausk, "the rejected piece of reality" that was the truth about Freud did require the mobilization of countercathexis.

Whatever the reason may have been that the rejected piece of reality made inroads, Tausk's self did not prove strong enough to endure a truth that had been successfully warded off until then. It also must be considered that, according to this model at least, the psychic apparatus would have had to cope with an inordinate quantity of psychic energy brought forth by the withdrawal of countercathexis. Thus a state of extreme damming-up of energy may have arisen.

edge, which, in turn, may be called pathological in itself, as happens in melancholia—can be the prelude to suicide. This will probably be advanced as a disproof of my assertion that the truth about the relationship between Freud and Tausk can be learned from the latter's farewell letter. However, close examination of the historical material will make the correctness of my assertion quite probable.

I have shown earlier how much autobiographical material is contained in Tausk's publications. This is no less true of many of his discussion remarks. About six months after he joined the group in Vienna, in commenting on a presentation by Stekel on the feeling of strangeness, Tausk made a remark that is recorded as follows (*Minutes 2*, p. 539f.): "On the basis of his own experience, Tausk suspects that the sense of estrangement is combined with a feeling of guilt. Perhaps the feeling of strangeness means nothing but this: *if I recognize myself, then I must kill myself*" [89] (emphasis added). This is a most surprising statement. It cannot have been derived from clinical observation, for at that time Tausk had not yet had the opportunity to make clinical observations for much longer than a few months; moreover, I think no one has ever confirmed this almost bizarre explanation of feelings of strangeness. It must have been the reflection of something that was eminently and uniquely true of Tausk.

Interestingly enough, the remark was made before there could have been any question of Tausk's energy having been exhausted by his fight with Freud and before he was supposedly humiliated by Freud. It flies right in the face of the consequences that Roazen has ascribed to Dr. Deutsch's abrupt termination of Tausk's analysis. Had Roazen taken cognizance of this discussion remark, he might have been more cautious in his interpretations, because Tausk's indirect confession clearly proves that Tausk's analysis —whoever might have conducted it—by leading to insight, would only have accelerated Tausk's suicide for, in his instance, self-recognition was apparently a signpost on the road to suicide.

I do not know whether the reader will agree with the foregoing presentation of the dynamics of Tausk's suicide. Originally

---

[89] The reader may recall that Tausk, in his posthumously published paper, assumed that Mr. B. had feelings of strangeness.

I had planned to end this section at this point. At that time I was still vacillating between the feeling that all the factors I have mentioned add up to a satisfactory explanation of Tausk's suicide and the feeling that my reasoning was somewhat forced and not convincing. Then chance brought me together with a person who had been close enough to Tausk and his fiancée to know the true proximate reason of his suicide.[90] It is impressive how frequently Roazen went astray when, in default of documentation, he relied on his common-sense guesses, for this information, too, shows again that Roazen erred when he wrote about Tausk's fiancée (p. 124): "With this woman he [Tausk] had wanted more than ever to succeed in love."

I had earlier heard that Tausk's fiancée was allegedly pregnant, but I had considered this to be nothing but a rumor, since the source of that claim could not be determined.[91] I had to change my mind, however, in view of later information from the person just mentioned, whose knowledge and reliability I have no reason to doubt, and who confirmed that Tausk's fiancée was pregnant. The woman had consulted Tausk professionally, and he had seduced her during her first visit; she was a virgin at that time. Tausk proposed marriage only after efforts to interrupt the pregnancy proved unsuccessful. The woman had a miscarriage a few months after Tausk's death.

Only now can one properly assess Tausk's inability to go through with this marriage. The reasons Roazen enumerates do not entirely lose their validity by virtue of this piece of information. A man who was as undisciplined as he was in his sexual relations had to anticipate serious difficulties in a second marriage; and if his doubts about the prospects of marriage should make it inadvisable for him to go ahead with it, there was no hindrance in post-war Vienna to breaking an engagement. However, Tausk had lost his freedom of action. The circumstances under which the relationship had begun and the pregnancy this time made it im-

---

[90] While this new information changes the relative weight of the factors that I had held responsible, I thought it appropriate to leave the text as it was, aside from remarking that the true reason of Tausk's suicide will be put forth later.

[91] A perspicacious mind would, indeed, have guessed that only a pregnancy could have kept Tausk from repeating what he had previously done more than once—namely, break the engagement.

possible to repeat the past incidents of breaking an engagement.

For a personality as excessively narcissistic as Tausk's—that is to say, for a man who was accustomed to conquer and then dismiss females, in accordance with his own wishes, and without any consideration of the welfare of others—it must have meant utter defeat to find himself in a situation without exit. This was the element, evidently, that triggered his determination to put an end to his existence.[92] But the new information will also help to clarify other details. The reader may recall that I have struggled so far with the explanation of why Tausk, prior to his suicide, exchanged his hostile attitude toward Freud for a benign one. I have until this point believed that this could be explained by a weakening of defense. In the light of the new information, the following may be added. What had happened between him and his patient must have caused in Tausk a feeling of guilt and failure. This time he was unable to shift responsibility, for the patient had come to him seeking help and trusting his professional integrity. In view of what did happen, it is inescapable that he must have developed a conscious feeling of guilt. At the same time, he very likely also felt that he had suffered failure, as a physician and as a psychoanalyst. Conscious feelings of guilt, shame and failure, however, frequently join to make a person more humble, and to decrease the narcissistic demands he puts on his environment.

If my reconstruction is correct, Tausk would have been following a path that one can repeatedly observe in the Old Testament. When the Jews were successful and victorious, they took it as a sign of the Lord's love, and felt free of sin; when they faced adversities, however, they gained insight and admitted their past sinful conduct. It is very probable that Tausk took the adversity of being coerced into marriage as a punishment; and that compelled him to reinstitute the father-imago in its own rights.

At the same time, marriage was somehow expected to undo the damage he had already caused. Roazen (p. 122f.) writes of a letter that Tausk wrote Freud, explaining his absence from the

---

[92] Roazen (p. 131) finds in the fact that Tausk committed suicide in two ways (by shooting himself and by hanging himself) the expression of his rage at two persons: his fiancée and Freud. In view of the new data, it is more probable—if one wants to interpret this detail at all—that the two persons at whom the repressed rage was aimed were the woman and the fetus.

Wednesday meeting preceding his suicide. In it, he said: "I shall probably soon be free again to approach you. I intend to appear with a minimum of neurosis." Why should marriage have made him "free again to approach" Freud? What he called "a minimum of neurosis" meant apparently "a minimum of guilt." Yet he was not strong enough to carry out the act of undoing, and instead succumbed to solution by flight.

Every person's life is, of course, studded with actions that warrant feelings of guilt. Freedom from feelings of guilt can be based only on deficient differentiation, sensitivity and self-awareness, or on powerful denial. But in Tausk's instance one is struck by the way in which he manifested and gratified his aggressivity as early as in his childhood, when he openly acted out a matricidal impulse without that degree of displacement that may be expected from the child. The adult who is strongly motivated by sadistic impulses finds in our society a variety of channels of discharge. What was it that compelled Tausk to abuse his profession, the one critical area in which abuse cannot be condoned under any circumstances, even though unconscious abuse cannot always be avoided?

It would be a grave mistake and an oversimplification to reduce the Tausk problem to one of sociopathy or delinquency, for he was, at the same time, evidently a morally sensitive person, as is affirmed by the assistance he gave to others, his letters of farewell, and his last deed.

Let me end this painfully written section by saying that I am awestruck whenever one man joins in his life seeming incompatibles and acts as saint, sinner, judge and executioner.

BEYOND THE GRAVE

WHEN ONE FINDS the author stating, at the beginning of his book (p. 8): "The Tausk story also clarifies in a humanly satisfying way Freud's whole career," one can only assume that this statement remained in the manuscript by mistake, since the author may not yet have known, when he wrote, it, to what conclusions his way of looking at the Tausk story would lead him. Otherwise, one would have to believe that the author's intention was to mock the reader. Moreover, even if in his book there were one single sentence of "humanly satisfying" clarification, it is impossible to understand in what way the Tausk episode would serve to clarify Freud's "whole career."

Roazen's book will not support, in the eyes of later historians, his thesis of "the powers that Freud's pupils magically attributed to their leader"; or that "quarreling with Freud was the most dreadful possibility imaginable"; that "to be cast out by him meant . . . psychic death"; that "the book would be closed, the candle snuffed out" (p. 7). Surely, the later historian's mind will not let itself be obfuscated by the sheer denial of facts—such as that Adler and Jung, who had quarrelled with Freud, survived and led worldwide schools (Adler's followers were actually far more numerous in Vienna than Freud's); that Stekel, who had quarrelled with Freud, also survived and had a flourishing practice; that Wittels, who had quarrelled with Freud (he even published, fourteen years later, a lustily aggressive book against Freud), also survived and maintained a splendid practice.

Will Roazen's book succeed in denigrating Freud's character? It may attract a good many readers by means of its indiscreetness. Without any necessity for it, the name of a patient, whom Paul Federn had come to the United States to treat in 1914, is divulged, along with his symptom, and the names of all except one of Tausk's sweethearts are similarly divulged—although two of them are still alive. In one instance, the incredible indiscreetness is committed of revealing the girl's former address as well. Information is accepted and reproduced as factual, without any consideration of the reliability of the source, so long as it is injurious to Freud and depreciates him in the reader's eyes. The wildest claims are made, against all probabilities, and without any reasonable attempt at proof or documentation. Freud is quoted in a misleading way, and in one instance the quotation is actually distorted, so that he seems to be saying the opposite of what he actually did say (see p. 455). The book is, in extensive parts, not much different from the gossip columns in tabloid newspapers; it falls into the category that Walter Kaufmann, in his Forward to Binion (1965, p. v), characterized as "going along with the fashionable journalistic prostitution of biography and history."

Yet it is cleverly written and for quite a while it may succeed in its purpose. The question is whether in the long run it may not have done a terrible disservice to Tausk's memory. After all, the literature on Freud is easily available, and the interested reader can readily obtain information that disproves almost all the author's claims about Freud. As to the personality of Tausk, that appeared in Freud's obituary in its best possible light.

After having read Roazen's book I, for one, was no longer able to feel about Tausk the way I did previously. A particularly bitter taste was left by Paul Federn's letter, which should unquestionably have been published only after Tausk had become a historical figure and no one who knew him personally was around any longer. I feel now even more strongly than did Federn, when he wrote that he was "no longer fond of" Tausk. Who could have imagined that the author of such papers as those "On Discounting the Motive of Repression" (1913), "On the Psychology of Deserters" (1916a), "On the Influencing Machine" (1919), was the carrier of such psychopathology as the author has here disclosed?

Yet where is the literature that I could read in order to regain my previous attitude toward Tausk? Roazen's book is at present the most complete biographical source, and the impression it makes cannot, for the time being, be rectified.

The author's (unconscious or conscious) motivation was apparently to lower the esteem in which Freud has been held, and to announce to the world that there lived a genius who easily might have rivaled Freud's fame, had his life not been snuffed out by the deliberate act of his jealous and envious teacher. Roazen evokes the sort of imagery that has found illustration in myth and legend (Kris and Kurz 1934), and that sometimes, I am certain, has come to pass as reality. There are not a few who—although it is a matter of legend—still insist that Schiller was poisoned by Goethe, as well as those who hold that Mozart suffered that fate at Salieri's hands. In these instances, it was a question of rivalry between two famous personages, yet the myth makes the same claims at times about master and disciple.[93]

---

[93] Prof. Anton Macku was kind enough to remind me of the myth of Daedalus, the great architect and inventor of manual art, who plunged his nephew Talos from the Acropolis, out of jealousy of the latter's inventive talents, which had brought forth the potter's wheel, the saw and compasses. This myth reveals undis-

Be that as it may, one could look at Roazen's book in still another way. One occasionally has the fascinating opportunity to observe the quasi-personal effect that the dead seem to be able to exercise from beyond the grave. At such times, one has the impression that the repetition compulsion, as postulated by Freud, is continuing its macabre rhythm beyond the grave in the manner of echoes that go on sounding long after the original voice has become silent. I once had the opportunity of studying how a testatrix—even though consciously she was well intended—by means of her last will forced a continuation of the quarrels that she had repeatedly initiated during her lifetime. It was uncanny to observe how the persons drawn into the imbroglio were forced to pursue the acting out, almost as if they were doing so under the dominance of a post-hypnotic command.

It is similarly quite striking to see how the repetition compulsion by which Tausk's tragic life was dominated still continues, even decades after his demise. One of the basic patterns of his life stood under the sign of the production of acrimony—whether this be his rebellion against school and father; his hatred of his father and father-in-law; his aggression against wife and children, as expressed in his desertion of them; or his abandonment of the many women by whom in turn he was passionately loved for a long time. The reader will recall his attacks against older colleagues, almost as soon as he joined the group; his aggressions against Freud; the argument he started with Federn. Wherever he went, conflicts speedily evolved; and he always seemed to achieve victory at first, only to hurt himself subsequently. He was forever achieving a new rise—until this drive toward self-destruction set the mortal wound. Yet even that final disaster was followed by an elevation, in the form of Freud's beautiful obituary.

Not only Freud's touching farewell, but also Tausk's own excellent last paper had guaranteed him the respect of subsequent generations of analysts. His reputation was not that of a genius who failed—a conception that Roazen wrongly ascribes to Dr. Kronold (p. 5)—but rather that of a man who was eminently

---

guisedly something that Roazen never asserts as crassly as all that, but which nevertheless underlies his own myth about Freud's relationship to Tausk.

talented, yet suffered from severe psychopathology (which is what Dr. Kronold indicated to me that he had told Roazen). The excellence of his achievements had gradually begun to cover over the memory of his disorder, when Roazen set in motion once again the repetition compulsion that had been the groundwork of Tausk's life. Intuitively, Roazen seems to have grasped the pattern of Tausk's "fate-neurosis" (cf. Helene Deutsch, 1930), and to have carried out what Tausk's unconscious had all along been craving for.

Once again, five decades after his death, Tausk is creating acrimony; moreover, he has at last seemed, at least for a while, to have succeeded in debasing authority—something he had regularly attempted to do during his lifetime. Yet Tausk's basic pattern was that of the destructive masochist, and only the future will show whether the extension of Tausk's unconscious into our time, in the form of Roazen's book, will also contain *sequelae* that regularly followed his victories.

Strangely enough, the final result of the author's book may be just the opposite of what he appears to have intended. Careful study of it makes us see Freud patiently dealing with a very irritating disciple, who owed to Freud everything he himself is. Freud never raises his voice, or loses his temper; his irritation does not lead to more than a slip of the tongue, or a critical remark that might otherwise perhaps have sounded somewhat softer. But it is Tausk's reputation that may have, in the end, received at Roazen's hands a grievous and permanent stain.

Recently, and too late to be adequately discussed here, an article by Roazen, with the title "The Legend of Freud," was published in the Winter 1971 issue of *The Virginia Quarterly Review*. There Roazen repeats some of his unwarranted accusations against Anna Freud, and then adds some new ones, along with various scurrilous implications. In this article, he nevertheless makes himself the torchbearer of historical truth, engaged in defending Freud against those who do him "no service" by minimizing his greatness through their idealization of him: "to mythologize Freud as a man in full control of all his emotions is to deprive us of the opportunity of identifying with him as a fighting man."

Is one to identify with Roazen's Freud, who makes "devilish

arrangements"; betrays the confidence of a patient and a pupil; is unable to master his own petty jealousy; maneuvers a disciple to suicide; raises a claim to a discovery that another man has made; plagiarizes; attributes to himself royal, even divine prerogatives; feels enraged by the originality of his pupils, and is eager for nothing more than to find a mirror picture of himself among his entourage? The reader must be seriously warned against identifying with this travesty of Freud. If Roazen really needed *that* picture of Freud in order to be able to identify with him—as he intimates in this article—what can that mean in terms of his own personality?

If Roazen now tries to take the tack that he has to teach the world what Freud had to *transcend*, in order to arrive at what he did become, he is coming too late. That was already presented in part by Jones, in his biography of Freud, and it found lasting formulation in Freud's book on dreams, as well as in the posthumously published letters (Freud 1960).

Furthermore, Roazen never did describe in the book any instance of success on Freud's part in transcending, but instead consistently presented a picture of a man who is defeated by what it would have been his duty to transcend, so that he actually acts it out—and in a morally reprehensible way.

Only if the reader of his book does not come across the paper in *The Virginia Quarterly Review* or vice versa does Roazen have a chance, slim as it may be at best, to survive as a trustworthy writer.

III

FREUD AND HIS PUPILS

Roazen has attempted, on the basis of the Tausk episode, to develop a new slant on Freud's personality profile. He therefore has to prove that the features he believes he has observed in that particular episode can be generalized. Consequently, he undertakes to examine Freud's relationship to such men as Adler and Jung. In this respect, however, he would have been far more original had he taken the opposite stance from the one he is here taking. The image of an irascible and despotic Freud, who does not tolerate contradictions and opposition, is a popular one; it is put forward by more people than it is rejected by.

It is precisely in the discussion of this area that one becomes painfully aware of how futile it is to publish anything about Freud's personality, unless it carries with it a hostile bias. Repeatedly Roazen (pp. 47–49, 51, 53f., 97, 113) ascribes to Freud the demand for "absolute surrender." This is nothing but the old myth of Freud's authoritarianism. In 1963, Robert Waelder wrote a penetrating paper, which he fittingly called "Historical Fiction"; it is devoted to a critical essay on Fromm's (1959) semi-biographical book on Freud. A substantial part of that essay (pp. 635–642) was devoted to a discussion of the frequent charge

of "Freud's alleged authoritarianism. Freud, it is said, was intolerant of opposition, 'expecting others to follow him, wait on
him, to sacrifice their independence and intellectual freedom to
him.' " (Waelder 1963, p. 635). The quotation that he took from
Fromm's book could just as easily have come from Roazen's
book.[1]

I invite the reader to read Waelder's beautiful essay and then
ponder about how it is possible for Roazen to go on filling page
after page with the now traditional invectives about Freud's "authoritarianism," without once referring to that paper, in which
is set forth not one man's opinion but a collection of indisputable
facts refuting the traditional reproach. Has Roazen never read
that paper? Does he dispute the correctness of the facts Waelder
gathered? One has the right to expect that, in a civilized academic
community, minimal standards of conduct will be maintained,
and that an author who feels compelled to denigrate a historical
figure will spend at least one sentence explaining why he disagrees
with someone who has refuted other such efforts at denigration,
by presenting a score of *facts*.

What is one to say about such a sentence as: "So Freud collected able people who would in effect be yes-men. . . . He
wanted them to mirror back his ideas" (p. 47). And then this
assertion is "supported" by the following two "proofs," whose
incorrectness can be ascertained with ease. Roazen (p. 47) calls in
Wittels as a witness to testify that Freud wished "to look into a
kaleidoscope lined with mirrors that would multiply the images
he introduced into it" (Wittels 1923, p. 134). Yet Roazen did
not manage to discover—or else he withheld from the reader—
the fact that Wittels himself, as has been mentioned earlier, took
back his past derogatory remarks.

Some of those derogatory remarks that Wittels (1933) felt
compelled to retract were that Freud had a "Jehovah complex;
that he [Freud] is a despot who will not tolerate deviations from

---

[1] Although the author proudly lets us know of all the wonderful places to
which three research grants made it possible for him to travel, one of which
was "a villa in the mountains outside Mexico City" (p. XIV)—which can only
refer to an interview with Dr. Fromm—he does not once cite Fromm's book.
Yet, Fromm, after all, must surely have told the author a great deal of what he
has to say about Freud's allegedly "authoritarian" way of dealing with his pupils.

his system; that he brings his disciples into hypnotic dependence upon him" (p. 362). He corrected this as follows:

> Among all psychoanalysts, myself included, he is perhaps the only one who is not intoxicated with the method and its results. It has always remained questionable to him whether psychoanalysis—a matter of which we, his pupils, are all firmly convinced—would change the spiritual face of the world. . . . If one speaks of his world renown, he answers not only with the wisdom of Solomon that this is vanity, but he reminds us that many an "immortal," together with his theories, has been forgotten in an incredibly short time. Therefore, it now seems to me that it is his disciples who bestow upon him a rank (*ipse dixit*) against which he does not defend himself because it is a matter of indifference to him" [p. 363].[2]

Thus wrote, a decade later, the man who had coined the "kaleidoscope" metaphor. Yet the author also quotes another informant who has not so recanted, to prove Freud's eagerness to have followers who "mirror" (p. 47):

> Freud was enchanted by a paper of one of his students. As he said approvingly, 'I feel as if a painter has done my portrait, and, when I look at it, it is better than the original.' The paper had systematized some of Freud's concepts, without suggesting any new formulations.

I wonder how many readers have checked the references at the end of Roazen's book (p. 211, n. 22). There they would have

---

[2] Roazen makes the most of a metaphor that Freud used in a conversation with Lou Andreas-Salomé (*Journal*, p. 38f.) and this to prove that Freud "was likening himself to an immortal God" (p. 49). I do not know whether he would have been more cautious had he taken cognizance of the deep regret Wittels felt at his rash, short-circuit conclusions. Metaphors, analogies and the like are important clues to the reconstruction of unconscious processes; but the technique requires psychological tact and, when that is lacking, the metaphor may only lead astray. Identifications with the Biblical Joseph in his childhood, later with some of his admired teachers, still later with Moses, and finally, with Jacob—these are highly probable; but the Zeus hypothesis appears most questionable. Still, if the author does believe that each metaphor reflects the equivalent unconscious process—that is to say, has to be taken literally—then Freud's letter to Jung (April 16, 1909), in which he writes that, after Jung's departure, the furniture is "like nature silent and godless before the poet after the passing of the Gods of Greece" (Jung 1961, p. 362), would prove that Jung meant to him a Greek god; yet this would undermine all of Roazen's theories about Freud's relationship to his followers.

found that the mirroring "student" was Robert Waelder, and
the paper referred to was not a paper at all but a *review* of Freud's
(1926) *Inhibition, Symptom and Anxiety*.[3]

Even though there are, of course, many analysts—and, by
the way, other writers as well—who mirror Freud's writings, to
connect the late Robert Waelder of all people in any way with
"mirroring" Freud is altogether incredible. For those who may
not know it, it should be said that Waelder was one of the most
original writers in the field of psychoanalysis. Freud's text was,
for most analysts in 1926, difficult to understand. Even at present,
many regard it as Freud's most controversial contribution, and
we know that Freud himself was not satisfied with it.[4] Thus
Freud was paying Waelder the greatest compliment that can be
paid to a reviewer when he suggested that it was the content of
the review alone that made the original comprehensible. It was
indeed an extraordinary accomplishment of Waelder's to succeed
in presenting the new, and at that time quite perplexing, thoughts
of Freud in a crystal-clear way, and it is open to question whether
anyone else would have been able to understand so quickly what
Freud meant with his new book, at a time when its contents
had not yet become integrated into psychoanalytic theory.

Roazen, who is a sociologist by profession, seems to believe
that to comprehend something is to be unoriginal and passive.
He rashly calls Helene Deutsch passive and receptive, on the
grounds that she agreed with Freud's basic concepts and theories
(p. 97).

I now have to turn to the Adler and Jung controversies, since
Roazen attempts to use them "to examine . . . how the pattern
of Freud's anxiety over Tausk's possible plagiarism recurs whenever Freud had difficulties with his students" (p. 161). These two

---

[3] Waelder's review was published in the *Zeitschrift* (1928) and in the *Journal*
(1929), in sections distinctly marked as book sections. It is listed in Grinstein's
(1956–1966) *Index* under "Book Reviews." To call this a paper, even though
I hear that Waelder presented it to Freud at a private meeting, is misleading.
In any case, I feel that the name of Robert Waelder should have appeared in the
main text; the informed reader would then have known immediately that Roazen's
interpretation of Freud's remark is nonsensical.

[4] Freud's comment was that in general it "is not good" (Jones 3, p. 131),
and Strachey (1959) said that "there are signs that Freud found an unusual
difficulty in unifying the work" (p. 78).

controversies will also give the reader an opportunity to examine whether Freud really did set himself against originality in his followers, as the author repeatedly asserts.

Alfred Adler was considered a prominent member of the Society. On November 7, 1906 he presented to the Wednesday Meeting, which Freud chaired, a paper ("On the [Organic] Bases of Neuroses") which he published in book form (Adler 1907). Retrospectively, it may be regarded as the starting point of a way of thinking that was later to lead to Adler's leaving the Society. The main point of his paper was that childhood neuroses are the consequence of organ inferiority. "A primary inferiority of organs" (*Minutes* 1, p. 36ff.) was, for Adler, the basic moving force in neurotic disorders. Whether or not one agrees with this view, its originality cannot be disputed. Hitschmann was the first speaker. (At that time the sequence of discussants was determined by lot.) He was essentially critical of Adler's theory. Looking back, one must agree with each point he raised and admire his alertness in perceiving quickly where the weaknesses lay in Adler's theory.

Yet Freud, who was the next speaker, "turns against Hitschmann. . . . He attributes great importance to Adler's work; it has brought his own work a step further. To judge from the immediate impression, much of what Adler said may be correct. He singled out two leading ideas as significant and fertile" (*Minutes* 1, p. 42). Thus spake "Zeus." Freud had only "one main objection," which concerned "the formal aspect of the paper." He thought that "the choice of the term inferiority, which he himself does not like, shows no great originality; it might, perhaps, be better to speak of a certain variability of the organs" (*Minutes* 1, p. 43). Variability of organs—that is the key term for the decoding of many an observation.

Little did Freud seem to know, at that point, that "organ inferiority" would ultimately, in Adler's hands, devour the whole theory of childhood sexuality and of the repressed. At Adler's later presentations, Freud's discussion remarks were always more positive than negative. Apparently, Freud's intention was to smooth out the growing differences between Adler's new theories and psychoanalysis. In 1910 he insisted that Adler be made President of the Vienna Society, although the majority of members evidently wanted Freud to be in that position. This is why Freud declined:

"He feels the need of putting himself in the background" (*Minutes* 2, p. 466); "It would be useful if a younger worker were to step to the head" (*ibid.*, p. 468).

What Roazen has to say about the final events that led to the split of the original Society and Adler's founding of a new society is historically incorrect. At no point does he cite, or even take into consideration, Colby's (1951) publication of that part of the *Minutes* that contains the few sessions of the Society before Adler withdrew, or Jones's report, which is based on historical documents.[5] When he writes that "here personal issues mushroomed into a theoretical debate," and that Freud forced the issue and "split his society," he distorts what can be learned clearly from Colby. By referring to the *Minutes*, one discovers that "Adler read three papers." After the last one, a discussion began. Freud, of course, objected to Adler's theories. It would lead far afield if I were to repeat here what can be read in Colby's paper, but this much may be quoted.

Freud said, according to the *Minutes* (Colby 1951, p. 233f.): "I do not consider these Adlerian doctrines insignificant and would like to predict that they will make a great impression, at first damaging psychoanalysis very much. The great impression has two sources: (1) it is obvious that a remarkable intellect with a great talent for writing is working on these matters; (2) the whole doctrine has a reactionary and retrograde character," etc.

A week later, on February 8, 1911, the discussion continued. The final meeting took place on February 22; it apparently ended with one member (Maximilian Steiner) declaring "that we might have to rename our society into whose program and framework Adler's ideas do not fit at all."

At the following committee meeting, it was Adler who resigned his position as president of the Society "because of the incompatibility of my scientific position with my post in the

---

[5] As in the case of the cocaine episode, (see later), Roazen seems to be unwilling to make use of objective well-documented historical data. He "proves" one point by reference to his interview with Dr. Richard Wagner and to my interview with the late Dr. Paul Klemperer, the transcript of which I had forwarded, at the informant's request, to Dr. Jones. It is quite evident from the transcript that Dr. Klemperer was mistaken in his recollection of many details of events that had taken place 41 years prior to the interview, and which had besides become peripheral to his main interests. He had since become a pathologist.

Society." According to the *Minutes* of a meeting of the Board of Directors, "it was proposed in reference to Adler's statement regarding incompatibility, that the Society clearly indicate that it was not of this opinion, [and that it] thank the recent president for his activities and regret his departure. Freud commented that they could spare Adler the remark on incompatibility, but the majority present voted for the motion" (Colby, p. 237).

Adler's last attendance at a meeting was on May 24 (Jones 2, p. 133).[6] When Roazen writes: "Everyone in the Society had to take a stand, one way or the other. . . . Freud violently denounced Adler, it was a trial, and the accusation was heresy" (p. 162), no reader can possibly guess that this "trial" took place *after* Adler had resigned from membership, *after* he had gone on to found his own society. In the fall of 1911 Adler had voluntarily, and counter to the expressed request of the Society, made a complete break; now the majority of members, to be sure expressing Freud's own desire, decided against dual membership and insisted that each member had to choose in which society he preferred to be a member.

Looking back, one cannot call this decision unwise. Even at present, almost six decades after the event, no psychoanalyst would feel motivated to ask for membership in an Adlerian society or vice versa. No harm was done either to the development of psychoanalysis, or to that of individual psychology. Indeed, it stood the latter in good stead. Adler's Society flourished in Vienna and gained the adherence of a large number of teachers. The major portion of that part of the intelligentsia who belonged to the Viennese majority party (Social-Democrats) were far closer to individual psychology than they were to psychoanalysis.

Yet the question must be raised seriously whether it was really Roazen's ignorance alone that led him to write of "excommunication" as a "penalty" and of Freud's "ostracizing Adler and his sympathizers" (p. 162), when in reality Adler had *already formed a new society* and it was solely a matter of each member having to decide to *which* group he wished to belong. Did the author really

---

[6] There are discrepancies between Colby's presentation and Jones's. Since Jones had more documents at his disposal, his description is probably more reliable, but the final decision will have to depend on the third volume of the *Minutes*, which has not yet been published.

venture on his book without taking minimal precautions against error? Why did he here disregard well-known sources in favor of imprecise recollections by two well-meaning witnesses (Drs. Richard Wagner and Paul Klemperer), whose testimony had lost accuracy with the passage of time?

It is fully evident from the historical record that no personal issue was at work here, at least on the part of Freud, who had put up with Adler as long as possible, trying hard to synthesize Adler's theories into psychoanalysis and paying him compliments even at the height of the debate with him.

And why did Roazen keep the reader in ignorance of what Adler himself had to say about his reasons for leaving the Vienna Psychoanalytic Society? Did not Phyllis Bottome, Adler's biographer, who had countless conversations with him, report that Adler had told her that he did not want to go on working with Freud, because he was afraid that he would be held responsible for psychoanalytic theories that he considered inimical to the welfare of mankind (Bottome 1939, p. 66)? Does this alone not refute Roazen's historical presentation?

In Freud's paper "On the History of the Psychoanalytic Movement," which was published three years later, he never denied Adler's merits. After describing his efforts to secure for Adler a prominent position in the Society, Freud (1914a, p. 50f.) continued:

> When I perceived how little gift Adler had precisely for judging unconscious material, my view changed to an expectation that he would succeed in discovering the connections of psychoanalysis with psychology and with the biological foundations of instinctual processes—an expectation which was in some sense justified by the valuable work he had done on "organ inferiority."

Any question of plagiarism or priority was, if it existed at all, wholly secondary. In the discussion with Adler and afterward, Freud, of course, had to examine the new terminology that Adler had introduced and to determine whether it referred to something relevant that psychoanalysis had overlooked or not taken into consideration, or whether it contained the adjustment of psychoanalytic findings to a biologizing psychology. If all of that means concern about plagiarism, then such concern is a proper part of scientific endeavors.

The same disregard of historical truth reappears in Roazen's discussion of the sequence of events that led to Jung's resignation from membership in the local and international psychoanalytic societies. Obsessed with the question of "plagiarism" in Freud's life, which the author needs so badly in order to establish the case he is seeking to make against Freud in the Tausk episode, he writes (p. 165f.): "The same issue of priorities played its part in Freud's break with Jung. Freud began to get upset at Swiss articles on psychoanalysis appearing 'without mentioning his name.' Freud did not take being slighted lightly." Roazen refers to an episode reported in Jones's biography (1, p. 317)—namely, Freud's conversation with Jung and Franz Riklin, a prominent Swiss psychoanalyst, on November 24, 1912, in Munich.

I shall have more to say about the Munich meeting, at which Freud did, indeed, behave in an unusual way; but first I want to mention that the subject of priorities was really introduced by Jung, as can be learned from early letters that were exchanged between Freud and Abraham (Abraham and Freud 1965, p. 33–37), at a time when Freud was doing his very best to avoid any incident that might arouse Jung's sensitivities. Furthermore, one of the earliest signs of Jung's abandoning the pathway of scientific psychology was brought to Freud's attention as early as July, 1908 by Abraham (see Abraham and Freud 1965, p. 44). Thereafter, the latter often had occasion to warn Freud against relying too much on Jung, but for a long time he was not believed by Freud.

The decisive factor is that between 1908 and 1912 evidence had already accumulated that Jung was turning away from psychoanalysis and that he definitely would not be the man to whom Freud could entrust the function of leading the young group—a function that Freud was most eager to pass on to someone else. I do not wish to list here all the disappointments Freud had to experience from Jung prior to their meeting in Munich. Suffice it to remind the reader that Jung had come out with his theory about incest being only a symbol of higher ideas. Moreover, it is very probable that Freud was deeply disappointed by a highly provocative statement Jung made shortly before the Munich meeting, in a letter in which he reported "how successful he [Jung] had been in making psychoanalysis more acceptable [in the United States] by leaving out the sexual themes" (Jones 2, p. 144).

It is evident that the question of whether he was being quoted or not quoted must have been among the least worrisome in Freud's mind. To be sure, it is an interesting question why Freud brought up the point at all at the meeting. Jones reports that, prior to that conversation, Freud and Jung had taken a walk for two hours, during which Jung had admitted to a personal resentment for an alleged slight of Freud's. It turned out that Jung had been mistaken, that Freud had never slighted him, but that Jung had been the victim of an error brought about by his own negligence. "Jung became extremely contrite. . . . Freud . . . did not spare him a good fatherly lecture" (Jones 2, p. 145).

It was at the luncheon after the walk that Freud brought up his complaint about not being cited sufficiently. Since, during their walk, Jung had "accepted all the criticism and promised to reform" (Jones 2, p. 145), it was, indeed, unreasonable of Freud to bring up a reproach about a more or less trivial matter. Jones further recalls that Freud was in a state of elation during the luncheon. Jung justified the omission of citations, but Freud "persisted, and I remember thinking he was taking the matter rather personally" (Jones 1, p. 317). Suddenly, Freud fainted.

It is plain that Freud's unusual behavior during that luncheon should be viewed in the light of the syncope that followed. As long as the nature of Freud's syncopes is not better understood (the late Dr. Schur's research does not rule out an organic factor, as mentioned earlier), Freud's behavior in Munich cannot be properly evaluated.[7]

I have gone into these details not only to demonstrate that questions of priority and plagiarism played a negligible role in the discord between Freud and Jung (the situation would not have been different in any way, even if Jung had cited Freud profusely), but primarily in order to show how difficult it is to interpret a single biographical incident. However, it is quite clear from Jones's description that Freud was on that occasion in a state that was not characteristic of him; this is confirmed by his subsequent physical reaction, quite independently of whether the syncope had an organic or a neurotic etiology.

---

[7] See Martin Freud (1957, p. 129) for an incident of apparent cardiac distress provoked by physical strain.

In order properly to evaluate the relationship of Freud to his followers, who were younger than he was, one has to read Freud's letter to Jung of April 16, 1909 (Jung 1961, pp. 361–363). It is most touching how seriously, and against his own conviction, he takes Jung's belief in a poltergeist[8] operating in his library, how he experiments, and then informs his younger colleague of the results of his experiment; how he admits having once been victimized himself by a kind of superstition, yet having rid himself of it by self-analysis. In this same letter, one also finds Freud's moving comment about a disagreement with Jung regarding psychoanalysis: "Well, that is how the young folks are; they really enjoy things only when they need not drag us along with them, where with our short breath and weary legs we cannot follow."

Brome (1968, pp. 125–129) stresses the homosexual factor in Freud's relationship with his collaborators and pupils. It goes without saying that homosexual conflicts are mutually activated in a teacher-pupil relationship. But the question can only be: how did Freud deal with this type of conflict, and how did the others?

A usually reliable yardstick of the degree to which a man controls his latent homosexuality is his relationship to his father and

---

[8] Bennet (1962, p. 36) disputes the veracity of Jones's version (3, p. 383f.) that Jung "displayed his powers as a poltergeist by making various articles in the room rattle on the furniture." He reports that Jung considered the story preposterous because he and Freud "took it for granted that the sound was due to inexplicable expansion of the wood of the bookcase." However, Jung's published report, as well as the letter, seem to confirm Jones's version.

In his *Memories*, Jung (1961, p. 155) wrote about that meeting with Freud that he had "a curious sensation. It was as if my diaphragm were made of iron and were becoming red-hot—a glowing vault." Then a noise occurred in the bookcase, which Jung explained to Freud as "an example of a so-called catalytic exteriorization phenomenon." Not having studied such phenomena, I may be mistaken when I interpret the remark as indicating Jung's belief that the noise was caused by him.

Dr. Bennet reports that Jung complained to him that Jones did not ask him about the incident. Dr. Bennet considers the poltergeist story as revealing an interest on the part of Freud's followers in finding "what they considered to be weak points in Jung's work and personality." Dr. Bennet wrote me, however, in response to my inquiry, that he found no contradiction between the two versions, the one Jung gave in his *Memories*, and the one Dr. Bennet reported having heard from Jung. The reader will have to decide whether or not there is a contradiction, when a person says on one occasion that a sound "was due to inexplicable expansion of the wood of the bookcase," and on another occasion writes that it was "an example of a so-called catalytic exteriorization phenomenon."

to his sons. It seems quite remarkable that nothing is known about a manifest conflict either between Freud and his father or between him and his sons, whatever Freud's inner processes might have been. Now this absence of outwardly observable conflict would not exclude a displacement of that type of conflict to other areas. But the harmony that apparently existed, at least on the surface, in Freud's relationship to father and sons would speak against the existence of uncontrollable impulses to act out in his relationship to males.

A close scrutiny of Freud's letters and of his book on dreams makes it clear that this control was acquired gradually, that in his earlier years he was combative and at times provocative. Suffice it here to record one passage from a letter of 1910 (earlier than the years of conflict with Adler and Jung) to Ferenczi, one of his closest collaborators; from it one can learn that Freud worked actively on the taming of this very impulse. He wrote (Jones 2, p. 83): "You not only noticed, but also understood, that I *no longer* have any need to uncover my personality completely, and you correctly traced this back to the traumatic reason for it. Since Fliess's case, with the overcoming of which you recently saw me occupied, that need has been extinguished. A part of homosexual cathexis has been withdrawn and made use of to enlarge my own ego. I have succeeded where the paranoiac fails" (emphasis in the text).

The last sentence, an early forerunner of Freud's famous statement, "Where id was, there ego shall be" (1933, p. 80), may on good grounds be interpreted as a sign that he had succeeded in mastering the homosexual conflict.[9] How else would it have been

---

[9] Brome (1968) is doubtful about such mastery. He explains Freud's fainting spells in terms of his homosexuality, quoting (p. 126) from Freud's letter to Jones of December 8, 1912, which apparently referred to the incident in Munich: "There is some piece of unruly homosexual feeling at the root of the matter." The fainting spell, if it was not organic, was, to be sure, a neurotic symptom; but what does an autoplastic symptom prove in terms of possible acting out in Freud's relationship with men? The data on hand reveal a Freud who does not deny inner processes, but actively works at them. Unless we assume all this to have been mere intellectualization, it speaks in favor of ever-increasing control.

Moreover, critics of Freud try to establish the existence in him of conflicts, and then draw the conclusion that these conflicts show up in areas of social conduct. If Freud had had no conflicts, he would never have become the genius he was.

possible for him to respond to Jung, at their first meeting, with unrestrained delight and affection, and later to be ready—without apparent conflict, at least—to let Jung take over the conduct of the entire psychoanalytic movement, he himself being at an age when jealousy and rivalry with the coming generation is almost the rule?

When the facts are examined, therefore, a Freud emerges who is tolerant and ready to compromise, and who himself makes efforts to resolve disagreements. This could also be shown in later years, when Otto Rank suddenly turned against him. To be sure, when all efforts at reconciliation and peacemaking had come to naught, and the other person had gone to such extremes as to make any further cooperation impossible, then Freud withdrew and gave the history of the disagreement in print. Of course, debates of this sort were not chess games for Freud, and he did not move arguments like pawns. Since his writings came also from his heart, these debates were not some abstract matter to him; he went into them with his magnificent temper.

What is most curious about Roazen's presentation is that the question of ideational content is put by him in a very subordinate place. That what was involved was an argument about whether reality was constituted one way or another—of this, the reader obtains only slight information. Instead, the impression is created that those episodes were a personal matter and depended entirely on Freud's character, biases, or whims. No cognizance is taken of the fact that Freud took great pains to avoid clashes, but only under the condition that this was not achieved at the expense of thereby allowing psychoanalysis to become eclectic; in short, that he did what every scientist ought to do—fight for what he is certain to be the truth. In other words, was Jung not correct in resigning as President of the International Psychoanalytic Association on the grounds that he had gained the conviction "that his views stood in such harsh contrast to the views of the majority of

---

The problem is what a genius does with his conflicts. When Brome writes (p. 126): "Thus it is possible that his [Freud's] sublimated homosexual impulse redirected his libido to the highest creative purposes," he himself makes a statement that would seem to reduce the probability of homosexual acting out, although genius, creativity, and acting out are not necessarily mutually exclusive. (For further comments, see Chapter VII).

members that he could not regard himself as a person suitable for the chairmanship" [10] (Abraham 1914)?

To be sure, there are occasional remarks in Roazen's book that do take a stand in favor of Freud, such as: "Freud was justified . . ."; "from Freud's point of view, Adler and Jung were endangering everything"; or "Freud might understandably fear . . ." (p. 167).

Roazen was, after all, in a rather difficult situation. If he had taken a stand on the question of whether or not Freud was *objectively right* in his dealings with Adler and Jung, his derogatory psychological implications would have come to naught. If he had said that Adler and Jung were right in their theories and for that reason alone quite justified in establishing their own schools, then many a reader would doubt Roazen's reliability, because he would have declared himself an opponent of psychoanalysis, and as such probably prejudiced against Freud. His book could be successful and induce a few analysts to lose faith in the solidity of Freud's character only if he interspersed positive remarks about him. This Roazen did with an uncanny journalistic flair, an art of which he is an estimable master.

How many readers would have taken seriously his remarks about Freud's relationship to Jung, for example, if he had reported the poltergeist incident and in so doing remarked that, after all, Freud had had an early opportunity to observe that Jung was lacking in the observation of minimal scientific standards and prone to be overawed by the arcane? Or if he had stressed that Freud nevertheless stuck loyally to his intended successor for three more years, and most reluctantly came to take cognizance of the fact that Jung was determined to break away from the psychoanalytic movement?

From Jung's (1961) *Memories*, as well as from Dr. Bennet's (1962) essay, many a passage could be quoted to demonstrate the deep-going ambivalence that separated Jung from Freud from the very beginning, and that made the final break between them inescapable. Once Freud had bestowed his affection, he could

---

[10] ". . . er habe sich überzeugen lassen, dass seine Anschauungen in einem so schroffen Kontrast zu den Auffassungen der Mehrzahl der Mitglieder ständen, dass er sich nicht mehr als die zum Vorsitze geeignete Persönlichkeit betrachten *könne*" (p. 405).

probably never completely withdraw it. He was the most loyal of friends. Dr. Bennet (1962, p. 56) reports the conclusion of a meeting with Freud as follows: "I then asked about the rupture with Jung. Freud, after a pause, said very quietly, 'Jung was a great loss.' No more was said." [11]

In characterizing Freud's relationship to his pupils and colleagues Roazen does not shrink from the grotesque. He pictures Freud as insisting on his collaborators' submission; apparently he not only wished that they become sycophants "but he gave it [his love] only if they came close to castrating themselves as creative individuals" (p. 113).[12] "But for one man to flatter another can be corrupting, and the best of Freud's male pupils left because the atmosphere was too narrow and ultimately degrading" (p. 48). All this is writen without anything like adequate documentation. If the author were the least bit correct, he should be able to cite some instances, or at least offer some indications. The freedom the author takes in making assertions that he should, after all, be able to document, if they are true, is excessive. Yet where he does try to document and one has the opportunity to check these efforts, one makes surprising discoveries.

Roazen asserts (p. 75) that Freud's pupils "were obliged to secede from psychoanalysis, if they had interests in other fields,"

---

[11] The following quotation, from Lou Andreas-Salomé's (1958) Journal, which contains her observations on Freud's emotional responses during the Munich Congress (September, 1913), when the break with Jung became acute, may be meaningful to the reader:

"At the congress the Zurich members sat at their own table opposite Freud's. Their behavior toward Freud can be characterized in a word: it is not so much that Jung diverges from Freud, as that he does it in such a way as if he had taken it on himself to rescue Freud and his cause by these divergences [author's emphasis]. If Freud takes up the lance to defend himself, it is misconstrued to mean that he cannot show scientific tolerance, is dogmatic, and so forth. One glance at the two of them tells which is the more dogmatic, the more in love with power. Two years ago Jung's booming laughter gave voice to a kind of robust gaiety and exuberant vitality, but now his earnestness is composed of pure aggression, ambition, and intellectual brutality. I have never felt so close to Freud as here; not only on account of this break with his 'son' Jung, whom he had loved and for whom he had practically transferred his cause to Zurich, but on account of the manner of the break—as though Freud had caused it by his narrow-minded obstinacy. Freud was the same as ever, but it was only with difficulty that he restrained his deep emotion" (pp. 168–169).

[12] I only wonder to what use a man who was, according to Roazen, puritanical and Victorian could have put so many eunuchs?

and refers in this connection to an interview with Dr. Richard
Wagner, the noted pediatrician. I could not understand why Dr.
Wagner,[13] who was the only student ever to register five times
in Freud's semestral lectures at the University of Vienna (Gicklhorn 1960, p. 178) should have been obliged to leave the Society.
As a matter of fact, as he himself has written me, he "resigned
from the society in a letter to Freud, which he [Freud] answered
very kindly," after he had moved to Strasburg and taken up the
study of biochemistry. This is another instance in which an informant was not able to confirm what Roazen published as his
having said.

To whom is Roazen referring when he speaks of "the best"
of Freud's pupils who left because they felt degraded? Freud, of
course, did not expect to obtain from his colleagues full agreement
concerning his own theories. The majority of analysts rejected his
theory of the death instinct, for example, without any consequences for their "standing." But was such a liberal attitude perhaps an exception, limited only to a theory that had offended even
psychoanalytic common sense? This seems the right moment to
offer one instance of how Freud was treated by his "sycophants."

At one meeting (February, 1908), Freud presented in a discussion a novel idea about trauma (*Minutes* 1, p. 336), which led,
twelve years later (Freud 1920a) to a far-reaching theory. Sadger
presented clinical material "proving the opposite." Stekel doubted
"that this ingeniously thought-out theory is correct." Adler did
not "think that matters are as simple as Freud described them."
The comments of two other speakers were not quite that negative.
I could give other examples. Of course, there were meetings when
Freud did earn laudatory comments. What should one expect
from a group that had the privilege, for example, of listening
to Freud presenting, for the first time, his ideas about Leonardo?

There is another incident recorded that demonstrates the
liberal atmosphere that prevailed in the early group, despite the
tensions that were unquestionably present there. When Lou
Andreas-Salomé arrived in Vienna, the fight with Adler was quite
fresh in everyone's mind and still an "acute" matter of discussion.

---

[13] M.D. 1912; *Dozent* 1924; Professor Emeritus of Pediatrics, Tufts University
School of Medicine, Boston; Guggenheim Fellow, 1960.

Yet surprisingly one reads in her *Journal* (p. 37): "Had a discussion with him [Freud] and Dr. Federn during the intermission, Federn defending Adler's theory of inferiority as applied to children." This casual remark throws a sidelight on the whole atmosphere of the early Viennese group, which belies Roazen's description. Here was one of Freud's closest collaborators agreeing with a principal thesis of Adler's, who had recently broken with Freud in a tempestuous way, and such "betrayal" ruffled their relationship not in the least!

Paul Federn's (1871–1950) relationship with Freud is, in general, an embarrassment for Roazen's theories, and much can be learned from the way he deals with it. As is well known, Federn was one of the first—I believe even the very first—to evolve a modified psychoanalytic technique of treating schizophrenic patients; he also developed a metapsychological system of ego processes that was independent of Freud's metapsychology and even different from Freud's metapsychological concept of the ego. It is precisely Federn's career and the confidence Freud had in him—as demonstrated, for example, by the fact that Federn represented Freud in the Vienna Psychoanalytic Society, after Freud's illness, up to the time of its dissolution—which shows that independence and originality did not in the least interfere with a harmonious relationship to Freud.

How then does the author extricate himself from this embarrassing situation? The way Roazen proceeds in this instance lays him open to the reproach of unfairness. As will be seen, he writes the truth, but puts it into the form of the negation of vicious acts—which necessarily leaves the reader with the impression that such vicious acts *might have been* perpetrated by Freud under a different set of circumstances, or even that they actually *were*, but that, as an exception, they did not occur in his dealings with Federn. I know I would feel highly uncomfortable if newspapers were to report that I had not committed a murder, even though that were indeed the truth.

It is a phenomenon that can be compared with a mirror image of an inner process that Freud (1925c) described in his paper on "Negation." There Freud proposed that linguistic statements in the negative form enable the ego to let repressed contents enter its borders. The equivalent mechanism on the social level is called apophasis. By using it, a speaker insinuates precisely the existence of what he denies he is saying—a device carried to a famous extreme by Shakespeare in Antony's funeral speech. Yet the way the author handles apophasis does not deserve praise. He writes (p. 189): "He [Freud] did not order Federn to stop trying with such [schizophrenic] cases, he simply did not want to participate in the work himself"; and further: "But Freud still sent Federn cases and never tried to drive him out of his circle." To this, I have only to add that the author did not beat up his wife last New Year's Day.[14]

It is precisely Paul Federn's career that completely disproves some of Roazen's repeated claims. Despite theoretical differences between them, his relationship with Freud was never clouded.

It is also understandable why Roazen consistently ignores Freud's reaction to Rank's theory of the birth trauma, which was fairly original and deviated profoundly from Freud's own theories. Rank was a man whom Freud treated almost like a son. If there was any trace of intolerance in Freud, it might have reared its head when Rank evolved a theory that, if correct, would have shown Freud to be wrong in basic conceptions of the working of the psyche. With seemingly unending patience, however, Freud tried to quiet Rank's disappointment that others did not agree with his theories, and he made the greatest effort to keep Rank from withdrawing from the psychoanalytic group; it was Rank who was intolerant and left (see Taft 1958; Waelder 1963). When Roazen tries to characterize Freud's relationship to his colleagues and pupils as that of an irascible and jealous egotist, he owes us documentation. In the one instance where he did try to construct a reaction of jealousy on Freud's part, because Tausk was allegedly "forging ahead of Freud," I was able to prove that he was grossly mistaken. Tausk was not forging ahead and the opinion that Freud expressed on that occasion reflected a conviction that he held not only with regard to Tausk's statement, but to the end of his life.

---

[14] This last sentence earlier read: "By the way, who knows?" I had to delete it because most readers understood the remark as if I wanted to cast aspersion on the author, whereas the "by the way" should demonstrate, ad oculos, the uncanny effects negative sentences, when skilfully manipulated, may have. One is reminded of a profound statement Nietzsche made about language when he said: "Every word is a bias" [Jedes Wort ist ein Vorurteil] (Nietzsche 1879–1880, # 55).

On another occasion Roazen even claims—again without doc-umentation—that "to Freud it seemed that anything his pupils thought of was ultimately his" (p. 93). How can Roazen main-tain such a reproach, in view of Freud's recording even those instances in which he used *oral* remarks made by a colleague? I shall cite only one instance. In discussing "the influence of or-ganic disease upon the distribution of libido," he remarked: "I follow a suggestion made to me orally by Sándor Ferenczi" (Freud 1914b, p. 82). Many such instances can be cited, which would not rule out those instances when Freud did not recall the stimulation he had received.

One passage in a letter to Abraham of December, 1910, which I shall quote, demonstrates an instance when Freud apparently thought that he had been original but found out that he was not. The passage documents at the same time how Freud responded when a pupil of his was actually forging ahead:

> My own work, just finished, is on Schreber's book and tries to solve the riddle of paranoia. As you can well imagine, I have followed in the direction indicated in your work on the psycho-sexual differences between hysteria and dementia praecox. When I was pursuing these thoughts in Palermo, I was specially pleased with the formula that megalomania signifies a sexual overestima-tion of the ego. On returning to Vienna I found that you had said the same in the clearest manner. Naturally I shall have to plagiarize you extensively in my work (Jones 2, p. 164).

"Plagiarizing" an author meant, for Freud, strange as it may seem, quoting him several times and stating besides that the au-thor's paper "contains almost all the essential views put forward in the present study" (Freud 1911a, p. 70, n. 1). If the reader should ever have thought that Freud did not want to be stimulated by his collaborators, this should be sufficient to prove that he was wrong. There is no doubt that Freud ardently desired that the future of psychoanalysis should not rest solely on his shoulders. He knew well that a real future was possible only when his collabora-tors made original contributions on which to build, and he was most eager for this, as the letter to Abraham proves.

A general remark may conclude this chapter. Roazen is not alone when he places the main responsibility on Freud for the fact that Adler and Jung left the psychoanalytic movement and started their own schools. I have a different view of the meaning of so many leaving that movement and becoming leaders of greater or smaller groups. It is, in my opinion, a proof of the greatness of Freud's work that it grew like a powerful trunk from which twigs branched off. I say purposely twigs and not branches, because all these other schools that emerged ended where they were, and did not produce new branches. Adler, Jung, Stekel, Rank, Sullivan, Reich, Horney, Rado—and all the rest whom I may not have enumerated—all their works are unthinkable without Freud's comprehensive writings, yet their schools did not produce any new schools in turn. They came to a halt, in a dead end. Oddly enough, whatever they themselves have produced can with some modification be assigned a place in the edifice Freud had built. They are more original in their denials than through the addition of any original values.

Purified of its bizarre part, Reich's work finds its place in Freud's psychology of drives; Adler investigated one area, covering a small part of Freud's ego and superego; even for Jung's psychology a corner can be found in the huge canvas that Freud had created. Freud was thus the only one who "disturbed the sleep of the world." For the third section of his "History of the Psychoanalytic Movement," in which he deals with Adler and Jung, Freud (1914a) chose as a motto Goethe's "Cut it short! On the Day of Judgment it is no more than a fart," which probably expressed the way he felt about these various interludes: they had been annoying and unpleasant—but not consequential for him. Personally, I see more in them; I see them as indirect expressions of the vitality that imbued Freud's work. But perhaps he was right here, too: after all, even what is vital does sometimes end in a fart.

IV

THE ROLE OF PLAGIARISM IN FREUD'S SCIENTIFIC HISTORY

ONE WHOLE SECTION of Roazen's book is headed "Plagiarism." In it, the author makes the astonishing comment that "the theme of plagiarism can be found almost everywhere one turns in Freud's career" (p. 88).

This and similar statements to be found in Roazen's book, in my opinion, are not genuine biographical discoveries, or insights that the author has gained during the course of his studies; instead they are, as the context shows, constructions designed to prove Freud's guilt in Tausk's suicide of 1919.

I shall, in what follows, discuss separately those episodes in Freud's life that Roazen introduces in order to prove his point.

THE COCAINE EPISODE

CONTRARY to Freud's own statements on the matter, as well as to all historical evidence, and purely on the basis of a statement made by a former patient of Freud's with regard to a remark that Freud had allegedly made decades earlier, the author maintains (p. 88f.) that Freud arrogated to himself the honor of having made a discovery that he had, in reality, "missed by a wide margin." Roazen is here alluding to the cocaine episode in Freud's life, which led to Carl Koller's (1857–1944) epoch-making discovery of a method that made the performance of painless eye surgery possible.

In this instance, it is easy to give the author short shrift, simply by referring the reader to Freud's *Autobiographical Study* (1925b, p. 15), where he will find the following statement: "Koller is . . . rightly regarded as the discoverer of local anesthesia by cocaine, which has become so important in minor surgery." [1] Since Freud (1900) also reported several dreams in which Koller's discovery played a leading role and he nowhere indicated any claim to have made that discovery himself, and since such pupils as Wittels (1923) and Sachs (1944) heard Freud talk about Koller's discovery, it would be a sheer waste of paper to attempt to determine whether Freud told the truth about himself in his published autobiography or confided it to a single patient of his. Any unbiased reader would readily draw the conclusion that the patient's statement rests on a paramnesia. Surely, it is Roazen's duty to explain why he chose to accept his informant's tale, as against the overwhelming evidence to the contrary.

The reader will not mind, I hope, if I digress at this point to present a few details of the cocaine episode that have not been published up to now, and which may correct some points in the otherwise excellent presentations of that episode found in the literature (Jones 1, p. 78f.; Sachs 1944, p. 71; Bernfeld, 1953; Becker-Koller, 1963).

I cite these details from a letter Freud wrote in 1934 to Prof. Josef Meller (1874–1968), the former chief of the First *Augenklinik*, University of Vienna. Meller (1934) had written a paper commemorating the fiftieth anniversary of Koller's presentation of local anesthesia. Freud's letter was in acknowledgment of the receipt of the reprint that Meller had sent him.[2]

---

[1] See also Becker-Koller 1963, p. 339, quoting from Freud (1885).

[2] The letter is contained in the collection of The Sigmund Freud Archives. It is the Archives' policy not to make its collection accessible, for the time being, to the public. The Board of Directors has given me special permission to deviate in this instance from this policy. The Archives' policy has been criticized. Those who are truly interested in the general question of the creativity of scientific

In June 1884 Freud published a paper on cocaine, summarizing the literature on the subject-matter, and reporting his own observations as well as his intention to do further research. In April of that year, he had formed the plan of investigating the drug about which there was very little reliable information. Freud put great hope in this new scientific project of his, even though it was outside his own field of neurohistology and neurological diagnosis, for he was in need of some conspicuous success in order to improve his rather desperate financial situation so that he could marry. In order to carry out his project, Freud purchased a substantial quantity of cocaine, at a much higher price than he had anticipated. As soon as he had tried out the effect of cocaine on himself by oral ingestion, he praised its beneficial effects to his friends, and used it therapeutically.

Once, when he was treating a colleague, who suffered from acute abdominal distress, with a solution of cocaine, "Koller, who had come with us, demanded also to taste the medicament. I gave it to him and thus brought about his first acquaintance with cocaine"[3] (Letter to Meller). Before leaving for Hamburg, where he stayed from September 2 to September 24, 1884 to visit his fiancée, Freud instructed Leopold Königstein (1850–1924), a close friend of his, who had held a lectureship [Dozentur] in ophthalmology at the University since 1881, "to try the substance upon the eyes of his ambulatory patients. I know that the evening before my departure [for Hamburg] I told Dr. Josef Breuer about it and heard from him the objection: 'Aren't you afraid of the trophic disturbances that could be the consequences of an anesthesia of the cornea?' But none of us pursued the thought to its end and no one of us reached the fairly obvious conclusion that one could make good use of this insensitivity for the performance of [surgical] operations. That step Koller took on his own and it

---

geniuses, or in the general psychology of creativity, will not be deprived by this policy, because there is outside the Archives a mass of material concerning other geniuses that has as yet remained untapped by research. Concern with Freud's life is, at present, rarely aroused by interest in the psychology of creativity, but rather by unscientific motives. Our times have evidently not yet reached that distance from Freud and his work that is necessary for the maintenance of minimal scientific standards.

    [3] . . . Koller, der mitgekommen war, verlangte das Mittel auch zu kosten. Ich gab es ihm und vermittelte so seine erste Bekanntschaft mit dem Cocain.

remains to his credit" [4] (Letter to Meller). When Freud returned from his journey, he found out that a paper by Koller about the anesthetizing effect of cocaine on the eye, and its application to surgery, had been read on September 15th, at a congress in Heidelberg.

The explanation of why Königstein had failed in his examination of the anesthetizing effect of cocaine was the following: "Cocaine gave at the time an opalescent solution. Königstein, disturbed by this totally irrelevant circumstance, requested from his pharmacist that he prepare a clear solution. The pharmacist not knowing the intended use of the fluid, added a drop of hydrochloric acid, and the patients screamed in pain when a drop of the clear fluid was instilled into them. Thereupon Königstein desisted from further experiments." [5] (Letter to Meller).[6]

When Königstein tried to salvage some acknowledgment for himself, Freud became angry with him.[7] Koller and Königstein agreed to submit the matter to a private arbitration committee, to which Königstein then designated Freud, and Koller, Wagner-Jauregg. In view of the decency and honesty that were still customary at that time in some academic circles, it will not come as a surprise to the reader to learn that "it then happened that I energetically rejected the demand of my client, whereas Wagner

---

[4] . . . das Mittel an den Augen seiner ambulanten Patienten zu versuchen. Ich weiss, am Abend vor meiner Abreise erzählte ich Dr. Josef Breuer davon und hörte von ihm das Bedenken: Fürchten Sie sich nicht vor den tropischen Störungen, die die Folge einer Anaesthesie der Cornea sein können? Keiner von uns dachte aber den Gedanken zu Ende und kam zu dem so nahe liegenden Schluss, dass man diese Unempfindlichkeit zur Vornahme von Operationen ausnützen könne. Diesen Schritt hat Koller selbstständig gemacht und er bleibt sein Verdienst.

[5] . . . das Cocain gab damals eine opalisirende Lösung. Königstein durch diesen ganz gleichgiltigen Umstand gestört, verlangte von seinem Apotheker, dass er ihm die Lösung kläre. Der Apotheker, unwissend über die beabsichtigte Verwendung der Flüssigkeit, setzte ihr einen Tropfen Salzsäure zu und die Patienten schrien vor Schmerz, wenn ihnen ein Tropfen dieser klaren Lösung eingeträufelt wurde. Daraufhin stand Königstein von weiteren Versuchen ab.

[6] Bernfeld (1953, p. 512), as well as Becker-Koller (1963, p. 341) who quotes from an unpublished paper by Koller, give a different version of Königstein's failure (cf. Freud 1960, p. 351, where Freud refers to Königstein's failure without spelling it out).

[7] See Becker-Koller (1963, p. 342) for the letter that Freud wrote Koller immediately upon discovering that Königstein did not want to give Koller full credit for his discovery.

took his side and caused our arbitrament to contain a certain measure of recognition for him" (Letter to Meller).[8]

When Freud (1884) ended his paper on cocaine with an announcement of future research, specifically referring to the anesthetizing effect of cocaine ("Some additional uses of cocaine based on this anesthetic property are likely to be developed in the near future" [Jones 1953–1957 1, p. 83][9]), he evidently had in mind the investigation that he later entrusted to his friend Königstein.

Thus, if Freud had remained in Vienna, he would have been present when Königstein made the mistake and, upon proceeding correctly, they would undoubtedly have observed that both the cornea and the conjunctiva were rendered insensible to touch. It would then probably have dawned on both of them that, under such conditions, surgical interventions can be made in the eye without causing pain. It is quite apparent that Freud did not miss making that discovery by a wide margin, as the author says with some sarcasm but only by one or two weeks, to to speak.

One puzzling question, however, remains unsolved: why did Freud not make use of the intervening time between finishing his paper in June and his departure in September? Why did he procrastinate and then, shortly before leaving, entrust the whole experiment to his friend?

Curiously enough, there is a high degree of probability that, if Freud had made that epochal discovery, it might have given his subsequent development an entirely different direction. World fame—acquired too early and by an accidental and, so to speak, unmerited success—might conceivably have become his undoing, as it probably was for Koller, whose scientific career ended in 1884, although he was an eminently gifted person, as attested by his two early embryological papers (Becker-Koller 1963, p. 319). "Nothing succeeds like success" is a principle that is believed in by many; it has even been recommended to us as the maxim of psychoanalytic psychotherapy. A closer look at life, and particularly

---

[8] . . . geschah es, dass ich energisch den Anspruch meines Klienten ablehnte, während Wagner für ihn Partei nahm und in unserem Schiedsspruch ein gewisses Mass von Anerkennung für ihn durchsetzte.

[9] Nevertheless, Jones asserts, on the same page, that "for Freud cocaine was an analgesic, not an anesthetic."

at the lives of the great ones, may make us somewhat wiser and perhaps keep us from this delusion of commonsense thinking.[10]

Yet let us return once again to Freud and our unfortunate author. One can easily imagine the crisis through which Freud must have gone! At that time Freud was still possessed by a burning ambition, yet his life circumstances were close to desperate, since he was separated from his fiancée and there was no prospect that his material circumstances would improve sufficiently to make marriage a probable event in the foreseeable future. A set of coincidences had placed a promising drug in his hands; he had had the right idea about how to apply it—"I guessed its usefulness for the eyes" (Freud 1960, p. 351)—and then the strangest accident, brought about by a friend's ineptitude, had snatched an incomparable success right from under his nose.

It would seem to be unavoidable that Freud should have associated with that success the opportunity for marriage and for the solution of the dire economic problems that were besetting him and his family at that time. Yet there is no trace of hostility visible, no reproach, not the slightest trend toward a paranoid reaction. In complete control, whatever might have been the repressed imagery, he continued his friendship with Königstein without any lapse in harmony, and one ought to read the letters of affection, care and friendship he subsequently exchanged with Koller (Becker-Koller 1963).

And did he really have no reason to be resentful of Koller's behavior? After all, it was he who had familiarized his friend with the drug, and they had been working together on an experiment measuring the effect of cocaine on muscular strength (Koller 1928). Freud had announced in a publication almost the same experiment that made his friend overnight a world-famous figure. Bernfeld (1953, p. 589) even maintains that Koller made his discovery after he heard of Königstein's experiments. Indeed, Koller acted with what I would call surprising haste. One witness to

---

[10] Freud, it seems, would not have agreed with the implications of my train of thought. Strangely enough, a mild feeling of guilt remained attached to the relative failure of the cocaine project of 1884. In a letter to Wittels (Bernfeld 1953, p. 594), he implied that his interest in cocaine had been a kind of hobby, which had distracted him from the path of duty; earlier (1900, p. 170), he wrote: "I had not been thorough enough to pursue the matter further."

Koller's crucial experiment reported, thirty-five years later, that it took place "one summer day," and Koller himself dated a brief preliminary note "in the beginning of September, 1884" (Bernfeld 1953, p. 590). Yet he had his paper read at Heidelberg by a representative, on the fifteenth of the very same month. Was it necessary for him to have the whole matter finished before Freud returned? Was he perhaps afraid that someone else might be on the trail of his great discovery?

It is not even known for certain whether the drug that Koller used was not Freud's property, which he had left with his friend for purposes of their joint studies. If present academic usage had been customary in those days, it would have been expected that Koller should notify Freud of his project and offer him at least co-authorship of the final paper. The historical record leaves no doubt that, by himself, Koller would never have thought of experimenting with cocaine, had not Freud called his attention to it. Was Freud's behavior—and at that time he was still dreaming of glory—characteristic of a man who worries about priorities? After all, this was a man who entrusted his friends with his scientific projects, and who with incomparable mastery and discipline let his friend enjoy world fame, without the slightest sign of a reproach for which, in my opinion, he had more than one reason.

Not yet thirty years old, he already had sufficient greatness of spirit to send his fiancée (October 10, 1884) the "pleasant news" that "a colleague has found a striking application for coca in ophthalmology. . . . I had advised Königstein a fortnight before I left Vienna to try something similar" (Jones 1, p. 88).[11] In his published works he could not, of course, tell the full truth, since that would have been all too compromising for his friend Königstein. Roazen, however, dares to assert that "as later in his conflict with Tausk, Freud sometimes imagined that he had thought out another's achievement" (p. 89), and offers that statement without any documentation whatsoever, aside from the questionable statement of a patient who had been treated by Freud decades before.[12] I shall close this episode by repeating my initial question:

---

[11] See Jones (ibid.) for a different interpretation of Freud's reaction.

[12] It also should be noted that Paul Federn in his lectures in Vienna presented the cocaine episode the way Freud described it in his letter to Meller. Federn must have received the information first-hand from Freud, additional evidence that Roazen's informant was mistaken.

Why has the author, in significant instances, assigned more trust to hearsay evidence than to Freud's unequivocal and repeated assertions?

THE FLIESS-WEININGER EPISODE

UNDER THE SAME heading of plagiarism, the author takes up the Fliess-Weininger-Swoboda affair, although it is unconnected with any question of plagiarism on Freud's part, but rather with an allegation of indiscretion. Again we shall observe the author's habit of disregarding primary sources and quoting out of context, thereby leaving an entirely erroneous impression in the reader's mind. The facts are as follows:

Otto Weininger (1880–1903), the Viennese philosopher who put an end to his own life, published in the year of his death a book that later on became a best-seller (it was translated into English under the title of *Sex and Character*). In the following year, one of his best friends, Hermann Swoboda (1873–1963) published a book on the role of periodicity in human psychology and biology. In 1906, a German librarian, historian and mathematician, Richard Pfennig,[13] published a violent attack against both Weininger and Swoboda, for alleged plagiarism committed against Wilhelm Fliess (1858–1928). In that publication, Freud was also denounced for allegedly having mediated the plagiarism. Swoboda, whose academic career was gravely threatened by Pfennig's denunciation, felt forced to reply, and did so in the same year. But Wilhelm Fliess (1906a) then published an attack of his own, of no less ferocity than Pfennig's.[14]

---

[13] I would have liked to familiarize the reader with Pfennig's personality. I owe thanks to Dr. Gerhart Maetze who with great effort and circumspection tried to collect the relevant data. But only little could be found. Pfennig was born in 1862; the date of his death is unknown. He studied classical and Romance philology and received a Ph.D. degree. From 1888 on, he was employed by the Royal (now State) Library of Berlin, whose *Oberbibliothekar* he became in 1909. He retired in 1927. His list of publications comprises three books and seven articles.

[14] The contemporary reader cannot help smiling about the whole episode; it is hardly likely that something of that sort—at least in that form—could happen at present. It is of interest to keep in mind how rapidly the temper of the times is changing. One hardly can avoid wondering about what a reader, sixty or

Wilhelm Fliess was convinced that Weininger had robbed him of his concept of bisexuality and Swoboda of his concept of periodicity—both thefts, he maintained, having been made possible by Freud's betrayal of Fliess's discoveries to the two authors. Fliess's accusations against Weininger centered on two discoveries that the young author had published as his own. One of them was "the existence not merely of embryonic sexual neutrality, but of a permanent bisexual condition . . . In this form the idea is entirely new . . ." (Weininger 1903, p. 7).[15] Weininger had asserted that each cell of the organism contains a different proportion of maleness and femaleness.

There is no reason to assume Freud's intercession in this instance. Fliess had practically published this theory much earlier, even though in 1906 he disputed this. In 1897 he had put out a book entitled *The Relationship Between the Nose and the Female Sexual Organs*, in which he proposed something that no one would have guesed from the title—namely, that two periodicities—for the male, 23 days and for the female, 28 days—were operative in the lives of both sexes.

He wrote of these periods: "Their existence consequently is not limited to mankind, but goes into the kingdom of animals and probably through the whole organic world. Indeed, the miraculous exactitude with which the time of 23 whole days and 28 respectively is maintained permits one to conjecture the existence of a profound relationship between astronomic conditions and the creation of the organisms" [16] (Fliess 1897, p. IV; my own translation).

After having demonstrated the operation of these periodicities in cats and horses as well, Fliess wrote, toward the end of the book: "The question of the extent and meaning of periodicities in man, animal and plant should find a detailed monographic

---

seventy years from now, will think about a reply like the present one to an essentially erroneous presentation of a historical figure.

[15] My own translation.

[16] *Ihre Existenz ist sonach nicht auf den Menschen beschränkt, sondern geht ins Thierreich und wahrscheinlich durch die ganze organische Welt. Ja die wunderbare Genauigkeit, mit der die Zeit von 23 bezw. 28 ganzen Tagen innegehalten wird, lässt eine tiefe Beziehung astronomischer Verhältnisse zur Schöpfung der Organismen vermuthen.*

elaboration adequate to their importance" [17] (Fliess 1897, p. 237; my own translation).

The formulations by Fliess and Weininger are so close that it is difficult to say with certitude whether or not Weininger's theory is already contained in these statements. After all, when Fliess suggested the possibility that the two periodicities pervaded the entire organic world, this was really tantamount to saying that each cell contained maleness and femaleness. Since Weininger had read Fliess's book, there was no reason to bring in Freud at this point, but only to castigate Weininger for not having cited Fliess on that occasion. Weininger, as a matter of fact, did cite Fliess briefly—in connection with the question of periodicity.[18]

There is no doubt that Fliess had the right to complain about not having been cited sufficiently by Weininger, and not at the right places; but his own previous publication rendered quite unnecessary the thought of an indiscretion committed by Freud. Yet Weininger had gone a step further and established a "law of sexual attraction," according to which a male will be attracted by a female who possesses the maleness that he himself is lacking. Of course, he would have to possess the femaleness lacking in the woman who possesses the maleness he is lacking. In this instance, there was nothing in Fliess's previous publication that would suggest anything of the sort.

Weininger himself cited Schopenhauer as a precursor, while still maintaining independence of authorship. Pfennig and Fliess regarded the claim of Schopenhauer's precedence as feigned, because Schopenhauer had asserted nothing of the sort. Both proved Weininger to be most inept in his handling of biology; they were certain that, with his mental powers, he could never have evolved either theory and that he had plundered Wilhelm Fliess's unpublished wealth of original discoveries through Freud, to whom Fliess had entrusted all his discoveries at their regular meetings prior to 1900.

Abrahamsen (1946, p. 130) has suggested that Weininger's

---

[17] . . . die Frage von der Ausdehnung und der Bedeutung der Periodicitäten bei Mensch, Tier und Pflanze eine ihrer Wichtigkeit entsprechende ausführliche monographische Bearbeitung finden soll.

[18] The English translation does not contain the Appendix with its Zusätze und Nachweise (cf. p. 499 of the German edition, for the brief remark about Fliess).

law of sexual attraction may have been based on the latter's homosexuality. Indeed, Abrahamsen may be right. Weininger was suffering, it can hardly be denied, from a schizophrenic psychosis. Yet the delusion of schizophrenics sometimes reflects the patient's distribution of libido.[19] If one adds the tendency toward concretization in schizophrenic thinking, the discovery of the "law of sexual attraction" becomes quite conceivable in a man who might have been otherwise inept in biology.

I owe to Dr. Ruth S. Eissler the following historical observation, which seems to me to be important: Fliess's conceptions of the distribution of maleness and femaleness are already contained in Plato's *Symposium* (189–193), where it is proposed that maleness and femaleness are contained in various members of the human species in various proportions. The only difference between Plato's and Weininger's propositions lay in their respective key to attraction between lovers: in Plato it is "likeness," and in Weininger "complementation." Plato's theory of sexual attraction demonstrates that theories of that sort can be evolved by someone who does not possess the skills and the versatility in handling biological data that are required of a contemporary scientist; also this disproves one of the arguments proffered by Fliess and Pfennig, who were certain that only an accomplished biologist could have arrived at the theory that Weininger had published.

The particulars of Pfennig's and Fliess's impeachment of Swoboda need not occupy us here. Fliess had published a detailed presentation of his theory of periodicity in 1897. During the next few years, he had greatly improved upon it; his own revised version was to reach the public in 1906(b). Swoboda, even though he devoted a few pages to Fliess in his own publication, tried (unfortunately) to prove that he had discovered the doctrine of periodicity independently of Fliess, that he was the first to have suggested and demonstrated the operation of periodicity in the normal psyche. He had also observed a rhythm of 18 hours in the recall of tunes. All this apparently infuriated Fliess. His suspicion that Freud had betrayed him to Swoboda makes all the

---

[19] See Freud (1911a, p. 78), where the content of a delusion is interpreted as "a concrete representation and projection outwards of [the patient's] libidinal cathexes."

less sense, since Fliess, as well as Pfennig, tried to prove that Swoboda published nothing but nonsense on the subject.

Yet did not Freud concede "that he had been tempted to steal from Fliess the 'originality' of this [bisexuality] concept" [20] (p. 89)? What Roazen has not reported adequately is an episode Freud himself reported in his *Psychopathology of Everyday Life* (1901, p. 143f.). It happened that in 1900 [21] he told Fliess, at one of their meetings, that the problems of neuroses are based on "the original bisexuality of the individual"; whereupon Fliess reminded Freud that years earlier he had told Freud the very same thing, "But you wouldn't hear of it then." The fact of the matter is that shortly thereafter Freud did recall the conversation of years past.

Here, at last, we do have a clear-cut instance of possible plagiarism—at least at the psychological level. Fortunately, before it could have been perpetrated socially, it was discovered and any unpleasant consequences that might have resulted therefrom were forestalled.

The effect of bisexuality upon the neuroses is really a major and far-reaching discovery. It would be understandable if Freud, who had devoted so much time and effort to the explanation of the neuroses (and had had to pay such a high price, in terms of personal anguish and pain, for that research), was indeed possessed by the wish to be credited with that discovery. But what did he do? He told the very man who had made that discovery that it was *his*. Can one conceive of a more honest, a more naive, I would say, a more innocent "unconscious"? Can any man be imagined who is more guileless than that? This, I think, is the

---

[20] This sentence was published by Pfennig (1906, p. 30). It was written by Freud in a leter to Fliess (July 27, 1904). As Freud wrote Wittels exactly two decades later (Freud 1960, p. 351f.), he had gone much too far in his self-accusation. Breuer had called his attention to a tendency of self-harming (Freud 1950a, p. 245), and he himself admitted to Fliess in 1902 "an habitual [self-] damaging urge toward honesty [*Aufrichtigkeitsdrang*]" (translated somewhat misleadingly "compulsion to honesty," *ibid.*, p. 342). Knowing how readily a person defends himself against the unconscious, Freud apparently sometimes attributed too great an effect to unconscious wishes. I do not doubt the existence of a temptation on Freud's part to steal ideas from Fliess at that time, but even when he wrote Wittels he did not recall that Fliess had already made his basic concepts of periodicity and bisexuality part of the public domain by way of his book of 1897.

[21] Cf. Jones 1, p. 314 for the correction of the year 1901, which Freud gave in his publication.

impression one gains from an episode that is directly relevant to the question of Freud's supposed ambition. How many are there who would even have been able to recover the memory of the original conversation, still less to acknowledge on the strength of that memory the friend's priority?

Freud rarely passed up an opportunity to learn from life, and so he added (1901, p. 144): "But since then I have grown a little more tolerant when, in reading medical literature, I come across one of the few ideas with which my name can be associated, and find that my name has not been mentioned."

What really had happened to Freud was the repetition of events that had previously victimized him without his being aware of it. Ernst Kris (1950, p. 315f.) has very engagingly demonstrated how Freud made discoveries that slipped away and were then rediscovered, only to be lost again, until they finally became permanent parts of his theories. Yet the final step, even though it was experienced "as a great and triumphant revelation," was nothing but a rediscovery of what had become subject to Freud's own forgetting. One may call such instances "self-plagiarism." [22]

But let us return to the course the episode took publicly. One cannot avoid the impression that Pfennig, who had written a study on a historical incident of plagiarism,[23] himself apparently desired to participate in a contemporary one. His brochure abounds in gross exaggerations.

Weininger was gone. His *Über die letzten Dinge*, published in 1904, already showed that he had been in the grip of a psychosis.[24]

---

[22] The unabridged publication of the Fliess letters will make it possible to determine whether the rhythm that Ernst Kris discovered was also at work with regard to Freud's forgetting Fliess's discovery of bisexuality; for in both January, 1898 and August, 1899 (cf. Jones 1, p. 315n.) Freud expressed himself enthusiastically about Fliess's great discovery. It is quite possible that Freud's forgetting followed the sort of rhythm to which creative thinking often seems to be subjected.

[23] Fleiss (1906a, p. 6) recommends Pfennig as a historian "to whom we owe the nice paper on the question of priority between Lagrange and Arbogast! Who first emancipated analysis from metaphysics?" [*Wer hat zuerst die Analyse von der Metaphysik emanzipiert?*] Festschrift for August Wilmanns. Leipzig, Otto Harrassowitz, 1903.

[24] If there had been any doubt about it, it was removed by the publication of the *Taschenbuch*, in which his friend reports that Weininger believed in the real existence of a double (Weininger 1921, p. 7f.).

This is a highly mitigating circumstance and should have been taken into consideration by Pfennig even though he was eager to secure for Fliess the acknowledgment he deserved.

Swoboda clarified the role Freud had in the whole matter by delineating precisely two incidents: In 1900, he told Freud [25] of his observations that it was not only fantasies about victory that aroused pleasure but also those about defeat, and that this can be detected in lyrical poetry. Freud thereupon advised him that the condition of being "now incubus and now succubus vis-à-vis events" is to be explained by man's bisexual *Anlage*.[26] Further, on another occasion, Freud called his attention to Fliess's publication of 1897.[27] This was the whole of the "betrayal" that Freud perpetrated on Fliess. Indeed, there was nothing that Fliess could justifiably hold against his friend.

Swoboda's description of Freud's share in the whole affair seems plausible, and I myself am convinced that it was correct.[28] Still, Fliess was unable to rid himself of the idea that his discoveries had been plundered, and for this he needed the conviction of continuous, egregious betrayal by Freud of what he had confided to him.

Freud met Weininger only once; at first, he denied this in his correspondence with Fliess. But at that meeting nothing essential regarding Fliess's theories could possibly have been divulged. Freud had read Weininger's first draft, which was quite different from the final book. In any case, one does not know

---

[25] Swoboda (1906, p. 7) says this happened during the course of conversation. Probably it took place during his treatment, but he apparently wanted to keep secret the fact of having been in analysis with Freud.

[26] However, decades later, in a letter to Wittels, Freud (1960, p. 352) said that this conception was not a matter of "an isolated conversation [with Swoboda] but a substantial part of a treatment" (Freud 1960, p. 352).

[27] Since Swoboda was doing research on the subject of periodicity, he was right in saying that it was Freud's duty to do so because, in view of the title of Fliess's book, Swoboda would never have come across it in his search through the literature.

[28] I had the chance to interview Professor Swoboda many years ago, and I gained the impression of a straightforward, reliable person. Of course, decades had passed since he had been denounced by Pfennig and Fliess, and an old man may create an impression that is quite different from what he was when he was young. But even as early as 1906, Swoboda had no reason to protect Freud, and a tendency that was critical, in fact resentful of Freud, can be felt in his vindication of 1906.

how much it may have contained of Fliess's ideas. Freud told Weininger that he should not publish the manuscript because it was "nonsense" [*Unsinn*] (Pfennig 1906, p. 29). What Fliess held against Freud was that the latter had not immediately informed him of Weininger's manuscript. I do not quite see why Freud should have done so, or how he could have done so, without abusing Weininger's trust. He evidently thought that the manuscript was so bad that it would never find an audience.[29]

I could quote many a statement of Fliess's that would prove he was victimized by a set of paranoid ideas. At the root of these ideas was the conviction—not in itself necessarily paranoid—that he was the innovator of biology, a kind of Newton, and that he had made of biology a natural science, one to which mathematics could be applied. This dream did not come true, and today Fliess's basic theories are, in general, rejected.

(It is my impression, however, that Fliess's greatness is also underestimated in psychoanalytic circles. Unfortunately, his voice in the correspondence with Freud is silent. My guess is that he had a far greater and more direct influence on Freud than one might conclude from Freud's letters to him, the only voice in the dialogue that has been preserved.[30] His seeming undoing was that his mind became caught up in the idea of the two periodicities, and most of his published endeavors went in that direction. Yet we have no way of knowing how often he might casually have made significant remarks to Freud, such as the one he made in 1897, when he recognized the dream of a female patient of Freud's about enormous serpents as homosexual (Fliess 1906a, p. 21). This happened at a time when the idea of bisexuality was still alien to Freud.)

Furthermore, in science (as in life), fate sometimes elevates the fortunate ones to great heights, only to let them tumble into the abyss of oblivion, and vice versa; and one day biology may

---

[29] Probst (1904, p. 14) reports that "a Viennese neurologist "described Weininger's appearance as follows: "A slender grown-up youth with grave features and a veiled, quite beautiful look in his eyes. I could not help feeling that I stood in front of a personality with a touch of the genius." In a letter of June 11, 1939 to Abrahamsen (1946, p. 207) Freud acknowledged that he was the author of this description.

[30] The contents of only two letters from Fliess to Freud are known (see Fliess, 1906a, pp. 19, 21f.).

discover, even though it looks quite improbable at present, that the totality of life is indeed regulated by rhythm, and that the sequences of biological phenomena that we can observe are variations of an all-embracing principle. That this principle could turn out to be the counterplay of two periodicities would not be altogether improbable in a world in which one or another form of dualism is constantly being encountered. Thus it is not inconceivable that Fliess may, in some far-distant future, come to high honors.

Be that as it may, not only Swoboda, but Freud too felt deeply hurt, offended, perhaps even threatened, by the Pfennig-Fliess publications. Here was one instance in which Freud had to protect himself for purely practical reasons. Yet it was characteristic of Freud that he shunned publicity even under circumstances, when, as far as can be reconstructed, right was completely on his side. What he did was nothing more than privately to ask two personages for their protection.[31] As can be observed in other instances, no change was engendered in the attitude that Freud expressed to others about Fliess, and in 1920 he wrote of Fliess's "magnificent" conception.[32] In writing to Abraham, he called Fliess "a remarkable, indeed fascinating man" (Abraham and Freud 1965, p. 100). There are not too many who would have preserved their objectivity and sense of loyalty, despite the terrible beating they had received at the hands of an erstwhile beloved friend, who had not hesitated to commit an egregious indiscretion by publishing letters that Freud had written in the spirit of old and intimate friendship, thereby causing him extreme embarrassment.

In the foregoing, I have touched only the surface of Freud's relationship to Fliess. The unconscious, deeper relationship has been the subject of several biographical endeavors, which have brought about partial clarification. Yet there are contradictions in Freud's last two letters, which Fliess published, as well as some

---

[31] See Freud (1960): Freud's letter to Karl Kraus (1874–1936), an eminent Viennese publicist, and Jones (1, p. 316), for a partial reproduction of a letter to Magnus Hirschfeld (1868–1935), the Berlin sexologist.

[32] Strachey translated Freud's grossartige Konzeption as "large conception" (Freud 1920a, p. 45), which, I think, does not do justice to the praise that Freud actually bestowed on Fliess on that occasion.

as yet unexplained actions. These are sufficient to justify the comment that an unsolved enigma still surrounds the relationship of these two men. Yet whatever the solution of that enigma may be, the facts do not substantiate the impression that Roazen has tried to evoke in the reader by his narrative. Freud had not supported plagiarism, nor had he committed an indiscretion.

The Fliess-Weininger-Swoboda episode has no rightful place in a chapter entitled "Plagiarism," and how it can shed "additional light on the controversy with Tausk" (p. 89) remains entirely obscure. In my opinion, the correct biographical approach would be to cite Fliess as the prototype of the scientist whose efforts are hampered by his paranoid tendencies, and who wastes time and effort in a useless and destructive fight about priorities —a fight that, if anything, actually makes him appear a fool in the eyes of posterity. After all, one paragraph in the introduction to his *Ablauf des Lebens*[33] would have been sufficient to set the historical record straight.

FREUD AND JANET

ANOTHER INSTANCE that Roazen cites in connection with the significant role that plagiarism allegedly played in Freud's life concerns the controversy between Freud and Pierre Janet. Actually, it was quite peripheral. The author compresses it into one paragraph (p. 91).

He writes: "By the 1920's Janet was bluntly claiming that Freud had plagiarized his ideas and simply altered the terminology." Since he does not add any comment to indicate whether he believes this to be true or false, the reader is free to assume that Janet was right, and that Roazen agrees with him. Of course, the reader cannot know that the author is here simply echoing Dr. Bennet (1965: "Janet himself was quite blunt and said explicitly that Freud plagiarized his ideas though he changed the ter-

---

[35] In the second edition of that book (Fliess 1906b), there is a summary of the entire affair. The first edition was not accessible to me; but Fliess did reproduce in his pamphlet (1906a) what he had published there about the matter. This would have been quite sufficient to protect his claim to priority and to make the pamphlet of the same year unnecessary.

minology"), while failing to note that Dr. Bennet's article was written in order to *disprove* this claim. Furthermore, Roazen ignores the fact that Janet himself had never claimed anything of that sort, that this was Bennet's wrong interpretation of some paragraphs in Janet's (1924) book (pp. 41–45). Janet never did accuse Freud of plagiarism, nor did he have any reason to, since Freud in fact cited Janet whenever there was an opportunity for him to do so. Had the author gone back to the original and not relied on Bennet, he would have found that Janet (1924, pp. 41–46), after delineating in one paragraph the alleged changes Freud had made in Janet's terminology, then goes on to devote four full pages to Freud's original contributions. Needless to say, Janet disagreed with all of them, but he never, as far as I know, openly accused Freud of plagiarism, although he seems never to have rejected that accusation and may even have personally thought that it was correct.

Roazen then continues: "Freud *naturally* resented 'the libel' being 'spread by French writers that I had listened to . . . [Janet's] lectures and stolen his ideas'" (emphasis added). What does "naturally" mean here? and why is the word libel put in quotation marks? If a conscientious reader should turn to the bibliographical reference the author gives for this sentence—namely, Dr. Bennet's article—he should not be surprised to discover that neither the word libel nor the quotation can be found in it at all. In this context, the word libel has a paranoid connotation. Needless to say, Freud never used it on that occasion in his printed work; despite the execrable slander he was exposed to during his lifetime, he never for a moment intended to bring any one of his numerous calumniators before a judge.[34] Lastly, the author says: "Janet had not followed along the path Freud took, so Freud said he had 'ceased to understand Janet's writings'"[35] (em-

---

[34] The author does not let the reader know that Freud's complaint was contained in a letter to Marie Bonaparte (Jones 3, p. 213f.). I shall come back to that letter, but wish to point out here that the word *Verleumdungen*, which Freud used, has no primary legal implication, as the word "libel" does in English, but lies somewhere between slander and calumny.

[35] The word Freud used was Janet's "*Ausführungen*," which is less than the general term "writings" of Strachey's translation; it means elaborations or expositions.

phasis added), the "so" apparently being intended to imply arbitrariness and subterfuge.

What are the facts? Let us start with Freud's ceasing to *understand* Janet. Freud refers to Janet some thirty-eight times in his published works. For the historian, it will be an interesting task some day to discuss each reference singly. Eleven of these references may be classified as positive; seven as neutral, or simply references; and about fifteen contain criticism. The rest contain both positive and negative implications.

In order to understand Freud's relationship to Janet, one has to take into consideration the fact that Freud had—and expressed —the greatest respect for Janet's work. From the beginning, of course, he also referred to the differences in their theories, as happens when two scientists conduct research independently of each other. Thus Freud could not align himself with the role Janet attributed to *idées fixes, insuffisance psychologique*, the splitting of consciousness, and other concepts. Yet no reader will discover in Freud's references the slightest trace of hostility, ridicule or denial of Janet's merits—not even when, in 1913, Janet suddenly launched, at the International Congress of Medicine in London, an attack against Freud and psychoanalysis, which Strachey (1955, p. xii) has rightly called "absurdly ignorant and unfair." One has to read the 69 printed pages[36] of ridicule, falsifications and errors, in order to appreciate the commendable simplicity with which Freud replied to this attack, never once denying or minimizing his early admiration of Janet's work.

The passage to which the author refers (Freud 1916–1917, p. 257) was preceded by a reference to the "very great credit" Freud had given Janet. To stop at that would have meant, after 1913, a public disavowal of psychoanalysis. The disagreement was reduced to the question of whether the unconscious is a live, actually effective force or nothing but "a form of words, a makeshift, *une façon de parler*" (*ibid.*). According to Freud's view, after 1913 Janet adhered to the latter conception of the unconscious, which is why he "ceased to understand" Janet—except that here the phrase is not used in the sense of "I do not get the meaning," but rather

---

[36] For a rebuttal, see Jones (1915).

as signifying "I do not understand *how, in view of the facts, such a statement can be made.*"

That Freud understood all too well *what* Janet meant is quite clear, for he set forth succinctly that part of Janet's theory with which he disagreed. What Roazen tries to prove is, to the contrary, that it was Freud's habit to find ideas "simply incomprehensible," when they did not fit his schemes—which alleged habit is then supposedly at play in a reproach of Freud's, when he writes to Lou Andreas-Salomé that Tausk's constructions regarding narcissism are incomprehensible to him.[37] In this context, his meaning was, of course, not what it had been in the controversy with Janet, but simply that he could not understand the meaning of what Tausk had said. It is precisely the controversy with Janet that shows how dignified and grand—I would say how "unparanoid"—Freud was in his polemics, for he had a very good reason to be personally angry with Janet.

In a letter to Marie Bonaparte (Jones 3, p. 213f.), Freud rightly pointed out that it had been unfair—at a time when the French press was maintaining that Freud had attended Janet's lectures during his stay in Paris (October, 1885–February, 1886) and upon his return to Vienna had plagiarized what he had learned from Janet[38]—for Janet himself not to state publicly that Freud had never met him during that time. It was because of this discourtesy that Freud refused to receive Janet in 1937.

It can be proven that the French press was wrong in its claim of Janet's influence upon Freud during his stay in Paris (see Bennet 1956; Delay 1963). Janet (1859–1947) completed his doctorate in philosophy in 1889. His first publication (1886) was on "Malebranche et les esprits animaux." His early papers in the field of psychopathology were devoted to the phases of the hypnotic state and hypnosis transmitted from a distance. He was for seven years professor of philosophy at Le Hâvre. He moved to Paris in 1890, when he became the director of the psychological laboratory at the Salpêtrière.

Even Janet's priority in print, which Freud mentioned so often,

---

[37] Cf. Binion 1968, p. 358f., Roazen 1969, pp. 63, 70.

[38] I have not been able to ascertain how frequently these false statements were made by the press. They were, however, repeated even in texts, such as that by Guillain (1955, p. 60).

has become open to question. Apparently Freud had forgotten that already in 1888—that is, one year prior to Janet's decisive publication of 1889—in an unsigned article in Villaret's *Handwörterbuch der gesamten Medizin*, he had mentioned Breuer's method of searching, through hypnosis, for "the psychical occasion on which the disorder in question originated" (p. 56).[39] In the light of the historical actualities, therefore, Roazen's opprobrious remarks about the Janet controversy go up in smoke, and Freud's dignity and composure are to be observed with clarity, in a situation where others might easily have felt disconcerted and even agitated.

FREUD AND MOLL

ANOTHER CLAIM—this time that "anyone coming close to Freud's own work ran the risk of incurring his wrath" (p. 91)—is also a preparation for Roazen's final attack against Freud in the Tausk affair. It is derived from Freud's discussion remark (*Minutes 2*, pp. 48–51), when Albert Moll's (1908) book, *The Sexual Life of the Child*, was being discussed at a meeting of the Vienna Psychoanalytic Society (November, 1908). Here the author has simply turned the situation into its opposite, for Albert Moll had been supposed to be the expert in matters of sexuality, as is evident from his volume on libido (1898), which Freud was repeatedly citing in his publications. It had been Freud (as well as Magnus Hirschfeld, by the way) who had weakened Moll's position as the eminent sexologist of the time. Moll apparently had tried to regain it by discrediting Freud, for in his book there was not one good word written about Freud. To judge from the English translation (the original was not accessible to me), he referred nine times to Freud and, except for one neutral reference, all of them were highly critical.

Childhood sexuality was the one great discovery of Freud's that he was certain was a fact. As a scientist he knew, of course, that, as happens with scientists generally, most of his findings

---

[39] Anderson (1962, p. 89f.) rightly points out that the therapeutic element of an abreaction was not mentioned by Freud in 1888.

might well be superseded by others after a time, and Freud was
rather pessimistic about what part of his findings would remain
a permanent, unquestioned part of knowledge. Just as Columbus
knew that he had discovered a fact—mistaken as he may have
been about its interpretation—so Freud, I would guess, while he
may have had his doubts about whether his theories of the etiology
of neuroses would endure, was convinced that, with the discovery
of childhood sexuality, he had discovered "a new continent." Even
though the interpretation of it would very likely vary in accordance
with the progress of research, its existence had been established by
him as a fact. Moreover, for no other discovery was he to pay as
high a price, in terms of isolation, criticism, and ridicule.

Now comes a man who, in a previous volume (Moll 1898),
had stated everything he knew about the development of sexuality in the human species, and he takes up the same theme, denies
the correctness of the significant research that has been made in
the meantime, and arrogates to himself originality, by clearly making capital of the very research that he is attacking and "proving"
to be wrong. Unless Freud were a saint or a masochist, or patho-
logically inhibited, he would most certainly have been bound to
be angry in the face of such provocation. I have not succeeded in
obtaining a picture of Moll's character. Historical veracity, however, would have required the author to let the reader know that
the *Minutes* do not make it clear whether some of Freud's criticism
of Moll was not in fact a repetition of what Magnus Hirschfeld
had reported to him from Berlin.[40]

At that time, there is no doubt, research on the child's men-
tality and on the perversions had more than scientific implications.
The liberation of the child (*Die Befreiung des Kindes*) was a
slogan with almost religious, but certainly political, implications,
coming as it did at a time when the majority of the European intelligentsia believed that reforms would banish the evils of their
time. In Magnus Hirschfeld, the combination of research with a
political *Weltanschauung* was far more pronounced than it was
in Freud, at least insofar as his printed work was concerned; but
when the *Minutes* record Freud's statement that Moll "never ex-

---

[40] The passage is as follows (*Minutes* 2, p. 49): "Moll's character is only too
well known. Hirschfeld has complained bitterly about him. He is a petty, malicious,
narrow-minded individual."

presses a firm opinion," he might very well have been alluding to that very state of affairs, for Moll's book was a step back, if judged with regard to *Die Befreiung des Kindes*. In Freud's *Three Essays* (1905a), if viewed in terms of the imagery they leave with the reader, the child has the right to his sexual feelings and their expression;[41] in Moll, although the harshness of previous decades (and centuries) has been mitigated, childhood sexuality and morbidity are still linked. Indeed, the dilution of truth aroused Freud's wrath sometimes more than outright error.

Furthermore, in evaluating Freud's reaction to Moll's book, one must take into account that Society meetings at that time were a kind of family affair, which permitted the free ventilation of personal feelings. In his papers, Freud continued to cite Moll as before and disregarded the personal affront to which he had been exposed, even though, I imagine, he strongly disliked Moll, as the quotation from Horace in a letter to Abraham may suggest: "*Hic niger est, hunc tu Romane caveto.*" [42]

I shall come back in the last chapter to Freud's capacity to hate, which in my judgment was most admirable, but I wish here to repeat that the historical evidence does not confirm the author's interpretation that Freud's wrath was aroused by Moll's coming close to his own theories but, if anything, by the opposite—namely, the fact that Moll, having been clearly under the influence of Freud's research, then went on to dilute his theories and, in view of his authority in Central Europe, might well succeed in curbing the progress—little as it may have been—that Freud and his group had brought about. The fact that such an authoritative figure wrote on the sexual life of children and asserted that Freud had published nothing but mistakes with regard to the subject-

---

[41] According to a footnote (1905a) added in 1915 (p. 162), the forces that restrain the sexual drive "arrive at the appropriate moment, as though spontaneously, when upbringing and external influences give the signal" [*auf die Winke der Erziehung*]—which adumbrates a far-reaching enlightened philosophy of the upbringing of children.

[42] ("That man is black at heart: mark and avoid him, if you are a Roman." Horace, *Satires* I, iii, 85. *The Oxford Dictionary of Quotations*, sec. ed., p. 261, 15). When Freud wrote to Abraham in the same letter (February 18, 1909) that several passages in Moll's book "really merit a charge of libel," I find in this the expression of the same anger, rather than a suggestion as to possible strategy of reprisal, for he adds that the best answer is "prudence and silence."

matter, not to speak of his bypassing Freud altogether when writing on perversions, was more than sufficient reason to respond with strong emotion. Yet once again we observe the same dignity and calm as we saw in Freud's response to Janet, and no outsider could have guessed from Freud's publications how deeply offended Freud may have felt, at least for a while.

FREUD AND McDOUGALL

THE REPROACH OF "subconscious plagiarism," which McDougall raised against Freud, is dealt with by Roazen in a footnote (p. 91). Its pursuit did not promise to shed any light on the Tausk episode. I myself have tried to ascertain whether McDougall was right, but have not succeeded in clarifying the point. If this was the only instance of unconscious plagiarism, then Freud must surely have had a literary guardian angel, for with such voluminous writing, unconscious plagiarism is absolutely unavoidable.

FREUD'S ALLEGED PENCHANT
FOR FALSE RECOLLECTIONS

AT ONE POINT Roazen writes (p. 92): "One way of coping with his [Freud's] own penchant for false recollections about his sources was simply to avoid reading." From what does Roazen derive what he calls Freud's "penchant for false recollections"? As is well known, Freud's dualistic theory of Eros and Thanatos was rejected by most analysts. Freud was all the more pleased when he found the same theory expressed by Empedocles, not quite two and a half millennia before. "I am ready," he continued, "to give up the prestige of originality for the sake of such a confirmation, especially as I can never be certain, in view of the wide extent of my reading in early years, whether what I took for a new creation might not be an effect of cryptomnesia" (Freud 1937, p. 244f.).

Even a reader who was most critical of Freud would have to admit that a doubt about absolute originality is justified in all instances, and that Freud was here expressing only the feeling that every creative person will share who has preserved at least a minimum of gratitude and humility. It is altogether unreasonable to derive from such a statement the existence of a "penchant" for falsification by way of cryptomnesia.

Yet Roazen does not stop at that, but alleges that Freud "deliberately ignored the works of Nietzsche, a clear rival as a psychologist of the unconscious," in order to cope with "his own penchant." The only reference Roazen gives in this instance is to Kris (1956, p. 631). It is made in order to prove the detail, quite subordinate to Roazen's basic denunciation, that Freud considered Nietzsche's self-knowledge to be more penetrating than any other person's; yet the way this reference is interpolated may easily be taken by the reader to refer to the whole train of thought, as if Kris were in agreement with the author about Freud's motive for not reading Nietzsche for a long time.

Freud twice referred to his relationship to Nietzsche. It was in 1914 (a, p. 15f.), that he wrote he was glad "to forgo all claims to priority," because he had denied himself the very great pleasure of reading Nietzsche, in order not to be disturbed in his psychoanalytic work by "anticipatory ideas"; two years later (1916, p. 333), when he published his paper on "the criminal from a sense of guilt," he duly informed the reader that this type of criminal had been known to Nietzsche, as "a friend has since called to my attention."

In his *Autobiographical Study* of a decade later (1925b, p. 59f.), Freud took up the same question again, and it is worthwhile recording this instance in detail. After refuting the possible reproach of having relinquished observation for speculation in his old age, Freud reports (*ibid.*) that the great extent of the coincidences between psychoanalysis and Schopenhauer[43] "is not to be traced to my acquaintance with his teaching. I read Schopen-

---

[43] Cf. Freud to Karl Abraham (January 20, 1911): "Juliusburger has done a very good thing with his quotation from Schopenhauer, but my originality is obviously on the wane," (Abraham and Freud 1965, p. 99). He is here referring to Otto Juliusburger's article of 1911. As with all great discoveries, those of Freud can also be traced to the past. This happens to most great discoverers, but usually only posthumously. Since the group around Freud zealously searched for predecessors, Freud had to acknowledge during his own lifetime the precursors of some of his ideas.

hauer very late in my life. Nietzsche, another philosopher whose guesses and intuitions often agree in the most astonishing way with the laborious findings of psycho-analysis, was for a long time avoided by me on that very account. I was less concerned with the question of priority than with keeping my mind unembarrassed." [44] Many a sparrow wants to teach the eagle how to build his nest.

REMARKS ABOUT FREUD'S BIBLIOGRAPHIES

A GENERAL REMARK may be permitted. If one wishes to express in a short formula the place of Freud's opus in the history of Western ideas, one may say that the majestic reconstruction of the human mind that he left in his opus rests on an awesome synthesis of the philosophies of Plato, Schopenhauer and Nietzsche. Usually the link with Plato is limited to the place that Eros takes in Freud's work; but the far more important link is with Plato's *Phaedrus* (246, 253, 254), in which a tripartite conception of the human personality is also anticipated. It stood Freud in good stead that he had not received a rigorous training in philosophy. If his anticipations with regard to the structure of the mind had been preempted by an integration of various philosophical systems, that would have severely hindered the freedom and directness of his psychological observation. From experimental research (Fisher 1954, 1959), the important influence of subliminal perceptions is known. I surmise that some philosophers had their bearing on Freud in the form of *subliminal* thought stimuli, and for that reason were able to have a creative rather than a restraining influence on the evolvement of his ideas. Otherwise, he might easily have become the representative of a particular philosophical school; the subliminal stimulation made possible the synthesis of the best to be found in philosophies that in their essence are disparate.

---

[44] The last word reads in German *unbefangen*, which covers an area from "unprejudiced" to simply "open." The implication is clearly: keeping my mind from *prejudging*—that is, from skipping "laborious findings" in favor of overhasty theoretical formulation—or keeping it open to the significance of clinical observations.

As far as Freud's bibliographical references are concerned, he was necessarily in an impossible situation. As long as a topic was a relatively circumscribed one, like dream or wit, he might have come close to an adequate bibliography; but the more he approached a general psychology, the more impossible it became to live up to bibliographical requirements. They might have included perhaps the major part of the past output of Western ideas—and this for a simple reason: there is a large number of historical papers demonstrating a particular connection of Freud's work with a particular philosopher or philosophical system, or showing that one of Freud's discoveries was anticipated in a particular literary product (even though it is highly probable that in many instances Freud was acquainted with none of these). The range will become even more extensive as historical research progresses. Since Freud presented almost the complete human cosmos scientifically, and since it is very likely that in literary masterpieces, as well as in systems of philosophy, at least a fraction of the human cosmos found a presentation that was true to reality—even though in most instances it was not presented in a scientific form—it is small wonder that "predecessors" are so frequently discovered. This, of course, does not prove that Freud's opus was actually influenced by them at all, subliminally or not; further, the fact that countless historical strands connect Freud's opus with mankind's cultural past does not prove any lack of originality on his part, but, to the contrary, the greatness of his achievement. I would even go so far as to say that the view that the totality of Freud's work contains a multidimensional, scientifically-correct presentation of the structure of the mind presupposes manifestations of relatedness with a large number of historical predecessors. But none of these comprised a scientific psychological system that could compare with his in terms of completeness, depth and rationality.

I cannot forgo closing these remarks with a really amusing specimen of Roazen's psychology. Freud was an avid, passionate and quick reader, and the author knows that he was famous for his splendid bibliographies: the first chapter of Freud's The Interpretation of Dreams, for example, is a masterpiece of bibliographic introduction. But this was done, according to Roazen, for the sake "of protecting himself against his tendency to forget his predecessors" (p. 92). Having acknowledged that Freud sometimes "began by citing every known authority on the subject," he then goes on to say, "Of course, this expository technique would at the same time establish his own claims to originality." I would not like to play poker with the author; I am almost certain that, with each round, he would announce the rules of the game anew, after every player had put his cards on the table.

A PLAGIARISM WRONGLY ATTRIBUTED
TO FREUD

IN A FOOTNOTE on page 88, however, we find new information, unknown up to now, that would adduce a concrete instance of unconscious plagiarism on Freud's part. Dr. Edoardo Weiss allegedly told Roazen that he "had an experience of his own in which Freud forgot one of his sources, in this case a paper by Weiss." From Dr. Weiss's answer to my inquiry as to which source Freud had forgotten, I have discoverd that Roazen's assertion is an instance of wrong recollection, and that Dr. Weiss never told him anything of the kind.

It easily may have happened that, from his numerous discussions with psychoanalysts, Freud obtained many promptings and pointers of which he was not aware, and it would be of the greatest importance for the psychology of the creative act if we were to know of one such instance. We might then have had the opportunity to draw some important conclusions from the difference between the contents of the prompting or pointer, and the content of what the genius made out of it.

UNCONSCIOUS PLAGIARISM

A GENERAL REMARK does not seem to be uncalled for here. Unconscious plagiarism is unavoidable; no one knows for sure where he received his stimulations or suggestions. It is up to the historian to try to find the exact links in the widely spread web of the history of ideas. Freud, of course, was particularly interested in the unconscious sources of his discoveries. He was apparently

quite surprised when he discovered that the method of free association—about which, I would assume, he had felt that he was
quite original—was almost a replica of an essay he had read during
his puberty (Freud 1920).

Even the objective historian meets great obstacles in recon-
structing correct historical sequences. Recently Jaki (1969) put
together the history of a paradigm concerning the explanation of
the seemingly obvious fact that it is light during the day and dark
at night. It is a most impressive piece of historical research; but
it also implies that the researcher, who is forever trying to take
into cognizance the true historical records, can thereby get bogged
down and lose the inner freedom to make great new discoveries
on his own. All one can do is to "keep the record straight" in
some halfway approximation.

Freud, in general, did more in that respect than the average
scientist is likely to do. Nevertheless, I am quite certain that the
future historian of psychoanalysis will find a fairly large number
of precursors of whom Freud either did not know at all or about
whom he had forgotten.[45] That is inherent in the living, creative
process. But I am also reasonably sure that unconscious plagiarism
will be found with lesser frequency in Freud's work than in that
of others, if for no other reason than that Freud was endowed with
an extraordinarily good memory.

FREUD'S UNCONCERN ABOUT PRIORITIES

AT ONE POINT Roazen tries to coerce Freud into serving as witness
against himself with regard to a pathological overconcern with

---

[45] A remarkable instance, discovered shortly after the publication of *The Interpretation of Dreams* (Mentz 1901), was brought to attention once again by
Bry and Rifkind (1962). There is a paragraph in the novel *Niels Lyhne* by J. P.
Jacobsen that clearly speaks of the wish fulfillment of dreams. Freud read that
novel and was deeply impressed by it at the time of his developing his wish
fulfillment theory of dreams (Freud 1950a, p. 128), but the reference is missing
from his bibliography. Freud did not tire of documenting instances that clarified
the history of his own discoveries. When he found out that Popper-Lynkeus
(1838–1921), a well-known Viennese engineer, author and sociologist had written
a short story (1899) in which the dream distortion was explained in a way almost
identical with his own, he delighted in commenting on originality in science
(Freud 1923, 1932).

priorities. He writes (p. 79): "After he [Freud] had begun to collect students, he complained that now he had to publish too quickly." The most ingenious reader could never guess that this was plucked out of the following autobiographical passage (which the author gives as his source), referring to Freud's early years of psychoanalytic research (1914a, p. 22): "My 'splendid isolation' was not without its advantages and charms. . . . My publications, which I was able to place with a little trouble, could always lag far behind my knowledge, and could be postponed as long as I pleased, since there was no doubtful 'priority' to be defended." [46]

Yet quite aside from the question of whether Roazen complied with the minimal standards of quoting on that occasion, it seems to me that a remark by Freud, to be found in the Minutes of the meeting of the Vienna Psychoanalytic Society on February 3, 1908 (*Minutes 1*, pp. 298–305) should have been brought by Roazen to the reader's attention, if he was seriously interested in inquiring into Freud's attitude toward plagiarism. Part of that meeting was devoted to a discussion of the "intellectual communism" that existed in that brave little community of pioneers. Apparently there was no copyright attached to ideas, and everyone in the group felt entitled to use any idea that had been stated in lectures and discussions. It was Federn who made the motion that this "intellectual communism" should be abolished: "No idea may be used without the authorization of its author. Otherwise, one would feel inhibited in freely discussing." In the ensuing discussion, Freud made completely available whatever he said at meetings. "He [Freud] personally waives all rights to any of his remarks" (*Minutes 1*, p. 302)—which the editors correctly explicate as "they are available for general use." No man who is concerned about priorities would ever speak like that. In the discussion, one finds a remark by Wittels that is quite revealing: "He [Wittels] himself is incapable of writing anything without using the Professor's ideas; he does not always give the source." This, I trust, was true not only of Wittels.

Just as Freud constantly absorbed what he observed and read,

---

[46] A literal translation of certain parts of the sentence gives it more inner strength. Freud stressed the difficulty he had in finding "Lodging" [*eine Unterkunft*] for his papers; this was done "with some trouble" [*mit einiger Mühe*].

for use in his creative processes, so he constantly gave freely to others the ideas that he himself had developed. Wittels was the only one who freely acknowledged this. That Freud's free offering of all his discussion remarks was not a mere gesture on his part, and that the members of his group did accept and act on Freud's liberal offer I can now prove by an example that I came across accidentally. I am certain that systematic comparison of the *Minutes* with the psychoanalytic publications of the same or later period will reveal a few more.

The example I came upon has to do with a case report that J. Sadger, an early collaborator of Freud, published in 1910. I shall come back in the final chapter to the patient whose case history he presented on three evenings. Suffice it at this point to note that it was a case of multiple perversions combined with episodes of hysterical absences. During the discussion of the second evening, Freud put forward a far-reaching and quite original thought (*Minutes* 2, p. 313):

Being enamored of oneself (of own's genitals) is an indispensable stage of development. From there one passes over to similar objects. In general, man has two primary sexual objects, and his future existence depends on which of these objects he remains fixated on. These two sexual objects are for every man the woman (the mother, nurse, etc.) and his own person; and it follows from this that [the question] is to become free from both and not to linger on too long with either. Usually, one's own person is re- placed by the father—who, however, soon moves into a hostile position. It is at this point that homosexuality branches off (*Minutes* 2, pp. 312–313).

The remarkable thing is that this same passage can be found almost literally in Sadger's paper without any reference to Freud. Sadger wrote (1910a, p. 112):

Being enamored of one's own person, behind which hides the fact that one is enamored of one's own genitals, is a developmen- tal phase that is never absent. Only from there one goes over to similar objects, and his further life depends on whether and upon which he finally remains fixated. For the male these two objects are the mother (that is to say, the first nurse) and his own person. In order to remain healthy, he must get rid of both, not to linger on too long with them. Only for a short time is the own person replaced by the father, because he, as the primary rival with the mother, soon moves again into a hostile position. It is from here that inversion then branches off [my own translation].

Freud had said on the same occasion that "Sadger's comment with regard to narcissism seems new and valuable." Thus Sadger was at that time perhaps slightly ahead of Freud, who would write his famous paper on narcissism only four years later, and who would therefore have had reason to feel "threatened" and jealous—character traits that, as we shall see, Roazen attributes to Freud. Therefore, I wish the reader would keep this instance well in mind, since it is a documented proof of Freud's generosity toward his collaborators, his unconcern about questions of priority. It should also be remembered that Sadger was by no means a favorite of Freud's but rather someone about whom Freud quite often felt justified in complaining.

How liberal and easy-going Freud was in giving credit to his collaborators can be observed in a footnote to his famous paper on the psychosis of the Presiding Judge Schreber (Freud 1911a, p. 70, n. 1): "Abraham's short paper contains almost all the essential views put forward in the present study of the case of Schreber." Freud was referring to Abraham's paper of 1908, three years earlier. In comparing the two publications, the reader will see that Freud went much further in giving Abraham credit than was necessary.[47]

Freud was also unusually magnanimous in sharing his ideas with others. In 1908 (*Minutes* 1, p. 336), he confided to the group an idea about trauma out of which he was to form, twelve years later, his famous theory of traumatic neurosis. Further, in a letter to Yvette Guilbert, Freud (1960, p. 404) presented an entirely new theory about the psychology of stage acting, with which a less creatively rich mind could easily have filled a book. Yet he merely set it down in a letter; its fate evidently did not concern him in the least.

---

[47] However, on page 41, n. 1, Freud had recorded that Abraham had attributed to him an "influence upon the development of his [Abraham's] views."

Just as we shall never know the full scope of Freud's sources, so we shall never know the full extent of his fertilization of others. This is the hallmark of the true genius: he owes more to the world than he and the world know, and the world owes to him more than he and the world know. In Freud's instance, it is my feeling, the balance is in his favor: he gave more to others than he received from others. But the future historian will have the final word in that matter.

A SEEMINGLY PROVEN CASE
OF PLAGIARISM

I WANT to refer briefly here to what happened to Robert Bárány (1837–1936), the Viennese otologist who became Nobel Laureate in 1914. He was denied academic advancement in 1916, because of "gross negligence with regard to the consideration of the mental property of others" [grobe Fahrlässigkeit bei der gebetenen Rücksicht auf das geistige Eigentum anderer] (Burgher et al., 1922, p. 381)—which may be called roughly the reproach of plagiarism. And although Bárány had to admit that "he had made himself guilty of an error by having totally forgotten the paper by [Joseph] Breuer" (Burgher et al., p. 386), it is highly questionable whether Bárány ever did commit an act of plagiarism, even though Bergler (1932) did not hesitate to cite the incident under the rubric of "plagiarism without participation of consciousness."

I have thought it suitable to cite the case of Bárány here because it shows: (1) that it was not very easy for a member of the faculty of the University of Vienna to commit plagiarism, since the academic authority evidently kept an eye on the maintenance of proper standards; (2) that even if an investigating body does reach the conclusion that a scientist has committed plagiarism, that judgment ought to be accepted with great reserve.[48] It is highly probable, almost certain, that the academic senate made

---

[48] I do not know what the senate's final verdict on Bárány's case was.

an error in Bárány's instance. Be that as it may, if the senate had passed judgment on Freud, as it did on Bárány, we can be quite certain that Roazen would not have hesitated to cite it as evidence injurious to Freud's character.

V

CONTRADICTIONS,

ABSURDITIES AND ERRORS

A BOOK that is completely without contradictions would be a rare achievement. Close scrutiny of any text that deals with a complex matter of human affairs is bound to unearth points at which epagoge and logic do not click. Since life is so full of contradictions and may well be a contradiction in itself, why should books that reflect specific sectors of it be expected to be free of life's most significant ingredient?

Yet there is a type of contradiction that is the result of nothing more than inconsistency. By no means does it stem from the depths to which the inquirer's gaze has penetrated in his search for the truth, but rather from his looseness of thinking, his lack of information, and his own emotional entanglements. More often than not, such contradictions stem from an author's lack of awareness of the unconscious motives behind his eagerness to compose a scientific piece of work.

The position that Roazen takes initially with regard to Freud and Tausk is this: "The two men formed an uncanny pair of opposites" (p. xx). Yet, less than half-way through he switches horses: "Part of the whole fascination of the Freud-Tausk struggle stems from their personalities being so similar" (p. 93). The two statements, whose contrariety is witness to the author's carelessness (the first appears in the introduction without inner necessity, but rather as a rhetorical embellishment), together reveal an essential misunderstanding of the historico-psychological situation.

In general, to be sure, great men do need the proper antagonists in order to establish their greatness. If Churchil had not found in Hitler an antagonist worth his efforts, his place in history might have been a rather minor one. Roazen's statements are aimed at giving Tausk the distinctive role of antagonist in Freud's life. Yet that he never was. There was, between the two, neither the relationship of oppositeness nor that of similarity, since the relationship between talent and genius never falls into either of these categories. They are examples of two altogether different types of creativity.

Tausk was an accident in Freud's life. Freud's life history would not have been different in any way, if Tausk had stayed in Berlin and Freud had never met him. On the other hand, posterity would probably never have heard of Tausk if he had not joined the early group around Freud. In the eyes of posterity, Tausk is little more than a reflection of Freud.

Tausk was talented in his own right, of course, and it is conceivable that he might have acquired some degree of prestige as a journalist. But many reasons could be adduced that make it probable that the profession of journalism would have harbored grave dangers for such a personality as Tausk's. It is a moot question. The fact is that Freud was bound to attract disciples, and one cannot therefore ascribe to any one of them individually the role or function of either protagonist or antagonist necessary to his rise.

Another peculiar contradiction occurs in relation to Roazen's initial statement about Freud's "extreme isolation" (p. 25) prior to 1906, when followers were gradually beginning to gather around him. This is put forward by the author at the moment of describing Tausk's decision to become an analyst; it is obviously intended to imply the sacrifice that Tausk made—an implication that is certainly not vaild for Tausk, even though it may be for most of the others, as has been mentioned before. However, this "extreme isolation" later becomes "surely in part self-imposed, and indeed somewhat exaggerated [by Freud]" (p. 92).

The intent of this change of opinion is apparent; for on the latter occasion the author is discussing Freud's not having read Nietzsche—which, strangely enough, seems to have implied, in Roazen's eyes, a "self-imposed" isolation. However, I suggest that the author would have done better to let Freud decide for himself the degree of the isolation he had to bear.

When Tausk studied medicine (contrary to the author's claim, this was not a "requirement," the practice of psychoanalysis by non-medical persons having been customary from the very beginning), this necessitated financial assistance by Freud and a few of Tausk's colleagues. Tausk's decision is linked by the author to Freud's "wish to triumph in the medical world" (p. 28)—that is to say, it is made to appear once again as a sacrifice made by Tausk on behalf of Freud.

The author quite specifically states, on this occasion, that a follower was "all the more useful to the advancement of psycho-analysis" when he possessed "the respect of the medical profession and of hospital psychiatry in particular" (ibid.). Yet he says that Helene Deutsch, who held an important position at the Psychiatric University Clinics, allegedly "soon realized she would have to give up her position in Wagner-Jauregg's clinic" (p. 73) when she entered her training analysis with Freud, because "Freud looked on official psychiatry as his enemy" (p. 74), and "Freud could be like a demanding lover; he wanted all of her" (p. 102).

About Freud's attitude toward psychiatry, which is here mis-construed by the author, I shall have more to say presently. But just how wrong Roazen is can easily be found out by merely check-ing the membership lists of the Vienna Psychoanalytic Society. There one will find the names of Heinz Hartmann, Paul Schilder, and later Erwin Stengel, all of whom held prominent places at the Psychiatric University Clinics and were greatly welcome in the Society. Yet the author really reaches the peak of absurdity when he writes, after reporting that Dr. Deutsch became an as-sistant at a neurological clinic upon leaving the psychiatric service: "Neurology, having nothing to do with psychoanalysis, would be less threatening to Freud. It was also closer to Freud's own earlier

interests, since it had been his field before founding psychoanalysis" (p. 75).[1]

The truth of the matter is, as Dr. Deutsch assured me, that
Freud had said, in his first interview with her, no more than that
she might have to face a conflict of loyalties, if she were working
at the University Clinic and as an analyst at the same time. She
left the University Clinic, she told me, because there was no
chance there of advancement for her. At that time she needed one
year of neurological training, in order to be able to fulfill the requirements of what was the equivalent of an American Specialty
Board; and she changed clinics because the University statutes
made it impossible for her, as a woman, to acquire the title to
which she aspired, one that she was able to receive at the clinic to
which she transferred. The author's audacity of distortion sometimes goes beyond the expectable average.

Imagine Freud feeling "threatened" by Dr. Deutsch's remaining at the University Clinic, after he had spent considerable money
on Tausk's medical studies, in order to gain by Tausk's prestige
as a psychiatrist, and had even favored Tausk's permanent tie with
the University by way of a Lectureship (Dozentur) in psychiatry!
There seems to be no limit here to the preposterous. And from
where does Roazen obtain his insight into Freud's most intimate
emotions? He really writes as if he had been a daily guest at
Freud's table, or an intimate friend, to whom Freud confided the
secrets of his heart. After all, even those who did have the privilege
of such closeness cannot possibly have known when Freud felt
threatened or flattered (another emotion the author assigns to
Freud "free for the making"), and yet many an experienced reviewer of Roazen's book has accepted its author's biased free associations as if they were indeed documented facts.

One wonders whether it is called for even to mention, not
to speak of discussing, such a statement as: "Little of what Freud
did to Tausk was deliberate sadism; there was no special pleasure
in his cruelty to Tausk" (p. 148). After all, when a historian writes
in such a vein, which amounts essentially to defamation by negation, he is feigning objectivity, almost as if it were he who was

---

[1] For other absurdities contained in Roazen's book and not enumerated here,
see the review in the (London) Times Literary Supplement of August 7, 1970.

defending Freud against a detractor. Does such a statement perhaps have the intention of making the reader forget that it was the author himself who accused Freud of the very misdeeds of which he now speaks so moderately, with the purpose of securing the reader's assent to his picture of Freud's culpability? Was it not Roazen who earlier called the therapeutic setup Freud had recommended for Tausk a "devilish arrangement," designed for the purpose of "triumphing" over him (p. 103)? It is difficult to see how such a thing could be done without "deliberate sadism" and "pleasure in cruelty." Roazen even openly accuses Freud of "disregard for human life" (p. 159), and finally speaks of Tausk's "destruction at Freud's hands" (p. 158).

He enumerates all the things that Freud had done for Tausk, but then adds: "Freud did this more for the cause than for the man" (p. 158), as if this were a reproach. For what other reason should Freud and his colleagues have spent their hard-earned money on Tausk's medical education? "When Tausk began to infuriate him [Freud], he simply brushed Tausk aside" (p. 158), the author continues. We know that it was not "simply," and that it did not consist of brushing Tausk aside. It was a matter of Freud's disqualifying himself on good grounds as a suitable analyst, which the author denies with stubborn consistency, although he himself acknowledges why it would not have been advisable for Freud to take the first generation of his followers into psychoanalysis. That "Freud as their analyst would only complicate already hyper-involved ties" (p. 65) he seemed to have known very well, when he conjectured why Tausk had opposed obligatory didactic analysis at the Budapest Congress, shortly before asking for an analysis himself.

How strongly the author is identified with Tausk's aggression against authority can be seen from Roazen's insistence that Freud deliberately refused to comprehend Tausk's original ideas. This reproach is based on nothing more than a sentence Freud wrote Lou Andreas-Salomé (January 31, 1915), saying that Tausk's "constructions [on narcissism] were entirely incomprehensible to me" (Pfeiffer 1966, p. 30), as if it were impossible for Tausk ever to have expressed himself in a way that was difficult to understand! On other occasions, Freud was ready to acknowledge Tausk's merits. Yet the author writes gratuitously (p. 62): "Freud *had* to admire Tausk's work" (emphasis added), as if he knew that, in order to do so, Freud had to overcome an inner resistance.

Dr. Robert Jokl told Roazen that "Freud had spoken well of Tausk's most recent work on schizophrenia" (p. 70). The author was here in a dilemma: having declared Freud's criticism of Tausk to have been unjustified and born out of Freud's antagonism, then he had to record Freud's positive remarks—in an area of "rivalry," to boot, since Freud was also working on the subject of psychosis at that time. Well, the author did not remain nonplussed for long; he had no need to, since he was ever ready to produce a piece of legerdemain. In order to get over that hurdle, he wrote: "Freud may have harbored old jealousies because of Lou, but the erotic tie between Tausk and Lou had been over for five years now" (p. 70).

Here we are once again in the midst of one of those breathtaking absurdities. The author almost writes as if the fact that at that time Freud approved of a theory of Tausk's proves that he had been jealous of Tausk's liaison before. Furthermore, it should not be forgotten that the author had claimed that Freud had sent Tausk to Helene Deutsch at that very time, precisely because of his old jealousy and revengefulness. Even Roazen seems to have harbored, this time, some doubts about his absurd construction, and he therefore quickly adds a no less absurd one (p. 70): "To the external world Tausk at this point had nothing, and he came back from the war needing help," thus implying, I would guess, that Freud could talk well of a "threatening rival" only when the latter was prostrate.

Enough. If I have not convinced the reader by now that the author's book is a biased and malicious attack against Freud, I never shall—even if I should pile on more examples. However, an interesting point is raised when Roazen comments (p. 112) that "Contact with Freud meant more to each of his pupils than to Freud himself." At first reading, one might agree with this statement; one would then be thinking of the famous teacher surrounded by his pupils, he being irreplaceable to them, but none of them meaning that much to the teacher.

Yet it is highly questionable whether this image reflects the truth about Freud. After all, there is evidence that Freud was ready to surrender the leadership of the international organization to Jung, and that of the Viennese group to Adler. Only under the strong pressure of the Viennese membership did he finally make a compromise in the latter case, and allow himself to become "scientific chairman" (*Minutes* 2, p. 470). To his disappointment, however, Jung and Adler did not fulfill the functions that had been entrusted to them, and he had to devote himself once again to tasks that he would gladly have left to others.

This problem existed not only with regard to administrative functions, but also with regard to matters of science. There is evidence that Freud had hoped that Jung would carry out the necessary research on psychiatric disorders, just as he had also expressed the hope that Tausk would use his particular interests and knowledge for the psychoanalytic examination of philosphical problems. It is evident that Freud was well aware of what still had to be done for the growth of the new psychology, which was far more important to Freud than any narcissistic gratification.[2]

It is by no means certain for how many psychoanalysts this would have been true at that time. Indeed, it is reasonable to ask how many analysts there have been at all, for whom the welfare and growth of psychoanalysis has been more important than their narcissistic gratification, in terms of prestige, success, and personal advancement. When this absolute subordination of Freud's own narcissistic advantage to an objective frame of values is taken into account, it is questionable whether contact with his pupils did mean less to Freud than it did to them. It is more than likely that, whenever he met a talented and promising analyst, the hope arose in him that this would be the man who would solve the riddles of the mind more effectively than himself—Freud being, most often, dissatisfied with his own achievements. Of Abraham, he wrote: "I have no substitute for him" (Abraham and Freud 1965, p. 400); and there were a number of analysts about whom he might have said the same thing. About one discovery of his own, on the other hand, he wrote (Freud 1960, p. 361) that "one

---

[2] How far he was ready to step into the background can be observed from his apparently having agreed with Ferenczi, when the latter put forward, at the second Congress in Nuremberg (1910), "the necessity for all papers written or addresses delivered by any psychoanalyst to be first submitted for approval to the President of the Association" (Jones 2, p. 69)—for which office Jung was destined. If this motion had been accepted, Freud's own position in the International Association would have been reduced to a secondary one.

ought almost to be ashamed [of it], for one should have divined
these connections from the beginning and not after 30 years."

Yet, if we put to one side the author's errors in detail, the fact
still remains that his inquiry is based on a principal misunderstanding that deserves to be set straight. The meaning and function
of friendship in Freud's life cannot be studied in his relationship
to his pupils. When the author writes reproachfully that "he
[Tausk] was never 'Victor' for Freud" (p. 128), he not only betrays his ignorance of and insensitivity to the customs of Tausk's
cultural milieu, but also gives voice to a misjudgment about
Freud's relationship to his followers. Freud, of course, never called
any of his pupils by their first names, and one may say, in general,
that none of them was his friend. I am not prepared to give
a definition of friendship, but one has to differentiate between
friendly feelings and friendship. He had very friendly feelings toward Rank, Abraham and Ferenczi, but I am certain that they
were never friends of his, as were Oskar Rie (1863–1931) and
Leopold Königstein (1850–1924).

In life, the give and take in relationships is not always mutual.
A person may be mainly giving to one person, and receive nothing
but thanks in return; in another relationship, the same person may
be mainly the recipient and be giving hardly anything. Yet, friendship, I believe, presupposes a fair balance between giving and receiving. We may say that a father is his son's friend, and in some
rare instances this may be true; yet while the general pattern of a
father-son relationship ought to be friendly, it will not be friendship in the narrower sense of the word. In the mythological sym-
bolizations of friendship, such as the Dioscuri, what I have in
mind is brought out with clarity; in that instance, the two are even
physically hardly different.

In view of the difference in age and disproportion between
giving and receiving, it is not probable that true friendship could
have developed between the man who had single-handedly given
birth to what had become "the breath of life" of the younger
ones, and those who were producing accretions to the treasure he
had made available to them. Nevertheless, from 1910 on, Freud
addressed Abraham in letters as *Lieber Freund*; Eitingon and
Ferenczi, too, acquired this form of address; the latter was occasionally called *Mein lieber Sohn*; Pfister always remained *Lieber*

Herr Doktor, but none of them would have dared to start his letter in an equivalent endearing manner. The one-sidedness of the form of address, its irreversibility, the fact that it never led to the use of the first name and the familiar *Du*—all this shows that in every instance a line of separation remained that was not compatible with friendship in the narrower sense of the word.[3] It is probably quite characteristic that the first name was used by Freud in his letters to Lou Andreas-Salomé and Marie Bonaparte. There we read, *Meine liebe Lou, Liebste Lou, Meine liebe Marie.*

The relationship of the younger man to the older, however—of the ambitious pupil to the accomplished teacher—harbored, even under optimal conditions, material for conflict, misunderstanding and disappointment. Freud felt most affectionate toward Ferenczi, and favored him wherever he could; nevertheless, even Ferenczi felt at times disappointed in this regard. How tactfully and how frankly Freud handled the complications brought about by the excessive demands of a younger collaborator can be learned from a letter (Jones 2, p. 83f.) that he wrote in 1910, after the return from Italy, whither he had gone in the company of Ferenczi. It contains a demonstration of Freud's superiority as a human being, and flies in the face of such superficialities as the assertion that "we increasingly know that Freud was dominating, captivating, peremptory, difficult at best" (Grinker Jr. 1970, p. 189). How uncalled for such a remark is, as well as many others that are critical of Freud's ability to maintain friendships can be learned from Binswanger's book of reminiscences. Within the professional setting, a friendship was formed with a man 25 years younger, with the older man placing high hopes in the younger one as someone who would follow and further psychoanalysis. As it was, the younger man's philosophical bent took him far away from psychoanalysis; yet no shadow was ever cast as a result on the relationship between the two. In one letter, Freud revealed what had made this possible: "Quite unlike so many others, you have

---

[3] Yet a letter that Freud (1960, p. 385) wrote to Ernest Jones on his fiftieth birthday may contain statements that challenge the accuracy of my reconstruction: ". . . the assurance that I always looked upon you as a member of my intimate family circle . . . which points . . . towards a fount of affection from which one can always draw again. . . . It is not in my nature to give expression to my feelings of affection, with the result that I often appear indifferent, but my family knows better."

not permitted your intellectual development, which has increasingly withdrawn you from my influence, to wreck our personal relations, and you have no idea how much comfort a man derives from such sensibility [*Feinheit*]" (translation by Mr. Collins; cf. Binswanger 1956, p. 85). A few months earlier Freud had written Binswanger: "Certainly I have had many fine things in my life; as a whole it was difficult, and I was eager to like others as I like you,[4] for instance, but many people made it impossible for me" (Binswanger 1956, p. 85).

Here Freud is unmistakably expressing himself in favor of friendship, and putting far less weight on the question of scientific agreement. Later research will have to decide whether Freud's relationship to Binswanger brought forth what might have been possible with many others, but could not become manifest in their cases because of the rudeness of those others—or was it an accidental occurrence, rooted solely in coincidences or exceptional qualities of Binswanger's character?[5]

My comments are, of course, quite superficial;[6] they serve only to indicate how complex is the problem of friendship in Freud's life. His relationship to Fliess was certainly essentially different from his relationship to Breuer or Jung or Oskar Rie. It would be quite impossible to place them over a common denominator.

Jones (2, p. 155) observed that the letters Freud wrote to friends and collaborators varied in tone from one to another. Yet one does not receive the impression that the writer of the letter is consciously trying to keep his communication within the boundaries that have been set by an external situation—as is necessary in a professional letter to a patient. The vast majority of Freud's published letters convey instead the impression of being saturated with his personality—even a letter as professional as the one written for the purpose of consoling the mother of a homosexual

---

[4] The German *lieb haben*, which Freud used on that occasion, is stronger than the English "to like."

[5] I shall later take up Freud's reaction to Alfred Adler's death, which has been held against him by many. I want to say here only that neither Adler nor any one of those who left the Society with him, for that matter, was anywhere as close to Freud as was Jung, Abraham, Rank or Binswanger.

[6] A more accurate and deepgoing analysis of Freud's friendships is found in Jones 2, pp. 154f., 419f.

son (Freud 1960, p. 423).[7] Furthermore, they testify to an instantaneous empathy with the person addressed, a rare delicacy of feeling. "Grace" might be the proper term, yet here one means it as entailing no loss of self-expression. This is true, of course, only of those letters that Freud wrote to people he liked. When Freud rejected a person, he could be terribly terse (cf. the letter to Silberer [Roazen, p. 157]).

Yet how does all that fit into Freud's relationship to Tausk? If one gives some consideration to the total picture, it is not only not puzzling, but not even a question at all. The initial reception was in the form of a full affirmation, in accordance with the usage prevalent at that time, when the selection of analysts was not yet subject to the stringency of rules: any talented person who was eager to join was welcome and could count on full support by Freud and his group. Unfortunately, the year of Freud's rejection of Bárány is not known; it may well have been one consequence of his experiences with Tausk. He may have become more selective after he learned that talent and eagerness alone are not sufficient to make a person an asset to the movement.

With Tausk the situation was essentially different from what it had been with Adler and Jung. Freud was surprised by their withdrawal, since it was unexpected; but on second thought the resurgence of their resistance, their desire to act out independence did make some sense and it did not, in the long run, cause any harm. After a short-lasting, even if excited, discussion everything feel into the old pattern, and the accustomed research continued undisturbed.

If Tausk had done the same thing and like them, withdrawn from the Society, there would have been no problem. But instead Tausk stayed on, affirming his agreement with psychoanalytic tenets, and with excessive ambivalence wooing for Freud's favor. Yet it seems that he hardly kept—as most others did—that min-

---

[7] The publication of Freud's total correspondence in chronological sequence will be a bounty for psychological research (the loss of his correspondence with his half-brother Emanuel and his sister-in-law, Minna Bernays, is grievous). There must be a large number of routine letters from which, too, probably much can be learned, although the letters that have been published sound as if there was, in Freud's life, no area one could truthfully characterize as "routine."

imum of distance that was necessary for a predominantly working relationship. He also acted out forcefully the hostile side of his relationship toward Freud and his colleagues, thus causing greater annoyance to the group, and threatening it more, perhaps, than any outsider would have been able to do.

Of course, ambivalence is imprinted on every human relationship, and not least that of a talented younger man to an older, more talented one. One may rest assured that, among all of Freud's collaborators and pupils, the mark of ambivalence would become visible, if we but knew their dreams. But, viewed socially, there still remains a gulf between a hostile wish or an impulse that is limited to the role of dream instigator, and one that enforces action.

Ambivalence was also present, in turn, in Freud's attitude toward the younger ones. Quite rightly, the author evokes an incident when Freud made a slip of the tongue that may have betrayed an unfriendly attitude toward Tausk. Lou Andreas-Salomé interpreted it immediately (*Journal*, p. 88) in that sense. Wittels (1933, p. 363) later regretted that he had used parapraxes and dreams that Freud had published, not as clues to unconscious processes, but rather as indices of character. And once the hostile purport of this error became clear to him, he had to admit: "If . . . a polemic purpose enters into the undertaking, precious little of scientific glory is left."

The insoluble difficulty with Tausk was that his ambivalence was not limited to parapraxes and dreams. Lou Andreas-Salomé spotted this too during her stay in Vienna, and she records that Tausk "rudely jostled" Ferenczi during a discussion.[8] Freud knew of the ambivalence that existed among his followers. Lou Andreas-Salomé (*Journal*, p. 98) reports Freud's remark: "Rank disposes of the negative aspect of his filial love by means of this interest in the psychology of regicide; that is why he is so devoted." Freud may have been right or wrong, but it did not in the least disturb his liking of Rank.

---

[8] How aggressive Tausk must have been can be seen from the very term Lou Andreas-Salomé used (German edition, p. 73): "*Ferenczi, den Tausk unnütz in der Diskussion anrempelt . . .*" ("anrempelt"—much stronger than "picking a quarrel" as translated [*Journal*, p. 78]—is vernacular for jostling someone with particular force and rudeness.

But what can be expected when a pupil—however talented he may be—loses control over his ambivalence and, without weakening his demands to be accepted as favorite, becomes openly aggressive and paranoid, at the same time continuing to offer assurances of his admiration? What is more, he starts acting out his ambivalence even professionally, as is claimed in Paul Federn's letter—that is to say, arouses far more pain than pleasure. There was nothing saintly in Freud. I even think that nothing would have been further from his mind than to evolve a cloak of saintliness. To have forgiven consistently Tausk's grave misdemeanors and annoying behavior would have been to be saintly—particularly after it had become clear that this was not a matter of a temporary crisis, but of permanent attitudes toward the members of the group and its leader. Under such conditions, I would assume, one attempts to reduce one's contact to the possible minimum and to fulfill only those obligations that are enforced by duty.

Tausk had made himself unlovable; no one in his professional group was apparently any longer "fond" of him. When such a person dies, one who has been for years the source of annoyance and pain, one feels regret and pity—but *mourning?*

Yet Roazen was in error not only with regard to the relationship that existed between Freud and his collaborators—in particular, Tausk—but also with regard to Freud's relationship to psychiatry.

The first point that is not clear from Roazen's book is whether or not he was cognizant of the fact that Freud was no psychiatrist and never did consider himself to be a psychiatrist.

I was amazed when I first discovered, in a brief by Wagner-Jauregg dated 1899, the statement that "Dr. Freud . . . has never occupied himself thoroughly in practice with psychiatry" [9] (Gicklhorn and Gicklhorn 1960, p. 30) and would therefore not be eligible to serve as acting chairman of the psychiatric-neurological department, in case of need. I took it as an open sign of hostility that Wagner-Jauregg was declaring the author of *Studies in Hysteria* to be unfit to function as acting chief—until Heinz Hartmann corrected my error.

---

[9] Dr. Freud . . . hat sich nie praktisch mit Psychiatrie eingehender beschäftigt."

Wagner-Jauregg was, of course, right. Freud did not fulfill the requirements that had been established for holding such a position. His University appointment was in neuropathology, which at that time covered the field of neurology—and in practice, aside from patients who suffered from neurological disorders, only the neuroses—whereas the practice of psychiatry, as can be proven by a study of contemporary textbooks, included the treatment and research of the psychoses, but did not include those of the neuroses (Eissler 1966). The neuroses were regarded as being functional disturbances of the nervous system, and therefore apparently the legitimate area of the neuropathologist, whereas the psychoses were apparently held to be types of disorder that required a training quite different from that of the neuropathologist.

How little this is understood can be seen from Sherwood (1962); in all seriousness, he criticizes Freud for having occupied himself with the neuroses, although his Paris travelling stipend permitted him only the study of neuropathology. If he had read Freud's *Interpretation of Dreams*, he would have found, right at the beginning of the Preface to the first edition, a sentence that clarifies the situation (Freud 1900, p. xxiii): "I have attempted in this volume to give an account of the interpretation of dreams and in doing so I have not, I believe, trespassed beyond the sphere of interest covered by neuropathology." Yet the reader will exclaim, "The man who had an effect on psychiatry such as no other man ever had was not himself a psychiatrist?" It would not be the first time in the history of science that an expert has a tremendous effect upon a field in which he is no expert at all.

Anton van Leeuwenhoek (1632–1723), by profession a manufacturer of microscopes, made discoveries of such basic importance to medicine that one might well say they have never been matched by any expert in the field. There is hardly anyone else to whom modern therapy owes as much as to Louis Pasteur (1822–1895), yet he never graduated from a medical school. In the light of such examples, it is not as surprising as it may sound at first to hear that Freud was not a psychiatrist but a neuropathologist—someone who was supposed to know everything about neurology and such diseases as hysteria, neurasthenia and their like. Consequently, it is an error when Roazen asserts that (p. 74) "Freud looked on official psychiatry as his enemy."

If only those who arrogate to themselves the right to pass judgment on Freud would first read his writings! Did not Freud write (1916–1917, p. 254f.), after showing that psychiatry and psychoanalysis are "one supplementing the other": "What is opposed to psychoanalysis is not psychiatry, but psychiatrists. Psychoanalysis is related to psychiatry approximately as histology is to anatomy"? Now how could a histologist ever look at anatomy as an enemy? Furthermore, the reader must be reminded that, contrary to contemporary teaching in the United States, anatomy was considered by the Vienna Medical School as the "principal" subject of instruction. Once a student had passed his examination in anatomy, he could feel practically certain that he would graduate. Histology, by contrast, held a subordinate place in the curriculum. Freud's comparison therefore proves the high esteem in which he held psychiatry, and with what sense of balance he thought about psychoanalysis in its relation to the former.

I am reasonably certain that he would never have approved of the present custom in this country's teaching of psychiatry, with its negligence—indeed in many instances omission—of what is called "classical" psychiatry, and with its immediate start on so-called dynamic psychiatry. And Freud would not have opposed this custom simply on the grounds that dynamic psychiatry is a debasement of psychoanalysis (cf. Gitelson 1956), but because, in his judgment, classical psychiatry was the foundation—the anatomy, so to speak—upon which alone the medical man could build his "histology" of the mind that was deranged by psychoses.

How misguided Roazen really is whenever it becomes a question of Freud's relationship to psychiatry can be observed when he commits the howler of writing (p. 180) that Freud "even maintained that 'the analytic study of the psychoses is impracticable, owing to its lack of therapeutic results.'" These words are, indeed, to be found in Freud's An Autobiographical Study (1925b, p. 60); but Roazen makes the mistake here, incredible as it may sound, of attributing to Freud as a negative statement what Freud had clearly said in a positive form. That is to say, he ignored the fact that the portion he quoted is preceded by "It would seem, however" and that what Freud proved in the subsequent sentences was that what would seem to be so is not confirmed by the facts. His train of thought culminates in the expression of his conviction (1925b, p. 60) "that so many things that in the neuroses have to be laboriously fetched up from the depths are found in the psychoses on the surface, visible to the eye. . . . It was thus bound to happen before long that analysis would find its way to the objects of psychiatric observation."

Why did Roazen try to convince the reader that Freud's belief was the very opposite of the one that he actually held? [10] Freud's works abound in statements that underscore the great hope he placed in psychoanalytic investigation of the psychoses. Indeed, he strongly recommended that such an investigation be undertaken. As early as 1914 (b, p. 82), Freud wrote: "Just as the transference neuroses have enabled us to trace the libidinal instinctual impulses, so dementia praecox and paranoia will give us an insight into the psychology of the ego." What does Roazen know that could have induced Freud to change his mind in this respect?

In his Introductory Lectures (1916–1917, p. 422f.), he even played down the significance of his own discoveries and predicted that "it is likely that we shall have a low opinion of our present knowledge of the vicissitudes of the libido, which we have gained from a study of the transference neuroses," when psychoanalysis will have achieved "the analysis of disturbances and disruptions of the ego" encountered in the psychoses. Regretfully, he noted (1916–1917, p. 423): "We psychoanalysts see too few psychiatric cases." Approvingly and hopefully, he informed his Viennese audience of the start that was "being made in America, where

---

[10] In being thus surprised by Roazen's ignorance, I am perhaps doing him an injustice. Charles Rycroft, whose name can be traced in the membership list of the British Psychoanalytic Society for at least 20 years, and who is responsible for the psychoanalytic education of the readers of The Observer, published (April 26, 1970) a review of Roazen's book under the sensational title of "Freudian Triangles." Since Rycroft takes exception in his review to nothing but two of Roazen's interpretations, and to the fact that Roazen accepts "uncritically the Freudian view of man," I must conclude that Freud was in error when he recommended only that psychoanalysts should go on with their own analysis every five years, without adding that they should also take reading courses in his works at least once every decade. Roy R. Grinker, Jr. (1970, p. 190)—who, by the way, has recommended in print that Roazen's book be read by all students of psychiatry—has only this to say about Roazen's quotations: "A number of quotations from Freud are used out of context, significantly altering their meaning" (emphasis added).

very many leading psychiatrists lecture to students on the theories of psycho-analysis, etc." (*ibid.*)

Roazen even goes so far as to write (p. 188): "The study of ego psychology began under Tausk and Federn with the treatment of psychotic disorders." One sentence from Freud's earliest paper, which contained a section devoted to psychiatric disorders, will suffice to prove the erroneousness of this claim. Freud wrote (1894, p. 59): "One is . . . justified in saying that the ego has fended off the incompatible idea through a flight into psychosis. . . . The ego breaks away from the incompatible idea, but the latter is inseparably connected with a piece of reality, so that, in so far as the ego achieves this result, it, too, has detached itself wholly or in part from reality." And shortly thereafter Freud was already operating with a concept that later, when ego-psychology came fully into its own, would take a central place—namely, the *alteration of the ego* (Freud 1896, p. 183), which the ego may sometimes suffer under the impact of a psychosis. I could quote many such passages to demonstrate Freud's early thrusts into ego psychology. One quite remarkable such attempt is to be found in a posthumously published manuscript of 1895 (Freud 1950b, pp. 322–324). Furthermore, in Freud's *Introductory Lectures* (1916–1917) it becomes visible what great strides Freud had made into ego-psychology since his early years. The important concept of the "tendency to conflict (that) is as much dependent on the development of the ego as on that of the libido" can be found in the XXII Lecture (p. 352) and the reader will encounter many a statement about the structure of the ego throughout the text (e.g., pp. 427–429). When one further reads in Freud's *Introductory Lectures* (p. 351): ". . . only the study of the narcissistic neuroses[11] . . . promises to give us an insight into the structure of the ego," then one recognizes the full extent of Roazen's error. There can be no doubt that Freud had early acknowledged the decisive importance of the psychoanalytic investigation of the psychoses, from which he expected to gain insight into the structure of the ego, as he was unable to do to his satisfaction through the analysis of the neuroses.

---

[11] This was the term used by Freud for those disorders among which schizophrenia belonged (see Freud 1916–1917, p. 420).

Yet all this does not give the full history of Freud's researches within ego psychology. Much as one can learn about Freud's early research in the field of ego psychology from his published works, they still contain only his global approach—extensive as it was. The depth of that preoccupation and its subtlety will be recognized only after all his private papers have been published. There are a few small-sized booklets in Hampstead, which Freud used as a kind of diary between 1903 and 1910, with each page carrying one or two short notations. Under the date of December 29, 1909, Freud wrote: "Inhibition = inner resistance without symptom formation. Model: inhibition in dream." [*Hemmung = inner Widerstände ohne Symptombildung. Vorbild: Traumhemmung.*] And under the date of January 29, 1910: "(The) basis for repression is always the excess of libidinal excitation that is anxiety of the ego" [*Grund der Verdrängung ist immer das Übermass der Libidoerregung d.h. Angst des Ich.*]

These terse entries indicate that, already in 1910, Freud was actively engaged in observations and theory formation that were to become the center of one of his finest elaborations on ego psychology (1926). In order to become cognizant of how far ahead Freud was in the area of ego psychology, however, one does not need those diary entries; one has only to compare Freud's paper (1911b) with what Tausk had to say about the ego in his lecture of 1912 (see Chapter VIII).

Roazen's errors are always tendentious. In this instance, he needs a Freud who is averse to any analytic involvement with the psychoses, so that he will be able to demonstrate Tausk's superiority over Freud, in view of Tausk's (1919) paper (which does hold an important place in the history of psychoanalysis) on a specific schizophrenic delusion. If he had informed the reader, however, that Tausk was carrying out what Freud had set up as a program, so to speak, for future psychoanalytic research (a program parts of which he himself had fulfilled), he would have had to fear lest that fact reduce Tausk's greatness in the reader's eyes.

The same tendency to arrogate for Tausk a greater place than was due him in the history of psychoanalysis becomes apparent when Roazen writes (p. xix) that Tausk "was the first member of the Vienna Psychoanalytic Society to study the psychoses clinically." In order to indicate the extent of Roazen's error, I need but add to the brief account of Freud's early involvement with the psychoses which I have given. In a lengthy discussion remark, following a paper "On the Megalomania of the Normal Person," Freud related "the extremely instructive case of an exquisite *paranoia*" (*Minutes* 1, pp. 57–59); author's emphasis). This took place in November, 1906, i.e., three years before Tausk joined the group. Since Freud's remarks cover two-and-a-half printed pages, they must have been the result of a prolonged period of investigation. During the same meeting, Adler gave a report on "three cases of paranoia which he had occasion to observe" (*Minutes* 1, p. 59f.); and Reitler mentioned "the case of a paranoid woman," whom he evidently had treated. Two years later, Adler presented extensive observations on paranoia (*Minutes* 1, pp. 288–297), and in the same year Stekel reported to the Society on two cases of psychosis. These were published in the 24th chapter of his book (Stekel 1908). To conclude this brief survey, I should like to add only Wittels' case presentation of a man suffering from a delusion; and Hitschmann's paper of 1908 partly devoted to paranoia.[12] I am rather certain that a careful scanning of the literature would reveal some more instances. How could it have been otherwise? Following the publication of Jung's book, *The Psychology of Dementia Praecox* of 1907, the psychoanalytic investigation of the psychoses had become popular. Already in the second volume of the *Jahrbuch für psychoanalytische Forschungen* of 1910, the review articles contain thirteen references to psychoanalytic papers on psychoses. Any member of the Viennese group who had the opportunity Tausk enjoyed at the University Clinics, where schizophrenia and melancholia abounded, would surely have made the psychoanalytic investigation of the psychoses his concern. Since the other members were not affiliated with a psychiatric hospital, however, they had to depend on the accidental opportunities of private practice. If Roazen

---

[12] Roy M. Whitman, a member of the American Psychoanalytic Association and active in a university Department of Psychiatry, repeats in a review of Roazen's book (1970, p. 386) that Tausk "had been the first member of the Vienna Psychoanalytic Society to study the psychoses clinically." Whitman leaves all of Roazen's errors uncorrected; he also adds one more of his own when he says that Tausk was "treated coolly by the analytic group."

had written that Tausk was the first one of Freud's Viennese colleagues to publish a major, so to speak, systematized paper on a
schizophrenic delusion, this would have been a correct description,
even though of little historical significance, since the same thing
had been done by Freud (1911a), before.

In his effort to "build up" Tausk—if Roazen had kept to the
historical truth, he would have had enough "good" things to report about Tausk's scientific history—he presents Tausk as a
therapist superior to Freud. Thus he writes: "Tausk was far more
willing than Freud to approach psychotics and to learn from them.
As a therapist he was less austere, more accepting of human
weakness, more able to identify with a patient and care for him.
. . . Tausk represented a broadening of therapeutic interests for
psychoanalysis. . . . Tausk wanted to extend the area of psycho-
therapeutic treatment" (pp. 185–187). All this is pure fantasy on
Roazen's part, so that the reader may be surprised to learn that
not one line was ever written by Tausk about the treatment of
psychotics or neurotics, and that there is no evidence whatsoever
that he ever had a schizophrenic patient in analysis.[13]

One finds it hard to understand how it was possible for Roazen
to have misinformed the reader so extensively about Tausk's endeavors with regard to the therapy of psychotic patients. Freud's
writings are, to be sure, voluminous enough to make it difficult
for one person to be able to keep before him the total output of his
psychological writings; and this may explain Roazen's ignoring
Freud's early writings, in which he reports psychoanalyses of
patients whose illness belongs in the group of schizophrenias.

Tausk's oeuvre, however, is a relatively small one. There are, all
in all, only eighteen papers by him in the psychoanalytic litera-

---

[13] When Roazen writes (p. 188): "The analytic method, Tausk thought,
needed to be changed to make these [psychotic] patients accessible to treatment,"
it sounds as if he is referring to something Tausk had published. When I was
unable to find what I was looking for in Tausk's works, I inquired of others; but
no one—not even an analyst who had known Tausk personally—could tell me
anything about a suggestion by Tausk to adapt the analytic technique to the
psychoses. It finally dawned on me that perhaps Roazen had mistaken something
Freud wrote as having been written by Tausk, for Freud did say (1916–1917, p.
423): "The narcissistic neuroses can scarcely be attacked with the technique that
has served us with the transference neuroses. . . . *Our technical methods must
accordingly be replaced by others*, and we do not know yet whether we shall
succeed in finding a substitute" (emphasis added).

ture, and together they add up to fewer than 170 printed pages. This relative smallness of output should have made it rather easy to keep all the relevant data in mind. Moreover, of these eighteen papers, only three deal with psychoses, as a study of the titles will show; and of these three, one is concerned with a toxic psychosis (Tausk 1915), one with war psychoses (1961b), and one (1919) with schizophrenia.

The last one is based mainly on the observations Tausk (1919, p. 529) made on a thirty-one-year-old patient, Miss Natalya A., who had "been completely deaf for a great number of years . . . and can make herself understood only by means of writing." Tausk was able to examine her only twice. "On her third visit, she became inaccessible and only stated that the analyst, too, was under the influence of the apparatus" (ibid., p. 531). It is plain—how could Roazen overlook this?—that Tausk's famous paper on the schizophrenic delusion of the influencing machine was not based on clinical experiences gained during the course of a psychoanalysis, but on an amazingly small number of interviews, which did not go beyond the scope of psychiatric interviews and were totally divorced from any therapeutic attempt.

Moreover, there are reasons why it is unlikely that Tausk was involved at this point in therapeutic deliberations, since his main interest was in establishing the correct point of fixation in libidinal development. He suggested, on theoretical (by no means clinical) grounds, that the delusional system of his patient "may be regarded as a defense against a libido position corresponding to the end of foetal existence and the beginning of extrauterine development" (Tausk 1919, p. 545), and certainly at that time such early fixations were considered to be inaccessible to therapeutic intervention. Moreover, any psychiatrically-oriented analyst who was at all interested in therapy would surely have published the history of a patient whom he had had the opportunity to observe over a long period of time. In neither of the two papers in which Tausk does take up problems of melancholia, schizophrenia and paranoia is anything said that suggests long-term contact with a patient. All his comments are limited to chance observations and to theoretical deductions from Freud's theories about the psychoses.

There is evidence, however, that Freud over and over again tried to find a way of dealing therapeutically with patients whose illnesses belonged to the group of schizophrenias. Right at the beginning of his career as a psychotherapist, Freud tried to apply his method to patients who were suffering from grave mental disorders, as his early writings (1894, 1896) testify. In his *Introductory Lectures*, he refers to experiences he gained from patients who suffered from delusions and were undoubtedly schizophrenics. It is not clear how extensive Freud's contacts were with those patients, but it is worthwhile to refer to a passage in Freud's autobiographical study, in which he acknowledges—apparently with pride and pleasure—that "the contributions of my pupils and collaborators have been growing more and more in importance" (1925b, p. 55). Therefore, he limited himself to "mentioning here [only] those new discoveries in which I still played a prominent part," one of which was "the application of psycho-analysis to the psychoses." Freud cannot possibly have had in mind only theoretical inquiries, since already in 1914 (a, p. 29), in demarcating his own contribution to the understanding of psychoses from that of Jung, he writes: "As early as in 1897 [actually it was 1896], I had published the analysis of a case of schizophrenia." I shall not enumerate here all the published instances that were ignored by Roazen, yet which prove him to have been in error when he wrote (p. 180) that Freud "steered clear of psychotics whenever he could." [14] Instead, I shall add one unpublished instance from my own experience.

In the late twenties, when Paul Federn had already evolved his own technique for treating schizophrenics, a classmate of mine, who evidently was a schizophrenic, was treated by Freud. I met

---

[14] Roazen likes to quote Wittels. Unfortunately for him, he regularly selects passages that Wittels later recanted. The following, I am certain, Wittels would never have recanted; to my knowledge, he never did—at least in writing. It would have been excellently suited to illuminate Freud's relationship to the treatment of psychotics: "I had the opportunity of seeing Freud for almost a year directly at work, for he treated a case of juvenile *dementia* [hebephrenia] in my presence for many months. The blunted sensibilities [*Stumpfsinn*] of the [female] patient made this possible. However, the patient's apathetic dullness also deprived me of the fruits of this enviable cooperation. Not much came out of it. My profit was only Freud's deep gaze, with which he looked at the imbecile creature, as if he had to turn this blind soul around and make it see" (my own translation; Wittels 1923, p. 122, German edition).

the patient's father later during the course of my work for The Archives, and learned that the patient had been committed to a hospital. The instance is of interest insofar as it shows that Freud accepted schizophrenics for treatment not only in his early years, when youthful enthusiasm may make the therapeutic difficulty appear to be smaller than it is in clinical reality; as an old man, even when he could have sent a patient to a colleague who specialized in the treatment of schizophrenics, he tried working with schizophrenics—despite some well-justified pessimism—if the conditions seemed to be favorable for the employment of his treatment technique.

At one point, Roazen goes so far as to leave the reader with the impression that Freud wrote only "one case history about a psychotic" (p. 181), and he adds, "but he never saw this man." No doubt, he is here referring to Freud's famous case history (1911a) of Daniel Paul Schreber. That publication was a real triumph for Freud, since doubts had previously been expressed about the reliability of the data that Freud reported obtaining from his patients. Here, however, was an independent record (Schreber 1903), written without any possibility of psychoanalytic influence. By means of this unusual document, Freud was able to provide for his theories at that time a far greater probability of acceptance than any reports could have achieved that were based on the secluded interchange between psychoanalyst and analysand.

Roazen's minimizing comment on Freud's paper on Schreber has to be compared, in this context, with his comment on Tausk's paper of 1919 (p. 193): "In this paper Tausk developed the concept of projection in a clinical psychiatric concept." The uninitiated reader would have to draw from this the conclusion that this was in contrast with Freud, who "never saw" his patient. But Roazen has ignored the fact that Freud had already in 1896 had "an opportunity . . . of undertaking the psychoanalysis for therapeutic purposes of an intelligent woman of thirty-two" (p. 175), and had found on that occasion that "in paranoia, the self-reproach is repressed in a manner which may be described as projection" (1896, p. 184, author's emphasis).

In one point Roazen is right. It seems that, to the very end of his life, Freud found himself rendered uneasy by patients who were suffering from grave mental disorders. I believe—and others have noted this, too, as Roazen reports (p. 189)—that it was the impression of uncanniness, weirdness, dismalness,[15] so significant of patients overwhelmed by serious mental disorder, that had this impact on Freud.[16]

Whether this was an idiosyncrasy of Freud's, therefore, or the uncontrollable response that sets in the therapist when man's archaic world appears on the surface without disguise, I shall not try to judge here. But it is testimony to Freud's greatness that, despite his own negative response, he succeeded, as did no one before him, in bringing light into the understanding of these disorders. What is more, he did not give up his therapeutic efforts, even though he had no obligation to persist in them, since he was no "psychiatrist."

I shall not tax the reader's patience any further by discussing Roazen's other errors about Freud's relationship to the psychoses and to psychiatry, but shall now turn to a discussion of what he has to say about one of Tausk's papers, in which the latter wrote about melancholia, and about an omission that Freud, according to Roazen (p. 192), committed in his own paper on that topic, by not citing Tausk's paper.

The reproach itself is untenable and could be raised only if the historical facts were—as in Roazen's book—ignored. Roazen takes cognizance of the fact that Freud wrote the first draft of his paper on melancholia (1917a) in February, 1915 (p. 191), as Jones (2, p. 329) had already reported. Yet Roazen then goes on to write that Freud "did not publish it for two years"; while he acknowledges that the war delayed publications, he then asserts ". . . in this case it was mainly *that Freud wanted to ruminate over his essay*" (emphasis added). But he did not tell us the sources of his knowledge, or his reasons for overruling Jones, who wrote (Jones 2, p. 234) that Freud's final draft was finished on May 4, 1915 and that "*because of the delay in publishing periodi-*

---

[15] The German language has for this the word *Unheimlich*—an emotional response to which Freud devoted an essay (1919c).

[16] In Chapter VII, the reader will find a letter in which Freud discusses this reaction.

cals occasioned by the war it did not appear until two years later" [17] (Jones 2, p. 329; emphasis added).

Freud's paper on melancholia was not the only paper of his whose publication was delayed by the effects of the war. War conditions, of course, played havoc with printers' schedules, and it is not known in what year Tausk's paper, which has the imprint of 1916, reached the reader.[18] Indeed, it is not certain that Freud ever read Tausk's paper, since it was published in the *Wiener Medizinische Wochenschrift*.[19]

Be that as it may, at whatever time Freud read Tausk's article, his own manuscript had long since gone to the publisher. Instead of this—all of which was surely accessible to Roazen—what the reader obtains from him is a false appearance of a Freud "ruminating over his essay" for two years.

Since Freud did not even have the physical opportunity to cite Tausk's paper, we might have dropped the whole matter. Yet Roazen has drawn further conclusions from the way in which *Tausk quoted Freud* in his own paper, as we shall soon see. The clarification of this point is an involved one, not only because of the intricacy of the situation, but also because of the vagueness and ambiguity that one finds in Roazen's assertions in this respect. Nevertheless, I believe that it is worthwhile to go into the following details—if it were only for the interesting facts one discovers when one sets out to verify a statement made by the author.

In order to decide whether Freud ought to have cited Tausk's name in his paper of 1917(a) at all, one has to take cognizance

---

[17] The title page of Freud's paper in the Standard Edition clearly puts 1915 in brackets at the side of 1917, thus informing the reader when the paper was completed.

[18] The fourth volume of the *Internationale Zeitschrift*, for example, has the imprint 1916/17 but it was actually printed in 1918, as the title page shows.

[19] Taking one of his many potshots at analysts in general, Roazen (p. 192) asserts that "consequently [as the result of Freud's failure to quote Tausk] Freud's pupils ignored Tausk's work on melancholia." This could have been written only by someone who knew nothing about Waelder's discussion of Tausk's paper, which was published in 1934. Aside from taking for granted the importance of Tausk's paper, Roazen does not consider the fact that Tausk's paper was published in a journal devoted to general medicine, and at a time, during the years of war, when most analysts unfortunately were at the front.

first of what Tausk's contribution to the problem of melancholia had been.[20]

As reported earlier, Tausk presented to the Vienna Psycho-analytic Society a paper on December 30, 1914, the exact title of which was, "Contributions to a psychoanalytic exposition of melancholia" (*Beiträge zu einer psychoanalytischen Exposition der Melancholie*). It is not quite clear from the title, however, what Tausk really had in mind. It was certainly not simply a paper on melancholia, as Roazen seems to believe (p. 191). The German word *Exposition* is ambiguous; it probably meant here either "introduction" or "outline." Since the *Minutes* of the Society contain only a summary of the paper, they may be misleading; yet the way the matter stands there, it is hardly possible to see what Tausk's original contribution to the problem was on that occasion.

He started with two suggestions that Tausk himself indicated he had obtained from Freud: "mania as substitute for mood, and the concept of the detachment of libido" [*Die Manie als Stimmungsersatz und das Wort von der Libidoablösung*]. He then undertook to deal with the relation between melancholia and mania, which is of no relevance in this context. By reference to two cases, he described the circumstances at the time of onset of melancholia: the anamneses showed the melancholic patients to have been narcissistic; they had a grandiose self-esteem, which took the form, however, of self-contempt; real megalomaniac ideas also occurred; these patients showed a fear of excessive punishments, which betrays links with sadomasochism. Then Tausk took up the relationship of melancholia to dementia praecox and, finally, he discussed anxiety in melancholia, which is limited, he asserted, to fear about the body.

It is noteworthy, to begin with, that Tausk did not cite Abraham (1911), even though Abraham's paper already contained some of the points Tausk brought up;[21] and comparing the *Minutes* with Abraham's paper one must say that—assuming that

---

[20] According to the author, however, Freud had that obligation in any case, because Tausk was "one of the few psychoanalysts then working on the problem" (p. 193). Such a demand, put forward without any further explanation, is really quite astonishing, particularly since Freud's paper was not a review, but mainly devoted to presenting his own findings.

[21] Rank, in his discussion of Tausk's paper, did refer to Abraham.

the abstract in the *Minutes* includes all of Tausk's main points —Abraham did rather better than Tausk. It is not clear from the abstract whether Tausk's paper was based on the actual analysis of melancholic patients, as were both Abraham's earlier paper and Freud's later paper, or was derived from observations at the psychiatric clinic. It is further not possible to know what Freud had in mind when he said that there was something new in Tausk's paper, because he did not expand on that comment, at least according to the *Minutes*. As reported in the *Minutes*, Freud's discussion remark was devoted mainly to an exposition of his own explanation of melancholia. Interestingly enough, during the course of it, Freud mentioned the successful treatment on his part of two patients who had been suffering frm the disease.

Now Tausk took up the topic of melancholia once again in a paper (1916b) that was not a psychoanalytic paper in the strict sense of the word, and for that reason was not published in the *Zeitschrift*. It was devoted to the symptomatology of war psychoses, for whose explanation Freud's discoveries were used.

Tausk's paper consists of two parts. In the first part, he presents his observations on some soldiers in whom, as he saw it, a full-blown melancholia and paranoia existed side by side. It is questionable whether Tausk was right in this. Kraepelin (1913, vol. 3, part 2, p. 1268) had already shown that the symptoms that, as Tausk asserted, formed a paranoia, belong instead to the depressive phase of manic-depressive insanity. Pilcz (1919, p. 7), interestingly enough, thought that such cases occurred during the war with greater frequency than in peacetime, but he, too, was of the opinion that such syndromes belonged to the disease entity of cyclic disorders. Be that as it may, the observation is more a question of classical psychiatry than it is of primary concern for psychoanalysis.

In the second part of the paper, Tausk tried to explain the simultaneous occurrence of melancholia and paranoia in terms of psychoanalytic theory. In looking for Tausk's originality in this paper (*in terms of psychoanalysis*), one could set forth the two following points he made: (1) Physical disease often precipitates melancholia. This Tausk explained by the detachment of libido that takes place, according to Freud, in states of pain and physical disease. (2) In melancholia, it is heterosexual libido that is used up; this is by contrast with paranoia, which constitutes, according to Freud, one of the vicissitudes of homosexual libido. The loss of feeling for nature was brought into connection "with the hetero-sexual libido situation" (1916b, p. 397). One may perhaps find one or another original point besides these in Tausk's paper, but I do not find in these points any connection with the problem of melancholia.

I should like, however, to comment on Tausk's proposition that melancholia is fed, as it were, by heterosexual libido. That hypothesis has never been confirmed by others. It is highly probable that it was the result of construction, based on global impressions, and did not grow out of observations made during the course of the live psychoanalytic process. How could it be otherwise? Tausk, as he himself reported, saw 1,500 cases in seven-and-a-half months under the trying conditions of military service. This was quite different from the situation with those analysts who did study phenomena that were specifically occasioned by military service and by exposure to trauma. In his paper on "Deserters" Tausk did follow that line—which is one of the reasons why that paper is superior to the one under discussion.[22]

Tausk's paper does suffer from a basic defect: it fails altogether to draw on the concept of defense. At the center of his proposi-tions stands the concept of a heterosexual and homosexual libido. It looks as if Tausk was thinking of a qualitative difference. It is more than questionable whether any such differentiation of libido is valid. Freud's theory (1911a) with regard to paranoid psychoses had centered on fixation, repression and the return of the re-

---

[22] The ease with which Tausk drew broad psychoanalytic conclusions, without the necessary previous laborious psychoanalytic research (this is observable even in his paper on "The Influencing Machine"), may have prompted Lou Andreas-Salomé's remark in her letter to Freud about the misgivings she felt with regard to Tausk's insistence on obtaining a university lectureship (Roazen, p. 144). Such a lectureship would have been combined with a permanent position at the clinic. Subsequent developments, particularly in this country, have demonstrated over and over again that psychoanalysts who spend half their working time or more in hospitals tend to lose something of their psychoanalytic sharpness. (This is not meant to belittle the fact that the community may benefit greatly from their dividing their professional activity between the couch and the ward.) By and large, I think Freud's assertion (1933, p. 153), which I have previously quoted, has been confirmed, even though it is strongly objected to by the majority of the profes-sion.

pressed; it had affirmed that the delusion of persecution constituted a defense against an intolerable wish for a homosexual love object. This was quite different from Tausk's train of thought. While Tausk did not overlook the importance of identification, to his way of thinking, it was the libido *per se*—whether it had been used for the cathexis of a heterosexual or a homosexual love-object—that made it susceptible to certain mechanisms or processes rather than others. This way of thinking was essentially non-analytical.[23]

At one point Roazen makes a remark that is quite puzzling. In his paper (1916b), Tausk quotes Freud's publications quite extensively; in addition, in instances of unpublished personal communications, he refers to Freud by name four times. Three times he limits these references to "Freud's verbal remark"; but once he speaks of "a not yet published conjecture of Freud (which I am free to use [*verfüge*] here with [Freud's] specific permission.)" (my own translation; cf. Tausk 1916b, p. 398.) This led Roazen to comment immediately after: "We can understand why Freud had to be cautious with this man." As indicated above, that comment is rather puzzling. One would assume that in this instance as in the others Tausk asked for and received Freud's permission to quote that particular discussion remark, or one part of a conversation that they may have had privately. But I fail to see in what way Tausk's comment at this point in his paper indicates anything about Freud.

Yet the whole matter, quite apart from Roazen's unexplained remark about Freud having "to be cautious" is even more confusing, as the reader will shortly see. The "not yet published conjecture" by Freud had to do, according to Tausk, with the predisposition to melancholia that "should be expected in in-

---

[23] Besides this, Tausk's paper shows another weakness. After all, he had seen a large number of soldiers whose illness had been either caused or precipitated by war experiences. It is noteworthy, therefore, that despite this he did not make any contribution to the problem of trauma. At the Congress in Budapest in 1918, when considerable time was devoted to a discussion of new clinical experiences that analysts who had served as psychiatrists in the Army had had, it may have dawned on him what opportunities for new research he had passed up because of his preoccupation with a syndrome that was long since well known from peace-time observations. This dawning awareness may have contributed to the severe psychopathology from which he was apparently suffering during his stay in Budapest.

dividuals who make their object choice on the narcissistic pattern" (Tausk 1916b, p. 398). Now what inferences is one to draw from this, when one reads in Freud's own article (1917a, p. 249) a statement to the effect that *he* has no title to this discovery; instead, he names Otto Rank (1911) as having asserted "that the object-choice [in these patients] has been effected on a narcissistic basis?"

Is it conceivable that Freud, if he did discuss it with Tausk, would have made it a special point to safeguard his priority with regard to this point, when in print he names Rank as originator? This is altogether improbable. My suggestion would be that in view of Tausk's great jealousy, he was quite unable to tolerate the priority of a brother-rival and that he was therefore willing—with exaggerated emphasis—to ascribe such priority to Freud rather than acknowledge Rank's contribution. Although Rank had called his attention, as mentioned before, to Abraham's paper on melancholia, Tausk still abstained from citing Abraham's name in his final publication.

At this point, it may be advisable to cast a glance at Tausk's idiosyncrasies with regard to quoting—a point that somehow failed to arouse Roazen's interest. In going through Tausk's published papers, one is struck by the almost complete absence of any references to the publications of his colleagues. To be exact, there is only one unambiguous citation (Tausk 1915, p. 426), and this to a paper by Federn.[24] If a psychoanalyst who has spent almost ten years in the midst of the heated and wide-ranging debates for which the early group is well known is able to find in seventeen papers of his own only one single occasion to refer in an unambiguous way to the paper of a colleague, then one can only deduce from that fact an excessive unwillingness to acknowledge that his own research has had precursors or that it owes anything to the stimulation of his peers. He apparently feels somehow diminished by the idea that he could owe anything to them; if at all, he is

---

[24] In his paper of 1919 he cites (p. 551) a paper by Ferenczi, but introduces it by the preamble, "After the completion of this paper, there also appeared . . ." In his review article of the psychoanalytic literature (Tausk 1914b), he of course had to refer to colleagues' writings that were the subjects of his presentation. Also, the title of Tausk's paper of 1916(c) does contain the title of a paper by Abraham, since that paper is devoted to the refutation and correction of Abraham's views on premature ejaculation.

able to acknowledge his indebtedness only to an authority of high charismatic order.

We shall see later Tausk hemming and hawing at times when he has to invoke *that* authority; but even though that too evidently pained him (probably in a different way)—namely, acknowledging charismatic authority—it apparently did give him, so to speak, "a compensation as a means of discounting that particular displeasure," if I may take off from the title of his paper of 1913. Thus he had to fight battles on two fronts—against sibling-substitutes, as well as against the father-substitute. The total omission of citations of the achievements of brother-substitutes shows the extremeness of his technique, as applied to that area of conflict. It is not a technique of compromise or displacement, but of complete erasure.

If Roazen had been aware of Tausk's first footnote in his paper on the symptomatology of war psychoses (1916b), he might have known that it is no longer possible to ascertain what was original at all in that paper. For in that footnote Tausk says that "this" lecture was given in January, 1916 (9 months after Freud had finished his paper), thus giving rise to the impression that the text is a reproduction of his lecture. Yet he goes on to add that later experiences have since then necessitated expansion and modification: "An essential part of the theoretical argumentation on the question of paranoia cum melancholia was added on the basis of a discussion held in the Viennese Psychoanalytic Society" (my own translation). Was Freud really the *only one* to speak in that discussion? Did no other member have anything to say that made any impact whatsoever on the content of Tausk's final paper? If not, then why was an "essential" part of his theoretical remarks added later "on the basis of a discussion"? And in the course of the discussion in Vienna, did not one really refer to Rank, in connection with the question of narcissistic object-choices?

All that can easily be answered. Tausk was apparently not only ungrateful to Federn, but quite unappreciative of the contribution of the rest of his colleagues. It sounds somewhat silly when one sees Roazen berating Freud for not using the right way of citing, in reference to Tausk. Yet the way in which Freud's paper on melancholia reached its final form shows the freedom and graciousness of his intercourse with co-workers. When Freud finished his first draft of the paper, he sent it to Ferenczi, asking him, after reading it, to forward it to Abraham (Jones 2, p. 329). Upon finishing his reading of it, Abraham sent Freud a letter that was filled with discussion and suggestion.[25] He pointed out the oral sadistic quality so frequently encountered in melancholic patients, and elaborates on their masochism; he reminded Freud of his own contribution, "not to assert my priority but merely to underline the points of agreement in our findings."

And how did Freud reply? "Your comments on melancholia are very useful to me, and *I unhesitatingly incorporated in my paper those parts of them that I could use*" (emphasis added). Quite aside from the fact that Tausk's ideas about melancholia, as he had expressed them in his 1916 paper, offered nothing to Freud, is it conceivable that such a correspondence as Freud entertained with Abraham would have been possible with a personality type like Tausk? Roazen seems to think that he finds in Freud's reaction to Tausk his (negative) response to Tausk's creativity. Yet a comparison of Abraham's letter, which contains far-sighted clinically-based views about melancholia, with Tausk's paper and its limitation of interest to homosexual and heterosexual libido (an unproductive track, for it is the *loss of object*—whether homosexual or heterosexual—that is the decisive factor) will demonstrate to an unbiased reader which of the two was the more creative in this instance. And Freud's eagerness to hear Abraham's comments, the freedom with which he tells him that he is using his suggestions—is there in this even the slightest trace of authoritativeness, or of a desire to abuse his co-workers as "kaleidoscopes"?

The reader may possibly have forgotten our starting point by now. Roazen inferred, as the result of Tausk's stating that he had special permission to quote a discovery of Freud's (a discovery that Freud himself ascribed, in fact, to Rank) that Freud had to be cautious "with this man." Roazen means by "this man" someone who "in addition to his having ideas of his own . . . would

---

[25] The reader should take the trouble to read that letter (March 31, 1915; Abraham and Freud 1965, pp. 215–218), if he wishes to find out who among Freud's co-workers, if any, was "ahead" of him, and with whom he ought to have been "cautious," if he had indeed had the paranoid and rivalrous bent that Roazen in vain attempts to ascribe to him.

rush ahead to fill out some of Freud's raw concepts with his own clinical material" (p. 192). Since Tausk's paper was published in English not too long ago (1969), it should be easy for a reader to form his own judgment on the quality of that clinical material. It was, to be sure, good enough for a medical journal; but I doubt that anybody can find anything unusual in these abbreviated case histories and chance observations—as cannot help being true when a military psychiatrist is working under the pressure of a hospital assignment during war years. If anything, one could say that, in this instance, "raw" clinical material was tacked on to Freud's subtle concepts.

As in other instances, so too in this one, one does not have to wait long to witness Roazen's self-defeating tendencies winning the upper hand. He comments (only a dozen or so lines later) that Tausk's paper had "spoiled his discussion by going into too many details of Freud's views, and he burdened his arguments with references to Freud's comments" (p. 192). In other words, it was not a good paper. Yet how much would have been left to the paper at all, if those "details" and "references" had been left out of it? Reviewing the total situation, it seems to me that Freud would have done Tausk a disservice by quoting—even if this had been physically possible—a paper of his that was below his usual standard and that it was to Tausk's advantage that Freud cited (1917a, p. 255) instead one of Tausk's (1913a) brilliant papers. Yet despite a seemingly deferential attitude that Tausk takes in the paper toward Freud, his profound ambivalence comes to the fore even there, as can be observed in the following instance.

When he raised the question of why melancholia leads to a reduction—and not to an increase—of self-esteem, he wrote: "*I found the answer to the problem in an observation made sometime ago and confirmed by Freud* to the effect that the melancholic's self-reproaches are only seemingly directed against himself; they are really intended for the love object he has abandoned" (Tausk 1916b, p. 395; emphasis added). Thus he was clearly asserting his priority regarding observations on which Freud's crucial theory of melancholia was based. In this instance there is documentary evidence that proves a tendency in Tausk to lay claim, in one form or another to mental goods that were none of his. The *Minutes* of 1914 clearly outline the insights Tausk had gained in his research on melancholia. It was Freud who had made subsequent to Tausk's paper the following remark: "The self-reproaches in melancholia are intended for other persons and are only turned against oneself." [26]

If Tausk had made this far-reaching observation before Freud, why did he not mention it when he presented his exposition of melancholia to the Society in 1914? A man of his astuteness would have caught on immediately and recognized that here were opened, clinically as well as therapeutically, new vistas on melancholia.

How difficult it was for Tausk to accept Freud's originality can be seen also from another passage. He wrote: (1919, p. 528): "Recently . . . Freud . . . stated that the complicated machines appearing in dreams always represent the genitalia. Having studied machine dreams analytically *over a long period of time*, I can fully confirm Freud's statement" (emphasis added).

I have earlier commented that many of Roazen's errors are of a tendentious nature and the example I have just given will confirm this. But this tendentiousness can also be observed when he extols Tausk as a therapist and belittles Freud. He does so, apparently, because from that vantage point he will be able, even though indirectly, to knock down Freud's moral stature. This he attempts to do by referring approvingly to what he erroneously believes to have been "an old Viennese adage" (p. 189): "Only a good man can be a good physician." [27] Freud is thus pictured as a man who, as the result of his preoccupying interest in research, is quite ready to sacrifice human welfare, and Roazen adduces Edoardo Weiss as witness to this—the latter having said of Federn that he would fight harder to help the patient than would Freud, who was more scientist than healer.

Yet, since this does not help Roazen, he then adds a quotation —which again proves to be wrong. "But in therapy," he writes (p. 189), " 'the scientific method is not always the best for

---

[26] *Die Selbstvorwürfe der Melancholie gelten anderen Personen und sind nur auf die eigene Person gewendet.* (As a matter of fact, Freud had observed this already in 1897 (cf. Strachey 1957, p. 240, and Freud 1950a, p. 207).

[27] It was Hermann Nothnagel (1841–1905) who said: "Only a good man can be a great physician" (cf. Lesky 1965, p. 314). Nothnagel was, by the way, one of the very few at the top of Vienna's medical hierarchy who held Freud in the highest regard.

illuminating a personality,' Tausk once maintained; 'art is often better suited for that purpose.' " If one turns to the source (*Minutes 2*, p. 388; January 12, 1910), one finds Tausk's comment as a discussion remark to a paper by Fritz Wittels, a rather debatable attempt to present a psychoanalytic interpretation of a contemporary Viennese journalist, Karl Kraus (1874–1936), who was then standing at the center of public attention. Of course, in such a presentation, no problem of therapy could possibly have been discussed, so that Tausk said not a word about therapy; what he maintained was that art is often better suited than science *for illuminating a personality*. How could Tausk, after having been at that time a member for only three months—which probably also covered the time of his practical psychoanalytic experience—have been in any position to make such a sweeping statement about therapy? It was thoughtless enough of him to attempt to say anything conclusive about the scientific method, but even his own characteristic rashness would very likely have recoiled from the notion of making any judgments about therapeutic method after such a short period.[28]

The reader, however, can conclude in what an embarrassing situation Roazen must have found himself when he set out to prove Tausk's therapeutic superiority over Freud. He was first compelled to convert a statement by Freud into its very opposite; and then he had to resort to a discussion remark that Tausk had made about three months after he started his psychoanalytic career, one that was unrelated to therapy, to boot.

There are only two instances from which one may be able to obtain a glimpse of Tausk's tact in his dealings with patients, and neither of these is in his favor. One of them concerns Mr. B., whose trouble with a pharmacist's wife and inability to identify Ibsen's bust the reader may recall from my previous reference to them.

When Mr. B., while standing before Ibsen's bust, asked who

---

[28] In Tausk's reaction to Wittels' presentation, one must take into consideration the fact that Tausk's father was a journalist, and that Tausk himself had given up his own attempts in the same field. It would not be surprising if Tausk had responded idiosyncratically to a quite unfriendly pathography of the most discussed journalist of those days. One could therefore read into his objection the statement that psychoanalysis would not be sufficient to explain his own difficulties.

that gentleman was, and Tausk suddenly understood that this and the preceding parapraxis were the result of Mr. B.'s shame and his intense aversion against being reminded of the pharmacist's wife, he did not answer simply "Ibsen" but "This gentleman is the pharmacist." According to Tausk, at that point, Mr. B.'s "eyes did not show a very happy expression" [*schauten nicht sehr glücklich drein*]. Was it really necessary to humiliate an acquaintance in such an offensive way?

After all, here is an instance in which Tausk, who was apparently very intuitive, was using the superiority that he derived from his knowledge of psychoanalysis to the disadvantage of another person (cf. Sterba 1941). His remark about Mr. B.'s unhappy expression sounds quite unpleasant—almost as though it was being said with malicious relish. One could say that Tausk himself, at the time of the incident with Mr. B., may already have been in the throes of his own crisis, and therefore not functioning at his best; but there has come to my attention an incident that occurred much earlier and is significant in the same regard.

In his 1917 paper, in which, as mentioned earlier, he analyzed one of his own parapraxes, he also reported one that had occurred to a young officer who "wanted to obtain my medical help." The patient had loafed for four years, instead of studying for a law degree. His father, a successful and respected businessman, had died years before, and his mother had continued to manage her husband's enterprises with energy and circumspection. But the son did not trust her, because "one has to be a man for such extensive work." Now the patient did not know what to do professionally.

When Tausk asked him whether he could not work in his father's business, he objected that his mother would never surrender the management of the business, and he would never be able to tolerate such a situation. "Then," Tausk continued, "there remains for you nothing to do but to wish your mother's death, etc." The patient, of course, protested. In so doing, he made a parapraxis that confirmed Tausk's interpretation. "The patient was honest enough to take seriously his slip of the tongue," Tausk ended the account. Despite the frequent occurrence at that time of quick and deep interpretation, to interpret a death wish against the mother in the first interview impresses me as being excessive and quite lacking in compassion.

Nevertheless, Roazen's proposition that a psychiatrist who extends his therapeutic effort to the psychoses is more human and charitable than one who prefers to limit his therapeutic effort to those disorders that are treatable by rational methods, founded on insight therapy, is interesting and deserves discussion. Of course, if Roazen had proposed simply that Tausk had a personality that was better suited than Freud's for the psychotherapy of schizophrenics, I think one might have to agree with him as I shall try to show.

In what follows, I shall be making a few remarks about the technique that is necessary in the psychotherapy of schizophrenic patients. The reader may forgive me when I treat this complex problem in summary fashion, and limit myself to the presentation, in the simplest possible form, of one aspect alone.

More frequently than not, the schizophrenic, particularly in his acute phase, responds in a positive fashion only to persons who possess a certain kind of *ambiance* and *mystique*, which can be characterized best as charisma. In order to describe the psychiatric charisma that is necessary for the treatment of schizophrenics, one has to make reference to the primary process. In the experience of many investigators, an interpretation or therapeutic transaction is successful only when the patient is made to feel the reflection of the therapist's own primary process.

To put it in a nutshell, no interpretation will become relevant to the patient unless it is presented to him in a magical form. Psychoanalytic theory is necessary, of course, in order for the therapist to be able to construct the correct therapeutic measure; but for that measure to be therapeutically effective, more often than not it has to be dressed in a magic garb—that is to say, the therapist's own emotionality has to become the carrier of the therapeutic action. The availability of charisma "at the schizophrenic's bedside," so to speak, presupposes absolute conviction on the therapist's part with regard to his own power and omniscience. No matter how much he may feel, in general, in doubt about the prognosis of the disease, when he is in direct contact with the patient all that must be forgotten and he must act with unwavering conviction the role that the clinical constellation calls for.

From the rich literature on the subject, I want to quote only one writer to back up these brief remarks. Searles (1963, p. 636f.) reports that many writers on the subject "have emphasized that the therapist must be able to provide in generous measure an intensity of emotional response" that is essentially different from the climate of the basic situation on which classical psychoanalysis, as devised by Freud, is founded; or in explaining the maternal aspect of the therapist-patient relationship, he writes (1958, p. 238):

> In this symbiotic form of relatedness, the patient's and therapist's feelings towards one another fluctuate, so that now the latter, now the former, is in an omnipotent-mother position; thus the therapist must be as open as possible both to his own infantile dependency needs and to his feeling subjectively omnipotent in relationship to his needful-infant patient.

Tausk, I believe, might well have been just the personality type for such a technique. His flamboyance, his dash, his seeming conviction of self—all that, if fitted into the requirements of the clinical situation, might have paved the way to a good many therapeutic successes.

It is obvious that Freud's personality, in which rational processes prevailed—what psychoanalysis characterizes under the summary term "secondary processes"—was unsuitable for such a technique. It is significant that the young schizophrenic of whom I spoke earlier, who was in treatment with Freud, was a shy person. Even though he did make himself conspicuous by bizarre behavior, he was sincerely devoted to his studies and at the same time, as far as one could judge from the outside, suffering from inner anguish. He was apparently a schizophrenic who would not, it seemed, have required the magic gesture or the magic phrase, to the same extent as more acute patients regularly need it. He might have recovered under the soothing effect of transference to a benign, kind father-figure, who conveyed insight. Needless to say, this is my reconstruction; but what I subsequently learned from the patient's father does not contradict this view.

Yet here one has to record a surprising observation that can occasionally be made about those who have been famous for their psychiatric charisma. It cannot be an accident that, of the two psychiatrists I have known who were most successful in their treatment of schizophrenics, one was a homosexual and the other a sociopath—that is to say, both were suffering from disturbed object-relationships in their own lives. I am far from seeking to generalize this observation; but I anticipate that investigation would reveal that a surprising percentage of those who are out-standingly successful in the psychotherapy of schizophrenics show particularly ambivalent and stormy relationships with the persons of their own immediate environment. (This may become quite different, however, with the successful use of pharmaca in the treatment of schizophrenics. The "correctly drugged" schizophrenic is far more accessible to rational psychotherapy than the "undrugged" one [Ostow 1962]).

Consequently, even if Tausk had worked hard at the extension of psychoanalytic psychotherapy to the schizophrenics—which he never did—and even if Freud had been uninterested in the structure of schizophrenic psychoses, as well as in the extension of psychoanalysis—which is not correct, as can be proven by considerable documentation—even if the situation had really been as Roazen has erroneously presented it in his book, he still would not have been correct in drawing the conclusions that he does, with regard to the character of Tausk and of Freud.

From all that is known about Tausk, it can be seen that he was not what is called, in ordinary parlance, "a good human being." By now, the reader should surely know by heart which of his traits prove the absence of goodness in him. Nevertheless, he was a master of the great rescuing gesture, of which more will have to be said in the next chapter. With some, of course, who had been the recipients of his not infrequent rescue actions, he had a reputation for goodness. But it would be a gross mistake in psychological judgment if one were to equate acts of rescue with the presence of goodness. Yet someone whose central urge seems to gravitate toward the dramatic rescue is likely to find far more gratification in the therapeutic struggle with down-trodden schizophrenics than will a personality type whose center of affective gratification lies in the steady, loving care of his next of kin and his friends.

An episode such as the following, which took place early in Freud's life, is hardly thinkable in Tausk's. As he wrote Martha

Bernays (August 9, 1883, Freud 1960, p. 49), a friend of his had left a message with him, requesting from him "another" gulden. He himself had no more than eight pennies in his pocket, at that time, yet he went into action and ran around raising the gulden. After some failure, he did succeed; but it was too late to help his friend. Freud raised no complaint on this score. "But," the letter continued, "don't you think this is a funny kind of gypsy life, Marty? Or does this sort of humor not appeal to you and make you weep over my poverty? Don't take it to heart, etc."

Here we see the 27-year-old Freud responding, without a second thought, to a friend's request for money, at a time when he himself was in dire need of it. This, by the way, did not seem to have been a solitary event, for one learns from the same letter that another friend owned Freud money. Such actions do not fall into the category of "rescue"—with its drama, its exhibitionism, and the recipient's obligation of gratitude. It is an action of generosity, which will hardly be noticed because it occurs, after all, in silence. The fact is that, if Martha Bernays had stayed in Vienna and Freud had not had the opportunity to write his daily letters to his faraway sweetheart, posterity would never have known about it. How different from Tausk's exclamation, "Only Freud and God know!" (p. 27), when he was faced with the question of his summer vacation being in jeopardy!

The therapy of schizophrenics affords a splendid opportunity for narcissistic self-aggrandizement—which is why those who harbor such needs will have a better chance of clinical success than someone who has renounced forever his infantile wishes. Let us assume that the author was right in his assertion that Tausk was more compassionate than Freud toward his patients. Should Roazen not have asked himself what might have been the reason why a man who showed so little compassion for father, wife, sons, father-in-law, and a long list of women—why just such a man would evolve an inordinate charitableness toward patients who suffered from grave mental disorders? I am always skeptical when I have to evaluate psychologically acts of "goodness" that yield a great narcissistic gain.

When I spoke of the psychiatric charisma that personality types like Tausk possess, I did not mean to question Freud's charisma (cf. Brome 1968, p. 131). But his was of an entirely different kind. I have been surprised to learn from many informants who had only superficial contacts with Freud that they would not have thought of Freud as a genius, after meeting him briefly, if they had not known his great achievements. By and large, it was only those who had the privilege of a longer acquaintance who discovered behind the great works an equally great personality. If someone were to have met Tausk and Freud together for the first time, without knowing their identities, it might very well have happened that he would have taken Tausk for the genius.

I once interviewed a man who had been personally acquainted with a good many great men. He had known Freud fairly well, but he assured me that Freud as a person had never given him the impression of being a genius. When I asked him who, among the many whose path he had crossed, had most strongly given him that impression, he named Otto Weininger, a person who contributed to the furtherance of philosophy or science almost nothing. Why Freud did not leave an impression of genius on a significantly large number of people who had only superficial contact with him, I may be able to succeed in explaining in the next chapter. But before closing, I want briefly to mention what strikes me as being a mistake in principle, which Roazen makes in his comment on Freud as a therapist.

A detailed study of Freud as he was before his trip to Paris evokes the impression that the therapeutic intent was quite strong in him. And I have been told of incidents that occurred in his practice, even when he was an old man, that were extraordinarily clever in their practicality. Thus, he told a woman whose lover had consulted him about a sudden occurrence of sexual impotence that, the next time her lover approached her, she should refuse him intercourse, pretending that it hurt her. The patient's impotence disappeared as soon as she had the opportunity to follow Freud's advice. Only someone who possesses a strong therapeutic impulse could have devised such an extraordinarily ingenious therapeutic move. The historical truth, as I see it, is that as soon as Freud discovered that true insight into oneself—the recognition of self—coincides with the therapeutic optimum, he consciously renounced the therapeutic ambition per se, which must have been quite strong in him, even though he felt himself to be free of it.[29]

It is an undue simplification, which may easily be misunderstood, when I condense the rock-bottom basis of classical psychoanalysis, as created by Freud, into the formula: insight is health. Nevertheless, Freud was certainly not part of the nineteenth-century philosophical tradition of rationalism and of the European enlightenment, even though there are historical strands that lead from both systems to psychoanalysis. It would take us beyond the limits of this book if I were to enter into a discussion of the meaning that the formula referred to above holds in Freud's theoretical edifice. In any event, my assertion that it was gained by Freud at the cost of a personal sacrifice will not find agreement among many.

Yet, whether I am right or wrong, the primary process, as I shall presently show, held in the classical situation an entirely different place from the one it now holds, to judge by what can be observed in present trends of psychotherapy. In the classical analytic situation, the remote echo of the primary process can be found in the analyst's maintenance of "free-floating attention": the patient, by way of uninterrupted chains of free associations, comes closer and closer to undisguised revelation of the primary

---

[29] After completing the manuscript, I was shown a letter that Freud had written at the age of nineteen, after his return from a trip to England; to some extent it seems to support my proposition. In it he wrote: "Last year I would have answered, if asked what my great wish is: a laboratory and free time; or a ship on the ocean, with all the instruments a scientist needs. Now I am trying to decide whether I should not prefer to say: a huge hospital and plenty of money, in order to reduce or eliminate from the world a few of the ills that afflict our bodies. If I wanted to make an effect upon a great number of people, instead of on a small group of readers and co-scholars, England would be the right country for such a purpose. A man who is respected and supported by the press and the wealthy, could perform miracles to assuage physical sufferings, if he were enough of a researcher to enter into new ways of healing.

[Voriges Jahr hätte ich auf die Frage, was mein höchster Wunsch sei, geantwortet: Ein Laboratorium und freie Zeit oder ein Schiff auf dem Ocean mit allen Instrumenten, die der Forscher braucht; jetzt schwanke ich ob ich nicht lieber sagen sollte: ein grosses Spital und reichlich Geld um einige von den Übeln, die unsern Körper heimsuchen einzuchränken oder aus der Welt zu schaffen. Wenn ich also auf eine grosse Menge wirken wollte, anstatt auf eine kleine Schaar von Lesern und Mitgelehrten, so wäre England das rechte Land für einen solchen Zweck. Ein angesehener Mann von der Presse und den Reichen unterstützt könnte Wunder thun, um körperliches Leiden zu hindern, wenn er Forscher genug ist, neue Wege der Heilung zu betreten.]

process; the analyst, by putting himself totally at the service of the subject, is totally absorbed in the unraveling of the obscure meaning of what the subject is presenting. In the state of mind that Freud advised the analyst to adopt, however, it was the classical Apollonian tradition that gained full victory.

The historian who prefers abstract generalizations, which are usually quite remote from historical reality, or the historian who tries to deduce from a confusing multitude of facts a crystal-clear evolvement of ideas, may think that he is able to perceive a straight line from the Greek oracle to the classical psychoanalytic situation. When the ancient Greek wanted to know the truth, he had to listen to what the "inspired" priestess was uttering. "For prophecy is a madness, and the prophetess at Delphi and the priestesses at Dodona, when out of their senses have conferred great benefits on Hellas, both in public and private life, but when in their senses, few or none" (Phaedrus 244, emphasis added). Here truth is gained by the prophetess's surrender to the primary process; to this procedure the analyst is the true antipodes.

The analyst relies on his "unconscious memory" (Freud 1912, p. 112). Without straining, he keeps himself in the state of "free-floating [gleichschwebend] attention," thereby making it possible for all the patient's free associations to be absorbed by his own unconscious, which will return the right interpretation at the right moment. "Unconscious memory" and "free-floating attention" are the reliable tools of therapy; even though they are not fully divorced from the primary process, nevertheless they are structured entirely in accordance with the requirements of the secondary processes—that is to say, the primary process is ideally tamed by the rational self.[30]

In the treatment of the psychoses, the therapist does not regress to the level of prophetic madness, but he does yield a significant area in himself to the effect of the primary process. I have devoted my own small share to the technique of harnessing the primary process in the service of treating acute schizophrenics. Yet at present the demand for a surrender to the inroads that the primary process may make on the self, the demand for its dis-

---

[30] For ego control of primary process, see Kris (1934), Kris and Gombrich (1938). For the complexity and manifoldness of the problems involved in psychoanalytic technique, see Greenson (1967).

charge in whatever form it makes its appearance within the boundaries of a therapeutic setting—these demands have become increasingly strong and, in my opinion, have converted therapy into a *Walpurgisnacht*.

It all started, to be sure, with concessions to the gravely ill who seemed untreatable, except in terms of their being temporarily absolved from the claims of rationality; but it has ended with "encounter groups" and therapists who also demand the Dionysian instead of the Apollonian in the individual treatment situation. It is impossible not to see, in this degeneration, a concomitant to the long-smouldering process of corrosive dissolution of the Occident. Historically, it is most impressive to note that, in the month Freud closed his eyes, the evening glow of Western culture took its brutal beginning.

VI

REMARKS ON FREUD'S
PSYCHOPATHOLOGY

IN THE STUDY of those individuals to whom mankind has accorded the honor of genius—the rarest of human phenomena, and one that I shall try in the next chapter to define—one regularly discovers psychopathology, in most instances even severe psychopathology. The difficulty in the psychoanalytic investigation of the genius's psychopathology lies in the fact that two kinds of psychopathology are to be differentiated here: the common variety, such as the genius shares with the rest of mankind, and the psychopathology that is inherent in the creative process and therefore particular to genius. It is not easy to keep the two apart; at this point, I want to delineate, without striving for completeness, the psychopathology that has up to now been known about Freud with certainty, because it is well documented.

From Jones's biography and from letters published posthumously, it is known that, as a young man, Freud went through a stormy period—his *Sturm und Drang* period, as it were. It covered the four-and-a-quarter years (June 17, 1882–September 14, 1886) of his engagement to Martha Bernays, later to be his wife. Prior to his falling in love with her, at the age of 26, he seems to have been vacillating in his interests, doubtful about his place in the world and mildly hypochondriacal. During the time of his engagement, almost certainly a period of sexual continence, he was passionately ambitious, acutely rivalrous and suffering from spells of short-lasting, almost pathological jealousy. He was frequently subject during those years to depressions about the hopelessness of his external situation, which at times mounted to despair. (More will have to be said in the next chapter about these quite remarkable years.)

After his trip to Paris (October, 1885–February, 1886), his marriage, and the inception of his medical practice, however, he seems to have become quieter. The area of conflict moved gradually to his scientific undertaking: the theoretical explanation of the wealth of observations he was making during the course of his practice as a psychotherapist. This was the period approximately covered by the letters to Wilhelm Fliess (1887–1900 [1902]; cf. Freud 1950a). As is well known, these letters also give insight into Freud's neurotic symptomatology of that time, which consisted mainly of swings of mood and psychosomatic symptoms. It is difficult to determine which of them were organic and which were due to conversion or hypochondria. During those years Freud's self-analysis took place.

With the successful termination of his self-analysis and the settlement of the father-conflict, which were involved concomitantly with the writing of The Interpretation of Dreams at the end of the last century, Freud developed the personality that was to become known to posterity. It is best represented in Ferdinand Schmutzer's (1870–1928) engraving—the portrait of a man of complete mastery, with deeply penetrating eyes, skeptic, even pessimistic. There is tragedy and sadness in the face, but no trace of despair. Schmutzer's engraving conveyed the truth, but not the whole truth, for Freud, of course, did share some of the frailties of civilized mankind.

He suffered from anxiety about missing trains, yet this did not prevent him from enjoying traveling; he suffered from migraine headaches, and at times from a superstitious-like preoccupation with numbers referring to the age at which he expected to die; all his life he suffered sporadically from constipation. There occurred at least four syncopes (Schur 1966a, p. 68). An instance has been described by Freud when he felt nauseated in a situation of great psychic stress, occasioned by a patient's sudden hemorrhage and near death. After the situation had been brought under control, Freud left the room, he related, drank a bottle of water and "felt rather miserable" (Schur 1966a, p. 57). Whether his love of smoking should be called an addiction is difficult to decide; he called himself "a passionate smoker" (1960, p. 403) and was unable, against all medical warnings, to abstain from smoking during creative spells, even though smoking had caused cancerous changes in the oral cavity.

The following observations, even though they fall outside the area of neuroticism, nevertheless belong to the subject of Freud's psychopathology. Occasionally, Freud adhered with great stubbornness and against all evidence to a conviction clearly disproved by facts. Thus he was "almost convinced that in fact Edward de Vere, Earl of Oxford, is concealed behind his [Shakespeare's] pseudonym" (Freud 1925b, p. 64). In this context, Freud's (1925b, p. 64) adherence to Lamarck's theory of the inheritance of acquired characteristics (Jones 3, p. 309, and Jones 1956, p. 29) is also to be cited. However, I am not certain whether Lamarckism, which is rejected at present, may not be confirmed in the distant future by new biological discoveries. One is reminded of Aristotle's concept of a finite space which also seemed to be disproved by Newtonian physics, and is nevertheless very seriously considered by physicists today. At any rate, Freud's occasional stubbornness in clinging to a doubtful—or even more than doubtful—theory is well documented. Freud also shared group biases with his fellow-men. Thus, after having visited in 1909 the United States, where he was singularly honored, he maintained a marked aversion against this country, evidently based on prejudice. Also, during the early phases of World War I, he indulged in a highly subjective view of the turn history was taking, and expressed in his letters plainly nationalistic opinions.

According to Jones, he was occasionally given to being indiscreet, and lacking in a practical knowledge of man (Menschenkenntnis). If Jones meant the latter as a general statement, I would doubt its validity, for there are many instances showing Freud as a superior Menschenkenner. However, as early as 1900 (p. 483) Freud himself remarked that a childhood pattern had a bearing on his relationship to men, and this may have led to instances of misjudgment. Freud was referring to his nephew John, one year his senior, "the playmate of my earliest years" (Freud 1900, p. 424). They loved each other and fought each other, and John had many "reincarnations" in later life.

Freud was probably a mildly compulsive character, disliking interferences with daily routines and insisting on punctuality. On rare occasions, he could become very angry. When one of his daughters died, he complained that he was unable to mourn adequately. One blatant diagnostic error is well documented (Jones 3, p. 105f.), and Jones reports a few instances of credulity toward absurd statements by patients (Jones 2, p. 429). Scrutiny of the literature, I am sure, will bring to light more signs of neurotic or other symptomatology. When Stefan Zweig (1931) drew an idealized, even though simplified, portrait of him, Freud himself replied with a description of his own psychopathology, as he saw it, and the reply provides delightful reading (Freud 1960, p. 402f.).

Freud's neurotic symptoms, taken together, do not amount to all that much. Phobias, headaches, and superstitions are the usual triad one finds in intellectuals. In general, one must say that the average intellectual shows neurotic symptoms of greater frequency and intensity than Freud did, at least after his self-analysis. Moreover, some of the symptoms may even appear, on closer scrutiny, in a different light. Thus Schur (1971) suggested that what has been regarded as neurotic cardiac anxiety of a hypochondriacal form (particularly during the Fliess period) might have actually been the symptom of an organic disease.

I myself (1965) have made a rather surprising observation with regard to the so-called number superstition.[1] Like most human beings—or, perhaps more correctly, like many human beings—Freud would have liked to know in what year he would die. He did make two or three guesses, which did not prove correct. But in 1899 he analyzed (1901, p. 242f.) a number that had come to his mind with seeming arbitrariness. The analysis revealed the wish to have twenty-four years added to his working life. Is it a coincidence that it was exactly twenty-four years later

---

[1] Roazen asserts that Freud "admitted a belief in the magic of numbers" (p. 171). The reference he gives, however, does not seem to support this.

that the first signs of a cancerous growth were diagnosed? It was due only to surgery that he did not die that very year.[2]

It is not impossible that the biological potential of man's lifetime is somehow represented in the unconscious. This would not, of course, include an unconscious knowledge about the effect of such accidental factors as the progress of medical technology. Freud (1924b, p. 174) was probably right when he wrote: "His [the individual's] organic disposition may already contain the indication of what he is to die from." If this is true, then it may no longer be superstitious to maintain that the time of biological death is contained in the unconscious. By free association, Freud might have obtained, without intending to, the true answer to the question of his biological lifespan, which had eluded him as long as he tried to solve the puzzle by way of ratiocination.

I have elaborated on this point because it is a suitable example of the sort of psychopathology of which one cannot say for certain whether it should be assigned to the common variety or to that of the genius. When Roazen calls Freud's search for the year of his death "numerological nonsense" (p. 105), he is, of course, following common sense. Yet subtlety and the understanding of genius may here discover a valid branch of Freud's indomitable urge to extend his inquiries into the remotest and most obscure territories.

The central issue, however, is that the neurotic symptoms Freud shared with the rest of mankind did not make him essentially different from the members of his social group, or from his contemporaries in general. That, at least, is the impression one receives from documented historical source material.

Freud's own psychopathology was, if anything, to him the signal for increased self-observation, and it might well have been also the instigator of creative action. When Plato (*Republic* 3, 408) says that a skillful physician had better be not of robust health, but should have had experience of all kinds of diseases in his own person, this may, to a certain extent, be applicable to Freud's neurosis.

One detail that Freud himself singled out as an occasional

---

[2] Thomas Mann was convinced that he would die at the age of 70. If a malignant pulmonary growth had not been removed in that year of his life, his conviction would have come true.

prerequisite of his productivity has to do with a quite different frame of reference. In 1896, he wrote Fliess that he was idle, because the medial degree of discomfort that he needed for intensive work was absent (Jones 1, p. 145). In 1895, during a phase of heightened creativity, he had written to Fliess (Freud, 1950a, p. 129): "One strenuous night last week, when I was in the stage of painful discomfort in which my brain works best, the barriers suddenly lifted," and in the same year, "In some peculiar way I'm never more productive than when I have mild symptoms. . . ." (Schur 1966a, p. 58). In 1918, he wrote that he was feeling physically too well during his vacation to have any new ideas (Freud, 1960, p. 323). The necessity for a certain optimal degree of physical discomfort as a prerequisite to creativity was apparently part of the psychopathology of creativity in Freud's case. It would be quite wrong to measure such a phenomenon in terms of the common variety of psychopathology, which can be studied in textbooks.

Further, it is almost certain that if someone had "cured" Freud of this "symptom," his creative potential might have been thereby reduced. The need for optimal discomfort was apparently no serious barrier to productivity on Freud's part, and in any case discomfort was sufficiently available to keep the creative processes going. Whether the psychopathology involved caused a sporadic lull is difficult to determine in view of Freud's enormous creative output.

The foregoing examination of Freud's psychopathology has been presented in the form of an enumeration of symptoms and does not lead to a uniform picture, from which the structure of Freud's neurosis could be inferred. This would have gone beyond my knowledge and, furthermore, is unnecessary in this context, since I have not been aiming at presenting a biography of Freud. The relevant points are that the single symptoms from which Freud suffered were unusual neither in their appearance nor in their intensity. With some minor exceptions, his psychopathology impresses me as the minimal price which a highly differentiated human being living in Western society has to pay, when—in his decisions and actions—he takes for granted the highest attainable ethical and moral standards.

It is also important that Freud was not a victim of denial.

If anything, he was rather strict or even severe in self-criticism, and was determined to eliminate the defects which he had noticed in himself. A comparable attitude can be observed in Goethe, who also suffered from a variety of neurotic symptoms. Not being a scientific psychologist, Goethe tried, whenever neurotic symptoms barred him from achieving his goals, to overcome them by training, that is to say, he repeatedly exposed himself to anxiety-arousing situations until the anxiety reaction subsided; Freud used insight instead for that purpose.

Still another feature is noteworthy. Just as the fear of missing trains did not prevent Freud from greatly enjoying travel, so by and large his psychopathology did not impair his ego functions. The syncopes were rare events without consequences; the migraine headaches, so far as is known, led to no interruption to speak of in his professional life. Thus, his psychopathology almost never stood in the way of his reaching his goals and did not reduce his creativity, with the possible exception of two occasions, discussed later in this chapter. It was never a barrier to action in the broadest meaning of the word. The nationalistic bias at the beginning of World War I barely shows up in his paper of 1915(c), although Freud had not yet shed it at the time of its writing. Freud's partiality for Lamarckism did not have a bearing on the theories which he developed. Their validity is not called into question, regardless of whether Lamarckism is disproved or not; he never wrote an essay on Shakespeare's identity, although this subject would have been quite challenging.

It looks as if Freud knew intuitively when to pursue his "credulity," and when to keep it at the level of a personal conviction. One could counter that at least once Freud was a victim of his credulity, even in his scientific work: that was when he thought he had discovered the etiology of neurosis in seduction. Strachey, as reported by Jones (2, p. 430), made a very relevant comment on this matter. Any other investigator than Freud would have dismissed the patients' tales about seduction as a sign of the all too well-known untrustworthiness of patients in general. Freud took them seriously, however, and his doing so was apparently an unavoidable stepping-stone toward his discovery of the importance of unconscious fantasies and of the existence of repressed infantile eroticism. The one area, however, in which

Freud may indeed have been less successful in eliminating psycho-pathology than he was in others was the area of his relationships with some of his friends. As he himself reported, he was apparently unable to escape the repetition of an early childhood pattern.[3] Nevertheless, Freud made two remarks from which one may draw the conclusion that pregenital symptomatology or, more precisely, fixations had at times a reductive effect on his creativity. In a letter to Ferenczi of April 23, 1915, he tried to explain the heightening of his productivity during the early stages of World War I by an improvement in evacuation: "My productivity probably has to do with the enormous improvement in the activity of my bowels. I will leave it open whether I owe this to a mechanical factor, the hardness of the present-day bread, or to a psychical one, the changed relationship to money that is forced on us" (Jones 2, p. 183). He then reports the amount of money he had to withdraw from his savings because of his diminished practice. This makes it probable that a dysfunction of bowel activity might have had at times an adverse effect on his creative momentum.

More serious consequences seem to me to be attached to Freud's "admission that his passion for smoking hindered him in the working out of certain psychological problems" (Jones 2, p. 189). In this instance, it was not a matter of a temporary hindrance, but possibly a permanent limitation of psychological understanding, even though only within a narrow compass, enforced by an oral fixation. How far-reaching the effect of enforced abstention from smoking was can be learned from a letter to Eitingon in 1926, in which Freud wondered—in view of a myocardial affliction supervening the cancer—how much longer he would be able to continue his professional work, "especially since renouncing the sweet habit of smoking has resulted in a great diminution of my intellectual interests" (Jones 3, p. 121).

Freud thought that his creative output was subject to periodicity, but he was not certain whether this was caused by developmental or organic factors, as he remarked in a letter to Abraham of January 25, 1915 (Abraham and Freud, ed. 1965). That the quantity of Freud's creative output as well as the mo-

---

[3] I shall have more to say about this in Appendix C.

mentousness of its content varied is undoubtedly correct. But when compared with other scientists, one would say that in Freud's instance it is the relative steadiness of his creativity rather than periodicity that would deserve investigation. One obtains the impression that Freud's creative personality was not cyclic but rather progredient, with thrusts of varying intensity.

A general remark about Freud's self-analysis does not seem out of place here, especially since I have never seen this viewpoint discussed in the literature. Usually—and quite rightly so—Freud's self-analysis is heralded as a great accomplishment, which was brought about at the expense of anguish and pain. Its consequences were most clear-cut and beneficial, with regard to his gain in insight, as well as the elimination of his neurotic symptoms. What is overlooked, however, is the ease with which this heroic undertaking might have misfired, and thus led to an aggravation of the very problems with which Freud was wrestling.

Evidently Freud had developed, from childhood on, a strong superego. His discovery of all the contents and impulses of which he became aware during the course of the self-analysis and which must have struck him as "evil," might have discouraged, rather than encouraged, a personality weaker than his. Nietzsche made a far-reaching observation, which is pertinent to this problem. In an aphorism that he titled "Conquest of Passions" [Überwindung der Leidenschaften] he wrote: "The man who has conquered his passions has entered into possession of the most fertile soil. . . . To sow on the soil of conquered passions the seed of good works of the mind then becomes the pressing next task. The conquest itself is only a means, not a goal; if it is not so regarded, there soon grow, on the rich soil that has been left empty, all sorts of weeds and devilish nonsense" (Nietzsche 1879–1880, #53; my own translation; author's emphasis).[4]

The danger of instituting the conquest of passions for its own sake is by no means small, in a personality that is adhering to high

---

[4] Der Mensch, der seine Leidenschaften überwunden hat, ist in den Besitz des fruchtbarsten Erdreiches getreten. . . . Auf dem Boden der bezwungenen Leidenschaften den Samen der guten geistigen Werke säen, ist dann die dringende nächste Aufgabe. Die Überwindung selber ist nur ein Mittel, kein Ziel; wenn sie nicht so angesehen wird, so wächst schnell allerlei Unkraut und Teufelszeug auf dem leer gewordenen fetten Boden auf.

moral and ethical aims, as Freud's was. In that case, the danger would be great that *Teufelszeug*, as Nietzsche called it, would develop, in the shape of inhibitions, scruples, and a sort of moral hypochondriasis. This is clinically quite well known, with regard to persons who are seized by disgust with themselves, when they are brought face to face with the immorality that has been woven into their very texture, up to then. The degree of self-control that Freud achieved by way of his self-analysis was considerable, particularly if it is compared with the initial unruliness of his intensive passions. If to this degree of control is added the discipline that is imposed by a strict professional routine, one could easily conjure up the image of a man whose life was totally without enjoyment, because he had become so completely absorbed in the fulfillment of duties. However, there are no signs of Freud's having conquered his passions as an end in itself; instead, he followed Nietzsche's advice: the conquest of passions was used for sowing "the seed of good works of the mind," rather than for self-reproaches.

Yet the problem remains that Freud's life history does not show any traces of asceticism or of an inclination toward evolving an ascetic ideal, such as might be suggested by the epithet "puritanical" that has frequently been applied to him. It seems that Freud never lost his *joie de vivre*. In *The Interpretation of Dreams*, written in his mid-forties, one finds episodes that breathe an ability to experience intense joys; and, even as an old man, driven out of his homeland and approaching death, he was flexible enough to derive infinite pleasure from his new environs. Among other things, he fell in love with the garden that surrounded his new abode; he "was particularly fond of a superb almond tree which . . . was covered with blossoms" (Jones 3, p. 232). From some reports, one gains the impression that Freud had preserved the child's ability to derive enjoyment from simple things.

True *joie de vivre* always has at its core some remnant of an early developmental phase, marked by the child's unsophisticated surrender to pleasurable stimuli. Freud would not be alone in that respect; the same thing is reported of many another among the great. It has often been misunderstood, and even given rise to criticism. It is actually, however, correlated with the ability that many geniuses possess to regard the world naïvely—that is to say, as if they were perceiving the world for the first time. This enables them to be forever discovering new aspects, even in those things that they have perceived and observed repeatedly. Life never becomes routine for any man who is able at times to enjoy the world in the way he did when he was still a child.

Up to this point, none of the usual eccentricities—occasionally sharpened to the point of manifesting themselves as absurdities, irrationalities, or psychotic-like states, such as are so frequent in the lives of the great—have been reported or asserted by reliable biographers with regard to Freud. He seems in that respect to have been rather like Socrates, with whom he shares other similarities as well.

In the next chapter, I shall offer some conjectures about the reasons why genius is so often combined with more or less bizarre psychopathology. But are Roazen's new "finds" regarding Freud's psychopathology—a good deal of which (but certainly not all) would make Freud similar to other members of the genius class, rather than unlike them—tenable at all? [5]

A general remark about Freud's sexual life is warranted at this point, since many writers have included it in his psychopathology. The general opinion is that Freud was puritanical and a Victorian. Since in this context no writer had in mind the almost regular transgressions of the Victorian male, this description implies an alleged sexual inhibition in Freud.[6]

Granted the difficulty of differentiating the effects of the cultural habitat, the *Zeitgeist*, subjective bent, and psychopathology,

---

[5] When I now maintain that some of the psychopathology that Roazen has erroneously ascribed to Freud would be typical of a genius, the reader may take this as a contradiction of my harsh criticism of Roazen's book. However, much of the psychopathology that Roazen does postulate is of a sort that cannot under any circumstances be brought into meaningful connection with creativity. Those forms that he incorrectly alleges to have existed in Freud and which have been in fact observed in other geniuses, Roazen presents in a way defamatory to Freud's character and personality. Roazen is mistaken in both: the psychology of genius in general, as well as that of Freud.

[6] Many writers base their judgment mainly on the following sentence in a letter written by Freud to Fliess on March 11, 1900: "I have finished with begetting children" (Freud 1950a, p. 312). They drew the conclusion from it that Freud stopped having intercourse at the age of forty. I am reasonably certain that this was not the case. It is more probable that the sentence in question was the outgrowth of a temporary mood.

it cannot go unnoticed that, in the lives of many, perhaps even most, of the greatest minds about whom sufficient reliable data are preserved, intercourse held an inferior position, compared with its position among the majority. They were able to endure continence over far longer periods than the average man; they started later, or else did not partake of intercourse at all. Goethe, one of the most creative minds among the luminaries of the West, did not have intercourse before the age of thirty-eight, as can be proved by documents (Bode, 1921). He had a short-lived relationship at that age with the niece of an innkeeper who was working at the inn as a waitress (Carletta 1899). On his return to Weimar, he started a relationship with a girl sixteen years his junior, who became his common-law wife. She bore him five children, of whom one survived. He married her eighteen years later, at a time when, characteristically, he was no longer in love with her. As can be learned from his diaries, he stayed away from her during his creative spells. He loved many women passionately but had no physical relations with them. Leonardo da Vinci had no sexual contacts with women; in his youth, he may have had homosexual contacts, but even this is questionable. Michelangelo might occasionally have had genital experiences with younger men. Beethoven was very probably continent throughout his life.

This is not only true of geniuses who were artists; the greatest among all scientists, Isaac Newton, never had intercourse. Some diary entries make it probable that he did not even masturbate, and that his genital life was restricted to nocturnal emissions, which he considered to be grave sins. The Abbot Gregor Mendel very probably never had sexual relations. I am certain the list could be extended.

Why then should a pattern of reduced frequency of intercourse (when compared with the average) in the life of a towering personality of the last hundred years be constantly brought into connection with the life of a contemporary Queen who was born thirty-seven years before Freud and whom he survived by thirty-eight years? Goethe grew up in the rococo period, and he lived most of his life at a court most of whose members hardly fell behind the sexual morals of the present. Nevertheless, historical evidence proves that all this did not color his own sexual conduct in the least; instead, he seems to have reduced his sexual activity to the level that, for this type of genius, is apparently optimal for maximal creativity.

In terms of the psychology of genius, it would be misleading to reduce the sexual life of such mental giants as Leonardo, Goethe, Newton, and Freud to anything like puritanism or Victorianism, or their historical equivalents. After all, Tausk, Freud's alleged antagonist, was born twenty-three years after Freud, and he absorbed a full dose of Victorianism, but to no avail. He lived a dissolute sexual life, escaping all discipline and being defeated in the end by that very lack of discipline.

Jones (2, p. 422) remarks that "only social or psychological anthropology" can answer the question of whether the fact of Freud's being "peculiarly monogamous" is to be regarded "as representing the true normality of males." I am certain that one can say without further inquiry that it does not represent the true normality of males. It can be called normal only with regard to a certain type of eminently creative male. In a less gifted personality, this kind of sexual life would be a symptom of pathological inhibition; it would probably be quite dangerous to such a person, since it could lead to unproductive conflicts. Yet it strikes me as being the prerequisite for the flowering of many geniuses, such as Freud, and it may therefore serve as a sign of the qualitative differences between their psychic apparatus and that of the less creative persons whom we categorize as talents. In the case of geniuses, it would be an error to look upon it as inhibition: it is rather a hallmark of their being destined for a higher form of mentation.

Yet what I am saying in these pages about Freud's sexual life, and about the various problems that are connected with it, seems to be contradicted by an old rumor, which was recently revived— namely, that Freud entertained a sexual relationship with his sister-in-law, Minna Bernays, who lived in his household for forty-two years and accompanied him on many of his travels. Jones calls it "a malicious and entirely untrue legend" (1, p. 153). Some critics who take the relationship to be a fact seem inclined to find in it a blemish, and it is possible that they are right. Despite all the liberal changes that have occurred, in views about what is permissible in terms of sexual behavior, even today one would meet with raised eyebrows the idea of a man entertaining a sexual relationship for years with his sister-in-law, who is, to boot, a member of his household.

One would consider such behavior, to say the least, to be tactless and unaffectionate, if not outright cruel, toward the man's wife, and certainly to be a danger to the moral upbringing of his children—a reproach that would have all the greater validity for the period prior to World War I, when children were expected to behave when they reached adulthood in a far more restrained manner than adults are expected to behave nowadays. Freud would certainly have damaged the upbringing of his three daughters by such behavior. To say the least, it is predictable that in a household thus "divided" a harmonious atmosphere could not prevail. It can further hardly be imagined that, under such circumstances, a wife would be able to maintain a practically conflict-free relationship toward husband and sister. Such a household would be expected, unless it were libertine, to stand constantly under a cloud. Yet no one who was familiar with Freud's household has ever reported the existence of an atmosphere there that would be in the least reminiscent of Ibsen, Strindberg or O'Neill.

It is highly improbable that Freud—whatever his personal feelings may have been about his sister-in-law (and there is no documentary evidence of what feelings he did have toward her)— would have risked creating a source of constant conflict and disharmony, right at the heart of his family life—especially since he was so proud of it and it offered him so much compensation for the pain and anguish that were so great a part of his professional life.

I do not want here to go into a discussion of the quarter from which the old rumor found its recent nourishment; instead, I shall rely on the total picture. Moreover, without external necessity and with no implication of defensiveness, but quite spontaneously, Freud once, in a letter to Putnam, wrote a brief sketch of his own sexual life, in general terms that are incompatible with his rumored behavior: "Sexual morality as defined by society, in its most extreme form that of America, strikes me as very contemptible. I stand for an infinitely freer sexual life, although I myself have made very little use of such freedom. Only so far as I considered myself entitled to" (Freud 1960, p. 308). It is hardly imaginable that Freud would have considered himself to be "entitled" to a liaison of the sort referred to. I take the openness and the lack of concern that are significant in his relationship to his sister-in-law, as well as the absence of any signs of secrecy or clandestinity, to be proofs that there was nothing that called for concealment. A sexual relationship, particularly one with a close relative, and particularly under circumstances that would have made it impossible to keep it secret from wife and children, would have been so extremely provocative as to amount to a source of constant friction and irritation; yet in Freud's case, this has never been reported or observed by anyone. The idea can therefore be safely dismissed as a rumor—one that regularly and automatically arises whenever a man and a woman are seen together frequently, and all the more when they travel in each other's company.

VII

TALENT AND GENIUS

THE INTERACTION between Tausk and Freud is of psychological interest, among other reasons because in it the gulf that separates talent from genius can be observed and studied.

It was historically a step ahead when the qualitative richness of the world of colors was converted into quantitative variations of wavelength. But there is a way of thinking that tends to dissolve *all* differences into quantitative ones. Whether this principle of converting differences of quality into quantitative differences can be extended into the human world appears questionable to me. I object, for example, to the view that sees in a psychosis nothing more than an ensemble of exceedingly intense neurotic symptoms.[1] Likewise, the view that the difference between talent and genius is solely a quantitative one appears to me to be misleading.[2] It is

---

[1] Psychoanalysts do not have a uniform view on that point. Freud himself wrote a paper (1924c) from which I get the impression that he found the difference between psychosis and neurosis to lie in structure. However, in a letter to Marie Bonaparte (Jones 3, p. 449), he seems to come close to regarding it as a quantitative difference.

[2] Of the extensive literature on this subject, I shall quote only two authors. Moebius (1901, p. 33) maintained that while the difference between one talent and another is to be characterized quantitatively, talent and genius differ in

not only that the productions of talent and genius are different in quality; when one has an opportunity to look behind the surface behavior of the two, one can hardly fail to observe the qualitative difference of their private worlds.

In science, it has not been too difficult to assign a structural index to the achievements of a genius, since Kuhn (1962) introduced the concept of paradigm into the history of science. A paradigm is, so to speak, a new key with which to decode problems that the scientist meets with in his field. To cite an example, the assertion that the earth moves around the sun is a paradigm, perhaps the most consequential for mankind ever set up. Paradigms may be called models, thought-patterns that are of consequence insofar as they affect the whole of the existing science. Usually, upon the discovery of a new paradigm, all the previous propositions, hypotheses and theories of that science have to be profoundly changed or, at least, modified.

The discovery of these paradigms is, in science, the function of genius. Talents will perform permutations or combinations of paradigms; or they may clarify their consequences, or adjust to them areas that have not yet been explored in their light. At best, a talent will be able to modify or employ the paradigm that a genius has produced.

In the literary field, the function of the genius is to create a new world that might even compete successfully with existing reality in the minds of many. Shakespeare's plays—his tragedies and comedies—constitute a permanent cosmos in themselves, as real to the human mind and as infinite as the world that surrounds the individual. Homer, Dante and Shakespeare have at least this one aspect in common: they each enriched the world by the creation of a new and valid cosmos, which exists within or alongside the world of things and people that exists physically.

---

quality. Jones (1956, p. 6) clearly states, however, that the difference between genius and talent is quantitative. He justifies this by referring to "the regular laws of mental development," as discovered by Freud. Yet even in physics laws that are adequate under ordinary or average circumstances are inadequate when extreme conditions prevail. Freud himself studied what the genius shares with others, yet he never asserted that psychoanalysis is able to explain the genius's creativity. He may thus have been admitting indirectly that "the regular laws of mental development" are not enough to explain "the extreme conditions" that are, after all, present in every genius.

Much could be said about these humanly created worlds and there are many problems inherent in them, but I shall not pursue that thought further here.

Among the scientists who have created paradigms, a few have at the same time also thereby created a new world. Newton's paradigms led to a specifically Newtonian world, with its infinite space, its universal gravitational force, and its masses moving in accordance with the strength and the direction of the forces that impinge on them.

The same thing holds true of Freud. He is not only the discoverer of an as yet undetermined number of paradigms (Gedo et al., 1964), but in his psychological writings he too created a new world. Freud's works will be read at a time when many, most or even perhaps all the paradigms he created have been superseded. But it is just because his works are more than an aggregate of paradigms, or even a cohesive system of paradigms, that they will be read with admiration, awe and respect, as Plato's dialogues are now read, even though today's general reader would be at a loss to say what is true or false in the Dialogues. Freud's writings contain a new world, a cosmos comparable in its extension to those created by a genius before him—let us say, as in Shakespeare's plays. We find represented in this new world almost all the phenomena of the real human world. They are described and viewed in a new way, which strikes the reader as being original, individual and interesting, even fascinating, independently of whether the content is true or false.

The difference between the achievement of geniuses and talents consists also in the surprising fact that those of the former can rarely be grasped completely and therefore give occasion for an endless number of interpretations, whereas a talent's creations can easily be grasped and do not set in general a barrier to full understanding.

The presentation of genius as a special category often meets with opposition. The American democratic tradition is not well disposed toward the praise of great men. Particularly at the present historical turn, with its relativization of values, assertions about the extraordinary position of genius in mankind's history will readily meet with denial. It is, however, just as readily forgotten or denied that the development of culture and civilization depends

on more than the huge number of people who keep society going
and growing, by working toward technical fulfillments. Mankind
would still be living in caves or lake dwellings, had there not been
the few who were able to "unthink" the world as it was and to
"think" a new world—that is, to recreate one that is more gratifying, or more illuminating than the one they found. For Hamlet
is surely far more fascinating, deeper and more enigmatic than
any person that nature has so far been able to produce; and has
there ever existed a king who was so kingly mad as Lear?

The attitude toward genius varies with the historical period.
There are times when the trend goes in the direction of glorifica-
tion and idealization, so that nothing but goodness and nobility
is ascribed to the genius; there are other times when he is shrunken
or planed down to a level that is only slightly above the average.
Of course, the idiosyncrasies of an investigator must also be considered. As Freud remarked (1930b), the individual's attitude
toward genius depends on his attitude toward his parents, and
particularly toward the father. It is noteworthy that Frank Harris
and others have asserted that Carlyle, an ardent admirer and
idealizer of heroes, was impotent.[3]

Genius is now in disrepute with some people because of the
psychopathology that is found, almost to excess, in the bulk of
those who deserve that title. There can be no doubt that careful
scrutiny of the lives of most geniuses will unearth episodes, habits,
events that, if they made their appearance in the lives of others,
would have to be judged as manifestations of severe psychopathology. While they have to be called psychopathology in the life
of the genius as well, there they have to be appraised quite differently. The structure of the creative act of the genius is not
comparable to anything else: it has its own laws, and, in order for
it to come to pass, certain conditions are necessary in the psychic
apparatus that are very similar to those one observes in the non-
genius when he is suffering from a common disorder.

The best way I can think of to demonstrate the error of equating the psychopathology that is implicit in the creative act of the
genius with common psychopathology is an episode that Goethe

---

[3] The individual bent, even though it probably cannot be eliminated completely, can nevertheless be curbed with the help of psychoanalytic insights and
most careful documentation.

reports. For a number of weeks, during his early manhood, he tried every evening to stab himself—which would have to be taken under ordinary conditions as a sign of an apparently severe and malignant disturbance. But when one learns that, shortly thereafter, he wrote his masterpiece, the novel Werther—the subject of which is the suicide of a young man, presented in a heart-rending way as never before—then it becomes clear that what looked at first like malignant psychopathology was in fact an unavoidable prerequisite of the creation that followed.

Most, if not all, of what can be observed in the genius, in terms of bizarre behavior, anxiety, maladjustment, mood swings and what not, is by no means the common psychopathology that is described and explained in textbooks of psychiatry and psycho-pathology, but rather manifestations of the creative act or of its prerequisites. Of course, the genius too may suffer from common psychopathology, and it is not always easy to keep the psycho-pathology of creativity apart from the common garden variety. And still we do not yet know why superb creativity so often has its roots in seeming psychopathology, and why what is called a normal man is hardly likely to create the sort of values that posterity will ascribe to a genius.

By and large what is forgotten, I think, is how problematic —even unnatural, so to speak—is the existence of genius. The basic functions of living organisms are apparently survival and propagation, and their chances for survival are greatly enhanced by improved adjustment. But the genius does not adjust to reality: he is dissatisfied with it, like the rest of mankind and perhaps even more so; and he creates his own, a new reality, instead of adjust-ing to the one that already exists.[4] Such an act almost seems to contradict nature's primordial intentions, if a teleological phrase-ology may be permitted in passing.

Be that as it may, since the time when extensive and reliable documentation about the lives of geniuses has become obtainable, it has been possible to read about their great anguish and suffer-ings (Lange-Eichbaum 1927; Muschg 1948). Goethe said, quite openly, that if he had not been "condemned" to his talent, it

---

[4] A biological precursor of this performance may be found in the adaptation of organisms through active choice of the most suitable environment, as observed by Parr (1926; cf. Hartmann 1939).

would have been foolish of him to burden himself with the torment and the toil that are inherent in creativity (letter to Zelter, April 22, 1828); and at the age of seventy-five he confessed that, although he had been lauded as "fortune's favorite," he had experienced, all in all, hardly four weeks of real well-being (*eigentiliches Behagen*); (cf. Greenacre 1957). Many a reader of the works of a genius may feel an ardent wish to achieve an equivalent greatness on his own, but it is more than likely that he would not have been able to endure the pain to which most geniuses are subjected.

All his life long, Freud harbored a deep distrust of his intellectual powers; he was convinced that he owed his many discoveries to what was essentially strength of character and mental honesty (aside from good luck at times). Nevertheless, I believe that, behind these assets, one can discover in him an extraordinary ability to bear pain and frustration, as became generally known only after the publication of some of his letters to his fiancée. How early this capability for bearing pain sets in in a life of a genius, I do not know. The genius's childhood seems to be no more unhappy than that of others—if anything, perhaps happier. Freud recalls having been a happy child for the first three years of his life.

In the case of the genius, the period of childhood seems to be significant rather for the fact that processes take place that are valuable in terms of their harboring a highly constructive prospect. Greenacre (1957, p. 56) coined the felicitous term of "the propulsive force" of fantasies in the creative child. Indeed, much of what may have a retarding effect on the less endowed child will become propulsive in the creative child and will also provide him with great joy.

In Freud's life, two such propulsive forces can be reconstructed. It seems to me highly probable that, as a child, Freud identified with the Biblical Joseph to such an extent that that identification took on a reality feeling, along the lines of "I am the Biblical Joseph, destined to be a famous dream interpreter and to come to high honors." Identification with heroes, with whom the growing boy becomes familiar by hearsay or reading, is frequent in certain cultures. But the step toward a reality identification of this sort is less frequent.

In Freud's case (Shengold 1971), this was based on the fact that he was the oldest son of his father's second [5] and probably more loved wife—that is to say, he had the same position in his family that the Biblical Joseph had in his. Furthermore, in both instances, the name of the father was Jacob. Yet the similarity between Joseph and Freud goes beyond this, as Dr. Ruth S. Eissler has so keenly observed. In the lives of both, an older half-brother—in the one case, Reuben; in the other case, Emmanuel —held a father-like position (see Jones 1, p. 9). The number of homologous circumstances in the structure of their primary groups is striking, so that it is difficult to regard it as being merely a coincidence for a boy who grew up under a similar set of conditions (they conjoin but rarely) to revolutionize in his adulthood man's thinking about the dream. When a Joseph identification occurred in Freud's dreams, I would not think this to have been a retroactive effect of Freud's discovery as to the interpretation of dreams, but would instead conjecture that, next to Joseph, he did become the most famous interpreter of dreams, because as a child he had already formed a reality identification with the Biblical Joseph.[6]

In Goethe there probably also occurred a reality identification with Joseph (he wrote a Joseph epic in early years and stood as the model for paintings of a Joseph cycle his father had ordered —that is to say, he saw himself as Joseph in those paintings); and Newton probably formed a reality identification with Isaac, not only because of the identity of names, but also because he was told that he too had survived infancy only through Divine intervention, just like his namesake (Manuel 1968).

From these three examples I draw the tentative conclusions that one of the childhood processes that are relevant for the later evolvement of greatness is an identification, based on reality, with a historical figure of great renown. This general statement, how-

---

[5] Recently, it was discovered (Gicklhorn and Sajner 1968) that Freud's mother was the third wife of his father. Circumstances speak strongly in favor of the assumption that this fact was unknown to Freud, at least when he was a child.

[6] Such reality identification, if it is not combined with the sort of endowment that is necessary for its crystallization into achievement or success in reality, will, of course, lead to disturbances of a grave nature. (For the role of identification in creative people, see Greenacre 1957.)

ever, needs qualification. In all three of the instances referred to above, the reality that the child introjected was the figure of a good son.

The Biblical Joseph, for example, even though he is arrogant to his brothers, is an obedient son, since he resists temptation by a seductive mother. He is free of oedipal guilt.[7] The Joseph identity is a particularly propitious and ego-strengthening one, since despite defeats Joseph rises to glory, without incurring oedipal guilt. Identification with Christ, on the other hand, a son purer and more ideal than Joseph was, would harbor great dangers for the ego. This is also partly true of identification with Isaac, who voluntarily surrenders his life to his father. It would not be surprising if research were to prove that Newton's relative ego vulnerability, as indicated by the fact that he suffered a transitory psychosis, was caused by identification with a masochistically tainted (son) figure.

Thus one may tentatively suggest that, given outstanding endowment, when the child's identification is with a historical son-figure who was not burdened by guilt and ambivalence, and when that identification is based on reality factors rather than only on fantasy or like psychic elements—such a combination may be a propitious beginning for later eminence. The documentation for such a process in Freud's life is meager (1925b, p. 8): "My deep engrossment in the Bible story (almost as soon as I had learnt the art of reading) had, as I recognized much later, an enduring effect upon the direction of my interest." I would strongly suspect that a statement Freud made in a letter to Thomas Mann (November, 1936), ostensibly relating to Napoleon's life, had an autobiographical meaning. There he wrote: "I keep wondering whether there was not a figure in history for whom the life of Joseph was a mythical prototype, allowing us to detect the phantasy of Joseph as the secret daemonic motor behind the scenes of his complex life" (Freud, 1960, p. 432; slightly altered by me).[8]

---

[7] It is not probable that a little boy would notice that Joseph, after so valiantly defeating the lures of Potiphar's wife, is given a spouse from the family of Potiphera—which may be interpreted as a return of the repressed, and therefore may arouse some doubt in the purity that the chronicler has ascribed to the youth.

[8] For a discussion of the problem of creative identification in a broad historical context, see Ernst Kris's (1952) basic text.

The other experience that is, in my opinion, propitious for later great intellectual achievements is found in one of Freud's early recollections. He mentioned it in association to his dream of the three Fates (1900, pp. 204–208): "When I was six years old and was given my first lessons by my mother, I was expected to believe that we were all made of earth and must therefore return to earth. This did not suit me, and I expressed doubts of the doctrine. My mother thereupon rubbed the palms of her hands together—just as she did in making dumplings, except that there was no dough between them—and showed me the blackish scales of epidermis produced by the friction as a proof that we were made of earth. My astonishment at this ocular demonstration knew no bounds."

Freud became later a master of the demonstratio ad oculos—to be sure, by way of words. Some, I think wrongly, have asserted his unsuitability for the experimental technique with which the mother had impressed him so much as a child. But later he knew well how to perform actively what he had experienced passively, and there were a few times when he was able to throw the world "into boundless astonishment" by his discoveries.

One may on good grounds recognize in Freud's childhood recollection (Freud's third sister was born at that time) a screen-memory for the child's envy of the mother's ability to create children; it contains the male's imperishable feeling about nature's having discriminated against him. But it is of decisive importance that the screen-memory already shows the earmarks of a high degree of sublimation. It does not refer to the mother's fecundity but to a non-physical aspect of her omniscience. In the screen-memory, the concealment of that envy's true nature leads to envy of mother's knowledge of death, a remote foreshadowing of the later construction of the death instinct and of repetition-compulsion.[9]

Be that as it may, the image of the creative mother was ap-

---

[9] It may be that Freud's later pejorative quotation, "the logic of soup, with dumplings for arguments" (1915a, p. 167), as characteristic of women with whom analysis is unsuccessful, is unconsciously still related to that early recollection, in which the mother impressed the child so deeply with an argument that later proved to be fictitious. As a matter of fact, the child was indeed made the victim of soup-and-dumplings logic (cf. the role of the dumpling in Freud's dream of the three Fates).

parently integrated into the superego. Ego identification with a guiltless, obedient and highly successful son-figure, combined with the organization of the superego around the image of the creative mother, impresses me as being a highly propitious beginning for the foundation of a creative personality.

The reader will already have noticed the essential contrast with Tausk's childhood, in which the terrible incident of pictorial matricide took place. Contrast in the relationship of the two to their fathers will be best illustrated, after what we already know about Tausk, by a statement that Freud's father allegedly once made about the adolescent boy: "My Sigmund is more intelligent in his little toe than I in the head; but he would never dare to contradict me" (Wittels 1923, p. 242, n. 32; German edition; my own translation). Here, if Wittels was correct, a boy had the rare good luck of having his father acknowledge the son's superiority, without aggressive acting-out being incited.[10]

From all we know about Tausk's childhood, there is no likelihood of his having been favored by events as propitious as those one finds in Freud's childhood. Of course, the question remains unsolved whether the genius's good luck in childhood is completely adventitious, or may not be in part already due to assets in the infant and child that arouse parental love to a larger degree than the average child does (cf. Coleman et al. 1953). It is to Tausk's merit that he was able to rescue his talents from a divided, torn, conflict-ridden childhood. In a discussion remark at the Vienna Psychoanalytic Society, following Freud's presentation of a paper on Leonardo (December 1, 1909), Tausk said that "as a child, he was always eager to hear how the parents, who often quarreled because of him, got together again." [11] Was he as a child already trying to arouse enmity between his parents, in order to witness their reconciliation? Does one not meet here an early pattern, to which the adult later became fixated?

The conflicts experienced by talent and genius do overlap in

---

[10] The boy's critical attitude toward the father, apparently successfully internalized, became attached to the father's story of an act of cowardice that he had committed upon being offended by a Christian on the grounds of his Jewishness. According to Freud's account, he was ten or twelve when he heard the story for the first time (Freud 1900, p. 197).

[11] . . . als Kind immer begierig war zu hören, wie sich die Eltern, die seinetwegen oft stritten, wieder einigten.

quite a few areas. Ambition; rivalry; the difficulty of accepting a subordinate position in the history of ideas and in life—these arouse conflicts and produce restlessness in them when such persons enter the adult world. Did Tausk ever acquire the ability to admit male superiority in a conflict-free fashion? [2] It is possible that he did succeed in doing so shortly before his death.

Freud, too, went through a phase of intense ambition; but toward the end of his stay in Paris, he wondered how he could ever have believed himself to harbor the potential of genius, and he acknowledged Charcot's greatness, apparently without conflict. The reader will perhaps also remember the sentence in Freud's letter to Jung, at the height of their friendship, in which he concedes to the younger man, apparently without resentment, that the latter is charging forward to peaks to which he himself cannot follow. But it had taken a period of unbelievable suffering before Freud had learned to accept the idea that his name would not become renowned.

This took place during the four-and-a-quarter years of his engagement, when month after month the fulfillment of any of his wishes seemed to keep moving ahead to a distant future, and he felt at times abysmally hopeless. His fiancée was living in faraway Hamburg, and it was altogether exceptional for Freud to possess the money needed for that journey. During these years, the frustrations were so exceedingly painful and the violence of his inner processes so intemperate, that even this giant feared for his sanity. Yet nothing could break his sense of duty, even during these years of turbulence; he did research and went through what may be described as a rotating residency, and he obtained the honor of a University Lectureship (*Dozentur*). Still, no effort on his part seemed to secure the income that at that time was believed to be a prerequisite to respectable matrimony.

Tausk also had his crisis. It was somewhat shorter, and frightfully painful; but it was unorganized and inorganic, being filled with a number of scattered attempts to find "a content of life," which finally forced him to take refuge in a hospital. Tausk's letters during that period are pathetic; they urgently cry out for pity; Freud also described his sufferings in detail, but he did not ask for pity. Tausk's letters to his wife concealed the secret of an ongoing love affair; in his letters to Martha Bernays, Freud imposed upon himself that candor and honesty that were to remain an outstanding feature of his later career.

When Tausk recovered from his crisis, he was able to start his psychoanalytic career. But had he changed during the crisis? The symptoms had disappeared, to be sure; but, as his later behavior demonstrated, irresponsibility, dependency, aggressive acting out, depressions and suicidal thoughts still remained ready at hand. Yet the four-and-a-quarter years of Freud's crisis released him as a man whose personality had undergone a structural change, and not only a symptomatic one—the most outstanding change being the elimination of his wild and probably pathological ambition.[12]

He was at last able to visualize himself as happy and contented with being fully absorbed in his relationship with Martha and the support of a family, without the need for a rise to fame to adorn and justify his existence. That this was more than a reaction formation can be strikingly observed in a statement he made to the effect that, if fate were to knock at the door, it would find him ready. Thus he was ready to fulfill an eminent task, should one present itself to him; but he was also ready to live in contentment without it. At that moment, he had reached a state of ripeness and fitness to become the great man he will forever be known as in the history of science.

Of Freud too one may say what Goethe, meaning himself, said of Wilhelm Meister: "Saul, the son of Kis, went out to search for his father's she-asses, and found a kingdom." As long as Freud was striving toward greatness, he failed to achieve it; but when he lowered his aims to those of other mortals, great discoveries fell into his lap, one after another. It may be very true of many geniuses that, even though they go out to seek she-asses, they reap kingdoms, while the talents venture out for the conquest of kingdoms, yet come back with no more than asses.

As soon as it was no longer a matter of striving feverishly for opportunities for glory, as was the case during the time of the cocaine episode, which is so very characteristic of Freud's "ambi-

---

[12] Freud himself was aware of the change that took place in him during these years. Cf.: "Even a year ago, I would have been speechless with agitation, but now I am different; I was not in the least frightened" (Freud 1960, p. 78); or, "I am changed more profoundly than I myself knew" (Freud 1960, p. 125; my own translation).

tious" period, the problems started to seize *him* and to a certain extent he lost his creative autonomy; whereas in the ambitious period he had tried with great effort to direct the creative impulse toward outstanding achievements, the impulse now dominated him. The most remarkable observation, however, to be made about those gloomy four years of Freud's engagement is the fact that something that was the equivalent of the discoveries that were later to make him famous had already come to pass during that earlier period.

It is interesting to note that, as early as in the premarital letters to Martha, Freud was almost constantly engaged in a keen observation of the people around him, and that he was already formulating general observations—in a unscientific way, of course; casually, without being aware of their full meaning. He was even observing his own dreams—an unbecoming kind of "hobby" for a medical man, especially one who was allegedly interested solely in neuropathological histology, in preparation for medical practice, and who was eagerly striving for a full measure of financial independence.

It looks as if, side by side with the problems that were filling his conscious mind, his unconscious was working at something quite different—namely, the problems of man and his mind. What will later, during the Fliess period, become scientifically observed, described, organized, explained, was at this time being pre- or unconsciously preformed as the raw material—the unbaked bricks, as it were—out of which the palace would be built during the subsequent four decades.[13]

If the reader agrees with me that the foundations for Freud's

---

[13] For specific examples, see Jones (1, p. 191 and *passim*); and Eissler (1964, pp. 203–205). The late Ernst Freud showed me the following passage in a letter of Freud, in which he had made an inkblot: "Here the pen dropped out of [my] hand and made this secret sign. We beg to be excused and [to suggest that one] not trouble oneself [with finding] the interpretation." [*Hier ist uns die Feder aus der Hand gefallen und hat dieses Geheimzeichen gemacht. Wir bitten um Entschuldigung und sich nicht um die Deutung zu bemühen.*] This passage would not be particularly remarkable if it had not been written in 1882—that is to say, nineteen years before the publication of *The Psychopathology of Everyday Life*; at a time when nothing could have been further removed from Freud's clinical and theoretical researches than the interpretation of parapraxes. Even if the word "interpretation" may refer here to the result of a parapraxis, this still does not diminish the historical importance of the remark.

stupendous discoveries later on were laid during those four years —even though this took place without his being aware in what direction his unconscious mentation was taking him—then he will perhaps also agree when I say that it must have been a relevant and even decisive aspect of the total situation that, almost certainly, the full duration of Freud's engagement was spent in total sexual continence.

The sex life of genius has occupied a good many researchers. It is a cardinal question, insofar as one may learn through it the energic prerequisite—the underpinning, so to speak—on which genius flourishes. When Schopenhauer says, "If Petrarch's passion had been gratified, his song would have fallen silent" (van Dovski 1959, p. 45),[14] he is putting in a nutshell the reason why the quality of accomplishment of the great poets is favored by sexual continence—and may even be made possible by it.

Yet this seems also to be true of the genius in science. One may conjecture that the genius's psychic apparatus produces extraordinary results only when the main and most cherished avenue of discharge is closed off. Reconstruction of Tausk's sex life suggests (I think this is typical of talent) that his psychic apparatus would never have been able to bear up under the degree of damming-up that the genius has to tolerate in order to create the extraordinary. It cannot be accidental that the seeds of that new psychology that was destined to have such a profound bearing on Western thought and to give the history of ideas a new direction took shape during a time in Freud's life when he was suffering maximal frustration. After all, he did not even have the solace of his sweetheart's company, yet he came to understand that this additional sacrifice, against which he had initially rebelled, had been in fact quite beneficial. This proves that also the unconscious gain of these four years would have been much smaller if his sweetheart had in fact been living in Vienna.

---

[14] A vulgarization of this idea is to be found in an anecdote about Balzac. He is said to have remarked, after a night in which he had a wet dream: "Another masterpiece lost to French literature," for he would not "be able to conceive any good story for at least a fortnight, yet I could certainly write a masterpiece in that time." I found the story in Frank Harris (1925, p. 247) and doubt its authenticity; but it seems to be a historical truth that Balzac did recognize the damaging effect that the prolonged closeness of the beloved woman would have on his creativity (van Dovski 1959, p. 119).

At first, he had taken the separation from Martha to be the consequence of an unnecessary step, enforced solely by her mother's selfishness and arbitrariness. In August, 1884, he was even driven to write bitter and cruel words: he felt that he had been "deeply injured" [schwer geschädigt]; and "I feel incapable of reconciling myself to her [Martha's mother], whose heartlessness and caprice I hold responsible for your departure" (Freud 1960, p. 123).

Yet by the spring of 1885 he knew better (Jones 1, p. 131f.): "In one thing I was in the wrong and I think I can now admit it. That is, I can no longer reproach anyone that you had to be away from Vienna in these years. I know I would have borne it still more badly had you been here and not belonged to me. My thoughts would have been always with you, and I should have had no peace in my work." And shortly thereafter he wrote: "I am able to be so reasonable, to work and to bear deprivation, only because I don't see you." These excerpts not only demonstrate Freud's chivalry of soul, its impartiality, but they also show an enormous change in the structure of his personality, the progress of his insight into his self, along with the evolvement of an incredible degree of self-discipline. It is just this sequence that seems to prove that the change of personality that took place later, during the course of his self-analysis, was built up on the previous one, which had taken place during the bitter years of extreme suffering, and may have been even more consequential than the latter.

It goes without saying that civilization imposes on every person sacrifices of drive gratification of one sort or another, yet the kind and the degree do vary. Deri (1939) and others have made the very interesting suggestion that sublimation is fed mainly by libido stemming from pregenital zones, and that genital libido is exempt. I wonder whether this is true of the genius (cf. Lantos 1955; see also Deutsch 1927). One gets the impression that the latter's sublimations, as distinct from those of talented persons, rest mainly on phallic energy—pregenital channels (Freud's quasi-addiction to smoking; Goethe's anal compositions and his daily intake of a bottle of wine; Mozart's obscene letters to his cousin) being kept open as a kind of substitute for the genital gratification that is being blocked off, or at least reduced.

But more. After a production phase has reached its conclusion, the genius's mind quite frequently falls into a state of tranquility and peacefulness, comparable to the moods that would follow sexual gratification. This is quite puzzling: during those peaks of production, no physical discharge has taken place; and yet, when the high-pitched mental activity has come to an end, the subject is left in a state in which he feels as he would have if a physical discharge had indeed taken place.

I therefore suggest that the structure of psychic discharge is different in talent from what it is in genius. In the genius, mental activity is apparently so highly integrated and so intensely charged with energy that it becomes equivalent to physical genital discharge. We then understand better why there are eminently productive minds that are quasi-addicted to creativity, their life being an almost uninterrupted stream of creations of the highest quality. Yet this very condition may precipitate conflict and therefore require all kinds of measures—which have the appearance of, and are therefore easily taken for, neurotic and even psychotic psychopathology—before the way has been opened for a productive breakthrough.

I earlier stressed the sexual continence that was aggravated by the love object's absence, in a decisive phase of Freud's development. I must now add that this was also a period of maximal outer directedness, in the shape of maximal craving for the passionately desired and loved woman, even though clouds of jealousy and ill-temper did make their appearance at times in Freud's relationship to his fiancée. If it was indeed during those years that Freud gained the basic stuff out of which psychoanalysis was later to be formed, then one may tentatively suggest a general formulation. It seems that an eminently gifted personality reaches its highest degree of creativity at a time when maximal frustration coincides with maximal directedness toward the world.

Is the talented person a genius in miniature? No. Nor is he a genius who has failed. In the life of the genius, victory and defeat are intertwined. Almost any other person would have collapsed, regressed or become embittered under the burden of those four-and-a-quarter years through which Freud had to go. Yet what is the undoing of others is given constructive form by the creative impulse that is inherent in genius. Behind all the rifts and conflicts that are so significant of the genius, there lies a latent harmony. For the genius can rely on the voice of the unconscious —sometimes called "the daemon"—which usually misleads others.

When Freud chose a theoretical discipline, such as neurological histology, as his principal field of endeavor, and later chose Martha Bernays, offspring of one of Germany's foremost Jewish families, to be his bride, even though she would not bring any dowry with her, he was acting against common sense, the voice of reason and, I am certain, the counsel of both family and friends. Nevertheless, contrary to all probability, both choices proved later to be eminently beneficial to him.

A famous instance of reliance on the daemon, against all reason, and thus flying in the face of the reality principle, was Goethe's taking residence at Weimar. All who knew him, of course, predicted—on seemingly good grounds—the detrimental effect that would follow when a member of the upper middle class established a permanent alliance with a rococo Duke. Yet this alliance led to an unusual flowering of literary output. Goethe himself seems to have been aware of the daemonic nature of his decision. His autobiographical work ends with the moment when he decides—against all obstacles—to go to Weimar. We read:

> As if whipped by invisible spirits Time's sun-horses run away with the light carriage of our fate and nothing is left to us but, courageously poised, to hold the reins tight and to steer the wheels now to the right, now to the left, away from a rock here and from downfall there. Whither it goes, who knows? He hardly even remembers whence he came (my own translation).

Nietzsche verbalized it when writing to a friend in 1879: "The good daemon in us is more powerful than disease and pain— whatever he may be called, this 'good daemon'!!" [*der gute Dämon in uns ist mächtiger als die Krankheit und der Schmerz wie er auch heissen möge, dieser "gute Dämon"!!*] (author's emphasis; Pfeiffer, ed. 1970, p. 57).

By contrast, when Tausk was driven to relinquish his career as lawyer and judge, he was probably being grossly misled by his daemon. If he had stayed in law, he could certainly have brought good fortune to many more people than he ever did as a psychoanalyst. When his daemon took him away from Vienna to Berlin, the crisis to which he was subjected there did not add strength to him: it did not consolidate his loose structure, nor did it immunize him against the poison of masochism. When his daemon led him back to Vienna to join the then avant-garde movement of psychoanalysis, this seemed to be a propitious beginning, and yet here too the daemon led him astray: he was not to bear for long an existence that brought him so close to what he regarded as the burning bush.

Rightly, one may say that the daemon does not act so cruelly with all talents. And there were many—indeed, the majority—in close proximity to Freud, who were talented and felt grateful to their daemons. Yet perhaps in the instances of those other talents who, having joined Freud, stayed with him and flourished, this was not so greatly a daemonic decision as it was with Tausk, but rather one of reason, even if not entirely of practicality. After all, Tausk's life story may show, in stronger relief than is observable in other instances, some essential features of the psychology of talent.

When I now proceed to discuss a mechanism that was apparently quite strongly activated in Tausk, namely, that of rescue, I enter momentarily into an area of speculation. This mechanism was prominent in his relationship to the young Serbian widow who was arrested by an Austrian platoon and freed by him. Already, as a lawyer, he had rescued from the gallows a Moslem girl who had killed her illegitimate child (p. 12) and, during the war, he rescued quite a few from the firing squad. He apparently also rescued his sister from an unhappy marriage (p. 109).

By sharp contrast with this, no vestige of rescue fantasies can be found in Freud, unless we are to regard his expressed denial thereof as being a sign of defense. "I have no knowledge," he wrote (1927a, p. 253) "of having had any craving in my early childhood to help suffering humanity. My innate sadistic disposition was not a very strong one, so that I had no need to develop this one of its derivatives. Nor did I ever play the 'doctor game.'" He accepted the truth of the bon mot that "educating, healing, and governing"—that is to say, just those undertakings in which the rescue fantasy can best be gratified—are "three impossible professions" (1925a, p. 273; cf. 1937, p. 248). Oddly enough, without being motivated by a rescue fantasy, Freud did "rescue" a large number of people and did succeed in creating an instrument whose potential for "rescuing" is enormous.

It would be important to know whether we are dealing here with a significant difference between genius and talent. Freud was generous in his personal life, in regard to giving to others; Tausk, as we noted above, could not give to those who were close to him, such as his wife, his sons and his sweethearts.

Annie Reich has written on the function of rescue fantasies in psychoanalytic work, and has dealt with the conditions under which they are helpful or cause damage. The rescue fantasy is a highly important psychic structure, on which the socially valuable behavior of many people depends. Yet the fantasy is the outgrowth of ambivalence (Freud 1910a, pp. 168–173; Sterba 1940); it makes social behavior dependent on the object's being in a critical condition. A person has to be in dire distress before the appropriate social action is initiated, and the positive object relationship is usually discontinued soon after the object's full restoration. The man who is preoccupied by an excessive rescue fantasy seems to say: "If you want me to love you and to win my affection, you must first jump into the lake." It is noteworthy to observe how often subjects in whose lives rescue fantasies occupy a prominent place, are deficient in affectionate behavior toward members of their immediate environment.

The exhibitionistic, narcissistic background of the rescue fantasy is evident: accomplishment in the service of the object leads to a narcissistic elevation of the self. In Tausk's instance it is striking that rescue actions were more often than not combined with a considerable aggression against authority. It is hardly possible to estimate what might have been the stronger motive in Tausk's case: the rescue of a person in danger, or the showing up of abusive authority.

My speculation is that pronounced rescue fantasies will be found more frequently in the life stories of talented persons than in those of geniuses. The rescue fantasy impresses me as being often the result of a tendency to isolate; it reduces the area of social action to narrow segments—which in itself interferes with a broad, free-flowing relationship toward the world. The latter relationship is marked by a minimum of ambivalence, whereas the preoccupation with rescue, even under optimal conditions, presupposes a heightening of ambivalence. May I repeat that this suggestion with regard to the relationship of genius and talent to rescue fantasies is merely a speculative one.[15]

One reaches concrete ground again when the question is raised of Tausk's achievement. It is typical of talent. As I have proposed above, the hallmark of genius is the creation of a universe and the discovery of paradigms. The former is quite exceptional for the scientist, and in Tausk's case there can be only the question of whether or not he did succeed in creating paradigms. It is difficult to answer that question, since the concept of paradigm is not as precise as one would wish it to be. In a previous paper (Eissler 1969b), I asserted that Freud was the only analyst who succeeded in the discovery—or creation, as the case may be—of paradigms, and I may, therefore, as I conceded on that occasion, be called prejudiced on that score. If paradigms are viewed in their historical context, however, as clustering within the process of a scientific revolution, then my generalization is correct.

Freud's work initiated a scientific revolution—that is a historical fact, quite independent of the degree of Freud's originality. Some authors, like Bailey (1956), try to minimize Freud's originality, by placing stress on his predecessors. This, I am certain, is a methodologically wrong approach. Freud was a great synthesizer, so that traditional elements are quite numerous in his work. Despite its revolutionary effect and content, psychoanalysis fits at the same time organically into the development of Western psychology. Among all the new psychologies, it is in psychoanalysis alone that the concept of association—the cardinal point of pre-Freudian psychologies (Bühler 1926)—has preserved a central position. Freud's greatness lay in his belonging among those of whom Gillispie (1960, p. 202f.) was speaking, when he said that "every science has its orderer in the structure of history, one who first framed objective concepts widely enough to reorient its posture: Galileo for kinematics, Newton for physics, Darwin for biology." The greatness of such an "orderer" is not diminished by his having had predecessors, as Gillispie (1960, p. 7) recognized

---

[15] Mrs. Dorothy T. Burlingham, who was kind enough to read this manuscript, has called my attention to the fact that not all rescue fantasies or rescue actions can be put over the same denominator. Evidently the problem is more complex than I have presented it here.

when he noted: "Everything, indeed, or nearly everything that Galileo put together may be found in the writings . . . of some predecessor," implying that, despite that fact, no historian would doubt Galileo's greatness and originality.

Furthermore, it can often be observed that new discoveries and ideas are rejected for a long time and, subsequently, when they are accepted, their originality is disputed. Something of that sort can already be observed in the evaluation of the work of Thales of Miletos, who was the first to introduce a scientific viewpoint into the history of ideas in the West, when he said that everything has developed out of water. Yet Homer (*Iliad* V, 206) had already said, a couple of centuries before Thales, that Okeanos is the origin of all things, and some historians have therefore disputed the originality of Thales.

Capelle (1935, p. 4) has rightly stated that it makes an essential difference whether an idea is presented in a mythical-magic-animistic context, or is set forth in a rational-scientific one. Posterity may easily underrate the grave labor that it took to purify an idea of its mythical-magic-animistic dross. The historian who looks for what is common to two events, two cultural elements or ideas, may vastly underestimate the mental distance that lies between an idea as set forth by Homer and one put forth by Thales—even if the two had appeared to be quite identical (which they were not). It is conceivable—though not probable—that, for every scientific discovery, precursors can be found within the mythical-magic-animistic orbit. Thus the sequence seems to be that the "orderer" of a science is at first ignored or rejected because he disturbs the relative pleasure inherent in mythical-magical thinking; after the idea has been accepted, however, many a historian will feel inclined to minimize the qualitative difference between his work and that of his precursors.

The mythical-magic construction, according to Capelle (1935, p. 31), should serve the historian as a foil to bring out, in full prominence, distinction and vividness, the magnitude of what we would now call a paradigm or a set of paradigms. Only acceptance of this methodological approach can lead to a proper appraisal of Freud's work.

However, the scientific revolution that Freud brought about consists of two phases: in the first, inquiry centered on those

areas in which the ego has been reduced in activity and over-
mastered, as happens in dream, parapraxis, drive, neurotic symptom, laughter; as a result, more (but not exclusive) attention was
paid to processes in the repressed and their derivatives within the
ego sphere. In the second phase, Freud's inquiry centered on the
psychology of the ego itself. No claim has been made with regard
to Tausk's having contributed paradigms to the first phase, but
the reader may recall Roazen's grave (and tendentious) mistake
in having "the study of [psychoanalytic] ego psychology" start with
Tausk's and Federn's treatment of psychoses (p. 188).

This, of course, would have been quite impossible, if for no
other reason than that Tausk never treated psychotic patients.
But, aside from that, I want to refer now not to Freud's early
papers, in which he conveyed his ego-psychological observations,
but to his paper of 1911(b), which contains the theoretical presentation of "the developmental process which affects the ego"
(1911b, p. 224). This paper marks the official introduction of ego
psychology into psychoanalysis, even though the scattered beginnings of psychoanalytic ego psychology can be found in Freud's
psychological writings from the start. The reader may also be
reminded of Freud's diary, which I cited earlier.

The so far unpublished portion of the *Minutes* of the Vienna
Psychoanalytic Society contains (March 27, 1912) a summary of
Tausk's paper on "Sexuality and Ego." There the problem of ego
is limited to the (antagonistic) interplay of sex- and ego drives,
and the ego is considered "an artificial concept" (*artifizieller
Begriff*); in Freud's paper (1911b) on the two principles of mental
functioning, by contrast, an ouline of the later ego psychology in
terms of structure is already visible. On October 26, 1910 (Jones
2, p. 312), Freud presented the essence of his ideas to the Society,
even though they were not yet as clearly formulated as they were
to be in the final product. It is of historical interest that even
that group of pioneers did not perceive the seed of greatness that
was contained in the newly introduced concepts, such as pleasure-
ego and reality-ego.

At that time, Tausk had announced, as reported earlier, that
he had reached similar conclusions previously; yet one-and-a-half
years later, when he himself addressed the Society on questions
of the ego, there was no indication that he had made any use of

the turning point that had been made in Freud's paper of 1911. Tausk was still discussing the problem of the ego from the vantage point of a position that Freud had already left behind, even though he himself was to use the old terminology until 1920.

The forthcoming publication of the *Minutes* of that meeting in October, 1910 will serve as a significant example of the difference between genius and talent. Here was a group at whose disposal there were, by and large, the same observational data. All of them were in agreement that resistances stand in the way of correct insights into the working of the mind; all of them had taken cognizance of these resistances in themselves to a varying degree, and all of them were eager to make new discoveries. Their intellectual sharpness, of course, varied, yet it is not certain that Freud's intelligence, if it had been tested in the way that is now customary, would have shown the highest scores among all members of the group. At least, most of his life he complained that his intelligence was not what he thought it should be.

Yet, from the observational data that he shared with the rest, he initiated a new set of paradigms (the second since he had taken up his psychological research), and no one of those present even noticed that here the foundations were being laid for a formidable extension of psychoanalysis. Curiously enough, it is highly probable that all of us who now profit so greatly from this second set of paradigms would have been as much lacking in discernment had we been present at that memorable evening.[16]

Tausk was also present at that meeting and, as we have seen, intimated that he had himself thought something of the kind Freud had presented, though in a different context—with a different index, as it were. Yet Freud's paper does not seem to have opened any new vista for Tausk, as the summary of his 1912 paper shows. Tausk was an excellent observer, and there can be no doubt that he used Freud's paradigms productively. This can be seen, for example, in the paper in which two dreams of a ten-year-old boy, who was evidently his older son (Tausk 1913b), were in-

---

[16] It may be that it is some awareness of that essential difference, between the genius' inner necessity to create paradigms and the talent's ability, which is limited to the *productive* use of those same paradigms, that has produced the need to deny the existence of any essential difference between talent and genius, thereby eliminating in the former any basis for a feeling of shame.

terpreted. Such a paper could have hardly been written more pene-
tratingly. In addition, the delineation of the sexual activities
during the boy's latency period is excellent.

Tausk was ever-ready to compound existing paradigms into
new ones. In the analysis of another dream (Tausk 1914a), he
tried to keep separate the representation of the affects and of ideas
—a very engaging proposition. There is no doubt that, within the
small group surrounding Freud, Tausk belonged to that still
smaller group in which the Freudian paradigms lived what one
may describe as "an active existence," always on the lookout for
extensions and new combinations. However, there is the question
whether he went beyond that point in two papers through which
he acquired a permanent place in psychoanalytic literature, along
with the posthumously published one, which aroused less general
interest.

In one of these papers (1913a), Tausk raised the question of
how it is possible for an idea that has been forgotten (temporarily
repressed), because of the displeasure attached to it, to be brought
to consciousness by means of free association. He proved, by way
of two clinical examples, that the idea that has been temporarily
lost reappears in the subject's mind as soon as an association has
provided a compensation, usually by way of a narcissistic gratification, and has thus reduced the displeasure originally attached to
the idea, which the subject now tries to regain. Tausk's paper may
impress many a reader as containing a paradigm. However, the
application of the pleasure principle to the recall of memories was
described by Freud as early as 1899 (p. 317). There, it was a
matter of explaining the recollection of early memories: "It seems
. . . as though the recollection of the remote past is in itself
facilitated by some pleasurable motive," and he added a quotation
from Virgil (Aeneid, I, 203): *Forsan et haec olim meminisse
iuvabit* [one day, perhaps, 'twill please us to remember even this].
Yet, more importantly, Freud demonstrated in his book on *Jokes*
(1905b) some specific techniques by means of which the repressed
can make its reappearance within the boundaries of the ego. Thus
the technique that Tausk described follows a pattern that is
similar to one previously described by Freud, and Tausk ought to
have cited on that occasion Freud's book of 1905.

Waelder, if I have understood his paper of 1951 correctly, assigned a paradigm to Tausk's credit,[17] inasmuch as—according to Waelder—Tausk was the first one to claim "*isomorphism* of symptom and defense mechanism" (Waelder 1951, p. 173; author's emphasis). That is to say, countercathexis, defensive structure and the return of the warded-off material all have the same formal characteristics. I myself doubt that the law of isomorphism is correct; but if it should be, the historian would once again have to assign the priority to Freud. In an early paper, Freud (1907, p. 34) proposed that "it is precisely what was chosen as the instrument of repression . . . that becomes the vehicle for the return." Even though in a reduced form, this contains the essence of the law of isomorphism.[18]

Now let us turn to that paper by Tausk (1919) for which he is known to every student of psychoanalysis who has graduated from a reputable institute in this country—namely, his paper on the origin of the "influencing machine," a highly interesting delusional system that occurs not too frequently in patients who are suffering from process schizophrenia. This is, undoubtedly, Tausk's best paper; it is rich in clinical observations and theoretical propositions.

The extent to which Tausk's main idea, that the delusion of the influencing machine is the result of a projection of the patient's body, has been anticipated by Freud, is usually overlooked. I owe thanks to Dr. Maurits Katan for having called my attention to a passage in Edward Bibring's paper of 1929, in which Tausk's theory is linked with Freud's case history (1915d) of a female patient who suffered from paranoia. Freud explained the patient's delusion as a projection of her clitoris onto a clock. This historical antecedent, although it would have deserved to be mentioned in

---

[17] It is ironic that it was precisely Waelder, whom Roazen attacked so unjustifiedly as one of Freud's many "mirrors," who did so much to protect Tausk against oblivion. His paper proves that there was no bias at all against Tausk's work among the analysts who worked directly with Freud.

[18] One could possibly read into a later sentence of Freud's (1911a, p. 65f.) a revocation of his earlier intimation of the existence of what Waelder called the law of isomorphism. "We certainly have no right to begin by assuming that these two mechanisms [the mechanism *by which the symptoms are formed* and the mechanism *by which repression is brought about*] are identical, and that symptom-formation follows the same path as repression, each proceeding along it, perhaps, in an opposite direction. Nor does there seem to be any great probability that such an identity exists" (author's emphasis).

Tausk's paper, does not, of course, reduce the merit of his theory.

In Tausk's paper the term "ego boundary" appears for the first time in psychoanalytic literature, and this, at last, might be considered the introduction of a true paradigm. However, the coining of a new term must not be equated with the formation of a paradigm.[19] Tausk used the term in order to explain the conviction of some schizophrenics that their thoughts are known to everyone; he called it "a loss of ego boundaries." Yet Freud had explained this symptom five years earlier by a structural change in the ego (1914b, p. 95), without, however, giving any special name to that change.

Furthermore, a scrutiny of other documents shows that the term was apparently taken for granted in the psychoanalytic jargon. I shall quote only two instances. One of them has been translated into English (Freud 1960, p. 310); it appeared in a letter that Freud wrote to Lou Andreas-Salomé (July 30, 1915) about a "substitute for the surrender of the boundaries of the ego, which can be painful enough." [20] The other is found in an untranslated letter of Lou Andreas-Salomé to Freud, in which she writes (July 2, 1917) of "negating the ego boundaries and the environment" [21] (Freud 1966, p. 66). Probably one could find more instances.

Sarton (1957, p. 219) rightly rejected the idea that marginal notes should be taken at their face value and incorporated into the history of science. This rejection may be extended to the content of correspondences. If one does so, the historical merit of Tausk's having been the first to use the term in official literature would not be lessened, unless one has to draw the conclusion that the term itself was indeed current among analysts at that time.[22] Be

---

[19] In certain phases of the development of a science, the tendency is observable to coin new terms rather than to discover paradigms. It may even happen that a paradigm remains unnoticed, while a new term—even though it signifies nothing more than a different statement of well-known facts and relations—comes into prominence. This occurs, it seems to me, when a science has reached a plateau.

[20] *Ersatz für das Aufgeben der Ichgrenzen, das schmerzhaft genug sein mag.*

[21] *Negierung der Ichgrenzen und der Umwelt.*

[22] This is quite probable not only in view of the letters cited, but also because Paul Federn (1926, p. 30) used the term as if it were a current one. Paul Schilder (1914) was already writing of a central ego (*Zentrale Ich*) and the depth of the ego, and Freud's metapsychological aspect of topography made "borders" indispensable—particularly his frequent description of the censor as

that as it may, in Tausk's paper the term has mainly descriptive value. It was only during the course of Paul Federn's ego-psychological research that the term gradually came to life—if this metaphor may be permitted—and proved its great heuristic value (Federn 1952 *passim*).

Another possible paradigm may be derived from Dr. Jacobson's (1964, p. XI) footnote, with regard to Tausk's having introduced the term "identity" into the psychoanalytic literature. She was there referring to Tausk's statement (1919, p. 543): "It is this stage of identity that precedes the first projection, etc." It is questionable that Dr. Jacobson is correct in her comment. In the passage to which she refers, Tausk did not use the term "identity" in the sense in which it is used in psychology and psychopathology. He meant only that the neonate "is completely identical with himself" [23]—that is to say, that it "knows nothing of the outer world" (Tausk 1919, p. 543).

Even though Dr. Jacobson may have been wrong in thus ascribing to Tausk the introduction into psychoanalytic literature of the term "identity," she was historically correct in pointing to a sentence in his paper of 1919, in which he took a step that was genuinely original. Tausk wrote (1919, p. 544):

> We must definitely understand that throughout life the ego develops with constant shiftings in the narcissistic libido position, *that man in his struggle for existence is constantly compelled to find and recognize himself anew*, and that the acquisition of narcissism is immanent in culture and is conceivable only on the basis of intact inborn narcissism that serves as a source of nourishment and regeneration (emphasis added).

Tausk here went as far as a talent can go. From the foundation by Freud of ego psychology, he derived the outlines of a new problem. The grave effect that paranoid psychoses may and do have on the sense of identity was described by Freud, without his using the technical term. Thus he wrote, as early as in 1911 (a, p. 72): "In paranoia the liberated libido becomes attached to

---

being located between conscious and unconscious, which inescapably implies a border. As the matter stands now, it is hardly possible to decide who actually coined the term.

[23] . . . *ist er ganz identisch mit sich.* Dorian Feigenbaum omitted this sentence altogether in his translation.

the ego, and is used for the aggrandizement of the ego"—an idea he elaborated further three years later (Freud 1914b, p. 80; see also Abraham 1908, p. 75). The new suggestion introduced by Tausk has to do with the repeated necessity in man's life of acts of self-recognition.

It is important, however, that, where Tausk is writing about the patient's disease *per se*, he keeps himself within the conceptual framework that Freud had established for the purpose of explaining paranoid psychoses: defense mechanism—particularly projection—fixation, auto-erotism, primary narcissism. Thus in no way did he overstep the path of thought patterns that were customary at that time among analysts.[24]

When Tausk's paper was published, Freud was already deeply steeped in the inner evolvement of new paradigms: the structural viewpoint; the death instinct; the repetition compulsion—a triad of which one may say that it includes his greatest constructions. Nowhere in Tausk's work, however, or in that of any other contemporary analyst, was anything visible that would have suggested that *he* was on the verge of recreating the analytic world, as it were, anew; of viewing the discoveries made until then under a new aspect, that was to give psychoanalytic research a new momentum, whose centrifugal power has not yet come to rest fifty years later.

Even though it may be a triviality, one has to restate something that is all too well known—namely, that under the touch of genius, everything becomes a token of eminent mastery. Oddly enough, Freud's potential for scientific genius showed up with his very first attempt, when at twenty, as a beginner, he received a grant to carry out a histological examination of a puzzling organ in male eels. The late Professor Gicklhorn—even though he was a critic of Freud, and indeed almost no less unrelenting than Roazen —spoke in the most glowing terms about the incredible feat of the young student—the fact that he dissected 400 eels. Professor Gicklhorn assured me that no person inexperienced in the field could possibly have an adequate notion of what such an accomplishment means, in terms of endurance, zeal and self-discipline. It also should be repeated here that Gicklhorn (1955) proved

---

[24] In Appendix A, I shall add further remarks about Tausk's contribution to the problems of identity.

Freud's publication (1877) to have been of great significance. Thus Freud's first student paper may be already counted as evidence of his later greatness.[25]

Yet, great and promising as were these groping endeavors of the tyro in the field of science, the real miracle is revealed in one of Freud's earliest preserved letters (Freud 1960, pp. 5–6). Its content is most remarkable, since the writer's future is anticipated in negative terms. Thus he wrote toward the end of that letter:

> I don't mean to suggest that if you find yourself in a doubtful situation, you should mercilessly dissect your feelings, but if you do, you will see how little about yourself you are sure of. The magnificence of the world rests after all on this wealth of possibilities, except that it is unfortunately not a firm basis for self-knowledge.

When, sixty-six years later, Freud reaches the end of his life, he will have made "dissection of feelings" the only firm basis for self-knowledge.

Yet all the interpretive possibilities that are dormant in that letter's content may be less significant than its linguistic aspect. Here the German language is wielded by the seventeen-year-old youth in an inimitable way. Out of disparate thoughts a literary unit is forged; the beauty and maturity of its language are truly bewitching. In reading this letter, one becomes convinced that it was the linguistic function that was the carrier of Freud's genius.[26] Great as were his powers of observation and ratiocination, what

---

[25] Talents either start out with a surprisingly promising production and never again reach that level; or else they work their way gradually toward a peak. In other words, among them eminence, if it occurs at all, is unpredictable. The steadiness in Freud's work, however, which was of eminent quality throughout decades of a good deal of production, is characteristic of a certain type of genius. I wonder whether it is only my own reaction that, in reading Freud's publications in the field of psychology, I almost regularly reach the point of believing that the one I am engaged in reading is the best he ever wrote. However, this statement needs qualification, since Freud's productivity in the field of psychology started approximately in 1893 at the age of thirty-seven—that is to say, long after he had reached maturity. On the other hand, a study of his letters, so far published, will also show "a bent toward perfection," so very characteristic of genius. The myth of Midas always impressed me as being applicable to genius: whatever they touch is turned—almost effortlessly in some instances—into gold.

[26] About Freud's language cf.: Hesse (1930), Muschg (1939), Schönau (1968). Particular attention should be paid to Politzer's (1969) review of Schönau's book.

made him truly distinguished from others who had been pioneers in fields of science was his ability to use language. I wonder whether the historians of German literature will agree, when I venture the proposition that the language of this seventeen-year-old lad was superior to Goethe's language at that same age.

A psychological explication of Freud's genius will, I think, have to center in his language. His power to observe, to judge, to draw inferences—indispensable as these were to the greatness of his work—nevertheless, in my opinion, have to take a secondary place to the genius of his language. I even anticipate the possibility that one day someone will be able to demonstrate that what Freud presented to the world in the organized form of his scientific papers—which seem to contain the results of innumerable as well as of single observations, of intensive meditation and deliberations, of subtle working through, checking and counterchecking, comparing and returning over and over again to the raw observational data—that all this was in the end the refined and scientifically correct presentation of what had been linguistically preformed earlier. By means of scientific inquiry, it became possible to present in an objectively valid form what the unconscious had hoarded and scraped together, and had already poured into exceptional linguistic forms.[27]

A proposition of this kind, which places the unconscious as the main source of Freud's work, and then goes on to assume the preformation of linguistic structures that are only secondarily brought into harmony with the cut-and-dried data of clinical experience and observation—such a proposition would seem to displace psychoanalysis from the scientific sphere, where its founder wanted it placed, and to move it over to the artistic. Freud regarded that view as a fresh turn taken by resistance and as a rejection of analysis (1920b, p. 263). To be sure, psychoanalysis *is* a science, wherever it had its origin. In my opinion, it is so very true precisely *because* it grew out of the depths of a genius's unconscious.

---

[27] This is also suggested by the form of Freud's manuscripts. Even in those on such complicated subjects as are dealt with in his metapsychological papers, a correction is a rarity. They convey the impression rather of a process of pouring out than of planned composition, based on careful ratiocination, which so easily goes astray and almost invariably needs improvement.

As long as Freud was striving actively for truth, by way of observing the world with the aid of the modern technical instrumentarium—the staining method; the microscope; the experiment; the clinical diagnosis—he achieved appreciable and relevant successes. All this remained, however, *relatively* separate and isolated from his own unconscious. It was only after he tumbled, so to speak, into a situation in which he was forced to devote attention and awareness to the world's flow into his psychic apparatus, and this became the principal issue of his professional life, that he became able to use the fusion of the human world's rich tapestry with the projection of his own creative unconscious. In his case, the two always fitted together to perfection, even though in most instances he was unaware of the unconscious root. To his own amazement, he found out that one of his greatest achievements—the technique of free association—was an almost exact replica of what he had read in an essay during his puberty but had completely forgotten (Freud 1920b), despite (or perhaps because of) the deep impression it had left on him.

It is one of the hallmarks of the works of genius that they are the outcome of the reverberation of the total personality. I have elsewhere called such states "unifunctional" [28]; they are characteristic of geniuses not only in the field of the arts, but also in that of science. The talented person can work with only one part of his energy. Usually he has to protect himself against the intrusion of disturbing stimulations stemming from the interior of the psychic apparatus, whereas in the genius the whole personality conjoins toward the creative act. In complete misunderstanding of such creativity, some writers have held it against Freud, upon discovering the unconscious roots of his discoveries. They should instead marvel at that degree of harmony that surrounds the achievement of genius, insofar as the end-product is a synthesis of the infantile and adult worlds; of repressed contents and those approved by a demanding, self-critical ego; of the irrational and the rational, which stands up, even under the most rigorous scrutiny that it might have to submit to, in terms of objective reality.[29] The talent

---

[28] Jones (1956, p. 17) wrote of "an unusual, and often only temporary, fusion of all the elements in the mind in a peculiar degree of harmony."

[29] The synthesis of psychologically quite dissimilar contents into a great, objectively correct scientific discovery has been convincingly suggested by Manuel (1968) with regard to Newton.

usually never succeeds in harnessing the unconscious into the
service of creativity, to an extent that would even approach that
which the genius is *compelled* to achieve. Because of what I would
metaphorically call at this point rigidities of internal structure the
talent's products, excellent as they so often are, nevertheless emerge
as fractions and fragments, when placed alongside those of genius.

When, following the turmoil of the engagement period, Freud
renounced his earlier ambitious plans and settled down to daily
practice, in order to support his newly-founded household, a series
of seeming accidents brought him close to the hitherto unexplored world of the unconscious. I can imagine that the initial
effect on him of that confrontation must have been fright and
perturbation. In Wilhelm Fliess, he found what was to be a kind
of ideal transference figure, whom he used productively to carry
him through the trying period of organizing the bewildering in-
flux of initially confusing observations. With his self-analysis,
which stood in the shadow of the father's sickness and death, he
took the final step that was necessary to bring about the full
flowering of his genius.

Here is the point at which more has to be said about the sufferings and the mental pain to which geniuses are regularly exposed. It is apparent that the creation of new values of that greatness for which no lapse of time can reduce mankind's admiration
—such creation is an extraordinary task, which places the psychic
apparatus under incomparable stress and strain. Yet these stresses
and strains more often than not produce pain, in some instances
even excruciating pain. In Freud's instance, the pain from which
so many of the truly great ones had to suffer was made particularly
great by his self-analysis.

The heroism—one is inclined to describe it so—that was necessary to carry out such an undertaking has not yet been sufficiently
appreciated. But anyone who has ever undergone a personal analysis will know how strong the impulse is to take flight from insight
into the unconscious and the repressed, how painful it is when
accustomed defense mechanisms are temporarily silenced and the
ego has to endure the inroads of what is repellent to it. Freud
had to find the strength to persist in this process without that
assistance which every analysand receives. It was his self-discipline
and his determination to find the truth that made him go on

where anyone else would have faltered and finally given up. Freud's self-analysis will one day take a place of eminence in the history of ideas, just as the fact that it took place at all will remain, possibly for ever, a problem that is baffling to the psychologist.

The quality of created values can be appraised according to two dimensions, one of which is their originality. Newly-created values of the sort that remain within the bounds set by present and past values stem from talent, not from genius. What the genius succeeds in doing is to create a new universe, distinctly different from anything that existed previously. The talent will succeed at best in adding something to such a universe, or else he may create a new value, which will dissolve one part of tradition. In the latter case, he is an innovator, who prepares the coming of genius.

The creation of a new universe presupposes not only a profound dissatisfaction with the world as it is, but also the ability to black out its appearance; for in the realization of a new universe, the conservative part of the personality—the inherent tendency to fall back on what is known and perceived—serves only as an obstacle, the overcoming of which requires unusually great efforts. Dissatisfaction with the world as encountered, and the effort to disregard its actual appearance are apparently two roots of deep suffering.

But the creation of new values also contains the dimension of fatefulness [*Schicksalsschwere*] (cf. Eissler 1969a), which often becomes visible only after many generations, but of which the genius may have a presentiment. One would imagine that there is hardly any occupation better designed to calm the nerves and to contribute to tranquillity of mind than watching and counting, within the protecting confines of a monastic garden, the colors and sizes of successive generations of plants; and yet Gregor Johann Mendel (1822–1884), for whom the famous laws of inheritance are named, developed in his later years—despite his biographer's denial (Iltis 1924)—an almost systematized aggregate of delusional ideas.

To be sure, the result of his great experiments remained completely unknown during his lifetime and, in addition, ecclesiastical advancement put an end to his scientific inquiries (which is always dangerous in the case of the genius). Yet whatever may have caused and contributed to the final derangement, I believe that the creative strain may also have been an etiological factor. In Mendel's case, it might have been the factor of fatefulness; for he was the genius who, by setting up fundamental paradigms, laid the foundation of genetics, which, once started, led somewhat like a chain reaction during the course of only two generations, to the formidable possibility that mankind might some day acquire the tools to construct as well the molecular structure of its genetic material. This would dwarf in its "fatefulness" anything that science has achieved up to now, and would no doubt thoroughly eclipse the work of Freud and his school.

To be sure, it is usually assumed that Mendel himself was not aware of the impact of his discovery; but since he was a rather reticent man, we do not really know what his daydreams, premonitions, and inner warnings may have been. Whereas the originality of an achievement can be appraised—in principle, even though not in practice—as soon as that achievement has been accomplished, its fatefulness often unfolds many years or even decades after the genius's death. Consequently, my proposition that the fatefulness of a scientific discovery also forms part of the strain that the creative act puts upon the psychic apparatus is not without mysterious admixture—one reason why it will not find ready approval.

Originality and fatefulness, however, were both profusely present in Freud's work, as soon as he turned from neurology to mental science. When he became aware that he had discovered the key to the psychological explanation and understanding of dreams, he was compelled to perceive his work within the larger context of the history of ideas, in which the problem of man's nightly dream life has been present since early in his history. But the stress of creativity had already burdened Freud far earlier, shortly after he started his scientific career.

It is puzzling to read that he twice quoted Macbeth, in a way that strongly suggests his identification with that most culpable and wicked of Shakespearean characters. The first quotation, relating to IV, 1, 117, appeared as early as 1878 in a letter to a friend (Freud 1960, p. 6),[30] and the second, relating to V, 5, 51, in

---

[30] I have tried to reconstruct the circumstances that precipitated that quotation (Eissler 1965).

a letter to Pfister on March 6, 1910 (Freud 1963, p. 35). I am here referring to a problem of sheer, inexhaustible depth: the feeling of guilt—that guilt that has been splendidly set forth in the ancient myths of Prometheus and of the building of the Tower of Babel,[31]—that seems to have plagued the minds of geniuses.

In talented persons as well, severe guilt reactions can occasionally be observed that have been brought about by their thrusts into science, even though the talent more frequently than not basks in the enjoyment of his accomplishments and the acclaim he receives. Yet the guilt reaction—as can be seen at least in Tausk—is, among those who are talented, of a far more personal nature and less sublimated than it is in the case of the genius, who knows that he has disturbed the peace of the world.

The problem of suicide in the genius is far more complex and can be dealt with here only superficially. It is surprising, in fact, that suicide does not occur more frequently among geniuses, in view of the inordinate stress to which their psychic apparatus is subjected; moreover, to so many of them was denied the succor contributed by the narcissistic gratification of success. In general, the true genius will commit suicide—if he does so at all—only when the pathway to creative acts is permanently blocked, and that can usually be brought about only by exogenous interferences. The genius's ingenuity in the circumvention of external blocking is sometimes incredible. When Emil Nolde (1867–1956), the great German expressionist of "wild colors," was forbidden by the German government to paint, he changed his accustomed technique—which made it possible for him to continue his art work without being discovered. The amazing consequence, however, is that these later paintings are even superior to his earlier accomplishments, when he was able to paint without the encumbrance of government interference.

The genius knows how to shape the unserviceable and even the malignant into a new creative channel. It is perhaps the crea-

---

[31] The punishment ordained in the form of the "confusion of tongues" has been undone by mathematics and its internationally understood language. This brought to an end the limitation that, according to the myth, the Divinity had imposed upon mankind's quest for knowledge (for symbolism of the Tower, see Politzer 1968).

tive momentum that cannot be halted that is most significant of genius; talents are far more vulnerable to blocking—that is, to defeat. The image of Pasteur dictating a paper the day after he was stricken, or of Freud going on with work, despite his malignant illness and the concomitant pain, are splendid examples of the victory that creative minds achieve over terrible physical handicaps (cf. van Dovski 1959, p. 16).

A general discussion of guilt reactions in productive personalities, whether they be talents or geniuses, would lead to a different aspect of Tausk's suicide, which would take us beyond the strictly personal. Even though the suicide rate is no higher in the medical profession than it is in others, the suicide rate among psychiatrists is the highest of that among all medical specialists (Blachly et al., 1968). It is necessary to reflect whether or not the suicide rate among analysts during the early phase was higher than statistically expectable. Aside from Tausk, there were Otto Gross (d. 1920), Honegger (d. 1911), Karl Schrötter (1887–1912) and Herbert Silberer (1881–1923) who put an end to their lives.[32] I have made several efforts to clarify the circumstances and motives of these suicides, but I have not gotten very far.

Of Otto Gross (cf. Jones 2, p. 29f.), Freud once said that he was the only truly original mind among his followers, aside from Jung (Jones 2, p. 133). He was treated by Jung for schizophrenia —a diagnosis that Stekel (1920) disputed. According to the obituary that Stekel wrote, for which I owe thanks to Professor J. Angst, Gross was a neurotic addicted to opium and cocaine. The case history at Burghölzli has remained inaccessible to me, on the grounds of medical discretion. Since he committed murder before ending his own life, and was the son of a prominent father, his death and the surrounding circumstances must have caused a public sensation, but I have not been able to find any newspaper reports of it as yet. A psychiatric study of his (1907) testifies to his extraordinary endowment. One receives from this single publication the impression that he would have become one of the leading theoreticians. He held a university lectureship (Dozentur) in Graz, from which he resigned for unknown reasons. I have not

---

[32] I owe thanks to Drs. Paul Parin and Fred Singeisen for having tried to provide me with data regarding Otto Gross and Honegger.

been able to find out what was the frequency of his personal contacts with Freud; they seem to have been rare.

About Honegger (cf. Jones 2, pp. 68, 86), I could not ascertain even the date of his birth. Karl Schrötter (*Neue Freie Presse*, May 9, 1913, p. 12) poisoned himself, two days after his fiancée committed suicide by shooting herself; he was at that time studying medicine, after having attained a Ph.D. Jones (1924, p. 482) even claimed that "Schrötter was chiefly known for his opposition to psychoanalysis." Silberer (cf. *Neues Wiener Journal*, January 13, 1923; *Neue Freie Presse*, January 12, 1923; *Zeitschrift* 1923, vol. 9, p. 119) was known in Vienna as a sportsman and an author. He himself was an enthusiastic pilot, and known as the editor of an aeronautic magazine. In the newspaper reports referred to above, nothing was said about his relationship to psychoanalysis. He was said to have shown for some time traces of nervous illness. Perhaps Gross and Schrötter should not be called psychoanalysts; and it may be that, for Silberer, psychoanalysis was a more or less peripheral subject of interest.

Evidently much depends on who should be considered a *bona fide* member of the psychoanalytic movement, and therefore the question of statistical preponderance must remain at present a moot one. Yet it is worthwhile considering the possibility that, in Tausk's case, other reasons aside from the strictly personal played their role. Those talented people who were keen enough to recognize Freud's genius earlier than the vast majority of the intellectual elite—they, too, had to bear something of the same guilt he suffered, although, of course, the initiator of the new science experienced it with a greater sharpness than they did.

A remote echo of that becomes audible in a letter of Freud's to Romain Rolland (Freud 1960, p. 370): "Unlike you, I cannot count on the love of many people," he wrote. He, who wanted only to "uncover a small piece of the truth" (*ein Stückchen Wahrheit*), had not contributed to the general pleasure and consolation. One of the consequences of the feeling of guilt, for having torn the veil from what has hitherto remained hidden, which is observable in the lives of the greatest, concerns a process of undoing setting in toward the end of their lives, if not earlier. This can be seen almost openly, as I have tried to demonstrate (Eissler 1971) in Shakespeare's *Tempest*; in that farewell play, the terrible

crimes that some of his earlier characters had committed are replaced by acts that appear, at least on the surface, to be friendly
and conciliatory.[33]

A tragic split of a scientific career, into one part that is devoted
to doing, while the other constitutes an undoing, is manifest in
Newton's life. Born in 1642, he went through "the marvelously
creative period when he was about twenty-three, the *annus mira-
bilis*" (Manuel 1968, p. 1). In September, 1693, after passing his
fiftieth birthday, "he sank into delusion" (Manuel 1968, p. 214).
He went through a psychosis from which he recovered, not without having undergone some personality change (see, however,
Manuel 1963, p. 11).

His external circumstances also changed. He was named
Warden and, soon after, Master of the Mint; this was followed
by his assuming the Presidency of the Royal Society. His time
became filled with the persecution of forgers, for whose punishment he mercilessly insisted on execution. Many samples of excessively strange behavior could be adduced, such as no one would
ever have suspected to be possible in the man who was undoubtedly
the greatest scientist the West has produced. Curiously enough,
an inquiry into the manifestations of his severe psychopathology
would have more to teach us about the psychology of the genius's
personality than an investigation of Freud's at least outward
serenity, in the midst of one of the most critical periods of
Western history.

Furthermore, what can be observed in Newton's life seems to
be far more characteristic and typical of the lives of geniuses than
Freud's serenity. Roazen really had a difficult time making plagiarism an issue in Freud's life; he had to ignore salient facts, distort
a few remarks, and inflate a statement that a former patient of
Freud's had made, against all historical evidence. How easy
Newton would have made it for him! Half of Newton's life was
consumed in a vendetta against Leibnitz, because of an alleged
plagiarism which had probably never occurred. "Newton re-
gurgitated the case repeatedly in Latin and in English, ungallantly
pursuing Leibnitz beyond the grave—witness the five-hundred-
odd folios of manuscript in the University Library in Cambridge

---

[33] Something similar has been claimed about Verdi's last opera *Falstaff*.

devoted to self-vindication" (Manuel 1968, p. 327). Yet at this point I am not citing Newton in order to outline what psychopathology Freud's life story might have made the world expect in him, but rather because the postpsychotic period of Newton's life was devoted to historical studies (Manuel 1963).

It is not necessary here to go into the relationship between Newton, the physicist and mathematician, and Newton, the Bible exegete—who took the Bible literally, to boot. I only want to propose that one was the undoing of the other. The scientific discoveries Newton had made had the effect of undermining religion and the Church as did no one else's. He denied fervently that his physics was in any way in contradiction with the Bible; yet did he not have to devote himself to proving the literal truth of the Bible with all the greater intransigency, since his physics contained the seed of a new and unconquerable atheism? In Karl Marx's works, too, as some commentators have indicated, traces of undoing may be found (cf. Feuer 1968, pp. 17, 18f., 21, 23f.).

The talent does not need to undo. But the more Promethean the genius's feat, the greater his need to undo. I wonder whether one of the unconscious impulses that carried Freud to the height of ego-psychology was also a longing for undoing what he had produced during the three preceding decades.[34] For one short moment, it seems to me, Freud came close even openly to retracting what he had established earlier. This happened when he wrote (1927b, p. 53): "The voice of the intellect is a soft one, but it does not rest till it has gained a hearing. Finally, after a countless succession of rebuffs, it succeeds. This is one of the few points on which one may be optimistic about the future of mankind, but it is in itself a point of no small importance." It does not seem at all as if this hope of Freud's was based on clinical evidence. It strikes me as being like Shakespeare's *Tempest*—one moment of a deepfelt urge to give mankind a glimmer of hope.

Roazen refers to the effect—inescapable by the very nature of

---

[34] It is more than coincidence that, approximately at the age when a short-lasting psychosis initiated in Newton's life the change I have just outlined, Freud started to systematize ego-psychology. He was fifty-four—that is to say, only three years older than Newton was at the time of his psychosis—when he presented to the Vienna Society his first draft on the "Two Principles," which constituted his first step toward the systematizing of ego-psychology.

Freud's eminent creativity—that Freud had on the productivity of his collaborators, and contrasts its spurring with its delimiting consequences. I shall not go into the errors in his presentation here, but rather focus on the kernel of truth that lies at the bottom of his assertion. Often the work of a genius does have the effect of nipping in the bud that of his successors. After Shakespeare, no tragedy could be written in the English language (possibly in any language) that could hold up alongside his. One is here reminded of Nietzsche's (1879–1880, #109) rhetorical question of "What remains of German prose literature that deserves to be read over and over again," if one leaves out of account Goethe's writings.

Thus a genius may shackle the creativity of many generations through the very fact that his creations are unsurpassable. It can be well imagined how some of Freud's collaborators felt, when they realized that they would never be able to produce anything that would come near to equaling his writings. Freud himself was in something of the same situation on his way back from Paris to Vienna. Yet, as we have already observed, he accepted what he took to be the fact—namely, that he would not surpass the great Charcot.

By his accomplishments, the genius makes the lives of many talented persons more difficult. There are, it is true, geniuses who, being all too well aware of their superiority, play out their innate endowment against those who have been less favored by nature and thus provoke ill-feelings in their proximate vicinity. Freud did not fall into that category: the number of co-workers who turned against him was small, Alfred Adler openly stating his jealousy (Freud 1914a, p. 51); the majority of his collaborators felt attracted by his wisdom and charm.[35]

Freud was well protected against provocative behavior and arrogance by his distrust of his own intellectual power. If anything, he was inclined to admire others. Not infrequently he

---

[35] On what grounds does Roazen make bold to claim that "Freud had trouble with all his 'sons' in psychoanalysis" (p. 113), particularly after the publication of Freud's correspondence with Abraham and with Pfister, which offers deep insights into the subtlety and tenderness of his feelings for his pupils? One of his "sons," Ludwig Binswanger, strayed far away from the road that Freud traveled, without this "heresy" casting the slightest shadow on their personal relationship.

overrated their works, before becoming aware of the weaknesses that they contained. This is perhaps rather rare in the lives of geniuses; it certainly cannot be observed in Newton, who showed a quite different attitude toward his disciples.[36]

When Roazen ponders upon what Tausk's difficulties might have been as a creative person, he raises many a problem that illustrates the difference between talent and genius. There is, for one thing, "the discrepancy between his [Tausk's] ambitions and his capacities" (p. 115). Roazen acknowledges that this is a problem that Tausk shared "with other men of ability." And he is right. The genius suffers even more from this discrepancy than does the talent, because a state of higher perfection is represented in him that makes its appearance in the talent, and at the same time he is more aware of the distance that separates human frailty and shortcomings from the attainment of perfection. Indeed, one could cite a greater number of passages from Freud's letters which show his feelings of diffidence with regard to his works rather than those of triumph. The latter were probably not totally absent in Freud's life, but it may be significant that a dream of powerful and even exaggerated self-assertiveness was brought about by a residue of disgust, the feeling that a lecture was "completely devoid of any value. I was tired and felt no trace of enjoyment in my difficult work; I longed to be away from all this grubbing about in human dirt" (Freud, 1900, p. 470). It will never be known whether such an experience was exceptional in Freud's life or occurred frequently after 1900. It is highly probable that the genius derives far less narcissistic gratification from his accomplishments than the talent does. One can certainly observe in Freud, together with a firm and unshakable adherence to what he considered to be secured knowledge, a humility vis-à-vis the vastness of what still remains unknown and the limitations of his own endowment.[37] Thus, tentatively, one may outline the dif-

---

[36] If the published *Minutes* reflect correctly the main sociological processes that went on in the early group, then one has to draw the conclusion that Freud did not arrogate to himself and did not even try to arrogate a position that would have gone significantly beyond that of other members, who were prominent in terms of their frequent contributions and discussion remarks.

[37] No doubt, the tension created by actual accomplishment and the vision of what man's mind ought to accomplish is greater in the minds of the heroes of science than in its retainers. I shall have an opportunity to come back to this problem, when I discuss the relationship of the aged Freud to psychoanalysis.

ference in narcissistic injury to which possibly all geniuses and
many talents are subjected in the following way: like Moses, the
genius gains a glimpse of the ideal only from afar, but feels that
he can never reach it, even though it is so strongly represented
in him; whereas the talent suffers from the fact that in viewing the
works of the genius he believes them to be perfection which he
can never attain.

Roazen asserts that "every man must, so Freud taught, in some
sense slay his own father" (p. 114), and "a son must in some realm
dare to surpass his models." To be sure, the necessity of slaying
the father—which one may perhaps read into Freud's paper on
the "Dissolution of the Oedipus Complex" (1924b)—holds true
for some men, perhaps even the majority; but it is not true, oddly
enough, of the genius. Roazen twice introduces Kafka, and it
sounds as if he were identifying Kafka and Tausk because of the
similarity of their conflicts. Yet it is precisely Kafka who disproves Roazen's theory of the necessity for man to slay his father
internally if he wants to be creative, for if Kafka had ever done
so, he would never have been in a position to write his "Letter to
the Father." In this literary masterpiece, which is clearly autobiographical, an Oedipus complex is visible, marked by a gravity,
gloominess and desolation that exceed even that of Dostoevski's
protagonists. It is significant for a heaviness and a despair of such
intensity that one wonders how he could ever bear up under such
a weight.

From clinical experience, one would expect that, in defense
against such a crushing structure, criminality, psychosis or some
other quite grave form of psychopathology would have evolved.
Yet the genius forms out of this abysmal anguish a document that
I anticipate will one day be heralded as one of the greatest masterpieces of the century. The difference between talent and genius is
—aside from the difference in endowment—inequality in the level
of inner strength. The talented person needs a dissolution of the
Oedipus conflict, or at least a substantial reduction in its intensity,
in order to survive; whereas, as Kafka demonstrates, the genius is
not only strong enough to endure the stress of the severest conflicts, but actually needs intense conflicts as a *vis a tergo*, in order
to be incited over and over again to renewed accomplishments
(cf. Greenacre 1957, p. 58f.). In Freud, as in other geniuses, one

can observe the persistence of the Oedipus complex in the unconscious. What else can it mean when, after his mother's death, he writes about a new feeling he is experiencing (1960, p. 400): ". . . a feeling of liberation, of release, which I think I also understand. I was not free to die as long as she was alive, and now I am. The values of life will somehow have changed noticeably in the deeper layers." In this one sentence he reveals how very alive man's primordial tie to life remained in him—his love for his mother. The vicissitudes of his relationship to his father are less clear. In the essay on "A Disturbance of Memory" (1936), one learns of one aspect—the successful conversion of aggression into feelings of guilt (cf. Harrison, 1966); and a dream (1900, p. 558f.) that Freud had dreamed in his early sixties and succeeded in analyzing suggests that, along biological lines, the Oedipus conflict was shifting in his unconscious to his relationship to his oldest son.

Roazen speculates about what Tausk's *rationalization* might have been of "his refusal to lead a new school like Adler's or Jung's" (p. 115), and he concludes that, "without a rebellion against Freud, the creative part of Tausk would have been frustrated" (p. 113). Here aggression for its own sake is declared to be a necessity, independently of whether or not the object against whom the aggression is directed deserves it. Acceptance of authority *per se* is apparently declared to be pathological, since it supposedly has a necessarily inhibitory effect on creativity. This is certainly not true of all talents. The type of talent that flourishes only in the shadow of a great figure has been clinically described. Eckermann, Goethe's secretary, who is famous for his book on his conversations with Goethe, would be unknown to posterity, had he not put his talents exclusively into the service of a genius. His individuality was absorbed in giving color to his encounter with Goethe and he wrote a book that Nietzsche (1879–1880, #109) called "the best German book that exists" (*das beste deutsche Buch, das es giebt*)—praise that makes me think that occasionally it is worthwhile not to slay one's father.

Eckermann's behavior would have been impossible for Tausk, who was a type of talent, I surmise, that is more frequent than the Eckermanns. It is interesting that Roazen here—probably without intending to—presents Adler's and Jung's secessions as having been brought about by their psychopathology, and not by objective necessities. *Per contra*, Roazen makes it out to be a sign of ego weakness in Tausk that he remained in agreement with Freud's theories, since he criticized (p. 97) even Helene Deutsch for remaining "passive and receptive" toward Freud and his concepts. I think that Roazen is wrong in principle here, but he has referred to a conflict that Freud (1937a, p. 252) called the "bedrock" of the analyses of many males: in many instances the analyst "preaches to the winds," when he tries to persuade a man that "a passive attitude to men does not always signify castration and that it is indispensable in many relationships in life."

As Kris (1939) has pointed out, one observes in very creative personalities an acceptance of passivity and femininity. It is highly probable that this had also been Freud's problem prior to his journey to Paris, but he apparently solved it, whereas in talented males one can observe, over and over again, how their desperate compensatory fight against the acceptance of another person's superiority prevents them from optimal use of their potential.

Here we encounter a problem of the greatest consequence, which is pivotal in a comparison of talent and genius. I have briefly touched upon the possibility that the growing boy may have identified with the mother, who knows about life and death and who has the ability to demonstrate the truth; I have also mentioned that this strongly suggests identification with the life-bearing and life-giving mother. As a matter of fact, a large number of those who have devoted their efforts to the psychology of genius have pointed out the connection between motherliness and capacity for genius (cf. van Dovski 1959, p. 49). It is possible that some day it will be proven that much, or even perhaps most of male creativity stems from the sublimation of the maternal element in him.

I was surprised, however, to discover—or so, at least, it seemed to me—that, in an area where it would be least anticipated, Freud behaved in a way that can properly be called exquisitely maternal. This happened in politics, an area in which highly affective attitudes usually narrow a person's range of interests and tend to make him rigid. We do not know very much about what Freud's political convictions and opinions were, in terms of his voting record; but it is, however, known that he did sign a political appeal by the Social-Democratic party.[38] But he himself was not a Social-Democrat. Recently (Toch 1970), it became known that he made regular financial contributions to Hechalutz, a Zionist organization whose aim it was to provide young Jews desirous of settling in Palestine with preparatory training in the skills that would be needed in their prospective homeland.

According to Mr. Toch (with whom I have spoken), whenever he came to Freud's apartment, he was not simply given an amount of money; each time he also had to inform Freud about the main organizational events. Yet Freud was no Zionist, and no one could even have guessed at any activity on his part in support of Zionism.[39] If one adds to this picture Freud's appeal, mentioned earlier, for everyone to make a daily contribution toward the alleviation of the general economic plight in Vienna, and if one considers that, even at eighty-one, when he wished to retire, the reason he did not was that he had so many to provide for (Freud 1960, p. 435f.), then it is clear that here is a man who is meeting the world with maternal care.

Wherever he comes across groups that, in his opinion, deserve encouragement, he actively involves himself on their behalf, without insisting on identity of political convictions. So too, as we have already seen, whenever support is needed within the narrower familial orbit he takes on himself some form of responsibility. It looks as if—to formulate it in general terms—Freud's preponderant attitude toward the varied forms of human life was to turn to them with maternal care. Such an attitude is not necessarily characteristic of genius; and in Freud it may seem quite surprising, since he is usually thought of as being intolerant and one-sided.

I have brought up the possibility of strong maternal elements in Freud because that possibility may help us to understand a kind of thought process that may be significant of genius, as against talent. We usually think of men who have accomplished much

---

[38] I owe this information to the kindness of Dr. Harald Leupold-Löwenthal.

[39] However, on July 23, 1970 (p. 16) *The Jerusalem Post* published the following quotation from Freud, the source of which is not given: "I fully know how powerful and beneficial an instrument [Keren Hayesod] has become for our people in its efforts to establish a new home in the old land of our forefathers, a sign of our unconquerable will to live which, for two thousand years, has been standing up to severe persecutions. Our youth will pursue the battle."

with regard to finding the truth, as "truth seekers." Freud is usually depicted as one of these. Yet I doubt that this really does justice to the actual process of his mentation. "A man never mounts so high as when he does not know where he is going"— this saying of Cromwell was once quoted by Freud, and it reflects one aspect of Freud's thinking. He had the courage to let himself be impelled toward the truth, even when he was not seeking it.

Somehow, I doubt that the generally accepted principle of striving and searching as the means by which to accomplish the goal of finding the truth (a German adage has it: "Who searches finds" [Wer suchet, der findet]) is correct. Freud made his great discoveries when he *let the truth come to him*. This is not necessarily, of course, a predominantly passive process, insofar as it presupposes a readiness, an openness for the truth when it does reveal itself.

As is all too well known, reliability is still lacking in the assignment of particular mental traits to one or the other sex and it is evident that any assertion that a trait is male or female may be easily attacked—and usually on good grounds. Nevertheless, I would suggest that a certain style of mentation, which is characteristic of Freud, may be brought into connection with sublimated maternal elements—for example, his inexhaustible ability to wait until the solution to a problem emerges; or his apparently not forcing solutions, an attitude that it would not be altogether correct to describe as "passive." If it were not internally contradictory, I would call it an "active passivity."

For that reason, I also find that the term "truth-seeker"—to which Freud would not have objected—does not completely comprise Freud's relationship to the truth. I feel inclined to compare him rather with Moses, who did not seek God—but God sought him, and he was strong enough to bear it. Goethe in *Faust* has the Lord say: "Man errs as long as he is striving" [*Es irrt der Mensch, so lange er strebt*]—a profound truth. The talented person usually does strive and his effort is rewarded; but his reward does not compare with that of the genius at his peak—at the time when he apparently gives up his zeal, eagerness and forcefulness and instead opens himself so as to let even the terrifying messages from his unconscious take hold of him. It is obvious why

such attitudes have suggested, in the minds of many, the picture
of the lifebearing mother.

It is fascinating to observe that this very attitude then reappears as a legitimate part of psychoanalytic technique and is demanded of the psychoanalyst in the form of Freud's advice to him
to obtain the correct interpretation by surrendering to his own
free associations. It seems to me that here something is expected
that is not dissimilar to "actionless action" (Herrigel 1953, p. 56),
which seems to be so important in some sectors of Eastern life.[40]

Yet strong as may have been the part that maternal elements
played in Freud's personality and creativity, the masculine element
was, of course, also very intense. It is the full evolvement of readiness to accept reponsibilities, to advise, to lead, to impose one's
will, when necessary—in short, the unmistakable presence of those
qualities that until recently have been regarded in Western society as exquisitely masculine—that shows that the style of the
"good son," which the youth had clearly demonstrated, had not
led to a fixation to the filial attitude, as is so often observed in
instances of that sort. On the contrary, the potentiality for growth,
the readiness to evolve those qualities that are syntonic with the
particular biological phase—these are characteristic of the type of
genius to which Freud belonged (it is also, by the way, characteristic of Goethe, with whom Freud shared many features, including an almost equal lifespan).

Not enough is known to decide whether we are here dealing
with a biological or a psychological capability. It is quite possible
that the "good son" identification releases the juvenile with fewer
feelings of guilt than is usual, and in that way facilitates his later
growth into a fully developed and paternal responsibility. How
strongly masculinity was represented in Freud can be observed in
his magnificent courage in attack, of which we have many examples. Usually, one thinks of his courage in telling the truth, his
aversion to making compromises. But Freud was also courageous
when he was threatened by physical dangers. Martin Freud (1957,

---

[40] If it turned out that at a crucial juncture of psychoanalytic technique, which
is a scientific procedure, a pattern is built in that appears to be quite reminiscent
of Eastern ways of obtaining truth, or better of meeting the problems of life,
then psychoanalysis would be truly a structure in which East and West meet.

p. 71) tells of an incident in which he and his father were threatened "by a hostile crowd," for anti-Semitic reasons, during the summer vacation in 1901: "Father, swinging his stick, charged the hostile crowd, which gave way before and promptly dispersed, allowing him a free passage."

One may find nothing extraordinary in a forty-five-year-old man charging a hostile crowd, even though his physical strength was not his most outstanding feature. But when one hears that this same man, at eighty-two, met the Nazis who had invaded his apartment "in a way of frowning with blazing eyes that any Old Testament prophet might have envied" (Jones 3, p. 219—it actually accelerated the departure of the unsought visitors), then one receives the impression that Freud was free of physical fears, to the extent that this can be achieved.

One might thus discover, in a particular and rather felicitous synthesis of the paternal-masculine and maternal-feminine elements, another aspect of the eminence of Freud's personality. What specific effect, however, the superbly-evolved masculine texture of Freud's personality might have had on his creativity—a problem that is really the decisive one, in this context—I do not feel prepared to deal with here.

That Freud's thinking was actually characterized by two types of thinking processes is indicated by a passage in a letter Freud wrote to Breuer in 1892 (p. 147). He mentions in it "the discomfort" [das Unbehagen] brought about by "unremitting pains of thinking" [beständige Denkschmerzen]. This is in contrast to "the satisfaction" with which he had "guilelessly" [arglos] handed over a manuscript to Breuer. The last two terms probably refer to the subjective experience he had when writing the manuscript. Thus, satisfaction and guilelessness vs. discomfort and thinking pains may characterize phenomenologically two different styles of productive thinking in Freud.

Thus a conflict-free synthesis of the maternal and the paternal seems a prerequisite for high creativity in this type of genius. That such a synthesis was inaccessible to Tausk, since both paternal and maternal elements were bound up in conflicts and therefore remained inaccessible to sublimation, is evident from all we know about him. But in general I would surmise that more often than not one will find in talents an inability to harness maternal elements to the extent to which the genius does, in the service of creativity.

If Freud's personality may be regarded as being paradigmatic of a certain type of creativity, then degrees of the internalization of conflicts may be taken as a yardstick of creativity. During his ambitious phase, the motivation of success was apparently disproportionately intensive, when viewed alongside the quest for truth. The quest for success and the quest for truth do not mix well, because the former, being mainly concerned with the response of the community, is often quite prone to pass over a truth that may incur disfavor with those who decide upon success. Only when a person has made his own conscience the sole arbiter of his mental action are the chances for the realization of the highest values likely to be great. In such a case, questions of rivalry, prestige, appreciation of peers—even though they can probably never be eliminated—fade completely into the background. Once having lost their power to distract, they are no longer obstacles on the way toward fulfillment of the highest sublimated goals.[41]

It is therefore highly probable that the degree of internalization that the productive person is able to achieve is decisive for his creativity. Freud's development, at least, demonstrates a progressive course, during which creativity becomes increasingly autonomous and object-independent.[42] During the early years, his relationship to Martha Bernays and his daily letters to her were decisive for Freud's personality in all respects. Such teachers as Brücke, Breuer, Meynert and later Charcot became active agents in superego formation. The next step was the centering of the object-relationship that is relevant to creativity upon one single person. This was Wilhelm Fliess, whom Freud considered to be superior to himself.

---

[41] Goethe's work in the area of the physics of colors may serve as a famous example to show that ambition and rivalry, when they are principal motors of creativity, diminish the quality of the achievement. Goethe did not place a very high value on his achievements as poet and writer, but he was proud that—as he imagined—he knew more about colors than any physicist of his century. At the center of his optical studies lay a desperate fight with Newton, who represented in his eyes a hated father.

[42] In the child's development, the step from learning for a loved teacher to learning for the sake of acquiring knowledge is a decisive one (Ekstein and Motto 1969). It is well known how rarely this step is fully accomplished.

From 1900 on, however, Freud's creativity became immune to the vicissitudes of object relations. The quest for truth was maximally internalized, and Freud felt responsible to himself alone. He could rely on his conscience, which was a stricter judge than any outside force could ever have been. The responses of the world, successes and defeats, adulation as well as detraction, did not count any longer, or else they took an inferior place.

Degrees of object independence, as observed in Freud after 1900, would be quite exceptional in a talent; it is my belief that such a high degree of internalization is the privilege of the genius. The remarkable concomitant to this maximal independence, in Freud's case, was the preservation of the full spectrum of emotions. One might have expected that the combination of a mutilating, chronic and painful disease, making thirty-three operations necessary, the tempestuous times, and the many disappointments Freud had to suffer—that all these would result in emotional hardenings and rigidities. Yet not even the old age Freud reached succeeded in calcifying his strong emotionality. This can best be seen in Freud's capacity to mourn.

Whether Freud had suffered in previous years from a disturbance of his ability to mourn is questionable. Grief about the loss of the father was converted into the creation of the masterpiece of the interpretation of dreams. When his daughter died, a full mourning reaction did not take place. In this instance, two factors might have interfered. As he himself reported, he had been exhausted by years of intense worry about the fate of two sons who were active at the front, the elder having been listed as missing for several months. Furthermore, Freud was at the beginning of one of his most productive periods at the time when he lost his daughter Sophie.

It is the privilege of genius to be temporarily overwhelmed by the creative impulse, to such an extent that the voice of nature is muted. However, when a beloved grandson of Freud's died, a mourning reaction set in that probably lasted for the remainder of his life; it was of such intensity that even in Freud the creative potential seemed threatened for a moment.[43] Here one can see

---

[43] Mrs. Dorothy T. Burlingham suggested that the intensity of Freud's reaction of mourning to the grandchild's death may have been connected with the fact that Freud was unable to mourn fully his daughter's death, which had preceded it by three and a half years.

that the full capacity for object love remained unimpaired. Any conflict about his own fatal disease paled before the hideous monstrosity of nature's murder of an unfulfilled young life. Yet not only did Freud's ability to mourn remain unimpaired, it is equally true of his empathy with the bereaved.

About a letter that he (Freud 1960, p. 386) sent at the age of 73 to Binswanger, when the latter lost his oldest son, Waelder (1963, p. 643) correctly remarked: "In the world's literature, I know of no more moving expression of sympathy to a bereft one." I have cited Freud's capacity for deep mourning in old age, because it is that emotional response that usually suffers the most during the course of aging. I therefore take the fact that this capacity had not been injured or reduced by the aging process as proof that all the other emotions had also retained their sharpness.

There is one letter that conveys with particular poignancy Freud's superb vitality, bound to readiness for a full emotional response. It is his reply, on the occasion of his seventieth birthday, to a congratulatory letter he received from Mathilde Breuer, widow of his erstwhile friend and teacher, to whom he owed so much and from whom he had separated in enmity. The letter consists of three sentences, which must have been written on the spur of the moment and with lightning speed. The "very great agitation" [die grösste Bewegung] that Freud asserted he felt is lost in the available translation (Freud 1960, p. 369f.).

In one superbly constructed sentence, he covered the period from the moment when he saw Mathilde Breuer for the first time up to the time of his writing the letter—including the incredible vicissitudes he himself had experienced during that period. In the background one feels the pressure of a complex emotion—a belated feeling of gratitude to the man whose death had occurred less than a year earlier, as well as to the fate that had permitted Freud to live so long.

In examining the orbit of Freud's emotional responses, it is impressive to take note of its wide circumference. It is particularly important that the circumference of his emotions also contained within it the emotion of hatred. Freud belonged among those who did have the ability to experience strong hatred.

As he wrote to Eitingon in July 1931, Freud set up once a list of persons he hated (Jones 3, 159f.). It contained seven or eight names. People in general deny the presence of such an affect, unless they feel protected by group support. Thus there was hardly anybody in the West who would not have felt free to express hatred against Hitler, but it is rather rare for a person to aver a hatred that is the result solely of his personal inclination. Since other geniuses have left no known record of people they hated, one cannot determine whether the figure of seven or eight persons on Freud's "hate list," as he called it, ought to be appraised as high or low. I regret that only one name has been identified on that list. Knowledge of who the others were would be one of the most important keys to understanding one aspect of Freud's relationship to the world.

The name Freud gave away was that of Theodor Lessing (1872–1933) a philosopher of history who was later killed by German fascists. Lessing had called psychoanalysis "a monstrosity of the Jewish spirit" [eine Ausgeburt des jüdischen Geistes]. Freud, thinking that the author was a descendant of Gotthold Ephraim Lessing (1719–1781), the famous exponent of Central European enlightenment, reminded him of the memory of his great ancestor. When Lessing replied that he himself was a Jew, "I turned away from him in disgust" [angewidert] (Jones 3, p. 160). It is significant that Freud remained comparatively unruffled, as long as he thought that psychoanalysis was being reviled by a Christian because of the Jewishness of its founder and of most of its adherents (as was the case at that time), yet could not tolerate this same type of defamation coming from a Jew. In trying to reconstruct the names on Freud's "hate list," only one other name comes to mind. It is that of Alfred Adler. This is suggested by a letter Freud wrote to Arnold Zweig on the occasion of Adler's death. It seems that Freud was not able to forgive Alfred Adler for having left the Society. Why Freud responded in that instance quite differently from the way in which he did to Jung's and Rank's resignations, I do not know. But that is of no importance in this particular context, in which the question at stake is Freud's general emotional responsiveness. Suffice it to say that the passage indicates strongly a feeling of aversion, amounting to hatred. It is as follows, in Jones's not quite correct translation (Jones 3, p. 208): "I don't understand your sympathy for Adler. For a 'Jew boy' out of a Viennese suburb, a death in Aberdeen is an unheard-of career in itself and a proof of how far he had got on." [44] The German term *Judenbube*, which Jones has translated as "Jew boy," does not carry the highly derogatory and racist connotations that the translation evokes in the United States. Translating the term as "Jewish boy" would have been more correct. This is not to deny that Freud was angry and expressed his own contempt for Adler. Freud's reaction, of course, has shocked some critics, such as Sperber (1970, p. 294), who launched an avalanche of unparalleled abuse against Freud for this sentence. Ellenberger (1970, p. 648) exclaims indignantly, "Could Freud have forgotten that he himself had been 'a Jew boy out of a Viennese suburb'?" No, Freud never forgot his Jewish ancestry; it was Adler who did, as his conversion to Protestantism shows, and Freud's sentence must be read in that light. For any Jew, like Freud, who was ready to bear the "stigma" of his ancestry, a baptism such as Adler's constituted flight by denial and escapism.[45]

In view of the indignation aroused by Freud's admission of hatred in his letter to Zweig, some explanatory comment is needed as to what I mean when I speak of Freud's ability to hate. The ban on hatred is particularly strong in Judeo-Christian civilization, as if the presence of that feeling in itself constituted a grave violation of man's ethical standards and of his dignity. As has been repeatedly stated, the works of such thinkers as Nietzsche and Freud contain the seeds of a new ethics, which has not yet been spelled out and which still lies dormant, buried in their opera. Little as we may yet know about what will be the terminal point of the course that was started by such thinkers as Nietzsche and Freud, of one thing we may be certain: the establishment of freedom of emotion.

---

[44] Cf. Jones 3, p. 208. Roazen intimates that Jones tried to protect Freud by excluding some of the available material from his biography. The fact that Jones published this passage for its own sake, so to speak (he did not need it for the clarification of any event in Freud's life), proves to my mind that he was guided by the conviction that there is no detail of Freud's life history that needs to be concealed in order to protect Freud.

[45] I shall briefly take up the question in Appendix D. By the way, Ellenberger, despite his effort to grasp sociological shades, made a mistake in his rhetorical question: Freud never did grow up in a suburb of Vienna.

Man will be granted the right to feel (and to express his feelings?), in accordance with his own inner processes. The ethical opprobrium that is still attached to some feelings will have been lifted, and man will perhaps be able at last to hate and to rage, without incurring a feeling of guilt. The second freedom that will be brought about, mainly through Freud's work, has to do with the freedom of fantasy: no ethical ban will be put on any fantasy that man may evolve.

There is good reason to hope that these two freedoms will enable man to organize his actions in ways that will be more social than he was capable of achieving, during that historical period in which anti-social actions might well meet with a greater chance of being institutionally condoned than would some of man's feelings and fantasies.

No human being is capable of existence without hatred; if the sporadic presence of that emotion is inacceptable to him, the most he can do is to repress it. Some analysts have not resisted the temptation to preach an ideal of "pure love," purified of all traces of enmity and hostility. Indeed, some analysts seem to take the position that the presence of hatred is in itself indicative of disease. Hatred may, of course, be the result of disease—when it dominates a person's life, or when it makes strong ties to objects impossible through the heightening of ambivalence.

Of all this, Freud was quite well aware, and a substantial portion of his writings was devoted to dealing with problems of ambivalence, sadism, hostility and destructiveness. But there is no reason to believe that Freud equated health with the absence of hatred, or that he thought a vision of man as incapable of hatred to be a desirable one. Be that as it may, it is my impression that it was his inner freedom with regard to the full range of emotions —including hatred—that made it possible for Freud to remain to the last the great psychologist he was.

At one point, the right to hate entered indirectly his printed works, when he launched an attack against "Thou shalt love thy neighbor as thyself" (1930a, p. 109ff.). The right to hate does not, however, include the right to resort to aggressive action. Freud's occasional remarks about the prevalence of aggression that he observed in the behavior of his fellowmen, and the grave disappointments that he himself had to suffer, have been utilized to present him as an embittered pessimist. Pessimist he may have indeed been in his judgment of man and on the course man's history had taken, and would take. After all, he foresaw with amazing clarity what history is now confirming with frightening precision. But in his personal life all avenues for a positive approach toward the world remained open.

Indifference makes the process of aging more tolerable for those who have to bear it. Many a genius, however, does not share in this solace that nature has provided. From the late paintings of Titian, who reached a high old age, as well as from the late paintings and self-portraits of Rembrandt, in which he looks so very old (he died at the age of 63), one does not obtain the impression that they were created by men who had become indifferent, but just the opposite—by men who have acquired a new sensitivity, and to whom the world has revealed a new depth of perception and insight, which had remained closed to them earlier.

One further thought about Freud's ability to have feelings about the world. In what was possibly his last letter—one that was written in an hour when he must have known that his life was limited to only a few more days, if not hours—one finds the words: comforting [wohltuend] and tender joy [innige Freude] (Freud 1960, p. 460); both these expressions refer to the sudden news of a welcome turn in a friend's fate, about which he had been worrying for quite a while. This should make it unnecessary to spend any more time on the question of Freud's emotionality and his ability to love even in his old age.

And yet there is a peculiarity that has, in my opinion, been misunderstood by such authors as Roazen, and which is not only of psychological but also of historical relevance. It has to do with Freud's attitude toward patients. There is evidence that does not need to be cited—because it can be taken for granted—of empathy, humaneness, loyalty and devotion. But there are also remarks, usually referring to patients who were treated by others, that need to be considered. The one that may sound the strangest to contemporary ears was made by Freud when he said, at a meeting of the Society in 1910, about a patient whom Sadger had presented, that he was an "absolute swine" (Minutes 2, p. 379). Roazen quotes this passage (p. 187) and holds up against Freud's comment Federn's "stressing 'the likeable impression' that the man created" (*Minutes* 2, p. 297).[46]

The way Roazen cites Freud in this instance is, to say the least, misleading. At an earlier meeting, Freud had said that what had been uncovered in this patient was "the regular constitution of all men" (*Minutes* 2, p. 311). During the final discussion, however, Freud mentioned "the poor impression" afforded by Sadger's presentation. This, he maintained, lay "for the most part in the subjects that Sadger usually has [as patients]. This patient is an absolute swine, a case of infantile and homologously inflated sexuality. *We have so many repressions within ourselves that, when faced with that, we feel aversion*" (emphasis added). Once one knows the context in which the remark was made, one obtains a different impression, for it is evident that on this occasion Freud did not have a moral judgment in mind, such as would be primarily deprecatory of the patient, but rather the emotional response that the therapist is forced to experience because of his own repressions.

But if what Roazen wanted to do was to bring to our attention the fact that Freud felt free to pass moral judgments on patients —something that is now strictly tabooed—he would have been correct. When in 1922 Freud wrote Edoardo Weiss (1970, p. 37) that "only a few patients are worth the trouble we spend on them," he put his idea into a general formula that would probably be rejected by almost all present-day analysts. Yet Roazen here commits an essential mistake. Freud's moral judgment did not have to do with a patient's disease. It is misleading when Roazen states (p. 183): "Freud grouped them [psychotics] with delinquents, addicts, and perverts—none of whom were 'worthy' of analysis." There is nothing in Freud's own writings and in his letters to substantiate such a statement.

Freud judged a patient's character. When the patient was acting out in an anti-social way, when he was delinquent, unreliable,

---

[46] The case has been published (Sadger 1910a). It is rather difficult to find anything likeable in the patient. Federn's remark was made after the first part of Sadger's presentation. After the third part, during the discussion of which Freud's remark occurred, Federn, who preceded Freud in the discussion, spoke of the same patient as "this perverse individual" (*Minutes* 2, p. 378).

immoral, then Freud took a critical attitude that was quite independent of what the patient's disease might have been. Some
critics have, like Roazen, ascribed to Freud a condemnation of
homosexuality. That is certainly out of the question. I have cited
earlier a passage from one of his letters in which Freud referred
to a homosexual problem in himself. As early as 1900, he wrote
to Fliess: "As for communication with the friend whom one particular—as it were, feminine—side [of me] requires, that can be
replaced for me by no one else" (Mr. Collins' translation; cf. Freud
1950a, p. 318).[47] Furthermore, from a reliable source I have been
informed that a patient who was among those whom Freud personally liked best was a manifest homosexual. Last but not least,
Freud's famous letter (Freud 1960, p. 423f.) to the mother of a
homosexual should convey to any student of Freud's life what
Freud's true attitude toward homosexuality was.

However, in order to prove Freud's "own defensive repug-
nance" toward homosexuals, Roazen writes (p. 186) that Freud
commented "about one male homosexual case [that] if worst
comes to worse, one ships such people . . . across the ocean with
some money." When one turns to the source (Weiss 1970, p. 28),
one learns that this statement was made because of the patient's
character, and explicitly not because of his homosexuality. "I do
not even consider," Freud wrote, "the fact that he is a homosexual. He could remain that and still live normally and ration-
ally." It was the patient's "fantastically narcissistic, self-satisfied
ego, which is inaccessible to any influence" (Weiss 1970, p. 27)
that forced Freud to give the advice that Roazen evidently misunderstood.

At any rate, it is a challenging paradox that Freud, who enabled psychologists to investigate *sine ira et studio* the whole
spectrum of psychopathology—including those deformations of
character and those acts that are most offensive to man's moral
principles—was himself predisposed against that part of human
psychopathology that was at that time covered by the new obso-

[47] *Aber den Verkehr mit dem Freund, den eine besondere—etwa feminine—
Seite fordert, ersetzt mir niemand.* The translation of the crucial *etwa* as almost
(Freud 1950a, p. 318) is wrong. *Etwa* is a combination of probably, perhaps, and
as it were.

lete term, "psychopathic character" or "psychopathic personality." [48]

Freud stands at a watershed in the development of psychology, just as Newton did in physics. Newton needed a fundamentalist religious conviction, without which he would probably not have been able to forge that very science that would make religious beliefs crumble. Likewise Freud, I conjecture, needed strong moral convictions and a full belief in the absoluteness of certain values in order to forge the instrument that would make possible a psychology purified of moral values.

Freud described in his autobiographical essay (1925b, p. 27) a moment that was crucial to the birth of psychoanalysis. Upon awakening from hypnosis, a patient threw her arms around his neck, but "I was modest enough not to attribute the event to my own irresistible attraction." From then on, Freud was bound to discover transference and its nature, and the understanding of transference has become one of the essential parts of psychotherapy. But how many men would have had the strength of character to resist that temptation? Even at present, when analysts learn throughout their training about the nature of transference, and should therefore be prepared for what they will have to expect, there is a substantial number who ascribe the patient's positive statements to their own excellence, and the negative ones only to transference (see Bartemeier 1952).

Freud's response to the patient's attempt at seduction proves the superiority of his personality. The talented person would have taken flight out of a feeling of guilt, or else would have accepted the pleasurable opportunity and made the most of it.

Retrospectively, a connection between psychoanalysis and Vic-

---

[48] As an Army psychiatrist, I had to examine hundreds, if not thousands, of trainees. Officially I met only subjects who were suffering from anxiety, but not a single coward. I wonder whether Freud might not have drawn the line somewhere, and designated as cowards some of those who were being diagnosed by us as simple anxiety reactions. It goes without saying that I myself often thought that the soldier to be diagnosed was a coward, but I would never have been able to put it down as a characteristic of the soldier's personality, not to speak of stating it as a diagnosis. I did meet one Army psychiatrist who solved the problem in an incontestable fashion: he declared the problem to be a non-medical one, and therefore refused to deal with such soldiers at all. Their behavior disorder, he maintained, fell within the competence of the sergeant.

torianism, which is usually overlooked, can be established. The discovery of psychoanalysis would have been impossible in antiquity or in the Middle Ages. In those times, the discussion of such "lurid" subjects as are inescapably dealt with during the course of a psychoanalysis would have aroused excitement of a sort that would have driven both participants toward sexual actions. I have only to remind the reader of the precautions that the Church had to take, in order to prevent excesses in the darkness of the confessional.

It is my impression that, even as late as the first half of the nineteenth century, the sexual drive had not yet been tamed—or weakened, as the case may be—sufficiently to permit such precarious circumstances as the psychoanalytic treatment situation does contain. The discovery of psychoanalysis was possible only at the height of so-called Victorianism.[49] It is one of those impressive paradoxes of history that psychoanalysis needed Victorianism in order to be born, and yet, at the same time, was among the factors that contributed in great measure to its ending.

It was mankind's good fortune that one of the truly great was living at that time—a man who had integrated everything that may have been good and beautiful in that period, but without being overwhelmed by it. He was fully an offspring of his time, and yet he was far above it. Such deep roots at one and the same time in antipodean areas goes far beyond the potential of a talent; only the genius has the synthetic power to merge seeming incompatibles into an inherently consistent system. The first step toward uncovering in detail the bestial nature of the ubiquitous repressed, as well as the varieties of its vicissitudes, would have been sufficient for anyone else's lifetime; but the genius was driven relentlessly until the beauty of the structural aspect emerged—to pay back, as it were, its due to Victorianism, without annulling one iota of what had been discovered earlier.

Here we return to the enigma of Freud's personality, to which

---

[49] The term Victorianism has lately acquired a different coloring. Whereas earlier it referred to an outlook on the world that denied the ubiquity and naturalness of the world of drives, more and more the term has come to evoke those violations of that outlook that seem to have occurred with fair regularity. It is evident that I am using that term in its former meaning—namely, as a way of referring to a historical period in which the accepted standards of the elite forbade any sort of irregularity of conduct.

I alluded initially. The stresses and strains to which his psychic apparatus was exposed during the course of his life were unusually great, even when measured in terms of what geniuses, as a rule, have to endure. If only that one moment is considered when Freud discovered, from the analysis of one of his own dreams, that he was harboring a death wish toward his oldest son, who had been at the front but was missing at that time, we can get some inkling of the shock and agitation to which his psychic apparatus was at times exposed. The courage it took to publish that dream, along with its interpretation, is hardly imaginable. On another occasion (1969a), I have called that deed the greatest self-sacrifice a man has ever made in the service of science.[50]

The stress involved in the creative act *per se* cannot be disputed. The originality and the fatefulness in Freud's work were of the highest. His findings had to be wrested in the face of his own extreme resistances—the self-analysis being comparable, in terms of the danger involved, to Benjamin Franklin's flying a kite in a thunderstorm in 1752, in order to investigate the laws of electricity. The next two persons who tried to repeat his experiment were both killed.

The incessant delving into the unconscious of others, which so often means tampering with one's own; the isolation and detraction, leading in 1934 to a public book-burning and to what amounted to a declaration of anathema; the lack of public recognition; the disappointments at the hands of one-time collaborators; the financial struggle; the disastrous years of war; the years of anguish about the survival of two sons; the sudden death of a daughter, and then the slowly progressing malignant disease; emigration and worry again, over and over—all that, one would expect, would have conjoined to defeat a man; to undermine the foundations of his existence; to make him irritable, melancholic,

---

[50] In my recent publication on *Hamlet*, I have tried to show that the root of that unavoidable hypocrisy that is spread throughout society is, to judge from that play, the older generation's denial of its own oedipal conflict. With the successful interpretation of the dream referred to, and its publication, Freud removed the shadow of hypocrisy that may separate not only one generation from another but also man from man. It proves Roazen's utter misunderstanding of genius, his lack of respect for the heroic mental deeds of the great ones, when he cites Freud's dream as an additional argument to prove Freud's guilt in Tausk's death (p. 112).

erratic, paranoid, embittered, if not worse. If one studies the life stories of his peers—Newton, Karl Marx, Nietzsche—what restlessness, what bizarreness, what severe psychopathology! But Freud? . . .

Roazen, even though with a different purpose in mind, seemed to have found at last the material that would make Freud, in this respect as well, equal to the majority of his class. But careful study of Roazen's presentation, and a detailed comparison with other sources, enforces the conclusion that he has not succeeded in uncovering in Freud's life story that psychopathology that is found almost as a rule in other geniuses.

Freud was aware of the enigma that surrounded his genius. He hit the nail on the head when he said to Marie Bonaparte, after she had referred to him as a genius, "Geniuses are unbearable people. You have only to ask my family, to learn how easy I am to live with, so I certainly cannot be a genius." (Jones 2, p. 415). And, indeed, who would ever have liked to share a household with a Newton, a Beethoven, a Nietzsche?

One may tentatively cite two sets of circumstances that at least contributed to Freud's relative freedom from severe psychopathology. The first was that he had carried out a partial self-analysis. Even though, as he averred in a letter I shall quote later, he had taken to neglecting his self-analysis, he was still evidently analyzing some of his dreams throughout his life. That may well have been an important barrier against the danger of an evolving psychopathology. But when we hear that the twenty-year-old student, left to his own devices away from home in Trieste, at a time when others are still sowing their wild oats, was already able to muster such zeal, devotion and endurance as are hardly to be found in an adult, attention may be drawn to another characteristic of genius.

Much as the genius is given to "letting himself go" and being driven by his wildness, nevertheless, in that particular area in which his gifts flourish, he shows incredible self-discipline. Michelangelo, despite his impetuous temperament and impatience, endured the hardship of painting the ceiling of the Sistine Chapel lying flat on his back for several years. There are few who would be able to live up to the physical demand alone.

The selfishness of genius, so often observed in his relationship to his environment, is absent in the work situation, in which one encounters almost no limits to his endurance and his willingness to sacrifice. This discrepancy—highly characteristic of a frequent type of genius—between an exacerbated narcissistic selfish behavior in everyday life, and an unending, inexhaustible devotion and sacrifice in everything that has to do with achievement, forms an engaging paradox that stands right at the center of the psychology of creativity.

There is a kind of circular causality or interdependence between the creator and his work. Already during the process of creation, what is being accomplished is having a retroactive effect on the creator. Furthermore, the genius grows with each of his own accomplishments. If we apply this to Freud, one has to note that, once he wished to create psychoanalysis, he had to abstain from acting out and instead endure the burden of internalization. The acting out that is imposed upon most geniuses and is their privilege—the prerequisite for their accomplishments—was incompatible with the creation of psychoanalysis. If unconscious processes were to be uncovered at all, Freud had to endure the burden of listening patiently day after day for eight to ten hours.

A general problem arises here that, as will be presently seen, makes for a bad prognosis for the furtherance and the growth of psychoanalysis. There is no other science in which the reliable collection of primary data necessitates a perfectly equilibrated personality. The making of far-reaching discoveries in the field of physics may be compatible with living a delinquent life; but that would not hold true of working in the field of psychoanalysis. It is generally observed that acting out and neuroticism, even though they may not necessarily impinge on the analyst's overt and, so to say, gross contact with the patient, do nevertheless have a bearing on the process of obtaining data, not to speak of their interpretation.

Highly talented people are restless; they feel the urge to manipulate, to change, to experiment, to pursue the improbable, to respond to the daydream—all of which would constitute roots of disturbance to the subtle interaction between psychoanalyst and patient, roots of falsification and error. The admissions committees of various psychoanalytic institutes, which are careful and cautious in the selection of candidates, have often been castigated for having rejected promising, talented applicants. In many instances, if even not in all, the negative decision may have been well founded, as Freud's may have been when Bárány wanted to become an analyst, even though the latter was a highly gifted person.[51] This incompatibility of restless creativity with the calmness that is necessary to the psychoanalytic profession has proven—and will probably continue to do so—to be a great detriment to the furtherance of psychoanalysis as a science.

If one applies this viewpoint to Freud, it must be recognized that in his case the task at hand required the mind of a genius, yet without permitting the evolvement of the psychopathology of the creative act. This may be called both the enigma and miracle of Freud's geniushood.

Without detracting from Freud's inner greatness, one is compelled to acknowledge that greatness was also favored here by external circumstances. A genius, in order to flourish, needs an aggregate of conditions, some of which are outside the range of his influence and some only partially subject to his choice. To begin with, there is the hereditary mass. Without certain constitutional factors, of which we are still ignorant, genius is not possible. Freud was apparently endowed with enough of these factors to build upon them his magnificent life and work. The question remains how many among the talented actually possess a constitution that is potentially endowed for geniushood, yet have never realized it, in part as a result of their own doing, in part through having been lacking in the proper opportunity.[52]

In view of the clustering of geniuses, as proven by Kroeber

---

[51] In a letter of 1915 to Ferenczi, Freud wrote that Bárány "seemed to be too abnormal" (Jones 2, p. 189). In the German edition (vol. 2, p. 228), one reads: zu abnorm und unsympathisch.

[52] The problem of the genius's biological endowment is an exciting one. Mozart, to a certain extent, might be the despair of the psychologist for already at the age of three he was starting to pick out tunes, and at six he started composing. Yet if the concept of quantity can be applied to biological endowment, then Saint-Saëns' endowment was greater than Mozart's, for the former was able to pick out tunes on the piano at the age of two-and-a-half, and he could read and write before three, at which age he composed his first piece. At five, he was analyzing the full score of Don Giovanni. And yet, if he had never composed, the musical world would not be very much the poorer. A comparative anlysis of Mozart and Saint-Saëns may one day demonstrate that even a full grasp of the biology of genius may not contribute as much to the understanding and explanation of genius as one might have hoped and expected.

(1944), it is highly probable that the potentiality inherent in the historical moment is another prerequisite for the flourishing of genius. This can be seen clearly in the rise of great statesmen. If Lenin had been born in Russia fifty years earlier, he would never have been able to develop into the greatest statesman of his times. Whether the biological endowment of genius is pliable, and would thus develop, no matter what the circumstances, into unusual achievements—wherever those "holes" in culture are situated that *need* the accomplishments of the genius—is not known. It is quite probable, however, that the endowment of particular individuals is suitable only for certain specific areas of cultural achievement.

The historical prerequisites for Freud are, of course, innumerable. If the Jews in Central Europe had not become emancipated during the years following the revolution of 1848, and if the universities had not been thrown open to everyone who possessed the proper educational credentials, Freud could never have become the great scientist that he did become. The fact that he was the first member of his family to attend a university may have given a particular lift to his zeal. But more. If the natural sciences had not made their great developmental leap, while leaving the psyche untouched—that is to say, if there had not remained this specific *terra incognita* on the map of human knowledge—Freud would not have been able to become the greatest psychologist of his times.

Yet it is the fact that he did so eminently fill the gap in mankind's knowledge that remains specifically his merit. Looking back, it is clear that science would have penetrated into the field of the human psyche, even if Freud had never lived; but it did make a great difference whether the task at hand was achieved by a Janet or a Freud. It is between these two poles—the inherited mass of genes and the structure of the historical moment—that there lie those innumerable chains of events that determine creative man's destiny.

One of these chains is the potential role of women in the genius's life. The first novel that Freud read, as a boy of thirteen, ends with the hero's being seized by madness (Freud 1900, p. 201): "He kept calling out the names of the three women who had brought the greatest happiness and sorrow into his life." The novel must have impressed the boy quite deeply; for, while he forgot its title and the author's name, he kept "a vivid memory of its ending." [53] This pubescent recollection was reported by Freud as an association to the dream of the three Fates, which referred to the important childhood recollection about the mother mentioned earlier (Freud 1900, p. 204).

One can well understand why a boy in the throes of early puberty should have been deeply stirred by the mystifying ending of the novel. Until that time, he had experienced only the blessing of one of the Fates. When Freud (1917b, p. 156) wrote that Goethe might well have given to his autobiography the heading: "My strength has its root in my relation to my mother," it is very likely that this idea may also be applied to his life history. Freud's mother must have possessed the qualities that were capable of bringing out the very best in her firstborn. His second Fate, in the form of Martha Bernays, was equally propitious. She was the ideal support for "the years of famine," as well as for those "of great plenty."

The former did not last as long as the seven Biblical years; they include only the four years of the engagement, when she bore with equanimity Freud's outbreaks of jealousy and despair. The subsequent years were not quite "of great plenty," as might have been expected, but Martha was richly rewarded for her endurance. In turn, she provided that background that was optimal for Freud's creativity, and thus she spared Freud the complications that are to be found in so many biographies of the great.

Yet destiny showed itself most bountiful in the third Fate, his daughter Anna. Here Moira had saved up its friendliest gesture, which compensated for those deepest pains that Freud had to suffer. Mythic imagery arose once again: Martha had been "my Cordelia-Marty" (1960, p. 40); Anna became "my faithful Anna-Antigone" (1960, p. 424). Without her, would Freud have had the strength to endure the loss of the beloved little grandson, the ravaging pain of the malignant disease, or the helpless dependency of old age, which he had feared all his life?

All this he did bear with magnificent fortitude, but he bore it against a background of constant and most tender loving care

---

[53] The identity of the novel has not been clarified. Its contents may contain many a clue to a better understanding of some important unconscious processes in Freud.

from a woman who was part of himself. "I of course rely," he wrote to Lou Andreas-Salomé (Freud 1960, p. 425), "more and more on Anna's care, just as Mephistopheles once remarked: 'In the end we depend on the creatures we made.' In any case, it was very wise to have made her." But he might just as well have quoted the last two lines of *Faust*: "The eternal womanly lifts us up." [*Das Ewigweibliche zieht uns hinan*].

It will not be easy to find another man, as great as Freud, whose relationship to women was so harmonious, untroubled, felicitous.[54] A man's relationship to women is a reliable barometer of the degree to which he has attained control of conflicts. I would say that his being free of conflicts in that area is the sign of a background of harmony. Fortunate as Freud was that Fate entrusted his welfare to these three women, and grateful as he was for that privilege and gift, they too reflect his goodness, and his sterling character. That the mother-child relationship is determined not only by the mother—that the child's character is also reflected in it—is well known (Coleman et al., 1953). If Freud's mother was able to bring out the best in the child, it was also to the child's credit that she was able to do so. And when Martha proved herself to be the eminently right spouse for him, that too was a reflection of the deep understanding that Freud had of her, and his practical wisdom in providing her with the frame she needed in order to be happy and contented. Finally, the daughter's devotion to her great father was not sacrifice, but self-fulfillment and joy.

Yet to return to Freud himself. There is something to be observed in Freud's later life that strikes me as being quite peculiar—indeed, unique. It would be rather surprising to me if it were to be found with any frequency in the lives of other great men. In the history of ideas, psychoanalysis and the name of Freud still remain almost identical; it is rare for a branch of science to have been for such a long time identified with the name of its founder. Yet, as Freud saw it, psychoanalysis was not his creation. In one single sentence this became more clearly revealed than anywhere else in his writings; but the fact that it is

---

[54] It may be worthy of note that the men in his environment do not seem—at least, as far as one knows about them—to have established any such harmony. See Stekel (1950); Brome (1968); Roazen (165 n.).

a single sentence is no reason to challenge the fundamental biographical meaning it contains.

After the death of Karl Abraham, Freud wrote to Jones: "We have to carry on and keep together. In terms of his personal qualities [persönlich] no one can replace the loss; but for what we are doing [Arbeit], there must be no one who is irreplaceable. I shall soon fall away; only much later, hopefully, the others. But the work [Werk] must be carried further; viewed against its magnitude, all of us, taken together, are small" (my own translation; cf. Freud 1960, p. 363; emphasis added). Here Freud viewed all those who were devoting themselves to gaining new insight into the human mind by means of the psychoanalytic method—and this included also himself—as less significant than the "work." (The English word reproduces only lamely the German word Werk; the latter has no connotation with labor, as work does, but is closer to the Latin word opus, and signifies in this context the totality of what has been built and created in an area of knowledge, as well as all accretions in the field that are suggested will follow in the future. The term is here used in a dynamic sense.)

This is a sentence of the kind that Freud was quite often able to write—simple and almost common-sense, yet encompassing the widest horizons, once one permits all its implications to burgeon. It says no less than that psychoanalysis is not, and never has been, the result only of his toil and ingenuity; that it is an objective structure, to whose service he and the others have been devoting their lives. The self-experience itself is at that moment dwarfed in the presence of that formidable structure we call science. At that point, Freud was envisioning himself and all his co-workers as dead; but he also saw subsequent generations alive, and nibbling away at the still huge mass of unknown things—until, in some unforeseeably distant future, even that bulky conglomeration of the unknown will have collapsed, and man will have brought light to all the dark corners of that universe he carries inside himself.

Thus Freud saw himself, in that instance, as reduced to a simple point, connecting a long past of human scientific endeavor with a still longer future that was devoted to the same aim, in much the same way as a man may visualize himself as being nothing but a link between the huge number of past and future generations. It is not infrequently that the wise man halts for a moment, and dissociates himself from what the seriousness of the immediate moment makes him believe to be weighty, in order to assess his nothingness within the eternity of time. Yet in the sentence quoted Freud went beyond that. He purified his relationship to his own work of that narcissistic cathexis that the originator of values generally attaches to his accomplishments.

Whatever may befall the products of talent or genius, they themselves tend to use their works to buttress their identity, to add value to their lives—sometimes, to provide the only meaning that personal existence has taken on for them. On the other hand, toward the end of their lives, they may have a low opinion of their accomplishments; in rare instances, they may even feel regretful about what they had created. Yet it never loses for them the special meaning of: "This came from me."

It is my impression that Freud succeeded in stepping so far back that even what had been initially "his" psychoanalysis dissolved into one sector of the culture in which he was living. Such a loss of his "property" must nevertheless be an exquisite esperience. The developmental arc that was covered by Freud was unusually large—spreading as it did from the young man who wanted to make his name famous by "discovering" cocaine, to the man who knew that one's own self does not count for anything, when set against the eternal kingdom of man's ideas.

Even though the reader may have felt that most of the laudable things I have here written about Freud have been sufficiently documented, I feel certain that he will say I have lost my bearing with my last conclusion—which is based, after all, only upon the one sentence Freud wrote to Jones following Abraham's death. He may even feel that I have spoiled this entire book by substituting romantic interpretations for biographical sobriety—even if it were only in this one instance. Perhaps. But if such renunciation of narcissistic gratifications may be unusual and may sound incredible, the genius's achievement is always unusual and incredible, and it may not be incompatible, therefore, with unusual and incredible structuralization in the genius's personality.

Be that as it may, even if Freud had only approximated such a state without fully attaining it, it would still explain the sen-

tence on Tausk that has puzzled many: "I had long taken him
to be useless." Add to that statement "for psychoanalysis," and
the sentence fits perfectly into all we know about Freud. At this
point, I shall not argue with authors who think that Freud meant
"useless to him personally" or "only to his [Freud's] own glory."
There was only one analyst who was consistently useful to Freud
personally, and that was Max Eitingon (1881–1943), his faithful
helper in emergencies. And "to Freud's own glory"? Here I am
puzzled again. When a pupil of his is allegedly solving the riddles
of psychoses, and extending the therapeutic orbit of psychoanalysis (what could have enhanced Freud's glory more?), we hear
that Freud was frowning in fearfulness and jealousy.

The knowledgeable reader, however, will quote from another
of Freud's letters to show that I have been wrong with my image
of a Freud who had withdrawn narcissistic cathexis from "his"
psychoanalysis. In an hour of apparent despondency, he wrote to
Stefan Zweig (Freud 1960, p. 438): "My work lies behind me,
as you yourself say. No one can predict how posterity will assess
it. I myself am not too certain; from scientific inquiry doubt is
undetachable; and more than a scrap of a fragment of truth has
certainly not been puzzled out. The proximate future looks
gloomy also for *my* psychoanalysis." (Partially my own translation; emphasis added.)

Despite the "my" before "psychoanalysis," however, I find
confirmation for my thesis in this very letter. In the letter to
Jones, the imagery referred to the proud progress of science and
the heroic plunge into ever new unexplored territories; that imagery was free of narcissistic cathexis. In the letter to Stefan
Zweig, however, the subject matter is psychoanalysis as a "scrap
of a fragment of truth" (*Bruchstückchen der Wahrheit*); and
as to the troubled future—that is to say, the rejection of psychoanalysis—that becomes "my psychoanalysis." [55]

---

[55] There is another passage among the many that can probably be adduced
against my position. Felix Boehm reports a remark that Freud made in 1938,
when Boehm had come to Vienna in order to report on the psychoanalytic situation in Berlin. After listening to Boehm for 3½ hours, Freud interrupted him
with a comment that allegedly ended with his saying (Boehm 1956, p. 181):
"I do not attach any value to the fact that my name is cited in Germany, if
only my work remains preserved" [*Ich lege keinen Wert darauf, das mein Name
in Deutschland genannt wird, wenn nur mein Werk erhalten bleibt*]. (For a

I still believe that Freud was privileged to attain the experience of "his" psychoanalysis being completely divorced from his own person. One wonders whether, for this particular area of the history of ideas, not only genius but a superior type of personality was necessary. An author and poet of our times has described, better than I can, this new type of man, who may be paradigmatic of a future still to come.

Certainly, what nowadays we understand by personality, is something quite different from what the biographers and historians of earlier times meant by it. For them, and especially for the writers of those days who had a distinct taste for biography, the essence of a personality seems to have been deviance, abnormality, uniqueness, in fact all too often the pathological. We moderns, on the other hand, do not even speak of major personalities until we encounter men who have gone beyond the original and idiosyncratic qualities to achieve the greatest possible integration into the generality, the greatest possible service to the suprapersonal.

If we look closely into the matter we shall see that the ancients had already perceived this ideal. The figure of the Sage or Perfect One among the ancient Chinese, for example, or the ideal of Socratic ethics, can scarcely be distinguished from our present ideal, and many a great organization, such as the Roman Church in the era of its greatest power, has recognized similar principles. Indeed, many of its greatest figures, such as St. Thomas Aquinas, appear to us—like early Greek sculptures—more the classical representatives of types than individuals.

Nevertheless, in the period before the reformation of intellectual life, a reformation which began in the twentieth century and of which we are the heirs, that authentic ancient ideal had patently come near to being entirely lost. We are astonished when the biographies of those times rather garrulously related how many brothers and sisters the hero had, or what psychological scars and blotches were left behind from his casting off the skins of childhood and puberty, from the struggle for position and the search for love. We moderns are not interested in a

slightly different version, see Schelkopf 1969, p. 190.) It would mean a great deal for me to know whether Freud said "my work" or "psychoanalysis" on that occasion. I have inquired of the still-living participants in that meeting, but none of them could remember the detail. I do not know whether Boehm paid special attention to the difference.

hero's pathology or family history, nor in his drives, his digestion, and how he sleeps. Not even his intellectual background—the influence upon his development of his favorite studies, favorite reading, and so on—is particularly important to us.

For us, a man is a hero and deserves special interest only if his nature and his education have rendered him able to let his individuality be almost perfectly absorbed in its hierarchic function, without at the same time forfeiting the vigorous, fresh, admirable impetus which make for the savor and worth of the individual. And if conflicts arise between the individual and the hierarchy, we regard these very conflicts as a touchstone for the stature of a personality. We do not approve of the rebel who is driven by his desires and passions to infringements upon law and order; we find all the more worthy of our reverence the memory of those who tragically sacrificed themselves for the greater whole. These latter are the heroes.

(Hermann Hesse, 1943; emphasis added)

Yes, the rebel who is driven by his desires and passions may be the talent. But an individuality that is almost perfectly absorbed in its hierarchic function, without forfeiting the vigorous, fresh, admirable impetus—that was Freud. Here we may also find the answer to the problem I alluded to before, of how it happened, relatively often, that people who met Freud only briefly, en passant, were not impressed with his personality. Apparently it took some time to discover the part of Freud that was alive behind the personality that was "almost perfectly absorbed in its hierarchic function."

There exists a letter written by Freud that shows with particular distinction how close Freud's development took him to the type of personality Hesse has presented in the foregoing quotation. It was written to the author (Hollós 1928) of a book, the gist of which was an appeal to adjust society to the world of the "insane."

Oct. 4, 1928

Lieber Herr Doktor:

It has been called to my attention that I have neglected to thank you for your last book. I would like to hope that it is not too late to correct that failure.

It did not arise out of a lack of interest in its content or in its author, whom I have learned to cherish as a friend of humanity on this occasion as well; it arose rather as the result of uncompleted trains of thought, which occupied me for some time after I finished reading the book, and which were essentially of a subjective nature.

Despite my unqualified recognition of the warmth of your feeling, of your comprehension and of the direction in which you are moving [*Tendenz*], I nevertheless found myself in a sort of opposition which did not become readily understandable to me. At last I admitted to myself that it came from the fact that I do not like these patients, that I am annoyed with them, that I feel them to be so far distant from me and from everything human. A curious sort of intolerance, which surely makes me unfit to be a psychiatrist.

In the course of time I have given up finding myself interesting, which is certainly incorrect analytically, and that is why I have not gotten any further in the explanation of this attitude. Are you able to understand me better? Am I behaving in this as physicians formerly did toward hysteria? Is it the consequence of an ever clearer partisanship toward the primacy of the intellect, an expression of hostility against the Id? Or what else besides?

With belated heartfelt thanks and many greetings,

Your
Freud

(Mr. Harold Collins' translation; with the permission of the Sigmund Freud Copyright, Ltd.; cf. Schur [1966b, p. 21f.])

When I read the letter for the first time, it immediately struck me as first-hand evidence of an incredible greatness of mind, greater than might have been expected even from Freud. As such, it needs no further comment; and yet a reader who has followed me to this point will understand my feeling that the Philistines will also take it out on this document. Hardly anywhere else in print has Freud shown so fully his humility, his awareness of how easily, despite all his effort, a scientist may go astray and be deceived by the never-dormant siren call of his own unconscious; hardly anywhere else has he so impressively shown his unyielding search for profoundest depths in himself. Here the reader can witness those sudden enlargements of visual angle and changes of visual line that the genius's incessant search for truth makes almost a necessity and of which only he is capable. At the same time, the reader of the letter is able to observe Freud recognizing the other person's superiority, without humiliating himself but instead with a full preservation of his own dignity—even though he does weigh the possibility of having himself been deceived by a weakness that in bygone times he had not spared when he observed it in others. And yet Freud was not born that way. It was as the result of a long hard struggle that he had become someone who deserves to be looked at—if Max Weber's conception may be applied—as approaching the embodiment of the ideal type of the modern scientist.

APPENDIX A

A HISTORICAL NOTE ON THE CONCEPTIONS OF NARCISSISM AND IDENTITY IN TAUSK'S WORK

CLEAR AS IS the evaluation of Tausk's use of the term "ego-boundary," in its relation to a paradigmatic value, just so difficult is it to obtain a clear picture of what Tausk's position was in the research on narcissism. From what is known with certainty, one can say that he did not go beyond what Freud had already presented in his papers on narcissism (1914b), on melancholia (1917a), and on the history of the Wolf-Man (1918). However, there is a significant footnote in a paper by Landauer (1914, p. 450), in which he states that Tausk was the first to suggest "the significance of the mechanism of identification for the character of narcissism and the preparation of object choice." [1]

According to Landauer, this happened on the occasion of Tausk's paper in München, at the Fourth Psychoanalytic Congress (September, 1913); its title was: "The Psychological and Pathological Significance of Narcissism" (*Die psychologische und pathologische Bedeutung des Narzissmus; Intern. Z. f. ärztl.*

---

[1] . . . *die Bedeutung des Identifikationsmechanismus für den Charakter des Narzissmus und die Vorbereitung der Objektwahl.* The occasion of the footnote was the report of a patient who, instead of mourning the loss of her father, regressed to a narcissistic object choice.

Psychoanal., 1914, 2:406). While the paper was at that time announced for publication in the *Zeitschrift*, it was never published.[2] I have not been able to find any summary of it, since the Congress reports, as the result of the resignation of the Swiss group, were highly incomplete.[3]

Tausk then read his Congress paper in full, under the title "Narcissism," to the Viennese Society on January 28, 1914. Again its publication was announced (*Zeitschrift* 2, p. 415) but not carried through. It is unfortunate that the *Minutes* do not contain any record of the meeting of November 4, 1914, at which Drs. Federn and Tausk discussed Freud's well-known paper on Narcissism, which he had presented to the Society on June 3, 1914. If Tausk's Congress paper and his discussion of Freud's paper were available, it might be possible to determine whether he was at that time ahead of Freud, as well as what differences existed between Freud's views and his on the question of narcissism, and whether or not he had gotten himself into a blind alley. If there did exist any documentation of these events, it might also be possible to obtain some evidence as to whether the reason why Freud found Tausk's constructions "incomprehensible," as he wrote to Lou Andreas-Salomé, was that they were objectively unclear, or simply that they had gone beyond the bounds of *his* comprehension. The content to which Freud's comment referred is just not known.

The reader will have to forgive the presentation of all these details. It has been necessary as a warning against Roazen's thoughtless and quick conclusions. In reality, however, it is not at all decisive whether Freud was right or wrong in his specific remark to Lou Andreas-Salomé. His main function vis-à-vis the early group was to stimulate research, and that he did to a quite considerable extent. Rarely has it happened in the history of science that so few have left so much to posterity through having worked under the guidance of one mind, whose each single pub-

---

[2] Cf. *Journal* (German edition, p. 279, n. 191). Ernst Pfeiffer, the editor, believes that Lou Andreas-Salomé collaborated on the paper with Tausk, since she describes it as "our paper" (*Journal*, p. 169).

[3] The secretary of the Congress, F. Riklin, was a member of the Zürich group and a follower of Jung. Jung had in general neglected his duties as President of the International Psychoanalytic Association (cf. Jones 2, p. 142).

lication was itself to provide sufficient momentum to banish any possible tendency toward staleness.

In general, one has to say that the generation that follows an innovator is often able to see some distance beyond his horizon, yet this may happen without either of them being aware of it. Something of that sort happened to Freud when he was the first to allude to the intersexuality of the eel. He was as little aware as his teacher was of how far-reaching his remark had been; he himself felt rather discouraged by the results of his research, and had no inkling that his student paper would hold an appreciable place in the history of biology.

It is equally difficult to evaluate properly Tausk's contribution to the psychology of identity and self, as that may be manifest or latent in his last paper (1919). The relevant portion of that paper, most of which I have cited in the main text, is not quite clear. What Tausk wrote about the primordial identity of the neonate was certainly not new. His assertion that man is forced by the struggle for existence to "find himself" over and over again is at least debatable. Because of the contemporary preoccupation with problems of identity, almost all analysts will probably be inclined to agree with the proposition; yet I still believe that this preoccupation is the result of the historical situation, and that the problem of identity, as it makes its appearance in contemporary psychoanalytic literature, important as it may be, is nevertheless no part of the anatomy—or better histology—of the personality.

It would be necessary at this point to discuss the psychoanalytic literature on the psychology of identity and self, and that cannot be done in this context. But this much may be said—that, while much that has been discussed in post-Freudian psychoanalytic literature under the headings of "self" and "identity" does, in my opinion, find its place in ego psychology, as outlined by Freud, it is certain that not all of it finds its place within the area Freud staked out. I do not know whether Freud would have accepted those problems of self and identity that do lie outside ego-psychology proper as valid problems of psychoanalysis.[4]

---

[4] Despite my uncertainty about this, I am, however, certain that Freud would have thought it utter nonsense if he had had an opportunity to read Peter Lomas'

It is my impression that Freud's unspoken main goal was the description, explanation and systematization of those psychic phenomena that are inherent in man as such, independently of time and history. This is not to deny that Freud was well aware that psychic phenomena can develop only in historical settings, which are in constant flux. Yet, despite the infinite variety of such phenomena during the course of man's development, one has the right to search for a sort of psychic skeleton that is common to all representatives of the human species, the individual members of which behave in such a bewildering variety of ways.

My conjecture is, as I have noted briefly above, that the contemporary psychology of self and identity no longer belongs to that area, but is an excrescence, having to do with a particular problem, which is characteristic of the contemporary historical constellation. In primitive society, identity was established by the social locus. When a member of a tribe became its chief, his ego changed in accordance with his new assignment. Vestiges of this socially determined ego identity can still be observed in contemporary societies, wherever remnants of primitive society can be observed: the Pope has the right to choose a name upon his elevation; likewise, the King of England determines his name upon his accession to the throne.

In ancient times, those who were captured in warfare, or kidnapped by pirates and sold as slaves, bemoaned their ill-fate, yet accepted their degraded status as a "natural" consequence of circumstances. Sexual identity was not autonomous, either; once enslaved, a man submitted to the demands of his master. In our times, the question of identity is looked at almost as the central issue of personality development; I doubt the general correctness of that approach.

Tausk's contribution to the psychology of identity has been overrated, chiefly because the term identity occurs in his paper. But whatever he did say about identity, it had, so far as I can see, no bearing upon what he had to say about his patient. His idea

---

verdict: "To have fully responded to Tausk as a person in need and as a theorist, Freud would have had to give up his sense of identity as a rational person who can stand back and look at problems in a detached way. This was a shift he could not make" (*New York Times Book Review*, October 12, 1969).

takes the form of an *aperçu*, which remained isolated from the rest of his clinical inquiry.

It is instructive that at that time Freud published a paper in which he delineated what I would call a psychoanalytic psychology of identity. I find this in Freud's comments on traumatic war neuroses (1919b, p. 209), which are characterized, he says, by "a conflict in the ego. . . . The conflict is between the soldier's old peaceful ego and his new warlike one, and it becomes acute as soon as the peace-ego realizes what danger it runs of losing its life owing to the rashness of its newly-formed, parasitic double." Freud did not use the term identity; nevertheless with this explanation of the traumatic war neuroses, he had taken a step right into the middle of the psychology of identity, a step I do not find recorded in most publications on identity. If one considers further that Freud then adds that the soil upon which the traumatic neuroses grow is a conscript army, that "there would be no possibility of their arising in an army of professional soldiers or mercenaries," there can be hardly any doubt that Freud himself had a problem of identity in mind.

Simmel (1918), whose book I have not been able to obtain, wrote, according to a review (Hárnik 1919), that neurosis arises "when the personality complex does not possess any longer the strongest emotional staying powers [*Gefühlbestimmung*] vis-à-vis all other sentiments [*Empfindungen*]." Where Simmel in his preanalytic phase uses the term "personality complex" in connection with his inquiry into the traumatic war neuroses, one would perhaps today say "identity."

It is important to take note of the fact that, in the instances I have cited, the concepts that refer to what is nowadays called identity are used in a dynamic sense. The "identity crisis" is here brought about, according to Freud, by competition and rivalry among different ego states (cf. Rangell 1963; Jacobson 1964).

It is of further historical interest that the brochure containing these papers and discussions of the Fifth International Psychoanalytic Congress of 1918 that referred to the war neuroses (Freud et al. 1919) is full of references to the very same problem. It was Jones, in particular, who set forth in detail the organizational processes that were necessary in order to convert the peacetime personality into one that was suited for wartime.

In an unpublished manuscript, in which I have tried to describe the psychopathology of army life, I made this the central issue. It seemed to me that most of the psychopathological symptomatology that could be observed among the recruits at an infantry training center was a reaction to or defense against the fear of transmogrification—that is to say, the fear of having to give up an identity they had accepted and taking on instead an identity they feared and rejected.

Because of the dearth of the data, it will probably never be known whether Tausk's comments on identity were included in the first draft of his paper (1919), which he read to the Viennese Society on January 6, 1918, or were added following the Budapest Congress, in which he participated.

APPENDIX B

NOTES ON FOLIE A DEUX
BETWEEN BIOGRAPHER
AND HIS SUBJECT

ROAZEN'S BOOK offers a splendid opportunity to confirm a connection that I had already assumed to exist, in a few instances, between a biographer and the person he has chosen as the subject of his presentation. The area of Roazen's biographical inquiry is, to be sure, defined by Freud and Tausk and their relationship, even though Tausk is the central figure of his book, with Freud providing the background. Yet the fact is that there is a triangle (which the author left out, even though he is at times preoccupied with the discovery of triangles); it is formed by author, Freud and Tausk. Only it is a spherical triangle: its nature is such that a person who is standing at any one corner of the triangle would be unable to perceive the other two.

Roazen never perceived Freud as he was; at one point he even perceived him as Othello and Iago in one. I doubt that he understood Tausk. Just as he assumes that Tausk used Dr. Deutsch in order to reach Freud, so his own interest in Tausk is apparently focused on the opportunity the latter provides him for detracting from Freud. In order to carry out his strategy, he quite often presents as a fact what very probably existed as a thought or fantasy (conscious or unconscious) in Tausk's mind.

The biographer's presentation of psychic reality (fantasy or wish) in his subject as an event of external reality is quite reminiscent of the disease psychiatrists call *folie à deux*. I do not mean to say that a psychotic condition is actually induced in a biographer by the subject of his story; yet the relationship between biographer and subject may have a structure that is equivalent to that of *folie à deux*. Something of the kind, to cite a famous historical example, may be said to have existed for a long time between Goethe and his biographers.

From Goethe's *Dichtung und Wahrheit* one might easily get the impression that he was a great lover. With the support of his biographers, who reconstructed his love life from the data he left, he became famous as a "ladies' man"—someone whose life was filled with amorous adventures from early manhood on. Yet, as mentioned earlier, it is now known that this was contrary to fact (cf. Bode 1921). As the result of Goethe's poetic mastery, he succeeded in covering up the truth without ever writing, on that score, anything that could be called an outright untruth. In this example, we see in a subject a strong wish that his life had taken a certain course—perhaps for a time even the illusion that it had indeed taken that course, and we see the biographer carrying out that wish and "proving" that things did in reality unfold in accordance with the subject's concious or unconscious wishes.

I shall now try to demonstrate a relationship between Roazen and Tausk that is comparable to that pattern. The first signs of this are his description of reactions in Tausk for which he has no proofs—or else he would surely have presented them—but which he takes as self-evident, as if no one could possibly dispute them. Thus, for example, he states repeatedly that Tausk felt humiliated, and that he was terribly insulted by being sent by Freud into analysis with Dr. Deutsch (p. 80f.). Of course, if we knew for certain that Dr. Deutsch's earlier (1954) statement is correct about Tausk himself having had the idea of going into analysis with her, then Roazen's idea would be proven *prima vista* wrong. If we do not assign reliability, however, to a statement that Dr. Deutsch is no longer able to confirm, then we are facing the possibility that the author may be right. We are, however, entitled under such circumstances to look for some confirmation from Tausk himself.

Although he told both Dr. Weiss and Dr. Deutsch of his conviction that Freud was draining off his ideas, Tausk did not mention anything about "insult" or "humiliation" in his last letter to Freud, nor did he mention anything of that sort to his therapist or to anyone else, insofar as we know. Could it have happened that he felt humiliated and insulted without apprising anybody of it? However, if someone were to assert—as Roazen does not—that this was Tausk's *unconscious* reaction, it would still be necessary to present those observations that would make it at least probable that Tausk did respond unconsciously in that way. Nothing of that sort is to be found in Roazen's book.

It is obvious that Roazen is certain that anybody *would have had* to react in that way. This is, however, incorrect, as I shall presently show; but it would seem to warrant the assumption that the author himself would have felt humiliated under such circumstances, and that he therefore took it for granted that everyone would surely have to feel that way under those circumstances. To lend some semblance to his description, he assumes that Dr. Deutsch was inexperienced in analysis and that Tausk was her first psychoanalytic patient (p. 71). The fact is, as Dr. Deutsch has told me, that Tausk was her third patient. In view of Dr. Deutsch's extensive psychiatric experience, her profound knowledge of Freud's writings and her having previously carried through the analyses of two patients she was not, by present standards and, all the more by those of that time, "inexperienced." [1]

Now Tausk had objected vigorously to any one of his male colleagues, and this negative reaction could be—rightly or wrongly—interpreted in terms of his anticipated humiliation if he accepted any one of them as his analyst. But a man who, like Tausk, had serious homosexual conflicts with father- and brother-figures, who was devoured by conflicts of rivalry, and who was unable to acknowledge the superiority of any man—such a person might feel considerably more at ease in a therapeutic relationship with a woman. Tausk might well have been able to ac-

---

[1] It is noteworthy to record that one of the patients whom Dr. Deutsch analyzed, before she started to analyze Tausk, was a close relative of Freud's. When Freud entrusted Tausk's analysis to an analyst to whom he had previously entrusted a close relative, one can be quite certain that there was no ambivalence attached to such a recommendation.

cept a maternal woman in the superior role of a therapist; at least, that minimum of submission that is unavoidable in a therapeutic relationship would be less painful under such conditions than it would be vis-à-vis a male figure.

After all, Tausk must have observed that Dr. Deutsch was an eminently gifted person, of rare brilliance, whose unique success at the University Clinics alone had proven her ability to be on a par with male professional excellence. Furthermore, the fact that she herself was in analysis with Freud created an imagery—to which Roazen correctly alludes—that permitted Tausk the illusion of actually being in analysis with Freud himself, without being drawn into the inescapable conflict of rivalry. Thus, the idea of being "rescued" by a maternal woman of Dr. Deutsch's stature and skill may easily have been—and very probably was—accepted by Tausk in a conflict-free way.

Objectively, moreover, there was no insult and humiliation involved at all, for we can rest assured that a person of such paranoid sensitivity as Tausk's would have responded to this reality factor with immediate vigor. The fact that he never showed any aggressive or reproachful reactions to Dr. Deutsch, either during or after his analysis, makes it all the more probable that Dr. Deutsch's 1954 recollection could, after all, have been quite correct, and that Tausk did consider himself responsible for being in psychoanalysis with her.[2]

Thus the idea of "terrible insult" and humiliation is solely the author's idea; it presupposes an identification with Tausk, along with the certainty that Tausk reacted as Roazen would have reacted under similar circumstances. Traces of the author's uncritical identification with Tausk were already visible when, contrary to the historical evidence, he asserted that Tausk—as must certainly have been his ambition—had "forged ahead of Freud" in a subject that had, in reality, loomed prominently in Freud's own *earlier* writings.

The author's overidentification with Tausk makes understandable his uncritical attitude toward Tausk's request to be analyzed

---

[2] The high regard in which he already held Dr. Deutsch, before she had even started her psychoanalytic career, can be seen from the fact that in 1915 he chose her and not Freud as a therapist for a beloved sister (p. 77).

by Freud. This request alone seems to me to show that Tausk's reality judgment was at least temporarily impaired. As I said before, if he was certain that there was any truth to his charge that Freud was taking his ideas, the only thing for him to do would have been to *stay away from* Freud as much as he possibly could; if it dawned on him, however, that that was a paranoid idea, he should have known, as an analyst, that a patient who has formed paranoid ideas about the therapist prior to treatment should never be taken into treatment by him. Yet Roazen continues to reproach Freud in the harshest terms, for having refused to accept Tausk as an analysand, and he does so in the way in which Tausk himself might have done it at one time or another.

There is one passage in which it becomes manifest that the author did become a victim of the sort of wishful thinking that is known to exist in *folie à deux*. He writes (p. 93):

Having heard complaints and accusations from both sides [Freud's and Tausk's], Helene Deutsch thought there was reality to what both felt. But in this struggle between them, it was Freud, she thought, who had taken the initiative.

Dr. Deutsch does not recall ever having said anything of the sort, or even having suggested anything resembling it. Since Tausk's struggle went back at least seven years, it is hardly imaginable that any analyst, within three months of the start of the analysis, could have developed any idea about who might have taken the first step in that struggle. This seems to be one of the instances in which the author's imagination ran away with him, and he took as a fact something that Tausk, we may be reasonably sure, ardently wished was historical truth.

What I have rightly or wrongly called, in a metaphorical sense, *folie à deux* led the author, at least once, into fallacious reasoning, as the following will show. At the Fifth Psychoanalytic Congress in Budapest (September, 1918), Dr. Herman Nunberg proposed that all *future* analysts should undergo a didactic analysis, before starting their practice. Even though Freud (1912) had already recommended such a procedure six years earlier, it was voted down—particularly as the result of Rank's and Tausk's

opposition.[3] Now, in discussing why the proposal of a didactic
analysis, as a prerequisite for all future analysts, was not welcomed
by the older generation of analysts, the author raises the question
—after reporting that Dr. Nunberg "had recently undergone a
brief therapeutic relationship with . . . Paul Federn" (p. 65)—
"Who, however, would be available to analyze Tausk or Federn?
[As if anybody had suggested didactic analyses for the oldtimers!]
Only Freud would have the appropriate seniority. Yet Freud as
their analyst would only complicate already hyper-involved ties.
Going to Freud for an analysis meant even more of a submission
than these men had already made to him. For the younger generation, and for the new recruits who would be even more distant
from Freud, a personal analysis might be more feasible."

This is a remarkable piece of argumentation, almost of soph-
istry, in view of the fact that Dr. Nunberg's motion was meant
exclusively for the new recruits. The author argues that the reason why these older analysts were against Nunberg's motion was
that they could not go to Freud for analysis. Rank was Freud's
favored pupil, and Tausk wanted to have that preferred position.
Tausk's opposition to a didactic analysis is especially remarkable,
since within a few months he himself would be asking Freud to
take him into analysis. The author even thinks (p. 70) that
"Tausk's stand on the issue might have represented his anxiety
lest Freud not take him into analysis"—which makes no sense
whatsoever, since an obligatory didactic analysis for training
candidates would, if anything, have given something of an added
weight and justification to Tausk's request to be analyzed by
Freud.

Roazen's argumentation—as little validity as it has as a reason for opposing Dr. Nunberg's motion—adds up to saying that
Tausk was motivated in 1918 by the fear that newcomers would
have the privilege of being analyzed by Freud, whereas he would
be excluded from such a privileged position. Thus it was the
envy that the older generation of analysts felt of the younger

---

[3] This incident is instructive, in that it shows once again the membership's
relative independence from Freud, so strongly disputed by the author. Here a
motion was made that was not only favored by Freud, but the appropriateness and
wisdom of which cannot be disputed. Didactic analysis later became the back-
bone of analytic training, yet, in 1918, it was rejected.

incoming ones—their fear lest they lose their privileged standing in relation to Freud—that caused the delay of this highly desirable measure. I can well imagine that the author very correctly guessed what were the unconscious motives of analysts like Tausk; but the strange thing, which makes me suggest the kind of mechanism that is active in folie à deux, is that Roazen presents these unconscious motives as if they were valid and reasonable arguments. Yet in general the folie-à-deux relationship of a biographer to his subject remains hidden and for that reason difficult to demonstrate. That also a reviewer may enter into a folie-à-deux relationship with the author of a book can be observed in the previously mentioned review by Sabshin (1970). The reader may recall his appreciation "of Roazen's excitment as he began to penetrate obstacles," although Roazen did not cite one single obstacle he had to "penetrate" in the course of his undertaking. In fact, the only three surviving psychoanalysts who had known Tausk shared willingly their knowledge with the inquirer. Had Roazen met with obstacles, we may rest assured that he would have let us know about them—possibly with a feeling of triumph —for they would have lent his assumptions a semblance of truth. As with some biographers, we observe in this case also the reviewer accepting what the author desires his readers to consider true reality, even though no documentation is provided to substantiate his claim. This is one of the fascinating aspects of the unconscious, in that it responds willingly to the subliminal message of an author's unverbalized wishes, but resists (more often than not) the insight gained through the tedious study of documents. Possibly what I have called here folie à deux is a rather vulgar form of that sublime folie à deux to which every susceptible reader, when he succumbs to the spell that is cast by the great poets, is subjected.

APPENDIX C

NOTE ON THE BIOGRAPHICAL
BIAS OF VOLUNTARISM

IN WRITING the life history of a subject, one has to disentangle
two sets of variables that Gabriel Marcel (1963; see also Schelkopf
1969, p. 171) believed to be almost inseparably intertwined: that
which happens in a man's life as a result of his wishing, wanting,
or willing it, and that which man has to endure, to tolerate, even
though it is discordant with his conscious and unconscious aspira-
tions and inclinations. Through psychoanalysis, the orbit of those
events in his own life that are—consciously or unconsciously—
wished for by man has received an extension that is not to be
compared, in scope, with any previous endeavor to explain a man's
life.

Indeed, from a certain point of view (a very doubtful one),
one may say that nothing can happen in a man's life without its
acquiring the meaning or function of a wish fulfillment. In the
deepest layers of the psychic apparatus, where the archaic is fully
regnant, and differentiation is lacking, the primitive psyche has
no choice but the one between devouring or destroying and dying
—that is to say, any event lends itself to a kind of either sadistic
or masochistic gratification. It is unnecessary to examine whether
or not such an archaic layer really exists in civilized man; that

question is irrelevant for the biographer because it is so far distant from the data he is dealing with. Yet the voluntaristic aspect of psychoanalysis, which is derived from the enormous force that it attributes to the unconscious and its imperishable wishes, facilitates a view that Roazen upholds indirectly in his book. By and large, one may say that Roazen looks at almost all events in Freud's life—at least, those that he takes into consideration—as having been wished by Freud and, if not actually wished, then directly or indirectly caused by him.[1]

I would say that the danger exists that an analyst, even when he is more cautious and sober than Roazen, may nevertheless find himself trapped by this pitfall. How does one go about protecting oneself against it in a biographical study? One of the several precautionary measures to be taken is to observe the frequency of events. When an event of a given type repeats itself, then the analytic biographer has occasion to search for a hidden wish.

Now it is very impressive to observe how well almost all those fared who had been in professional contact with Freud. In this context, it is worth mentioning in passing that, although psychoanalysis was on Hitler's list for extirpation, all analysts (with the sole exception of Sadger) escaped from Austria unharmed after the tragedy of 1938—and this not least by virtue of Freud's having stayed in Vienna against all advice. There is no doubt that if Freud had listened to the voices of self-preservation and of his friends, and had left Austria prior to 1938, few members of the Psychoanalytic Society would have escaped the concentration camp.

But is it not likewise impressive to consider the brilliant careers of all those who turned against Freud: Jung, Adler, Stekel, Rank, Horney, Fromm, Rado, and even Reich, whose tragic end cannot possibly be brought into any meaningful connection with Freud personally? If one considers the lives of those who were

---

[1] Even if a charitable editor had winnowed Roazen's manuscript and counteracted his propensity for the bizarre—for example, his equating of Freud and Henry II (p. 157), or his belief that Tausk acted out Freud's dawning theory of a death instinct—even were his tale thus purified of these and other bizarreries, it would still reflect a voluntaristic world, in which man cannot help but experience that which he secretly wishes. To a certain extent, one can see in Roazen's book a travesty of psychoanalytic theories.

close to Freud—whether they left Freud or remained faithful to him—one finds that they formed a group of people who were by and large favored by good luck (unless we regard the failure, on the part of those who left Freud, to arrive at the truth—a great misfortune for them). The statistical record would seem to suggest that to have been associated with Freud was equivalent to "having drawn a winning ticket." Tausk was really an exception. The repetition compulsion that Freud spread among his associates, as it were, was one of growth and success.

I can easily imagine the objections that most readers will raise at this point, and I therefore want to add quickly that I have put forth this remark chiefly because Roazen created the wrong impression—namely, that associating with Freud spelled tragedy for those who entered within the orbit of his charisma. It was the opposite that seems to have been the fact. If, however, the reader should draw the conclusion that I believe that single events do not sometimes reveal deeply repressed contents and strivings, that would be wrong. Clinical experience shows with some frequency that the analysis of a single event may lead one to the key to a major portion of a patient's neurosis. Nevertheless, the biographer must be cautious when he observes, on the part of his subject, an identical pattern of action, which he shows repeatedly at times when he finds himself in a certain type of situation. What if the biographer is then confronted with a situation that, even though it belongs to the same type, ends in an entirely different fashion than observed in the subject's past? When such an atypical ending is linked with an unusual circumstance—as was the case in the Tausk episode, by virtue of Tausk's severe psychopathology—then it would be stretching voluntarism beyond its limits if one were to profess to see in this unusual ending a reflection of the subject's unconscious strivings.

There is a series of similar events to be found in Freud's life, and yet I am not certain, although the evidence seems to speak so strongly in its favor, that this repetition necessarily grew out of Freud's unconscious. I have referred earlier to an autobiographical passage in Freud's *The Interpretation of Dreams*. It concerns John, Freud's nephew and childhood playmate, who was one year his senior: "All my friends have in a certain sense been reincarnations of this first figure. . . . They have been *revenants*.

. . . My emotional life has always insisted that I should have an intimate friend and a hated enemy. I have always been able to provide myself afresh with both, and it has not infrequently happened that the ideal situation of childhood has been so completely reproduced that friend and enemy have come together in a single individual" (Freud 1900, p. 483). If Freud had written this at a later date, I would think that he was here referring to his relationship to Fliess and to Jung. But it was written before 1900, when the friendship with Fliess was still undisturbed, and he had not yet even met Jung. Therefore, it is appropriate to ask which friendships Freud did have in mind when he wrote the passage just quoted. Could he have had Breuer in mind, since Freud's relationship to him had reached its nadir by 1900 (see Jones 1, p. 256)? But Breuer held the place of a typical father-figure in Freud's life. The nephew pattern, one would expect, would not include relationships to father images, since Freud made the special point that this pattern "had a determining influence on all my subsequent relations with contemporaries" (Freud 1900, p. 424). Or should one suspect that behind the nephew pattern lies the rule of the Oedipus complex?

Perhaps it was Freud's relationship to his brother-in-law Eli Bernays that was responsible for the discovery of the effect of the pattern that he had acquired in his early relationship to John. Eli was Freud's friend in the early eighties. Whether or not it was an intense friendship is not known. The conflicts—mainly brought about by Freud, according to Jones (1, p. 162)—were at times particularly severe. At any rate, it is a fact that many friendships in Freud's life followed the nephew pattern.

Three things are noteworthy in this respect. First, Freud had a number of personal friends, such as Rie and Königstein, the relationship to whom remained unencumbered by the pattern mentioned. Second, he had a great desire for friendship, and was highly appreciative of any kindness he obtained from friends. Third, when one examines the details—at least as far as they have reached us—of those relationships in which the nephew pattern seems to have held sway, one does not usually discover that it was Freud who caused the reversals. One obtains, instead, the impression that Freud was particularly eager to please the friend from whom he would later become separated.

It is possible, of course, that Freud's psychopathology was manifested in the mistakes he occasionally made in choosing a friend. After all, Abraham warned Freud repeatedly about Jung, and Jung himelf behaved in such a way as to make it quite clear that he was not a reliable scientist, at least in the way Freud thought a reliable scientist should be. It may have been that in his choice of friends he unconsciously laid the foundations for later discord, much as he may have struggled to avoid that very outcome, once the friendship had been established. One is inclined to say here: "Dark are the ways of the repetition compulsion."

I shall cite another example—this time, one of subordinate importance—that demonstrates how Roazen misapplies the voluntaristic aspect of psychoanalysis. He reproaches Freud whenever the latter was not able to understand something that one of his followers had written or said. In these instances, Roazen always draws the conclusion that it was out of unwillingness or hostility that Freud declared something that was contradicting his own theories to be incomprehensible. In relation to Federn, he writes: "As with Tausk earlier, Freud found Federn's formulations unintelligible." That Freud considered Federn's formulations to be incomprehensible has never, so far as I know, found its way into print, although it is very probably correct.

From clinical experience, it is well known that an inability to comprehend is often founded on resistance, manifest or repressed hostility, and such. Is the biographer therefore entitled, in any particular instance of the sort, to assume the operation of factors that are so familiar to the analyst from his clinical experience? If so, then the author could have made an important contribution to Freud's biography by demonstrating how easy it is to comprehend Federn's ego psychology; in so doing, of course, he would have proved Freud's stubbornness on an occasion when one of his adherents departed from his own theories.

Yet there is, after all, the question of reality to be considered, for there are many authors who lack the ability to convey to others, in a comprehensible form, what they themselves understand well. Paul Federn was one of these, as any reader will soon discover who takes the trouble to study Federn's papers on ego psychology. I myself attended Federn's courses on ego psychology, which he gave within the program of regular psychoanalytic training in Vienna, and can only testify that, along with many others, I was not able to follow them.[2] Roazen rarely misses an opportunity to contradict himself. After having convinced the reader that it was Freud's emotional attitude that made him find Federn's formulations incomprehensible, he writes (p. 190): "Federn was in such conflict that it handicapped his writing, and his concepts became clearcut *only long after Freud's death*" (emphasis added).

Let us now return to a more serious matter. There are areas in which it is extremely difficult to differentiate between fate and the fulfillment of a repressed wish. Roazen erred when he asserted that Freud had accepted it as his "task" to disturb the sleep of the world. On the contrary, he felt this effect of his writings to be unintended and indeed surprising; it was even a source of sadness to him. His conscious intent and wish were to enrich knowledge and thereby to add to that sum total of understanding of which mankind is most proud.

In a letter to Romain Rolland (1960, p. 370), one seems to detect the envy he felt toward the latter, because Rolland, at least, could count on the love of many people for having "pleased, comforted, edified them." And yet he had recalled in a letter to Martha Bernays that "even at school, I was always the bold oppositionist, always there where an extreme (position) had to be taken, and as a rule ready to atone for it" (my own translation, cf. Freud 1960, p. 202).

And when he chose as the motto for his *Interpretation of Dreams* Virgil's *Flectere si nequeo superos, Acheronta movebo* (If I cannot bend the higher powers, I will move the infernal regions), that may have been the echo of a strong unconscious striving that was intensely repressed, for he himself added speedily —evidently as an attempt at fuller explication of the quotation— "The interpretation of dreams is the royal road to a knowledge of the unconscious activities of the mind" (1900, p. 608).

In a letter to Werner Achelis (1960, p. 371), he says that he took the quotation from Lassalle—which is surprising, in the light of the fact that Freud was so eminently knowledgeable in

---

[2] This was in contrast to Federn's clinical seminars, in which the student was able to gain the deepest insights from the lifetime experience of a truly great clinician.

the classics. With Lassalle, Freud continues, it certainly "had a personal meaning," but he himself had used it to emphasize the main part of dream dynamics. He asks with surprise how his correspondent could have found anything "Promethean" in this motto. It is at least questionable whether the quotation does reproduce Freud's principal proposition with regard to dream dynamics; taken all in all, one may suspect that, even if they were unknown to Freud, Promethean forces were strongly at work in him.[3]

During the course of his analytic inquiries, Freud turned his scalpel onto the deepest layers, out of which have arisen not only culture and civilization, but also individual value judgments. The belief in the absolute validity of some moral values is an indispensable prerequisite to societal cohesiveness; and for Freud himself some values did have that very quality, even though he questioned the validity of others. Yet it is historically possible that it was his inquiries into the matrix of absolute values that have contributed to the present tragic trend toward discrediting any idea of a value system that would have absolute validity for the individual. Historically, a psychological inquiry into moral value systems may well have had the effect of casting doubt on their validity. The question of whether this effect was, after all, the result of a deeply suppressed wish in Freud is a challenging one to consider. One may reconstruct the following sequences: Freud apparently was a very active, not to say aggressively directed youngster, who was averse to conformism and insisted that those in power should live up to the ideals they preached—in which, as is well known, juvenile aggressivity finds an ego-syntonic outlet. In his early inclination to become a politician, one may also sense a revolutionary flavor. When he started out on his medical studies, he accepted the new ideal of science as taught by his favored teacher Brücke. That ideal had, to a certain extent, a somewhat revolutionary flavor, since it represented values that had not yet been generally accepted. But now authority and ideal coincided, and in his neurological phase Freud followed a program that was approved by authority. He thought that he was following the

---

[3] The Promethean myth undoubtedly symbolizes the conflicts that are inherent in extreme creativity. See van Dovski (1959, p. 7) and his comments on the fact that the myth of Prometheus was a frequent subject of literary masterpieces during the eighteenth and nineteenth centuries.

same pathway when the subject of his inquiry changed from the brain to the mind. We know today that he had indeed remained faithful to his earlier program; but others did not know that, and he was pushed, against his wishes and expectations, into the position of opposition, in which he had been so often as a youth. It seems to me that it was secondarily, under the influence of extraneous factors, that a revival took place of a phase that had seemingly come to an end, many years previously.

I feel inclined to draw the conclusion that if Freud was a revolutionary, one may safely say that he was a revolutionary malgré lui. But it is precisely this malgré lui that poses the greatest difficulty for the conscientious biographer. The poets have it much easier in this respect. Not only are they permitted to apply the voluntaristic bias whenever they wish, but they are obliged to use it in order to create the deepest effects in the reader. The world of magic is based on voluntarism. There, no man gets sick without having sinned or being tested by a superior power, and no death occurs without a murder. The poet partakes of this magic world and uses it for his particular purpose. There are literary masterpieces in which the poet does not hesitate to find in Christ himself the inspiration for the outrages that some churches have committed in His name. The reader requires no proof at such a moment; indeed, the artistic experience would be greatly impaired if the poet resorted to "documentation." All the poet needs is a suitable idea that fits into the magic world, and the persuasiveness of beautiful language.

But even though the poet so frequently grasps the truth much earlier and sometimes with greater ease than the scientist,[4] no rule has yet been found that might help us to distinguish between poetic license and the new insights that are revealed by poetic intuition. The conscientious, psychoanalytically-oriented biographer, even though he knows that he will hardly be able to evade completely the bias of voluntarism, will nevertheless—painstakingly, scrupulously and untiringly—pay the strictest attention to documentation. Only in this way can a line be drawn between the scientific biographer and a novelist.

---

[4] I doubt that Mr. Strachey was right when he understood Freud to have responded to a recognition of that fact with, "We may well heave a sigh of relief" (1930a, p. 133). I rather believe that what Freud meant by the term aufseufzen was "lament with sighs."

APPENDIX D

ANOTHER CRITICAL VIEW
OF FREUD[1]

DEPRESSING AS IT IS that a book like Roazen's can be written and published, I have found some aspects of Professor Ellenberger's book *The Discovery of the Unconscious* (1970) even more disheartening.

Professor Ellenberger is an existential psychiatrist. What he has presented in 932 pages is a history of that new view of man that in a variety of forms is accepted today in the field of psychiatry. The central part of his work is a unique presentation of the lives and works of Janet, Freud, Adler and Jung. He has not, it would seem, avoided any effort to obtain biographical data, pursuing the ancestry of each of his biographical subjects, and reporting on the proximate environment of each of them, as well as on the broad historical processes that took place during their childhood and adult years.

His style and art of presentation are beautiful; his apparent skill in handling the historical method will impress many as being impeccable. Whoever meets Prof. Ellenberger will be de-

---

[1] I owe thanks to Dr. Michael Beldoch for his kindness in letting me read the manuscript of his review-essay of Ellenberger's *The Discovery of the Unconscious*, prior to its publication.

lighted by his charm and sweetness, and will admire his complete devotion to the arduous task he set for himself—namely, the handling of such a mass of data and material as hardly anyone else would have thought himself able to integrate into a highly readable text.

Under such propitious conditions, one would be entitled to feel certain that objectivity will win the day, at least as far as that is possible in historical research. All the more saddened have I been to discover in his book an inadvertent distortion of facts—at least in his handling of Freud's life, which is marked by a definite prejudice against him.

To demonstrate this, I first have to discuss the following: In 1960, the late Prof. Gicklhorn and his wife published a collection of documents having to do with the history of Freud's relationship with the University of Vienna. The Gicklhorns had previously made a great contribution when, under the guidance of Siegfried Bernfeld, they discovered two Freud manuscripts, and their new project was most promising. Indeed, the publication of archival material is always commendable. But it was really upsetting to read the introduction to their book, in which they accused Freud of all possible sorts of things, in order to prove that the delay in his academic career (he had to wait for an unusually long time before he was given the title of professor) was entirely his fault, and in every respect quite justified.

Yet even an uninformed reader could not have helped noticing that there was something basically wrong with that introduction. The Gicklhorns asserted all of the following: that no discrimination had taken place against Freud, because his nomination by the College of Professors was handled by the Government in the same way as all other pending nominations; that the delay was in conformity with a ministerial decree; that it was caused by Freud's negligence as an academic teacher, as well as by his interest in money and his insufficient interest in academic advancement; that many members of the College of Professors favored his advancement; that he was lacking in such support because he had neglected his connection with the University. These were only a few among the authors' rather readily apparent self-contradictions.

In checking these, however, I made further surprising discov-

eries (Eissler 1966)—among them, that the text of the ministerial decree that formed a pivotal point in their argumentation,
as published by the authors had a different wording from the
original, *which did not support their thesis.* What they published
was an unsigned draft that never reached the College of Professors; yet this draft made it possible for them to build up an erroneous theory. I myself published two documents (they were
easily available in the University Archives, yet they were missing
from the Gicklhorns' collection—for which they had claimed
completeness), which proved that the College of Professors had
to renew their request to the Minister of Education with regard
to Freud's appointment, four (!) years after they had made their
first one—because the Minister denied ever having received it.
Such a denial was, I believe, a unique incident in the history of
the University. The Austrian bureaucracy, even though it was
often tardy and unfair, was certainly compulsively accurate in details of that order.

I further quoted extensively from Freud's published letter,
which proved that he had been told by an impeccable source
(Professor Sigmund Exner, 1846–1926) "about personal influences which appeared to be at work against me with his Excel-
lency [the Minister of Education]" (Freud 1950a, p. 343).

In addition, I was able to prove that the authors' tabulation
of Freud's semestral lectures was full of contradictions and errors
—one of them being their asserting in all seriousness that Freud
did not lecture in the academic year 1915/16, even though these
very lectures, in published form, had since been spread all over
the world in hundreds of thousands of copies.

I was further able to prove that the authors had consistently
derogated Freud's character by falsification. Of this, I want to
give only one example: they charged that Freud was a kind of
chronic complainer, and that was why he grumbled about the
food he got at the hospital, about which he had allegedly fretted
that it was the same as that of the gas-lamp lighter. From Freud's
letters so far published nothing can be learned about his reaction
to hospital diet. What the Gicklhorns had done was to ascribe
to Freud a remark that Bernfeld had made about Freud's salary
(1951, p. 211), which he figured out had amounted at that time
to that of the "gas-lamp lighter."

I fear that I may be accused by the reader, if I pursue this further, of being a chronic complainer about biographers of Freud. And yet I assure the reader that this is only a fraction—and possibly not even the worst—of the misinformation that the Gicklhorns published. What they did when they compared Freud with Wagner-Jauregg; or discussed the fact that Freud was never elected to the Academy of Science; or informed the reader what the Austrian laws were that regulated the administration of the University—all this is simply beyond belief. One cannot understand, as with Roazen's book, how a reputable publisher could ever have accepted such a manuscript for publication. My rejoinder to them (1966), incidentally, was apparently not burdened by grave mistakes, because it was never answered by Mrs. Gicklhorn, who had not hesitated to call Hanns Sachs a liar, because he had committed an error in his book of memories of Freud. The two authors attacked Jones in an unusually sarcastic way, even where he was right (they had never even read Freud's letters to Fliess—at least, they were never cited by either of them).

The reader may counter that one has to accept the fact that there are unscrupulous writers and publishers. And what harm have the Gicklhorns actually done? Few, if any (despite Sherwood's positive review), have taken cognizance of their book. It may, however, be different as the result of Ellenberger's book which, in view of its exquisite style, its aesthetic appeal, its digestion of a large mass of historical material, its seemingly sober and reliable use of the historical method, has an excellent chance of becoming a classic in the history of depth psychology.

Ellenberger now writes about the Gicklhorns' book as if it might indeed have contained the truth about Freud's academic career. He introduces the co-authors in a highly commendatory way, writing of the "basic value" of their "documentary" researches, "supplemented by Renée Gicklhorn's clarification of certain episodes in Freud's life" (p. 427). Most readers will probably therefore accept their explanations—some of which Ellenberger reports, such as "the secret decree," Freud's preoccupation with "his lucrative practice," and his neglect of his teaching function—all those things that allegedly caused the delay in Freud's academic career.

It is true that Ellenberger is courteous enough to mention that

I have "disputed point by point" these conclusions; but "disputed" is not the same as "disproved," and the decision is left up to the reader, whom Ellenberger has informed very scantily at this point.

There is no word about the Gicklhorns' misrepresentation in publishing a draft instead of an original; no word about all the passages I referred to in Freud's letters that prove his desperate fight for economic survival; no word about Freud's energetic steps with regard to the organization of his lectures—steps that were counteracted by the College of Professors as well as by the Government—or about his difficulty in obtaining a lecture-room (not to speak of complaints of even Theodor Billroth [1829–1894], who had been since 1867 the chief of surgery, and a luminary among the medical celebrities, that he had to drop some courses because of the insufficient number of participants.)

Furthermore, if one writes a biography, one tries to reconstruct social reality, and Ellenberger refers to what was going on concurrently in the world during the lifetime of his subjects. In my book, I quoted extensively from a paper by Solomon Stricker (1834–1898), professor of experimental pathology and a remarkable person of whom Wagner-Jauregg said (1950, pp. 11, 28) that he was "a quite outstanding scholar" [*ein ganz hervorragender Gelehrter*], "a passionate fighter, [for whom] truth was the highest" [*eine leidenschaftliche Kampfnatur, [dem] doch die Wahrheit am höchsten stand*]. Stricker was not ready to play ball with the univerity establishment and he had the courage to present a realistic picture of academic reality. If one takes cognizance of Stricker's paper, the whole situation of Freud at the university appears in a different light, and one gains a high respect for a man who resisted the moral corruption that surrounded him. I understand quite well why no reference to that paper is found in the book by the Gicklhorns, but its absence in Ellenberger's bibliography is disappointing.

On what grounds Ellenberger then attributes the delay in Freud's nomination to "bureaucratic *vis inertiae*" remains unclear. Does he really assume greater knowledge than Professor Exner, official representative of the College of Professors at the Ministry of Education, who had told Freud that there were "personal influences" at work against him? This is not a matter of interpretation—that always leaves an area of incertitude, small as it may be—but strictly one of fact. The reader will understand my despair about historical research within the field of Freud's biography, when it turns out that it seems impossible, with intelligent and seemingly conscientious historians no less than with the others, to correct errors of an elementary nature, such as should not have been made even by a beginner.

One point that Mrs. Gicklhorn raised, and which she cited as proof of Freud's indifference toward his academic career (1960, p. 31), is the fact that Freud never applied for an extension of his lectureship to include psychiatry; he had been appointed as lecturer in neuropathology. Here I have to give a few additional details. A University lectureship was one of the highest honors a physician could achieve in Vienna; it was difficult to obtain, and an elaborate network of conditions had to be met. Once a physician was a *Dozent*, it is true, he had the right simply to apply for an extension of that lectureship to other fields, without having to go through the usual rigamarole. Mrs. Gicklhorn holds up Wagner-Jauregg as an example, since he did apply for and receive such an extension for the field of psychiatry. He, too, had started like Freud in the field of neuropathology.

Yet what neither Mrs. Gicklhorn nor Professor Ellenberger mentions is: (1) that this was a subtlety of University politics that was apparently little known, and Wagner-Jauregg took that step only after his chief called it to his attention and advised him to do so; (2) that Wagner-Jauregg had worked as a psychiatrist for years and had already published a few psychiatric papers, whereas Freud's record never showed more than six months of psychiatric residency, and not one publication that would have been called psychiatric, in terms of the meaning that that specialty had at the time.

Consequently, even if Freud had known of the advantages that such an extension might have had for him, in order to meet the requirements he would have had to interrupt his psychoanalytic researches, and bury himself in a mental institution—which at the turn of the century and for sometime thereafter did not offer the possibility of psychiatric research in today's meaning, but would rather have meant spending himself in administrative chores, physical treatment and safekeeping of the patients. Yet

Mrs. Gicklhorn has in all seriousness maintained that all a *Dozent* had to do was to apply for such an extension—as if that application was merely a formality that did not demand any training in the field for which the extension was asked.

Thus the almost grotesque situation arose in which someone who apparently did not know what the field of neuropathology covered set herself up as a judge of Freud's character, and lectured Freud on how he should have organized his career. I called Mrs. Gicklhorn's attention a second time (1966, p. 66) to the nonsense she was putting into print. Nevertheless, Prof. Ellenberger—contrary to the elementary facts of the administration of a European university—writes as if Mrs. Gicklhorn's allegations could have been correct under any circumstances and, in summarizing his own conclusions, repeats (p. 454) that "Freud had been too absorbed in his self-analysis to see to his interests."

Prof. Ellenberger, I might say, should have had the sagacity to observe that, if Freud had indeed carried out Mrs. Gicklhorn's belated advice, she and her late husband would not have had the occasion for publishing their book on Freud's academic career. For a man who is ready to sacrifice years of his life solely for the purpose of academic advancement is likely to be one who has hardly any chance of doing something interesting enough to make him, in the eyes of posterity, worthy of a biography. In general, I would say that many a biographer who has written in a critical tone about the lives of the truly great would have had little or no opportunity to write a biography of that kind, if the subject of his literary efforts had actually acted in such a way as to provide no grounds for the biographer's critical remarks.

Prof. Ellenberger is also mistaken when he writes (p. 454) that now "Freud saw this one of his ambitions fulfilled. The title of Professor Extraordinarius was an acknowledgment of his scientific work." From a careful study of the Fliess letters, however, one learns that Freud regretted (and possibly felt ashamed) that he had not received the title in recognition of accomplishments, but through the use of "pull" (Freud 1950a, p. 342).

That Freud was right when he wrote his friend that he did not receive his title in acknowledgment of his scientific work can be learned from a document published by the Gicklhorns (1960, p. 126), in which the Minister's recommendation to the Emperor, requesting Freud's appointment, is reproduced. It says specifically that Freud should receive the title "in consideration of the many years of his activity as a *Dozent*" (Freud had been a *Dozent* for seventeen years), and not one word of any scientific achievement is to be found.

At the same time as the Minister submitted the recommendation in favor of Freud, he did it also for Dr. Emil Fronz, a scientific nullity who had been *Dozent* for only four years. In my book (1966, p. 89f.), I discussed this appointment at length, in order to demonstrate how biased the Gicklhorns had been. Thus Prof. Ellenberger had been given ample opportunity in my book to learn about the social reality of the University of Vienna during the years when Freud was *Dozent* there.

What Prof. Ellenberger covers with the innocent phrase "to see to his interests," when he reproaches Freud's alleged carelessness in the pursuit of his academic carer, also meant running after people in high position, flattering them, begging and kowtowing. Stricker (1894, p. 105) had warned specifically against the corrupting effect resulting from the fact that *Dozenten* had to curry favors in order to advance. As can be easily imagined, Stricker's call to honesty was not heeded, and it was not only as the result of economic conditions that the Vienna Medical School declined from being one of Europe's best to being a second- if not third-rate one within the next four decades.[2]

If all *Dozenten* had shown the degree of steadfastness that Freud showed during his academic career, things might have come about differently. The fact that he was defeated in the end and made the bitter visit to Exner, in order to inquire into the reasons for his being passed over consistently, was a violation of his personal morality (for which, I believe, he never forgave himself completely), and not a deviation from what was necessary and customary in those days. The contemporary American, who can hardly be expected to understand what all this meant, should take note that Billroth once wrote (1886, p. 43): "A Dozent who

---

[2] Cf. Wagner-Jauregg (1950, p. 85) about intrigues with regard to appointments "which introduced the decline of the medical faculty and should have important consequences." It should not be forgotten that even ten years after Wagner-Jauregg's death his memoirs could not be published unabridged (Wagner-Jauregg 1950, p. 74) because his "sharpness and objectivity" [*Schärfe und Objektivität*] might have hurt some people.

does not even become [professor] extraordinarius carries the dagger in his heart until he dies"[3] (emphasis added).

The way in which Prof. Ellenberger handles the Gicklhorn material, as well as the way in which he deals with the delay in Freud's academic career, is proof that he is biased against Freud. I want to repeat that I am not referring here to a matter of interpretation, but to a matter of fact. The historian who wants to be trusted has to present the facts that are available, while still having every "right" to err in his interpretations—something against which no one of us is sufficiently protected.[4] In view of the bias that is manifest in relation to this one episode, however, one does have reason to be distrustful of quite a few of the other conclusions and interpretations.

---

[3] *Ein Privatdozent, der nicht einmal Extraordinarius wird, trägt bis zu seinem Tode den Dolch im Herzen.*

[4] Prof. Ellenberger also discusses a rather complicated subject, which Renée Gicklhorn (1958) had handled incompetently. As the result of a paramnesia, Hanns Sachs (1944, p. 78) had reproduced wrongly a story that Freud had told him—namely, that he received the title of professor, only after a patient of his donated a famous painting by Böcklin (1827–1901) to a museum in which the Minister was interested. Jones (1, p. 340), repeating Sachs's mistake with regard to the painting in question, correctly recalled that the owner of the Böcklin was the patient's aunt. I called Mrs. Gicklhorn's attention to Freud's letter to Fliess (1950a, pp. 342–344), from which it is evident that Sachs had made a mistake and that no Böcklin was donated. I proved that the patient, as Freud had described it to Fliess, had donated a less valuable picture, probably after she had failed to persuade her aunt to donate a Böcklin. Beckh-Widmanstetter found the patient's letter of donation written to the Minister, in which she expresses her thanks without spelling out for what; that is indeed a strange thing for a donor to do. The letter of donation was never published. Ellenberger writes, as Mrs. Gicklhorn did, of the improbability of "bribery," in view of the small value of the painting that was actually donated. I spelled out twice (1958, 1966) why no one who was familiar with the customs of the times could ever call the affair "bribery." Even nowadays it would not be called that. Then, as now, it was an acceptable step in the game of seeking favors. It is plain that Freud would have had to wait much longer for his title, if the patient had not intervened. From a letter of Freud at the end of 1901, (1960, p. 243), we know that Exner was pessimistic about the possibility of Freud being appointed even after a year's time; yet Freud received the appointment two months later, and the patient "beaming" showed Freud the Minister's special delivery letter (Freud 1950a, p. 344) in which he carried out his promise that she would be the first one to learn of Freud's appointment. Neither Mrs. Gicklhorn nor Prof. Ellenberger has explained why the Minister found it necessary to inform the patient. The whole matter does not deserve even the printer's ink that has been spilled over it, but in my opinion the way in which Ellenberger presents it indicates an absence of unbiased reporting.

Prof. Ellenberger would probably agree, for example, with Roazen's appraisal of Freud's isolation. He believes that such isolation did not actually exist (pp. 450, 455), being only a subjective phenomenon during the time of Freud's illness (which he calls a creative one). Some of the proofs he presents are noteworthy: Freud had a large number of acquaintances; the household had three servants; Freud was not ostracized, because he did hold memberships in several associations, etc. If such external signs were really able to decide the question of isolation, then Freud would surely never have written about his years of isolation. But he could not have foreseen that some future historian would take the number of his household employees as a yardstick of his isolation!

It is worthwhile examining more closely the initial situation in which this isolation occurred, because it offers a suitable example for demonstrating Ellenberger's inadequacies of presentation and his bias in the interpretation of historical data. Let us therefore examine what Prof. Ellenberger has to say about Freud's relationship to Theodor Meynert (1833–1891), who had been Freud's teacher and was greatly admired by him before a break came about between them. A difference of opinion already exists regarding the meeting of the Viennese Medical Society in which Freud reported on the new things he had observed and learned at Charcot's clinic in 1886. The events of that meeting had a significant effect on Freud (1925b)—which is one reason why a reliable reconstruction of them is not without its importance.

Ellenberger (p. 439) used as "the best way to reconstruct what happened at the meeting" the reports—a kind of Minutes —that were subsequently published in a variety of medical journals. Of course, these reports have to be studied carefully; but it is, in my opinion, a methodological error to take such reports at their face value, since more often than not it happens that salient points of the speaker's presentation somehow manage to get lost in them. Moreover, the writer of a report may wish to spare the sensitivities of speaker and discussants. It is therefore necessary critically to evaluate the seemingly objective summaries that were published customarily.

Ellenberger draws the conclusion from them that Freud's presentation was critically received, among other reasons, because

(p. 441) he "had not conformed with the Society's tradition that the speaker bring something new and original." But is that correct? Ellenberger writes as if what Freud had brought as a novelty from Paris was the discovery that male hysteria existed. Indeed, the discussants also took that stand. Yet even according to Ellenberger (p. 439), what Freud had reported was that "male hysteria was more frequent than was generally assumed"—something quite different from announcing as a novelty the *existence* of male hysteria.

The text of Freud's presentation is not known. Ellenberger suggests that it was probably similar to the report on his trip to Paris that Freud wrote for the University (it was published posthumously in 1956). There, too, Freud does not write at all as if it was the existence of male hysteria that had been discovered in Paris, but rather stresses "the unsuspected frequency of cases of male hysteria" (Freud 1956, p. 11). That was, as I shall presently show, an important discovery, if Meynert's opinion about hysteria may be taken as representative.

Meynert (1889, p. 2) turned against the idea of male hysteria in "the sex without 'Hysteron' [Greek for womb]" and he suggested instead that one speak of "anatomical and functional paralysis of one side." Was this a purely semantic argument? In his *Clinical Lectures on Psychiatry* (1890, p. 177) he speaks of "female hysteria"; when, later on (pp. 186, 187), he speaks of hysterical patients, it is always in the female gender. However, it is plain that he was aware of hysteria among males, for he speaks (p. 186) of hysteria occurring among women *more frequently than* among men (see also p. 197).

How did Meynert explain this unequal distribution of hysteria among the sexes? According to him, hysteria is due to a functional hyperemia of the cortex, brought about by a decrease of arterial innervation. Meynert considered the blood of the females to be "more abundant in water [*wasserreicher*], poorer in solid parts," and brought this factor into connection with the differing excitability of different cortical centers. One can see from this alone that the observation of an equal or approximately equal frequency of hysteria among males and females would have relevant consequences.[5]

---

[5] It is not clear whether Freud suggested that hysteria occurred with equal

I shall not go further into discussion of details regarding hysteria, about which Ellenberger asserts—in my opinion, incorrectly—that they were well known in Vienna.

Furthermore, Ellenberger's imputation that Freud in his lecture showed a failure to recognize "the complexity and the practical implication" of the controversy that was dividing neurologists over the question of traumatic neuroses is not confirmed by Freud's report to the University. From this, it seems rather clear that Freud was well aware of these things, and that he had become convinced, by Charcot's clinical demonstrations, of the correctness of the part Charcot took in this controversy.

I am reasonably sure, however, that all this was of secondary importance. Freud must have made some remarks about hypnotism, since he also wrote about it in his report. As a matter of fact, in the 1886 meeting, the top representatives of the Viennese Medical School for the first time met the new spirit that had begun to spread from Charcot's Salpêtrière and that would take its triumphant course, in one form or another, yet would almost always be rejected by those who were carrying on in the tradition of the natural sciences. That tradition, which had had its inception in the nineteenth century, had brought about the stupendous rise of medicine by concentrating on physics, chemistry and the microscope—and totally disregarding the mind.

Prof. Ellenberger will, of course, take exception to such a view. He points expressly to the good relations that existed between Vienna and the Salpêtrière, and cites as an example Moritz Benedikt (1835–1920; by the way, also an outsider and in opposition to official medicine; see Lesky 1965, p. 390), who had introduced Freud to Charcot. He himself was a well-known psychiatrist in Vienna, and visited Charcot every summer (Ellenberger 1970, p. 440). But Ellenberger rightly observes that Central European psychiatry had become anxious about the trend of Charcot's more recent research (Ellenberger, *ibid.*). Yet it was exactly *that* research that Freud heralded at the meeting in question, and about which he must have felt that it stood at the watershed of a new period.

I cannot therefore quite agree with Jones who, anticipating

---

frequency among males and females. In his later work, Freud assumed that hysteria occurred more frequently among females.

Ellenberger by seventeen years (1, p. 230), thought that, on that occasion, Freud was oversensitive and naive. Looking back, one must say that Freud was quite right in feeling that he would not receive encouragement and stimulation from the medical hierarchy in Vienna, and that it might have been better for him to withdraw. What Prof. Ellenberger sees in all this is Freud's neurosis. Yet, before drawing such a conclusion, he should first have considered a passage in Wagner-Jauregg's *Lebenserinnerungen* (p. 72). After all, Wagner-Jauregg was a witness of those events, and he made specific reference to Freud's lecture, in which Freud "spoke of nothing but Charcot and praised him in superlatives. This, however, the Viennese bigwigs could not tolerate well. Bamberger[6] and Meynert had rejected Freud harshly and with this he had fallen into disgrace, so to speak, with the faculty. He was thus a practitioner in neurology without patients."[7] Although Wagner-Jauregg makes plenty of mistakes in his *Memories*, I do not see any basic reason for disregarding this passage.

It is instructive to follow the details of the relationship between Meynert and Freud. In a footnote in the preface to his translation of a book by Bernheim (Freud 1888b, p. 81n.), Freud criticized Meynert for "a general confusion" regarding the relations between hysteria and hypnotism. This referred to a lecture Meynert had given in 1888 in which he discussed problems of hypnosis, merely on the basis of clinical observations he had made in a patient who suffered from hysteria (see Meynert 1888, p. 453). Meynert's reaction to that footnote was most peculiar. It led to a shattering personal attack on Freud. After reporting that, in his own text, he was using a translation of Charcot, Meynert then went on to say that the translation had been made by Freud, "who, after having been honored by a University traveling stipend, is now active here as a trained practitioner in hypnosis" (Meynert 1889, p. 16).

It was most tactless of Meynert—and quite immaterial to the

---

[6] Heinrich von Bamberger (1822–1888) was a leading internist and chaired the meeting at which Freud spoke.

[7] . . . *in dem er nur von Charcot sprach und ihn in den höchsten Tönen pries. Das vertrugen aber die Wiener Grössen schlecht. Bamberger und Meynert wiesen Freud in der Diskussion scharf zurück, und damit war er quasi bei der Fakultät in Ungnade gefallen. Er war also ein neurologischer Pratiker ohne Krankenmaterial.*

issue at hand—to bring in the support that Freud had received from the University, as if the recipient had therewith incurred an obligation with respect to his future scientific opinions, or as if it were necessary to remind Freud that he had become acquainted with Charcot only through Meynert's indirect generosity toward him, in having voted in favor of his being the recipient of the grant. Furthermore, Meynert's designation of Freud as "trained practitioner in hypnosis," which sounds innocent to the contemporary ear, covered a devastating attack, for in a previous lecture Meynert had said of hypnosis that it was "the favorite specialty of unmedical charlatans [Lieblingsfach unärztlicher Charlatane]," that a shepherd would be able to practice this art just as well as a physician (Meynert 1888, p. 451). As if this were not enough to discredit Freud in the eyes of his colleagues, he then added, at the end of the footnote: "I find his [Freud's] intercession on behalf of suggestion therapy so remarkable for this reason—because he left Vienna as a physician exactly trained in physiology." [8]

Here Meynert openly declared that Freud was no longer a physician. Both statements were cruel thrusts, and posed a real threat to the beginning practice of the young physician, as well as probably causing irreparable damage to Freud's professional standing for many years thereafter. Is Prof. Ellenberger really so naive as to be completely unaware what it meant for Freud that Meynert singled out his name, among the few who were using hypnosis at that time in Vienna? But worse still was to come.

Toward the end of the paper, Meynert declared hypnotism to be a plague endangering the national health. His paper thereupon took a moralizing turn, and he did not hesitate to imply that hypnotism was the product of "a base character" [niedrige Denkungsart] (Meynert 1889, p. 29). It also took a nationalistic turn, when he wrote (p. 29): "We may predict, not without self-assurance, that in Germany this plague will come to an end before it does so anywhere else—and soon." This nationalistic flavor was carried even further: the whole people participates in Germany in the achievement of hygiene; the present generation as well as coming generations must be strengthened physically and psychi-

---

[8] Ich finde sein Eintreten für die Suggestionstherapie darum bemerkenswert, weil er als ein physiologisch exakt geschulter Arzt Wien verliess.

cally, for which he recommends gymnastics, swimming and other branches of sport. He contrasts with this attitude "the base and pernicious standpoint" that is revealed when a physician propagates conditions in which a person "loses his psychic equilibrium." The ending of the article was altogether devastating: a dog that is trained to deepest servility is an example of a freely rising mind [frei aufstrebender Geist], as compared with a hypnotized person.

This diatribe against hypnotism may have been precipitated by Forel's (1889) recent book, in which a psychiatrist of high prestige took a strong stand in favor of hypnosis; but it cannot have escaped Meynert's attention, nor can it be ascribed to accident, that he mentioned only Freud, and in a rather unusual and therefore conspicuous way to boot. That must have placed the danger to national health and the undermining of the nervous power of future generations right at Freud's doorstep, at least in the eyes of his Viennese colleagues. Why did not Meynert name others who were known to be practicing hypnotism, such as Krafft-Ebing (1840–1902), Moritz Benedikt and Heinrich Obersteiner (1847–1922)?

I also want to bring to the reader's attention a remark by Wagner-Jauregg (1950, p. 71): "With Meynert, the guilt was usually on Meynert's side." I cannot therefore see any sign of a particular neurosis, as Prof. Ellenberger does (p. 448), in the fact that, following Meynert's massive attack, Freud wrote to his friend Fliess (Freud 1950a, p. 58f.): "Because the attitude of all my friends demanded it, I had to be moderate in my criticism of Meynert, who in his usual impudent-malicious manner had delivered himself authoritatively on a subject of which he knew nothing."

Freud was undoubtedly correct here. When one reads now about Meynert's putting into his discussion with Charcot all his trust in the arteria chorioidea, or about his connecting agoraphobia with hyperaesthesia of the retina (Meynert 1890, p. 180), one can safely say that Meynert, although he was a great scholar, did not understand the particular subject of neuroses, on which he was behind his times. About the impudence and maliciousness of Meynert's massive attack against Freud, no word need be spared. As far as the restraining influence of Freud's friends is concerned, it may be said: "When a person is hurt, his friends are often quite reasonable until they themselves are hurt." But, in this instance, Freud's friends were probably worried about the inequality of the opposing forces. A young physician who is just starting out in practice must necessarily be crushed in a fight with the highest authority in his specialty—a man who was his former teacher, to boot. They feared lest Freud's reputation might be further hurt, if he were to take up the gauntlet. I must dispute Prof. Ellenberger (p. 448), when he uses this passage in Freud's letter to say: "A frequent feature in neurosis is the abundance of pejorative judgments." Pejorative judgments are frequently found in biased historians as well, but that is no reason to regard them as being neurotic.

Freud (1889) answered Meynert in his review of Forel's (1889) book on *Hypnotism*. The review consists of two parts, which were published separately in the *Wiener med. Wochenschrift*. The first part, the translation of which covers five printed pages in the *Standard Edition*, is devoted mainly to a criticism of Meynert's arguments against hypnosis, with special references to his personal remarks about Freud. Space forbids my quoting Freud's references to Meynert at length, and I must ask the interested reader to peruse those pages, in order to judge whether or not Prof. Ellenberger is right in speaking of Freud's "vehement attack on Meynert, whom he accused of being prejudiced" (p. 442). This should be compared with what Ellenberger has to say about Meynert's (1888) crushing assault on Freud: Meynert "added in a footnote that Freud's opinions were more dogmatic than scientific and contradicted Charcot's teaching" (Ellenberger 1970, p. 444).

Ellenberger, who disputes Freud's isolation, contradicts himself when he writes about the Meynert-Freud controversy: "Such episodes illustrate the atmosphere of isolation and distrust in which Freud began his career" (p. 442).

Here Ellenberger admits Freud's initial position of isolation in Vienna, although he lived in fashionable quarters and did have personal friends. Yet on the grounds of the very same features, as the reader may recall, Ellenberger called it a legend that Freud was living in isolation after 1895. The difference seems to me to be that Prof. Ellenberger believes he can impute to Freud his having caused the former—something he apparently would not succeed in doing with regard to the latter.

Is it really probable that a little-known scholar and physician, who had been so cruelly attacked by high authority, so openly discredited as Freud had been by Meynert, and for these reasons had found himself isolated, would already have overcome *this* status when, a few years later, he discovered facts and published theories that offended tradition to a far greater degree than had his initial undertakings? When one compares Ellenberger's presentations of Meynert's and Freud's behavior, one can only state that apparently any record that speaks in favor of Freud is assigned to legend, whereas anything that may lower his standing is accepted as historical truth.

The following might also be considered. Freud reports (1925b, p. 16) that he was excluded from use of the University's laboratory of cerebral anatomy, whose director Meynert was. We further know that he had trouble getting a lecture room assigned at the university; that students attended his lectures in a small number, if at all; that his practice was not lucrative, although the Gicklhorns and Ellenberger believe it to have been.

From the Fliess letters, we know that there were only brief promising periods of economic security. Most of the time he had a frighteningly small number of patients; finally not even non-paying patients came to consult him. We further know that one of the most powerful professors at the College (Nothnagel), of his own accord (and not after an appeal by Freud), promised to submit his name for a professorship, but was not certain whether despite his great influence he would get the majority to vote for Freud and that he was highly skeptical about the willingness of the Minister of Education to confirm Freud's professorship (see Freud 1950a, p. 191). Furthermore, for four years nothing happened in that regard, despite Freud's scientific output, and ultimately the responsible Minister even denied ever having received such an application. Why a scholar, working under such conditions, should not feel isolated, it is difficult to understand.

One must also take account of the fact that the general atmosphere in Vienna was anti-Semitic at that time.[9] Ellenberger underplays the intensity and extent of anti-Semitism. The evidence he offers is not convincing. He tries to prove his point by

---

[9] There seems to have been, however, no specific bearing of anti-Semitism on the delay in Freud's appointment as professor, as has been assumed by most of Freud's biographers.

indicating that neither reference to nor complaint about anti-Semitism is to be found in the writings of some contemporary prominent Austrian Jews. The absence of complaint, however, should not be taken as a convincing proof of the situation prevailing at that time. Anyone who has read Arthur Schnitzler's novel *Der Weg ins Freie* and his play *Professor Bernhardi* gets a distinct picture of the forms assumed by anti-Semitism in Austria around the turn of the century. But even such reading will not familiarize the reader with anti-Semitism's more vulgar forms, a few examples of which I shall give presently. Although no actual cruelties were yet being committed, the groundwork for the later excesses was being laid in Vienna during just that period. In 1898, one parliamentary representative proposed a *Schussgeld* for Jews —a term used for the premium paid for the shooting of game that causes damages. Another predicted that the Jews would be ground up into artificial fertilizer (Karbach 1964, p. 111). I am certain that this was mainly political propaganda at that time, and no one seriously contemplated the extermination of Central European Jewry. But it surprises me that an existentialist, in view of the fact that the political slogan of that day did become historical reality four decades later, would dare to speak of Freud's "extreme sensitivity to any (true or supposed) form of anti-Semitism" (Ellenberger 1970, p. 427). If anything, later events proved that Jewish "sensitivity" around 1900 was only too prophetic and might well have been even sharper. If the general atmosphere of rabid anti-Semitism, the way he was treated by the University hierarchy, the distrust of his colleagues (even manifested by the fact that scarcely anyone sent him patients) are considered, we can understand that Freud rightly felt isolated.

Ellenberger disputes the correctness of two accounts from Freud's pen that have been accepted as facts by psychoanalysts and by almost all of Freud's biographers.

The first one has to do with Freud's comment that his *Interpretation of Dreams* (1900) was ignored; he wrote (1925b, p. 48): "My *Interpretation of Dreams*, published in 1900, was scarcely reviewed in the technical journals." Ellenberger (pp. 452, 454, 783, 786) relies on the 1962 study by Bry and Rifkin, who reported that the book "was initially reviewed in at least eleven general magazines and subject journals." However, only seven of these were technical journals. Whether "scarcely" is commensurate with seven is difficult to decide. Freud may have thought of medical journals—which would reduce the number considerably. Furthermore, it is not known how many of the eleven reviews came to Freud's attention. Many references to Freud's book in newspapers were known to him, since some reviews are individually mentioned in his correspondence with Fliess, and he noted that a patient's father "has taken zealously to sending me every cutting and article in which there is a reference to me or the dream book" (Freud 1950a, p. 33).

Yet, it seems to me, the decisive fact is that the book was a publishing flop. In May 1900—that is to say, seven months after its publication—Freud wrote to Fliess: "The bookseller complains that the *Interpretation of Dreams* is going slowly" (Freud 1930a, p. 320). Although only six hundred copies (Jones 1, p. 360) had been printed, it took nine years to sell them. It was only thirteen years after its publication that it was first translated into a foreign language. When a book takes that long to arouse serious interest abroad, and only about sixty to seventy copies of the original sell annually for almost a decade, I still think that the impression now prevalent among analysts is justified. If one knows, further, that for the next four decades Freud's dream psychology was not taught in any department of the University, then one is entitled to say that—at least in Vienna, although I think it was hardly different at the vast majority of European universities—Freud's *Interpretation of Dreams* was ignored.

The other question whose factuality is disputed by Ellenberger has to do with the indignation and hostility with which Freud's sexual theory was greeted. Here the way the author goes about his "proof" is worth the attention of anyone who is interested in historical methodology. First he amasses all those items that do not fit into a society dominated throughout by Victorianism—for example, the writings of Arthur Schnitzler, the "leagues of free love" that flourished all over Tsarist Russia (p. 502), and the laxity of sexual mores in Vienna and Paris. The resultant impression is that Freud *could not have* offended the spirit of his times—first, because what he said was not truly original; and second, because around 1900 the European scene was satiated with scientific investigations of the sexual drive in all its forms, to such an extent that "the dividing line between scientific vul-garization and pornography was difficult to determine from the very beginning" (p. 299).

A host of interesting general problems, which cannot be satis-factorily discussed here, is linked with this view. It is the re-peated failure to discriminate sufficiently between the "orderer" of a science and his predecessors that also blurs the differences in society's reaction to the predecessors and the "orderer." One has only to mention the storm of indignation that met the publica-tion of Darwin's findings, even though he had many predecessors and was giving expression to the *Zeitgeist*. Galileo escaped tor-ture by the skin of his teeth and at the price of a revocation, despite the fact that everything he said had already been said by others.

Victorianism was still in full swing in 1905, when Freud's *Three Contributions* was published. The sociological phenomena that Ellenberger cities revealed to the discerning mind the signs of the impending breakdown of Victorianism. One could not suppress them to the extent to which those in power would have wished to do. In part, it was the tenets of Victorianism itself that prevented the instituting of Draconian measures such as Galileo had still had to fear, about two-and-a-half centuries earlier. But infringements upon the spirit of Victorianism were still being rejected and persecuted, when possible, by those who held power, and those who held power were the official representatives of Victorianism. Jones put together a list of how psychoanalysis was treated by the official representatives of psychiatry, and the record of these episodes can be checked.

One can learn, for example, about a personal experience that must necessarily have struck Freud as quite discouraging (al-though it will impress the contemporary reader as humorous rather than as tragic), through reading a letter he wrote to Fliess in 1901. He was invited to give a lecture in the Philosophical Society. In anticipation of an indignant reaction, it was arranged that he would give the lecture first to two representatives of the society. "They said that it was wonderful." A few hours before the appointed time, however, Freud received a special delivery letter, "saying that some members had objected, after all, and asking me to be kind enough to start by illustrating my theory with inoffensive examples, and then announce that I was coming to objectionable matter and make a pause, during which the ladies could leave the hall. . . . Such is the scientific life in Vienna" (Freud 1950a, p. 329). Of course, Freud refused to lecture under those conditions.[10]

By way of two examples I shall try to show that Ellenberger is lacking in historical acumen when he takes to interpreting the meaning of scientific texts.

Krafft-Ebing's famous book *Psychopathia Sexualis*, which was published in 1886 for the first time, is repeatedly mentioned by him as proof against the probability that Freud's sexual theories could have aroused indignation in Freud's contemporaries (although he does record that Krafft-Ebing's book would probably have cost him his honorary membership in the British Medico-Psychological Association, if Moritz Benedikt had not intervened in his defense [Ellenberger 1970, p. 299]). Furthermore, Ellenberger does not draw the proper conclusion from the fact that Krafft-Ebing had made extensive use in his text of the Latin language, in order to avoid reactions of indignation in the reader that he would have evoked otherwise; this fact alone, after all, is sufficient to demonstrate how careful an author had to be who did not want to endanger his good standing, just because Victorianism still exercised great power. Also, I think Ellenberger might have come closer to historical truth, if he had availed himself of the opinion of van den Haag who wrote an introduction to the translation of Krafft-Ebing's book. In it one finds the following statement: ". . . the relationship of his [Krafft-Ebing's] theories to psychoanalysis resembles that of the atomic theory of Democritus to nuclear physics" (van den Haag 1965, p. 18).

The other example I want to discuss briefly has to do with Emil Raimann's book on hysteria in 1904, which Ellenberger cites for the purpose of proving that Freud's theories were ac-

---

[10] It is appropriate to record that the violent reaction against psychoanalysis did not abate for a long time. Allers, who was a member of the University faculty (he became, after 1938, a leading representative of scholasticism in this country), requested, after the parliamentary system was abolished in Austria in 1934 and the Catholic Party came into full power, that suppressive measures be taken against such institutions as the child guidance clinics that were connected with psychoanalysis. He insisted that such institutions were not merely to be supervised, but had to "disappear" (Allers 1934, p. 17).

cepted in Vienna. While he cites the positive comment that Raimann (1872–1949) made in his text about Freud,[11] he fails to mention the fact that the motive for writing the book was to disprove Freud's theories. In his introduction, Raimann (p. 14) wrote: "From Vienna a theory went out into the world which proclaims the exclusively sexual origin of hysteria. . . . Universally [allseitig] (this theory) was more or less emphatically disapproved. Therefore it seemed appropriate to (make a) check-up at the same place in similar patients and to take a stand with regard to this theory."

It is instructive to compare Ellenberger's statement about Raimann's book with a contemporary review of it. Heinrich Obersteiner, a prominent representative in this field in Vienna, wrote in his review of Raimann's book that "severe opposition is taken to Freud's theories" [wird scharfe Stellung genommen] and that (according to Raimann) Freud's treatment is to be "avoided" (Obersteiner 1904). Is it really probable that a man like Obersteiner who knew both Freud and Raimann would have misunderstood Raimann so profoundly? Ellenberger finds it difficult to understand why Jones speaks on that occasion of Raimann's vitriolic attack against Freud. I was unable to find that remark in Jones's biography, but no doubt Raimann became later well known in Vienna for his indisputably "vitriolic" attacks against Freud, which he published twenty years later. Whether or not the epithet could be justly applied to Raimann's 1904 text, in which, after some general laudatory remarks, he totally rejects all of Freud's clinical findings, and all his theories, and at one point even asserts that what the patients told Freud was brought about by his method of interrogation and/or by suggestion— that the reader must decide for himself.

Even years later, Freud and psychoanalysis were still being ridiculed by Freud's colleagues at the University. Wagner-Jauregg (1950, p. 73) himself reports that Raimann gave—it must have been during the First World War—an official lecture on psychoanalysis, which consisted of "a collection of every form of spite

---

[11] Ellenberger (p. 784) quotes a very positive statement that Raimann allegedly made in his book about Freud's dream theory. I went through the book, but could not find it. I owe thanks to Mrs. Ruth Schorsch for also having gone through the book, but she was not able to locate the passage either.

and derision [one could think of]," [*Sammlung aller Bosheiten und allen Hohnes*]—not the sort of criticism that Freud was accustomed to listen to patiently.[12] Was there any other instance of a member of the Medical Faculty spiting and ridiculing, in an international course for the education of physicians, the work of a member of that same Faculty? We can well imagine, then, how Freud fared at the beginning of the century.

Ellenberger would very likely object to my summarizing the impression that his book may leave, on a reader who has had to rely solely on him, in the following way: "There were four men whose names loomed prominently in the history of modern psychiatry: Janet, Freud, Adler and Jung. Three of them were highly original and creative. Freud, who became the most famous, copied only what others, in particular Janet, had said before him." He would probably, in order to disprove my allegation, cite the passage (p. 547) in which he reports on "Freud's uncontestable innovation" (p. 549). But when he goes on to say that "Freud's most striking novelty was probably the founding of a 'school' according to a pattern that has no parallel in modern times, but is a revival of the old philosophical schools of Greco-Roman antiquity,"—then, by calling this historical fact "the most striking novelty," he has of course undone what he said in the preceding paragraph. Any reader, however, who goes through Waelder's paper of 1956 (which Ellenberger unfortunately has not taken into consideration) may gain a different view of even this allegedly "most striking novelty."

Ellenberger (1970, p. 445f.) ascribes to Freud a "creative illness" during the years of his friendship with Wilhelm Fliess; but when the result of this creative illness turns out to be nothing more than what Janet had earlier discovered, he has again undone the very term he has just applied. He has bitter words to say about the thefts committed upon Janet's work, which he compares with Pompeii: a buried city, he says, "may remain concealed while being plundered by marauders" (p. 409). It seems that this brutal attack was directed mainly against Freud. The Janet-Freud controversy has by this time become tedious. The

---

[12] It is significant that Wagner-Jauregg reproaches Freud on just that occasion with having been "one of the most intolerant men," who "punished every deviating opinion . . . with exclusion from the Society."

priority of publication has never been disputed by Freud. But Breuer's treatment of Anna O. had been completed four or five years prior to Janet's first publication on hysteria (cf. Ellenberger 1970, p. 413, n. 84). From Freud's letters (1960, p. 41) it is known that Breuer had already spoken with Freud about Anna O. in July, 1883. For that reason, it would be more correct to say that, if one measures by the actual historical sequences, not by years of publication, Freud owed little to Janet and very much to Breuer.

Freud had neither met nor heard anything about Janet during his stay in Paris; and he himself had already conducted a cathartic treatment before Janet's book *L'automatisme psychologique* was published in 1889. He therefore had every right to expect Janet to acknowledge publicly the fact that any influence on him by Janet could have started only in 1889. This, as shown earlier, was denied by the French press, which maintained that Freud had plagiarized Janet after leaving Paris in early 1886. Janet never corrected this false notion—which was why Freud refused to receive him when he visited Vienna in 1936.[13]

Janet's work is extensive, and I am not sufficiently familiar with it to say anything of importance about the subject in question. Perhaps Professor Ellenberger is correct in asserting that the early theories of Janet and Freud are similar in some major respects. However, since Janet asserted in 1889 that the phenomenon of falling in love was "a kind of illness that would not occur in a perfectly healthy or balanced person" (Ellenberger 1970, p. 401), and in 1929 that "love is nothing but a hypothesis transformed into a fixed idea" (Ellenberger 1970, p. 350, p. 412 n. 56)—these alone should prove that there cannot be any basic similarity between Janet's and Freud's work. While their starting points may have been similar, the end-products were far apart, as becomes evident after reading Prof. Ellenberger's chap-

---

[13] Ellenberger (1970, p. 557, n. 192) maintains that Freud did this because he believed "(quite incorrectly) that Janet had insulted him in 1913." Since Janet's lecture of 1913 was understood as saying that what was correct in psychoanalysis had been discovered by Janet, while all the rest was an aggregate of errors, I believe that would have been reason enough to feel insulted; but it is clear from a letter of Freud's to Marie Bonaparte (Jones 3, p. 215) that the immediate reason for Freud's unwillingness to see Janet was the latter's refusal to free Freud publicly from the charge of plagiarism.

ter "The Great Synthesis" (Ellenberger 1970, pp. 384–394), in which he presents the end-product of Janet's research.

Ellenberger also regards Adler's mind as having been far more creative and original than Freud's. He raises what he describes as a "perplexing question" with regard to Adler—namely, "the discrepancy between greatness of achievement, with massive rejection of person and work, and wide-scale quiet plagiarism [of Adler's works, by others]" (p. 645f.). He finds an answer to his question in a theory that contends that "genius is a microsociological phenomenon and a voluntary construction" (p. 646). "No isolated man," Ellenberger continues, "could acquire the distinction of being called a genius"—as if any person could be called anything, unless there was at least one other person to call him that. What makes a genius, according to this theory, is the group that surrounds him, "followers who not only proclaim his teachings, but create a reputation." [14] And that was the case, says Ellenberger, with Freud: his "followers propagated for him the positive image of the archetypal genius."

This explanation of Ellenberger's strikes me as being inadequate. Did Adler's pupils and collaborators lag in their efforts to idealize the founder of the school whose members they were? Adler himself was quite ready to take care of the image that posterity would obtain of him; but alas, he did not find a James Boswell, but instead only a Phyllis Bottome, when he wished that she should "write the story of his life, in conjunction with himself" (Bottome 1939, p. vii). Her book, apparently, did not leave the reader with an all too impressive image of Adler. Is it likely that Freud would ever have cooperated with anyone who was willing to write his biography, not to speak of wishing that it should be done at all? On the contrary, Freud demanded of Marie Bonaparte that she should destroy his letters to Fliess.

And in what way did Freud's pupils create an image of him in the popular imagination? Their eulogies remained primarily limited to publications in technical journals, which were read mainly by psychoanalysts, and they did not need to be told that Freud was a genius. Hanns Sachs's (1945) book of memories of Freud was not well received by the public; it was severely criti-

---

[14] I believe it was Lange-Eichbaum (1927) who was the first to suggest such a theory.

cized, even ridiculed, by outsiders. What Ellenberger probably regards as a damage had already been done, and Freud was already being looked at as the "archetypical genius," when Jones published his biography. Was it not Thomas Mann's (1936) paper, on the occasion of Freud's eightieth birthday, and Stefan Zweig's chapter on Freud in his book (1931), along with such terse statements as that by McDougall (1936): "He [Freud] has contributed more to our knowledge of human nature than anyone since Aristotle"—was it not these that had caused so many to become the victims of the "misconception" that Freud was a genius? I still think it was Freud's extraordinary achievements, rather than the propaganda of his followers, that were responsible for his fame.

But I cannot forgo referring to Ellenberger's further derailment. He cites Jean François Champollion (1790–1832), who deciphered the Egyptian hieroglyphics, and Georg Friedrich Grotefend (1775–1853), who deciphered the ancient Persian cuneiform scripts. The former is heralded as a genius and the latter almost forgotten today (Ellenberger 1970, p. 270), even though the achievements of the two men were equally great. All that may be correct; nevertheless Grotefend *is* a genius if Champollion was one, and anyone who is familiar with the lives and works of both will attribute to each of them equal greatness.[15] On the other hand, Alfred Adler's works have been read by possibly even more people than have Freud's. Consequently, the comparison with Grotefend, whose achievement is known only to a small group of experts, is altogether out of place.

Yet, according to Ellenberger, it is not only a sort of Madison Avenue technique that decides whether or not a man is to acquire the glory of genius. "Victimology, that newly founded brand of criminology that analyzes the personality of potential victims of

---

[15] Gordon (1968) does not hesitate to regard Grotefend's decipherment of the old Persian as an achievement superior to Champollion's. Thus he writes (p. 52): "Grotefend's task was more difficult than the decipherment of Egyptian, where an intelligible Greek translation provided the key. The decipherment of Old Persian was the work of a genius who sifted out the few essential texts and facts to solve with directness and economy of material and time a problem that seemed incapable of solution." This quotation alone is sufficient to disprove Ellenberger's theory of genius, for apparently whoever knows the facts and the literature in the field has no hesitation in according Grotefend the title of genius.

crimes" has proven that the personality of the victim is one of the causes of his becoming a victim, and this is also true of persons who are "persistently victims of bad luck or failure" (Ellenberger 1970, p. 646f.). Such people—and Adler was one of them —suffer from the so-called Abel syndrome. Having Adler in mind, Prof. Ellenberger continues (p. 647): "This is the case of the man whose superiority in a certain field is likely to attract envy, but who is not able or willing to defend himself." It looks as if Ellenberger himself belongs to the group who are victims of failure, because inadvertently he immediately goes on from there to disprove his entire thesis, by citing Jean-Jacques Rousseau as a classical example of the man who causes himself to be constantly followed by bad luck, to be defeated and persecuted. If Ellenberger had only not cited Jean-Jacques Rousseau as an illustration of victimology! Jean-Jacques Rousseau had not one single disciple to build up his fame, or to invent and spread legends about him; and he himself did everything in his power to blacken his name, by putting into print the sexual excitements he enjoyed when he was beaten by his governess, the homosexual seduction, the masturbation—and, if all that should not be enough, he let the world know that he deposited every one of his newborn children on the steps of a foundling home. Poor Rousseau! According to Ellenberger, he could never have acquired the fame of genius.

If Ellenberger wants to know why Adler is not usually regarded as a genius, he has only to read his own text. In it, he epitomizes individual psychology in the following sentence (p. 608): "This kind of pragmatic psychology . . . does not pretend to go into matters very deeply, but to provide principles and methods that enable one to acquire a practical knowledge of oneself and of others." [16] Even the ideal fulfillment of such a program could never provide the distinction of genius. Up to

---

[16] If only Adler had let Freud know from the start that what he was interested in was a "pragmatic psychology" of "practical knowledge"! I can hardly think of anything that is less "practical"—if I read Prof. Ellenberger correctly—than psychoanalysis. If Ellenberger is right, then Adler really did not have any legitimate place as a member of the Society of which he was President. After all, if someone's goal is to write a cookbook, he will remain forever an outsider in the company of chemists, even though the content of a cookbook does have to do throughout with chemical processes.

now, geniuses have *always striven* to go into matters rather deeply. I am afraid that not even Madison Avenue will be able to change that, even though I do not doubt that investment in some advertising agency could acquire for Adler the prestige of genius (the investment, to be sure, would have to be repeated annually).

Ellenberger tries to prove his point of view by presenting a comparative chart (p. 647) of Freud's and Adler's personalities. In it one finds a comparison of Freud's handsomeness and his imposing appearance (assisted by a well-groomed beard) with Adler's "not particularly handsome, unassuming" appearance. Wrongly, Ellenberger also claims that Freud "lived in the best residential quarter." Freud's "art collection" and of course the three servants are compared with Adler's residence "in a more bourgeois residential area," etc.[17] The temptation to reproduce the entire chart and to exercise my wit on it is strong, but I will single out just one of its items. Freud, as "a master of German prose and a superior writer, who knew how to use striking images" is compared with Adler, whose "works [were] written in ordinary style and poorly organized, with no striking images."

I must conclude from this that Ellenberger believes Adler's "ordinary style" was part of his Abel-syndrome. Bottome (1939, p. 60) reports that Adler countered a complaint about his lack of style by saying: "If the truth is there, bad writing won't hurt it." My contention is that Freud's style is a manifestation of genius, and that Adler, with or without an Abel-syndrome, had no chance whatsoever of developing a mastery of language comparable to that of Freud.[18]

I must forgo further discussion of Ellenberger's challenging errors: his belief that Individual Psychology is a child of enlightenment and Stoicism, while psychoanalysis is the child of romanticism and Epicureanism; his insufficient and one-sided description of Jung's personality. I must also forgo a discussion of Ellenberger's "distinction between two groups of dynamic sys-

---

[17] Here Ellenberger is wrong in the bare fact. The residential district of Adler's quarters was far more prestigious than Freud's.

[18] Quite rightly, the German Academy for Language and Letters [*Dichtung*] gives an annual Sigmund Freud prize for the paper written in the best scientific prose.

tems" (p. 890): those based on discoveries "obtained by means of objective clinical research" (Janet and Adler) vs. those whose "basic tenets originated from within, that is, from the experience of creative illness" (Freud and Jung).

I have gone into these specific details of error not in order to warn the reader—despite these shortcomings, Ellenberger's text is indispensable for anyone who is interested in the history of modern psychiatry—but because it demonstrates, in an even more striking way than Roazen's book, the present anti-genius drift. I could hardly think of anything more unpsychological than Ellenberger's Madison Avenue and victimological theory of genius—a theory that deprives the phenomenon of its uniqueness.

How greatly Ellenberger is basically mistaken can be seen from the following. He writes (p. 888): "The notion of the Oedipus complex and of its central place in human destiny was obviously derived from his [Freud's] own life history, and is also the reason why neither Adler nor Jung could accept it, since they had experienced quite different family situations in early childhood"; and (p. 888), "Events of his childhood led Adler to attribute a basic importance to the situation of the individual in the siblings' row, even more than to the early relationship with parental figures."

Ellenberger finds in Adler's relationship to his older brother and Freud's relationship to his father the main reasons for their differences in theory with regard to the Oedipus complex and to sibling influence. This supposition is not confirmed by the facts, however. The effect of the sibling relation was enormous in Freud's life. The father actually held the position of a grandfather in the boy's life (Jones 1, p. 9), and his oedipal strivings were directed toward his half-brothers Emanuel and Philipp, one twenty-three years and the other twenty years his senior. Thus, in terms of family constellations, Freud should have been the least "disposed" toward discovering the oedipal conflict.

Adler's brother was two years his senior. He is described as "a most intelligent and gifted person," "straightforward," "selfless to a rare degree" (Ellenberger 1970, p. 537). Phyllis Bottome (1939, p. 5), Adler's chief biographer, has the following to say about his relationship to the brother: "He [Adler] felt himself put in the shade by a model elder brother, a true 'first-born' who always seemed to Alfred to be soaring far beyond him in a sphere to which he—for all his efforts—could never attain. Even at the end of his life he had not wholly got over this feeling." [19] When it turns out that this older brother, who was soaring to heights unattainable by the younger brother—or so it seemed to him—bore the name of Sigmund, Adler's behavior toward Sigmund Freud may become better understandable.

It is more than an idle pastime to call attention to such an unfortunate coincidence of first names, as can be learned from a highly surprising sentence in Professor Ellenberger's text (p. 627): "It is certain that Freud influenced Adler negatively. During the Wednesday evening discussions, Adler seems to have used Freud largely as an antagonist who helped him to find his own path by inspiring him in opposite ways of thought." I must admit that this possibility never entered my mind; but I must also admit that if it had, I would not have dared to put it in print, since what it does is to question Adler's scientific integrity: it says no less than that Adler was not motivated primarily by the search for truth but rather by the desire for "opposite ways of thought." Under such conditions, of course, he could never develop "a creative illness," nor could he ever acknowledge Freud's pivotal discovery of the oedipus complex. Concomitantly, the question has to be raised: "How could Adler accept the Presidency of the Vienna Society under these circumstances?" If he was consciously motivated by the desire for "opposite ways of thought," then the reproach of lack of integrity is inescapable, because the president of a society ought to endeavor to help the group grow and flourish. If he was motivated unconsciously, and his own theory is applied, it would then be "an unconscious fiction" which was underlying his acceptance of the presidency —that is to say, an instance of severe neurotic acting out. It would also make it understandable why Adler later denied that he had ever been a psychoanalyst.

Furthermore, if Prof. Ellenberger's impression is valid, then it would reveal Adler's psychological work as primarily the result of his acting out a brother conflict. Such a revelation would remove any doubt that the full burden of those unpleasant events

---

[19] On the basis of this description, I would rather suspect a Cain syndrome than the Abel syndrome that Prof. Ellenberger diagnosed in Adler (see above).

that caused so much tension in the early Society would have to be placed on Adler's shoulders. This makes it even harder to grasp the meaning of Ellenberger's advice to the reader that "when studying Adler, he must temporarily put aside all that he learned about psychoanalysis and adjust to a quite different way of thinking" (p. 571)—the oddest advice I have ever encountered in a scientific treatise. Why, after all, should I put aside (if not forget) one set of theories, especially when I am studying another set, whose primary characteristic turns out to be that it is "opposite" the first?

That Adler's way of thinking was quite different from Freud's goes without saying; as he himself frequently stressed, his was meant to be a commonsense psychology. Since Freud was pursuing the pathway of science and Adler, according to Ellenberger, had to pursue "opposite" pathways, he did not have much choice: there was nothing left for him but to escape into common sense, that eternal bane of science.

When one studies biographical facts, rather than resorts to short-cut, feuilletonistic simplifications, of the sort that have both aesthetic and commonsense appeals, then one discovers that both Freud and Adler faced the same family problem—namely, the question of what determines the relationship of a boy to older brothers. In Adler's case, this meant a brother who was only two years older; in Freud's case, the problem involved two much older half-brothers.

Adler had a mainly negative relationship toward his mother (Bottome 1939, p. 9), by contrast with his relationship to his father. Phyllis Bottome (1939, p. 8) reports the following: "If any of the children were really ill, he [the father] would tiptoe into their rooms in the course of the night to see that they had all that they needed; and once, when Alfred was very ill indeed with pneumonia, his father harnessed a sleigh and drove across Vienna in the middle of the night to fetch the Kaiser's doctor to his little son's bedside." This speaks strongly in favor of a maternal imagery surrounding the father, who had thus saved the little boy's life. Whatever hostile impulse the young Adler might have felt toward the father was split off and directed instead against the older brother.

If Adler had thrust sufficiently deeper to recognize the full history of his relationship with his brother Sigmund, he would have had to acknowledge that he too, like all other male human beings, harbored not only affection but also hostility toward his father. Freud, after all, had been strong enough to take that step. Jones, who fully acknowledged the pivotal role of the half-brothers in Freud's life, has the following to say (1, p. 10f.): "There is every reason to think that Freud's conscious attitude to his father consistently remained, despite the latter's representing authority and frustration, one of affection, admiration and respect. . . . It therefore came as a great shock to Freud when forty years later he discovered his own Oedipus complex, and had to admit to himself that his unconscious had taken a very different attitude towards his father from that of his consciousness."

This digression was made necessary by the impression that Prof. Ellenberger may leave in some readers—namely, that there are several different and even "opposite" psychologies, all of them having validity in their own rights, and each of them being understandable only in terms of the idiosyncrasies of its founder.

The future biographer, however, will possibly be altogether interested in other details of biography, namely, those that are indicative of personality structure. Recently Manès Sperber (1970) published a book in which biographical material unknown to me about Adler has been made available. The most illuminating part of it seems to me to be an early recollection of Adler's, dating to his sixth year of life (Sperber 1970, p. 33f.). I shall not reproduce the whole memory; it is pretty elaborate, and refers to his daily walk to school, and the terrible anxiety that he suffered while passing a cemetery that he could not avoid, as well as his final decision to climb over the wall of the cemetery a few times, in order to free himself of this anxiety—an enterprise in which he succeeded. The recollection does not contain anything unusual; an untold number of children has experienced something similar. Only the act of self-healing, it is true, may be unusual in a six-year-old boy, and might be regarded as a precursor of the concept of training that plays such a considerable role in Adler's psychological system.

The whole matter, however, acquires a far different meaning when one learns that Adler found out, in his adult years, that the childhood recollection was untrue. There never existed any cemetery on his way to school. Suddenly, I understood the psychological root of many parts of his theory—for example, the assertion that mental and nervous diseases are "arrangements," as well as the frequent use of the word "tricks" in reference to symptoms and the general distrust of the patient's own words that is characteristic of Adler's approach.[20] Indeed, the role that Vaihinger's philosophy of as if and of "fiction" plays in his system becomes psychologically far more understandable from Adler's own childhood recollection than it does from the observation of neurotic patients. Yet this aspect may be of lesser interest to a future historian.

Early memories are often distortions or reversals, displacements and what not of real events. But what does it mean when an adult recalls repeated and quite detailed events that allegedly occurred at the age of six, and then it turns out they never did occur? If I should find such a clinical fact in a patient's history, I would take it as a sign of a pronounced disturbance in the ego.[21]

Further, let us assume that a patient reports, as Jung does about himself in his Memories (1961, p. 39), that at the age of twelve he went through a sort of religious crisis that found a preliminary solution when he had the courage to form a certain thought or fantasy. This was: "I saw before me the cathedral,

---

[20] Ellenberger himself writes about Adler's clinical acumen (1970, p. 594): "He would immediately detect the part of play-acting and mendacity on the part of his patients."

[21] A young man once told me that his earliest recollection as a child had been of the stork bringing him to his parents—which he professed to recall with great vividness. This "recollection" persisted undimmed even after he had learned "the facts of life." He was au fond a compulsive character. What made him remarkable was that the way he behaved and the way he appeared were characterized by an uncommon harmony. His idealism, without any element of masochistic acting-out, was one of his prominent features. I have always thought that this unusual "first recollection" was the result of an early attempt on his part to maintain a harmonious relationship with his parents. It was an eternal proof that parents do not lie and that one can trust them—a belief that must have helped him greatly in the evolving of his harmony and idealism. The successfully repressed ambivalence ought to have been considerable. Adler's screen-memory does not show the usual errors, displacements and distortions, but is significant by virtue of the absence of any equivalent in reality; nevertheless, it is given the appearance of a reality event, whereas the young man's recollection clearly belongs to the realm of fantasy. If the two memories are compared, the latter would appear to me to be clinically far less indicative of an ego disturbance than the former.

the blue sky, God on His golden throne high above the world—
and from under the throne an enormous turd falls upon the
sparkling new roof, shatters it, and breaks the walls of the cathedral asunder." In such a case I would be struck by the bizarreness
of content and the response to it, which impresses me as paradoxical, for twelve-year-old youngsters ought to feel guilty about
such blasphemous thoughts, rather than solve crises by way of
their production.

"Janet did not remember his dreams," writes Prof. Ellenberger (p. 888). Why not? Dreaming is a vital function; a person who never recalls dreams is doomed to living a rather restricted psychic life.

Thus I wonder whether the future historian will agree with
the personality profiles that Professor Ellenberger has presented,
and whether his evaluations of the four chief characters in the
drama of dawning modern psychology will not lead to quite different conclusions.

I have always been deeply impressed by a sentence that Freud
wrote to Jung in 1909 about an idea that haunted him during a
period of his life regarding the regular appearance of certain numbers (Jung 1961, p. 362): "Since I also have in my psychic system regions in which I am merely avid for knowledge and not
at all superstitious, I have attempted to analyze this conviction."
A Freud who was no longer able to form a superstition would,
indeed, have been a Freud whose psychic apparatus had lost its
resiliency and had stopped responding to life in a human way.
But a Freud who did not have the avidity to analyze his superstitions would have been anything but a great psychologist. I
have also been struck by the fact that, although Freud was an
uncompromising atheist, he did not lose the ability to understand
the role of religion. Quite apart from the fact that one finds
passages in his writings that suggest that he himself had strong
religious sentiments (which have nothing to do with prayer and
with attendance at services), what atheist has ever written with
such tenderness about the support that a child may obtain from
his belief in God (1918, p. 114f.): "In the present case, religion
achieved all the aims for the sake of which it is included in the
education of the individual. It put a restraint on his sexual im-
pulsions by affording them a sublimation and a safe mooring; it

lowered the importance of his family relationships, and thus protected him from the threat of isolation by giving him access to the great community of mankind. The untamed and fear-ridden child became social, well-behaved, and amenable to education."

It is quite likely that Professor Ellenberger in his reporting also tried to tip the scales in favor of those to whom he felt sympathetic. I have been able to observe this in at least two incidents in his biographical sketch of Adler, which would have been treated quite differently, had they occurred in Freud's life.

The first involves Adler's baptism when, at the age of thirty-four, he converted to the Protestant Church. Ellenberger's explanation for this is a gem of sociological rationalization: the Jews of the Burgenland, an Austrian province from which Adler's family hailed, became baptized, he says, because they did not have the feeling of being a persecuted minority (Ellenberger 1970, p. 575). He also quotes Phyllis Bottome (1939), according to whom Adler "resented the fact that the Jewish religion limited itself to one ethnic group, and he wished to belong to a universal one" (Ellenberger 1970, p. 595). He wanted, it seems, "to share a universal Deity with the common family of mankind" (Bottome 1939, p. 40). There is nothing one can say against that, but it does not provide, I would say, any justification for conversion in Adler's instance. At least, no proof has ever been brought forth that Adler really believed in the religious tenets of Protestantism or was able to find in them "a universal Deity."

Sperber (1970, pp. 49–51) reports that he never dared to ask Adler the reason for his baptism, even though their discussions frequently lasted until late at night. On what grounds Sperber was nevertheless absolutely certain that the conversion did not take place out of opportunism, he did not make clear. At any rate, some of the reasons he himself conjectured are not too far from opportunism. Yet the matter becomes even more bewildering when Sperber (1970, p. 49) reports that Adler was "the most radical freethinker" he had ever met, while Bottome (1939, p. 40) reports that Adler often said: "The idea of God is the most enlightened thought that has yet occurred in mankind." In Bottome's book, in fact, Adler appears to be a deeply religious person. How is one to explain this? Did the two biographers each project their own ideals onto him? Then their biographies would have to be distrusted. Or worse, did Adler talk to each biographer in accordance with what he felt his interlocutor expected from him? Sperber and Ellenberger intimate that Adler changed his views on religion during the course of his life. But did Adler really wish of Bottome that she should write his biography without ever telling her that he had once been a freethinker? Once again, we run into the question of Adler's honesty.

At any rate, until there is adequate reason to believe otherwise, one must assume that Adler's baptism constituted a sort of *mariage de convenance*—and that would seem to call for a characterological evaluation, rather than Ellenberger's sociological rationalization.

The other incident has to do with Adler's application for a *Dozentur* at the University. Wagner-Jauregg's opinion, in which he takes a strong stand against Adler's becoming a member of the medical faculty, has been published (Beckh-Widmanstetter 1965). It runs to four printed pages, and in it he sets forth the reasons why he considers Individual Psychology not to be a science and therefore not to be taught at the Medical School.

What is of particular interest here is a remark that Wagner-Jauregg makes in his introduction. After summarizing what Adler described in his application as his clinical experiences—among others, that he had been active as a psychiatrist—Wagner-Jauregg notes that Adler had failed to say in which institutes and in which positions he had worked. "This somewhat flippant way of putting it suggests that Wagner-Jauregg was not quite convinced of the reality of Adler's statements" (Ellenberger 1970, p. 585). Beckh-Widmanstetter, however, says in his closing paragraph (1965, p. 188): "Wagner-Jauregg's words are clear; he held back [*zurückhaltend*] only at the point at which it is a matter of the alleged clinical pratice and the study of psychiatry of the applicant. A person who is knowledgeable about conditions at that time can read between the lines [of Wagner-Jauregg's statement]: 'I, as chief of clinic, would have to know something of that, if it were true. Yet it does not matter any more [*Doch darauf kommt es schon nicht mehr an*].' As a matter of fact, archival studies show that it was not true" (my own translation). These archival studies have not been published by Beckh-Widmanstetter, as far as I know. On page 582 (that is to say, three pages before reporting

Wagner-Jauregg's "flippant" remark), however, Ellenberger sum-
marizes the archival studies Beckh-Widmanstetter undertook for
him.

No evidence was found that Adler ever received training in
psychiatry. The only activity of his that could be proven to have
taken place was his work in the Department of Ophthalmology
at the Poliklinik, a famous hospital in Vienna. Thus Wagner-
Jauregg was not intimating any doubts about the "reality of
Adler's statements," as Ellenberger puts it; he was expressing the
belief, as Beckh-Widmanstetter asserts, that "it was not true."
Since there were many other reasons of substance, in Wagner-
Jauregg's opinion, that made Adler's application inadmissible, he
paid no further attention to the question of Adler's training. If
Adler's application did, however, contain statements that were
not true, then Adler had made himself guilty of a serious breach.

Once again, we observe a problem of character that seems to
have gone completely unnoticed by Ellenberger. On the other
hand, it should be noted how Ellenberger reacts to a military
report on Freud's army service of four weeks in 1882. He reproduces in full (p. 450) all the highly commendatory things it
contains about Freud's personality, conduct and service. In a
footnote (p. 557, n. 177), however, he adds the comment of a
person whose name is not given but who was apparently Beckh-
Widmanstetter: "It proves that Freud was on good terms with
the officer who wrote the report." Perhaps Beckh-Widmanstetter
—if it was indeed he—was right. That is not the question, however. What is significant is that, in one instance, Prof. Ellenberger reports a personal remark that is unfavorable to Freud,
despite the fact that the person who made it must have had some
doubt, since he wished to remain anonymous; in the other, he
does not report printed words that would shatter the usual image
of Adler, even though the author of those words was certain that
they were correct.[22]

---

[22] I also would like to add a few words about Phyllis Bottome's biography of
Alfred Adler. I did not find in Ellenberger's book any expression of opinion regarding the credibility of her book. Since he quotes from it, one has the impression
that he trusts her reliability. If she has reported reliably, and Alfred Adler really
did say all the things she reported, this book will, in my opinion, prove to have
been of disservice to Adler. One of his alleged sayings invokes again the question
of honesty. According to Bottome (p. 66), Adler owned up to having said to

A critical mind might even wonder whether Alfred Adler had any rightful place in Prof. Ellenberger's book. After all, historically he came after Freud who, according to Ellenberger (p. 627), as mentioned before, "influenced Adler negatively." Thus it is understandable that the unconscious, which had to play such a large part in Ellenberger's presentation of Freud's work, had been reduced by Adler to the point where Ellenberger was able to write only one sentence about it: "Adler believed that the early childhood situations and events unconsciously determined the adult's style of life; he spoke of unconscious fictions and life goals." Consequently, if Prof. Ellenberger's book were truly devoted to "the Discovery of the Unconscious," as its title makes the reader expect, he could not have assigned to Alfred Adler and his work more than a footnote recording that, out of the school of Freud, there came a man who tried to undo most of the discoveries Freud had made in the area of the Unconscious. Nor does a psychology that aims primarily at practical knowledge of the surface of the personality (Ellenberger 1970, p. 608) have a rightful place in a volume whose subtitle is "The History and Evolution of Dynamic Psychiatry." [23] These few examples, which may impress the reader as being trival, when compared with the huge body of historical facts included in Prof. Ellenberger's book,

---

Freud: "Why should I always do my work under your shadow? He explained . . . that these words . . . were greatly misinterpreted by the psychoanalysts." He allegedly feared that he "was to be made responsible for the Freudian theories"; "he came to believe that the whole process of psychoanalysis was inimical to the welfare of mankind. This was the 'shadow' under which he could not work because he dared not be made responsible for what he feared might be the results of Freud's thoughts upon mankind." Incredible as it may seem, Phyllis Bottome seems to have accepted this explanation.

[23] I recently had the opportunity to observe how rampant is the prejudice that is still prevalent in Europe against psychoanalysis, and how useless it is to expect a half-way objective discussion of it. A noted Swiss historian of medicine published a review of Ellenberger's book, in which he sided on all matters with the author, and stressed Freud "plagiarism." I wrote to him, in order to find out the grounds for his accusing Freud's of plagiarism, and inquired at the same time why he agreed with Ellenberger's inclusion of Adler among the discoverers of the unconscious and the founders of dynamic psychiatry. In so doing, I presented the reasons I have given above. The historian's answer to my letter was not only surprising but ill-mannered. He wrote that, because of "your brilliant invention [Ihre geniale Erfindung] that Alfred Adler's work has no legitimate place in Ellenberger's book, discussing Freud with me would be as senseless as discussing the Immaculate Conception with a devout Catholic."

may, nevertheless, suggest that the sleep of the world is still being disturbed by Freud's writings.

But I may have done Prof. Ellenberger an injustice. After all, he may have proceeded along Aristotle's lines when the latter said about Plato: "Everybody may criticize him; but who is permitted to praise him?"

REFERENCES

Abraham, Hilda & Freud, Ernst L., eds. (1965), *A Psychoanalytic Dialogue. The Letters of Sigmund Freud and Karl Abraham* (1907–1926). New York: Basic Books.

Abraham, Karl (1908), "The psycho-sexual differences between hysteria and dementia praecox." In: *Selected Papers of Karl Abraham.* New York: Basic Books, 1953, pp. 64–79.

———— (1912), "Notes on the psychoanalytic investigation and treatment of manic-depressive insanity and allied conditions." In: *Selected Papers of Karl Abraham.* New York: Basic Books, 1953, pp. 137–156.

————, ed. (1914), "Korrespondenzblatt der Internationalen Psychoanalytischen Vereinigung." *Internat. Zeitschr. Psychoanal.*, 2:405–406.

Abrahamsen, David (1946), *The Mind and Death of a Genius.* New York: Columbia University Press.

Adler, Alfred (1907), *Studie über die Minderwertigkeit von Organen.* Vienna: Urban & Schwarzenberg.

Alexander, Franz (1966), "Sandor Rado." In: *Psychoanalytic Pioneers*, ed. F. Alexander, S. Eisenstein, & M. Grotjahn. New York: Basic Books.

Allers, Rudolf (1934), "Die neue Zeit und die Heilerziehung." In: *Der christliche Ständestaat*, 1:15–17.

Anderson, Ola (1962), *Studies in the Prehistory of Psychoanalysis.* Norstedts: Svenska Bokförlaget.

Andreas-Salomé, Lou (1951), *Lebensrückblick*, ed. E. Pfeiffer. Zurich: Max Niehans Verlag; Wiesbaden: Insel Verlag.

———— (1958), *The Freud Journal of Lou Andreas-Salomé*, trans. S. A. Leavy. New York: Basic Books, 1960.

Bailey, Percival (1956), "The great psychiatric revolution." The academic lecture. *Amer. J. Psychiat.* 113:387–406.

———— (1961), "A rigged radio interview." In: *Perspectives in Biology and Medicine*, 4:199–265.

Bak, Robert (1946), "Masochism in Paranoia." *Psychoanal. Quart.*, 15:285–301.

Bartemeier, Leo H. (1952), Opening address, Seventeenth International Psycho-analytical Congress. *Internat. J. Psycho-Anal.*, 33:250.

Becker-Koller, Hortense (1963), "Carl Koller and cocaine." *Psychoanal. Quart.*, 32:309–373.

Beckh-Widmanstetter, H. A., (1965), "Zur Geschichte der Individualpsychologie. Julius Wagner-Jauregg über Alfred Adler." *Unsere Heimat*, 36:182–188.

Bennet, E. A., (1962), *C. G. Jung*. New York: Dutton.

—— (1965), "The Freud-Janet controversy: an unpublished letter." *Brit. Med. J.*, Jan. 2, 1965, 52–53.

Bergler, Edmund (1932), "Das Plagiat." *Psychoanal. Bewegung*, 4:393–420.

Bernfeld, Siegfried (1949), "Freud's scientific beginnings." *Amer. Imago*, 6:163–196.

—— (1953), "Freud's studies on cocaine, 1884–1887." *J. Amer. Psychoanal. Assn.*, 1:581–613.

Bettelheim, Bruno (1960), *The Informed Heart. Autonomy in a Mass Age*. Glencoe, Ill.: Free Press.

Bibring, Edward (1929), "Klinische Beiträge zur Paranoiafrage II. Ein Fall von Organprojektion." *Internat. Zeitschr. Psychoanal.*, 15:44–46.

Billroth, Theodor (1886), "Wünsche und Hoffnungen für unsere medicinische Fakultät." *Wien. klin. Wochenschr.*, 1(36):733–736.

Binion, Rudolph (1968), *Frau Lou. Nietzsche's Wayward Pupil*. Princeton, N.J.: Princeton University Press.

Binswanger, Ludwig (1956), *Sigmund Freud: Reminiscences of a Friendship*. New York: Grune & Stratton, 1957.

Blachly, Paul H., Disher, William & Roduner, Gregory (1968), "Suicide by physicians." *Bull. Suicidol.* Chevy Chase, Md.: NIMH.

Bode, Wilhelm (1921), *Neues über Goethes Liebe*. Berlin: Mittler.

Boehm, Felix (1956), "Meine Begegnungen mit Freud." *Der Psychologe*, 8:176–181. Schwarzenberg, Switzerland: GBS-Verlag.

Bottome, Phyllis (1939), *Alfred Adler. A Biography*. New York: G. P. Putnam's Sons.

Breuer, Josef & Freud, Sigmund (1893–1895), "Studies on Hysteria." *Standard Edition*, vol. 2. London. Hogarth Press, 1955.

Brome, Vincent (1968), *Freud and His Early Circle*. New York: William Morrow.

Bry, Ilse & Rifkin, Alfred H. (1962), "Freud and the history of ideas: primary sources, 1886–1910." *Science and Psychoanal.* 5:6–36.

Bühler, Karl (1926), *Die Krise der Psychologie*. Jena: Gustav Fischer.

Burger, H., Forselles, A. A. F., Holmgren, G., Schmegelow, E. & Uchermann, V. (1922), "Bárány und die Wiener Universität." *Acta Oto-Laryngologica*, 3:379–393.

Capelle, Wilhelm (1935), *Die Vorsokratiker*. Stuttgart: Alfred Kröner Verlag, 1968.

Carletta, Giuliano (1899), *Goethe a Roma*. Rome: Editrice Dante Alighieri.

Colby, K. M. (1951), "On the disagreement between Freud and Adler." *Amer. Imago*, 8:229–238.

Coleman, Rose W., Kris, Ernst & Provence, Sally (1953), "The study of variations of early parental attitudes. A preliminary report." *The Psy-*

choanalytic Study of the Child, 8:20–47. New York: International Universities Press.

Delay, J. (1963), "Pierre Janet (1859–1947)." In: *Grosse Nervenärzte*, ed. Koller, C., 3:77–85.

Deri, Frances (1939), "On sublimation." *Psychoanal. Quart.*, 8:325–334.

Deutsch, Helene (1927), "Über Zufriedenheit, Glück und Ekstase." *Internat. Zeitschr. Psychoanal.*, 13:410–419.

———— (1930), "Hysterical Fate-neurosis." *Psycho-Analysis of the Neuroses*. London: Hogarth Press, 1932, pp. 29–49.

Eissler, K. R. (1955), *The Psychiatrist and the Dying Patient*. New York: International Universities Press.

———— (1958), "Kritische Bemerkungen zu Renée Gicklhorns Beitrag 'Eine mysteriöse Bildaffäre.'" *Wien. Geschichtsblätter*, 13 (73), No. 3.

———— (1965), "Ideen über Freuds Persönlichkeit. Mit besonderer Berücksichtigung des Schöpferischen und allgemeinen Bemerkungen über die Soziologie des Genies." Unpublished manuscript.

———— (1966), *Sigmund Freud und die Wiener Universität*. Bern & Stuttgart: Hans Huber.

———— (1969a). "Gedenkrede anlässlich der 30. Wiederkehr von Freuds Todestag, gehalten in Wien im Rahmen der Sigmund Freud Gesellschaft." Unpublished manuscript.

———— (1969b), "Irreverent remarks about the present and the future of psychoanalysis." *Internat. J. Psycho-Anal.*, 50:461–471.

———— (1970), *Discourse on Hamlet and HAMLET*. New York: International Universities Press.

Ekstein, Rudolf & Motto, Rocco (1969), *From Learning for Love to Love of Learning*. New York: Brunner/Mazel.

Ellenberger, Henri F. (1970), *The Discovery of the Unconscious. The History and Evolution of Dynamic Psychiatry*. New York: Basic Books.

Federn, Paul (1941), "Uber zwei typische Traumsensationen." *Jahrbuch für psychoanal. Forsch.*, 6:89–134.

———— (1926), "Some variations in ego feeling." In: Federn (1952).

———— (1952), *Ego Psychology and the Psychoses*, ed. Edoardo Weiss. New York: Basic Books.

Fenichel, Otto (1945), *The Psychoanalytic Theory of Neurosis*. New York: Norton.

Ferenczi, Sándor (1912), "Philosophy and psychoanalysis (Comments on a paper of James J. Putnam of Harvard)." In: *Final Contribution to the Problems and Methods of Psychoanalysis*. New York: Basic Books, 1955, pp. 326–334.

Feuer, Lewis S. (1968), "The character and thought of Karl Marx: the Promethean complex and historical materialism." In: *Marx and the Intellectuals*. New York: Anchor Books, Doubleday, 1969, pp. 9–52.

Fisher, Charles (1954), "Dreams and perception: the role of preconscious and primary modes of perception in dream formation." *J. Amer. Ps. Assn.*, 2:389–445.

Fisher, Charles & Paul, Irving H. (1959), "The effect of subliminal visual stimulation on images and dreams; a validation study." *J. Amer. Psa. Assn.*, 7:35–83.

Fliess, Wilhelm (1897), *Die Beziehungen zwischen Nase und weiblichen Geschlechtsorganen.* Leipzig/Wien: Deuticke.

—— (1906a), *In eigener Sache gegen Otto Weininger und Hermann Swoboda.* Berlin: Goldschmidt.

—— (1906a), *Der Ablauf des Lebens.* Leipzig/Wien: Deuticke, 1923.

Forel, Auguste (1889), "Hypnotism, its significance and management briefly presented." In: Woods M. & S. Monog., 5, New York, 1890.

Frederick, Calvin J. (1969), "Suicide notes: a survey and evaluation." *Bull. Suicidol.* (March). pp. 17–26. Chevy Chase, Md.: NIMH.

Freud, Martin (1957), *Glory Reflected. Sigmund Freud—Man and Father.* London/Sydney/Melbourne/Wellington: Angus & Robertson.

Freud, Sigmund (1877), "Beobachtungen über Gestaltung und feineren Bau der als Hoden beschriebenen Lappenorgane des Aals." *Sitzungsberichte der Akademie der Wissenschaften, Wien:* Math-Naturwiss Kl., Abt. 3, 75(4): 419–431.

—— (1884), "Über Coca." *Centralbl. ges. Therap.*, 2(7):289–314.

—— (1885), "Beitrag zur Kenntnis der Cocawirkung." *Wien. mediz. Wochenschr.*, 35(5):129–133.

—— (1888), "Hysteria." *Standard Edition*, 1:41–57. London: Hogarth Press, 1966.

—— (1888b), "Preface to the translation of Bernheim's *Suggestion.*" *Standard Edition*, 1:75-85. London: Hogarth Press, 1966.

—— (1889), "Review of August Forel's *Hypnotism.*" *Standard Edition*, 1:91–102. London: Hogarth Press, 1966.

—— (1889b), "Screen Memories." *Standard Edition*, 3:303–322. London: Hogarth Press, 1962.

—— (1892), "Letter to Josef Breuer." *Standard Edition*, 1:147–148. London: Hogarth Press, 1966.

—— (1893), "Charcot." *Standard Edition*, 3:11–23. London: Hogarth Press, 1962.

—— (1894), "The neuro-psychoses of defense." *Standard Edition*, 3:45–61. London: Hogarth Press, 1962.

—— (1896), "Further remarks on the neuro-psychoses of defense." *Standard Edition*, 3:162–185. London: Hogarth Press, 1962.

—— (1900), "The interpretation of dreams." *Standard Edition*, 4 & 5. London: Hogarth Press, 1953.

—— (1901), "The psychopathology of everyday life." *Standard Edition*, 6. London: Hogarth Press, 1960.

—— (1905a), "Three essays on the theory of sexuality." *Standard Edition*, 7:130–243. London: Hogarth Press, 1953.

—— (1905b), "Jokes and their relation to the unconscious." *Standard Edition*, 8:9–238. London: Hogarth Press, 1960.

—— (1907), "Delusions and dreams in Jensen's *Gradiva*." *Standard Edition*, 9:7–95. London: Hogarth Press, 1959.

—— (1910a), "A special type of choice of object made by men." *Standard Edition*, 11:165–175. London: Hogarth Press, 1957.

—— (1910b), "Leonardo da Vinci and a memory of his childhood." *Standard Edition*, 11:63–137. London: Hogarth Press, 1957.

—— (1910c), "Five lectures on psycho-analysis." *Standard Edition*, 11:9–55. London: Hogarth Press, 1957.

—— (1911a), "Psycho-analytic Notes on an autobiographical account of a case of paranoia (Dementia Paranoides)." *Standard Edition*, 12:9–82. London: Hogarth Press. 1958.

—— (1911b), "Formulations on the two principles of mental functioning." *Standard Edition*, 12:218–226. London: Hogarth Press, 1958.

—— (1912), "Recommendations to physicians practising psycho-analysis." *Standard Edition*, 12:111–120. London: Hogarth Press, 1958.

—— (1913), "Totem and Taboo." *Standard Edition*, 13: ix–162. London: Hogarth Press, 1955.

—— (1914a), "On the history of the psycho-analytic movement." *Standard Edition*, 14:7–66. London: Hogerth Press, 1957.

—— (1914b), "On narcissism: an introduction." *Standard Edition*, 14:73–102. London: Hogarth Press, 1957.

—— (1915a), "Observations on transference-love." *Standard Edition*, 12:159–171. London: Hogarth Press, 1958.

—— (1915b), "The unconscious." *Standard Edition*, 14:166–204. London: Hogarth Press, 1957.

—— (1915c), "Thoughts for the Times on War and Death." *Standard Edition*, 14:275–300. London: Hogarth Press, 1957.

—— (1915d), "A Case of Paranoia Running counter to the Psychoanalytic Theory of the Disease." *Standard Edition*, 14:263–272. London: Hogarth Press, 1957.

—— (1916), "Criminals from a Sense of Guilt." *Standard Edition*, 14:332–333. London: Hogarth Press, 1957.

—— (1916–1917), "*Introductory lectures on psycho-analysis.*" *Standard Edition*, 15 & 16. London: Hogarth Press, 1963.

—— (1917a), "Mourning and melancholia." *Standard Edition*, 14:243–258. London: Hogarth Press. 1957.

—— (1917b), "A childhood recollection from *Dichtung und Wahrheit*." *Standard Edition*, 17:147–156. London: Hogarth Press, 1955.

—— (1918), "From the history of an infantile neurosis." *Standard Edition*, 17:7–122. London: Hogarth Press, 1955.

—— (1919a), "James J. Putnam (obituary)." *Standard Edition*, 17:271. London: Hogarth Press, 19.

—— (1919b), "Introduction to psycho-analysis and the war neuroses." *Standard Edition*, 17:207–210. London: Hogarth Press, 1955.

—— (1919c), "The 'Uncanny.'" *Standard Edition*, 17:219–256. London: Hogarth Press, 1955.

—————— (1920a), "Beyond the pleasure principle." *Standard Edition*, 18:7–64. London: Hogarth Press, 1955.

—————— (1920b), "A note on the prehistory of the technique of analysis." *Standard Edition*, 18:263–265. London: Hogarth Press, 1955.

—————— (1921), "Preface to J. J. Putnam's *Addresses on Psycho-Analysis.*" *Standard Edition*, 18:269–270. London: Hogarth Press, 1955.

—————— (1923), "Josef Popper-Lynkeus and the theory of dreams." *Standard Edition*, 19:261–263. London: Hogarth Press, 1961.

—————— (1924a), "The loss of reality in neurosis and psychosis." *Standard Edition*, 19:183–187. London: Hogarth Press, 1961.

—————— (1924b), "The dissolution of the Oedipus complex." *Standard Edition*, 19:173–179. London: Hogarth Press, 1961.

—————— (1924c), "Neurosis and psychosis." *Standard Edition*, 19:149–153. London: Hogarth Press, 1961

—————— (1925a), "Preface to Aichhorn's *Wayward Youth.*" *Standard Edition*, 19:273–275. London: Hogarth Press, 1961.

—————— (1925b), "An autobiographical study." *Standard Edition*, 20:7–74. London: Hogarth Press, 1959.

—————— (1925c), "Negation." *Standard Edition*, 19:235–239. London: Hogarth Press, 1961.

—————— (1926), "Inhibition, symptom and anxiety." *Standard Edition*, 20:87–172. London: Hogarth Press, 1959.

—————— (1927a), "Postscript (to the question of lay analysis)." *Standard Edition*, 20:251–258. London: Hogarth Press, 1959.

—————— (1927b), "The future of an illusion." *Standard Edition*, 21:5–56. London: Hogarth Press, 1961.

—————— (1930a), "Civilization and its discontents." *Standard Edition*, 21:57–145. London: Hogarth Press, 1961.

—————— (1930b), "Address delivered in the Goethe House at Frankfurt." *Standard Edition*, 21: 208–212. London: Hogarth Press, 1961.

—————— (1932), "My contact with Josef Popper-Lynkeus." *Standard Edition*, 22:219–224. London: Hogarth Press, 1964.

—————— (1933), "New introductory lectures." *Standard Edition*, 22:7–182. London: Hogarth Press, 1964.

—————— (1935), "Postscript (an autobiographical study)." *Standard Edition*, 20:71–74. London: Hogarth Press, 1959.

—————— (1936), "A disturbance of memory on the Acropolis." *Standard Edition*, 22:239–248. London: Hogarth Press, 1964.

—————— (1937), "Analysis terminable and interminable." *Standard Edition*, 23:216–253. London: Hogarth Press, 1964.

—————— (1950a). *The Origins of Psycho-Analysis. Letters to Wilhelm Fliess, Drafts and Notes. 1887–1902.* New York: Basic Books, 1954.

—————— (1950b), "Project for a scientific psychology." Standard Edition, 1:295–387. London: Hogarth Press, 1966.

—————— (1956), "Report on my studies in Paris and Berlin carried out with the assistance of a Travelling Bursary granted from the University

Jubilee Fund (October, 1885—End of March 1886)." *Standard Edition*, 1:5–15. London: Hogarth Press, 1966.

———— (1960), *Letters of Sigmund Freud*, sel. and ed. Ernst L. Freud. New York: Basic Books.

———— & Pfister, Oskar (1963), *Psychoanalysis and Faith. The Letters of Sigmund Freud and Oskar Pfister*. New York: Basic Books, 1963.

————, Ferenczi, Sandor, Abraham, Karl, Simmel, Ernst & Jones, Ernest (1919), *Psycho-analysis and the war neuroses*. London/Vienna/New York: International Psychoanalytic Press, 1921.

Fromm, Erich (1959), *Sigmund Freud's Mission. An Analysis of His Personality and Influence*. New York: Harper.

Gedo, John E., Sabshin, Melvin, Sadow, Leo, & Schlessinger, N. (1964), *Studies on hysteria*. A methodological evaluation." *J. Amer. Psychoanal. Assn.*, 12:734–751.

Gicklhorn, Josef (1955), "Wissenschaftliche Notizen zu den Studien von S. Syrski (1874) und S. Freud (1877) über männliche Flussaale." *Sitzungsberichte der Österreichischen Akad. Wissenschaften* (Mathem.-Naturw. Kl.), Abt. I, Bd. 164, Heft 1 & 2.

———— & Gicklhorn, Renée (1960), *Sigmund Freuds akademische Laufbahn im Lichte der Dokumente*. Wein/Innsbruch: Urban & Schwarzenberg.

Gicklhorn, Renée (1958), "Eine mysteriöse Bildaffäre. Ein kritischer Beitrag zur Freudforschung in Wien." *Wiener Geschichtsblätter*, 13(73): 14–16.

———— & Sajner, Josef (1969), "The Freiberg Period of the Freud Family." *J. History Med.*, 24:37–43.

Gillispie, Charles Coulston (1960), *The Edge of Objectivity*. Princeton, N.J.: Princeton University Press.

Globus, Gordon G. & Pillard, Richard C. (1966), "Tausk's *Influencing Machine* and Kofka's *In the Penal Colony*." *Amer. Imago*, 23:191–207.

Goetz, Bruno (1952), "Errinnerungen an Sigmund Freud." *Neue Schweizer Rundschau*, 20:3–11.

Gordon, Cyrus H. (1968), *Forgotten Scripts. How They Were Deciphered and Their Impact on Contemporary Culture*. New York: Basic Books.

Greenacre, Phyllis (1957), "The Childhood of the Artist." *The Psychoanalytic Study of the Child*, 12:47–72. New York: International Universities Press.

Greenson, Ralph R. (1957), *The Technique and Practice of Psychoanalysis* Vol 1. New York: International Universities Press.

Grinker, Roy R., Jr. (1970), Book review of *Brother Animal: The Story of Freud and Tausk*, by Paul Roazen. *Arch. Gen. Psychiat.*, 22:189–190.

Grinstein, Alexander (1956–1966), *The Index of Psychoanalytic Writings*. New York: International Universities Press.

Gross, Otto (1907), *Das Freud'sche Ideogenitätsmoment und seine Bedeutung in manisch-depressiven Irresein Kraepelins*. Leipzig: F. C. W. Vogel.

Guillain, G. (1955), *J. M. Charcot, 1825–1893. His Life—His Work.* New York: Hoeber, 1959.

Hárnik, Jeno (1919), Review of Dr. Ernst Simmel's *Kriegsneurosen und "Psychisches Trauma." Internat. Zeitschr ärztl. Psychoanal.* 5:125–129.

Harris, Frank (1925), *My Life and Loves.* New York: Grove Press, 1963.

Harrison, Irving B. (1966), "A reconsideration of Freud's 'A disturbance of memory on the acropolis' in relation to identity disturbance." *J. Amer. Psychoanal. Assn.,* 14:518–527.

Hartmann, Heinz (1939), *Ego Psychology and the Problem of Adaptation.* New York: International Universities Press, 1958.

Herrigel, Eugen (1953), *Zen.* New York/Toronto: McGraw-Hill.

Hesse, Hermann (1930), "Notizen zum Thema Dichtung und Kritik." *Neue Rundschau,* December.

——— (1943), *The Glass Bead Game* [*Magister Ludi*]. New York/Chicago/San Francisco: Holt, Rinehard & Winston.

Hitschmann, Edward (1913), "Paranoia, Homosexualität und Analerotik." *Internat. Zeitschr. ärztl. Psychoanal.,* 1:251–254.

Hollós, István (1928), *Hinter der gelben Mauer.* Stuttgart: Hippokrates Verlag.

Iltis, Hugo (1924), *Life of Mendel.* New York: Norton, 1932.

Jacobson, Edith (1964), *The Self and the Object World.* New York: International Universitites Press.

Jaki, Stanly, L. (1969), *The Paradox of Olbers' Paradox.* New York: Herder & Herder.

Janet, Pierre (1889), *L'automatisme psychologique.* Paris: Alcan.

——— (1913). "Psychoanalysis." *J. Abnorm. Psychol.,* 9:1–35, 153–187.

——— (1924), *Principles of Psychotherapy.* New York: Macmillan.

Jellinek, S. (1947), *Dying, Apparent-Death and Resuscitation.* London: Baillière, Tindall & Cox.

Jones, Ernest (1915), "Professor Janet on psycho-analysis: a rejoinder." In: *Papers on psycho-analysis.* London: Baillière, Tindall & Cox, 1918, pp. 373–382.

——— (1919), "War shock and Freud's theory of the neuroses." In: *Psychoanalysis and the War Neuroses.* New York, London, Vienna: International Psychoanalytic Press, 1921, pp. 44–59.

——— (1924), Book Review of *Sigmund Freud: His Personality, His Teaching and His School,* by Fritz Wittels. *Internat. J. Psycho-Anal.,* 1:481–486.

——— (1953–1957), *The Life and Works of Sigmund Freud,* 3 Vols. New York: Basic Books.

——— (1956), "The Nature of Genius." In: *Sigmund Freud. Four Centenary Addresses.* New York: Basic Books, pp. 3–34.

Juliusburger, Otto (1911), "Weiteres von Schopenhaeur." *Zentralbl. Psychoanal. Psychother.,* 1:173–174.

Jung, Carl Gustav (1907), *The Psychology of Dementia Praecox.* Nervous and Mental Disease Monograph No. 3, Nervous and Mental Disease Publishing Co.

———— (1961), *Memories, Dreams, Reflections*. Recorded and edited by A. Jaffé. New York: Pantheon.

Karbach, O. (1964), "Die politischen Grundlagen des deutsch-österreichischen Antisemitismus." *Zeitschr. Geschichte der Juden*, 1:1–8, 103–116, 169–178.

Koller, Carl (1928), "Historical notes on the beginning of local anasthesia." *J. Amer. Med. Assn.*, 90:1742–1743.

Kraepelin, Emil (1913), *Psychiatrie*, 4 vols. Leipzig: Johann Ambrosius Barth, 1909–1915.

Kris, Ernst (1934), "The psychology of caricature." In: *Psychoanalytic Explorations in Art*. New York: International Universities Press, 1952, pp. 173–188.

———— (1938), "Ego development and the comic." In: *Psychoanalytic Explorations in Art*. New York: International Universities Press, 1952, pp. 204–216.

———— (1939), "On inspiration." In: *Psychoanalytic Explorations in Art*. New York: International Universities Press, 1952, pp. 291–302.

———— (1950), "On preconscious mental processes." In: *Psychoanalytic Explorations in Art*. New York: International Universities Press, 1952, pp. 303–318.

———— (1952), "The image of the artist." In: *Psychoanalytic Explorations in Art*. New York: International Universities Press, 1952, pp. 64–84.

———— (1956), "Freud in the history of science." *Listener*, 55:631–633.

———— & Gombrich, E. (1938), "The principles of caricature." In: *Psychoanalytic Explorations in Art*. New York: International Press, 1952, pp. 189–203.

———— & Kurz, Otto (1934), *Die Legende vom Künstler*. Vienna: Krystall Verlag.

Kroeber, A. L. (1944), *Configurations of Culture Growth*. Berkeley & Los Angeles: University of California Press.

Kuhn, Thomas S. (1962), "The structure of scientific revolutions." In: *International Encyclopedia of Unified Sciences*, 2 (2). Chicago: University of Chicago Press.

Landauer, Karl (1914), "Spontanheilung einer Katatonie." *Internat. Zeitschr. ärztl. Psychoanal.*, 2:441–459.

Lange-Eichbaum, Wilhelm (1927), *Genie, Irrsin und Ruhm* (4th ed.). Münich/Basel: Ernst Reinhardt, 1956.

Lantos, Barbara (1955), "On the motivation of human relationship." *Internat. J. psycho-Anal.*, 36:267–288.

Leavy, Stanley A. (1964), "A Footnote to Jung's *Memories*." *Psychoanal. Quart.*, 33: 567–573.

Lesky, Erna (1965), *Die Wiener medizinische Schule im 19. Jahrhundert*. Graz/Köln: Verlag Herlmann Böhlaus.

Lomas, Peter (1969), Book review of *Brother Animal. The New York Times*, Oct. 12.

Lorand, Sandor et al., eds. (1945–1954), *Yearbook of Psychoanalysis*, 1–10. New York: International Universities Press.

McDougall, William (1936), *Psycho-Analysis and Social Psychology.* London: Methuen and Co.

Mann, Thomas (1936), "Freud and the future." In: *Freud, Goethe, Wagner.* New York: Alfred Knopf, 1937, pp. 3–45.

Manuel, Frank E. (1963), *Isaac Newton, Historian.* Cambridge, Mass: The Belknap Press of the Harvard Univ. Press.

——— (1968), *A Portrait of Isaac Newton.* Cambridge, Mass.: The Belknap Press of the Harvard Univ. Press.

Marcel, Gabriel (1963), *The Existential Background of Human Dignity.* Cambridge, Mass.: Harvard University Press.

Meller, Josef (1934), "Gedenkworte zum 50. Jahrestage des Vortrages von Dr. Carl Koller über das Kokain, vor der Gesellschaft der Ärzte in Wien." *Wien. klin. Wochenschr.*, 47 (44).

Mentz, Paul (1901), Review of Sigmund Freud's *Die Traumdeutung. Vierteljahrschr. wissenschaftliche Philos. & Soziol.*, 25:112–113.

Meynert, Theodor (1888), "Über hypnotische Erscheinungen." *Wien. Klin. Wochenschr.*, 1:451–453, 473–476, 495–498.

———(1889), *Beitrag zum Verständnis der traumatischen Neurose.* Wien: A. Holder.

——— (1890), *Klinische Vorlesungen über Psychiatrie auf wissenschaftlichen Grundlagen.* Wien: Wilhelm Braumüller.

Moebius, P.J. (1901), *Über Kunst und Künstler.* Leipzig: Barth.

Moll, Albert (1898), *Untersuchungen über die Libido Sexualis.* Berlin: Fischers Medicin Buchhandlung H. Kornfeld.

——— (1908), *The Sexual Life of the Child.* New York: Macmillan, 1912.

Morgenthaler, Walter & Steinberg, Marianne (1945), "Letzte Aufzeichnungen vor Selbstmördern." *Beiheft z. Schweiz. Zeitschr. Psychol.* Anwend. No. 1.

Muschg, Walter (1930), "Freud als Schriftsteller." *Psychoanal. Bewegung*, 2:467–509.

——— (1948), *Tragische Literaturgeschichte.* Bern: Francke.

Nietzsche, Friedrich (1879–1880), "Der Wanderer und sein Schatten." In: *Gesammelte Werke*, 9:177–355. Munich: Musarion Verlag.

Nunberg, Herman & Federn, Ernst, eds. (1906–1915), *Minutes of the Vienna Psychoanalytic Society* (3 vols.) New York: International Universities Press, 1, 1962; 2, 1967; 3, in press.

Obersteiner, Heinrich (1904), Review of *Die hysterischen Geistesstörungen* by Dr. Emil Raimann. *Wien. klin. Wochenschr.*, Vol. 17 No. 44, p. 1184.

Ostow, Mortimer (1962), *Drugs in Psychoanalysis and Psychotherapy.* New York: Basic Books.

Parr, Albert Eide (1926), *Adaptiogenese und Philogenese. Abhandlungen zur Theorie der organischen Entwicklung*, 1. Berlin: Springer.

Peters, H. F. (1962), *My Sister, My Spouse. A Biography of Lou Andreas-Salomé*. New York: Norton.

Pfeiffer, Ernst (1965), "Die Historie von der Lou." *Neue Deutsche Hefte*, ed. Joachim Günther. No. 105, May–June, pp. 111–119.

—— ed. (1966), *Sigmund Freud—Lou Andreas-Salomé Briefwechsel*. Frankfurt/Main: S. Fischer Verlag.

—— (1969), "Lou Andreas-Salomé," In: *Handbuch der deutschen Gegenwartsliteratur*, ed. Hermann Kunisch. München: Nymphenburger Verlagsbuchhandlung, 2nd ed., pp. 53–55.

—— ed. (1970), *Friedrich Nietzsche, Paul Rée, Lou von Salomé. Die Dokumente ihrer Begegnung*. Frankfurt/Main: Insel Verlag.

Pfennig, R. (1906), *Wilhelm Fliess und seine Nachentdecker: O. Weininger und H. Swoboda*. Berlin: Goldschmidt.

Pilcz, Alexander (1919), *Lehrbuch der speciellen Psychiatrie für Studierende und Ärzte* (4th ed.). Leipzig & Wien: Franz Deuticke.

Politzer, Heinz (1968), *Der Turm und das Tier aus dem Abgrund*. Grillparzer-Forum Forchtenstein. Vorträge, Forschungen, Berichte. Heidelberg: Lothar Stiehm Verlag, 1969, pp. 24–42.

—— (1969), Review of Walter Schönau's *Sigmund Freuds Prosa*. *German Quart.*, 42:729–741.

Popper-Lynkeus, Josef (1899), *Phantasien eines Realisten*, Dresden: Carl Reissner, 1922.

Probst, Ferdinand (1904), "Der Fall Otto Weininger." In: *Grenzfragen des Nerven-und Seelenlebens*, 31:

Putnam, James Jackson (1912a), "Über die Bedeutung philosophischen Anschauungen und Ausbildung für die weitere Entwicklung der psychoanalytischen Bewegung." *Imago*, 1:101–118.

—— (1912b), "Antwort auf die Erwiderung des Herrn Dr. Ferenczi." *Imago*, 1:527–530.

Raimann, Emil (1904), *Die hysterischen Geistesstörungen*. Eine klinische Studie. Leipzig/Vienna: Franz Deuticke.

—— (1924), *Zur Psychoanalyse*. Berlin/Vienna: Urban & Schwarzenberg.

Rangell, Leo (1963), In: "Panel on the significance of intrapsychic conflict, rep. John C. Nemiah." *J. Amer. Psychoanal. Assn.*, 11:619–627.

Rank, Otto (1907), *Der Künstler. Ansätze zu einer Sexual-psychologie*. Vienna: Heller.

—— (1911) "Ein Beitrag zum Narzissismus." *Jahrb. f. Psychoan. Forsch.*, 3:401–426.

—— (1912), "Übersicht der bisherigen Leistungen der auf die Geisteswissenschaften angewandten Psychoanalyse." *Imago*, 1:91–99.

Reich, Ilse Ollendorf (1969), *Wilhelm Reich: A Personal Biography*. New York: Saint Martin's Press.

Ritvo, Lucille B. (1970), *Brother Animal: The Story of Freud and Tausk,* by Paul Roazen. *J. History Med.,* 25:366–368.

Roazen, Paul (1969), *Brother Animal: The Story of Freud and Tausk.* New York: Alfred A. Knopf.

Rycroft, Charles (1970), "Freudian Triangles." *The Observer,* April 26.

Sabshin, Melvin (1970), Review of *Brother Animal. The Story of Freud and Tausk,* by Paul Roazen. *Psychoanal. Quart.* 39:631–633.

Sach, Hanns (1912), "Über Naturgefühl." *Imago,* 1:119–131.

────── (1944), *Freud, Master and Friend.* Cambridge, Mass.: Harvard University Press.

Sadger, J. Isidor (1910a), "Ein Fall von multipler Perversion mit hysterischen Absenzen." *Jahrbuch psychoanal. & psychopathol. Forsch.,* 2:59–133.

────── (1910b). "Über Urethralerotik." *Jahrbuch psychoanal. & psychopathol. Forsch.,* 2:409–450.

────── (1913), "Über Gesasserotik." *Internat. Zeitschr. Psychoanal.,* 1:351–358.

Sarton, George (1957), *Six Wings: Men of Science in the Renaissance.* Bloomington: Indiana University Press.

Schelkopf, Anton (1969), "Aspekte der Psychoanalyse. Fritz Riemann— Versuch einer Biographie." In: *Aspekte der Psychoanalyse,* ed. Anton Schelkopf & Siegfried Elhardt. Göttingen: Verlag für medizinische Psychologie im Verlag Vanderhoeck and Ruprecht, pp. 171–211.

Schilder, Paul (1924), *Selbstbewusstsein und Persönlichkeitsbewusstsein.* Berlin: Springer.

Schönau, Walter (1968), *Sigmund Freuds Prosa. Literarische Elemente seines Stils.* Stuttgart: J. B. Metzlersche Verlagsbuchhandlung.

Schreber, Daniel Paul (1903), *Denkwürdigkeiten eines Nervenkranken.* Leipzig: Oswald Mutze.

Schrötter, Karl (1912), "Experimentelle Träume." *Zentralbl. Psychoanal. & Psychother.,* 2:638–646.

Schur, Max (1966a), "Some additional Day Residues of The Specimen Dream of Psychoanalysis." In: *Psychoanalysis—a General Psychology.* Essays in Honor of Heinz Hartmann, ed. Rudolph M. Loewenstein; Lottie M. Newman; Max Schur, and Albert J. Solnit. New York: International Universities Press, pp. 45–85.

────── (1966b), *The Id and the Regulatory Principles of Mental Functioning.* Journal of the Amer. Psychoanalytic Assn. Monograph Series Number Four. New York: International Universities Press.

────── (1971), *Freud Living and Dying.* New York: International Universities Press (in print).

Searles, Harold F. (1958), "Positive feelings in the relationship between the schizophrenic and his mother." In: *Collected Papers on Schizophrenia and Related Subjects.* New York: International Universities Press, 1965, pp. 216–253.

────── (1963), "The place of neutral therapeutic responses in psycho-

phrenia and Related Subjects. New York: International Universities Press, 1965, pp. 626–653.

Shengold, Leonard London (1971), "Freud and Joseph." In: *The Unconscious Today,* ed. Mark Kanzer. New York: International Universities Press (in print).

Sherwood, S. (1962), Review of *Sigmund Freuds akademische Laufbahn im lichte der Dokumente* by Josef and Renée Gicklhorn. *Dis. Nerv. Syst.,* 23:235–237.

Simmel, Ernst (1918), *Kriegsneurosen und "Psychisches Trauma." Ihre gegenseitigen Beziehungen, dargestellt auf Grund psychoanalytischer, hypnotischer Studien.* Leipzig Munich: Otto Nemnich.

Simon, Ernst (1957), "Freud, the Jew." *Yearbook II of the Leo Baeck Institute of Jews from Germany,* London: East & West Library pp. 270–305.

Sperber, Manès (1970), *Alfred Adler oder Das Elend der Psychologie.* Vienna: Molden.

Spielrein, Sabine (1912a), "Über Transformation." *Zentralbl. Psychoanal. Psychother.,* 2:478.

———— (1912b), "Die Destruktion als Ursache des Werdens." *Jahrb. psychoanal. psychopath. Forsch.,* 4:465–503.

Stärcke, August (1919), "The reversal of the libido-sign in delusions of persecution." *Internat. J. of Psycho-Anal.,* 1:231–234.

Stekel, Wilhelm (1908), *Conditions of Nervous Anxiety and Their Treatment.* New York: Liveright, 1952.

———— (1911a), *Die Sprache des Traumes.* Munich/Wiesbaden: Bergmann. (First part translated: *Sex and Dreams, the Language of Dreams.* Boston: Badger, 1922).

———— (1911b), "Die Verpflichtung des Namens." *Zeitschr. Psychother. & med. Psychol.,* 3:110–114.

———— (1914), "Die Verpflichtung des Namens." *Zentralbl. Psychoanal. & Psychother.,* 4:419.

———— (1920), "In memoriam (Otto Gross)." *Psyche & Eros,* 1:49.

———— (1950), *The Autobiography of Wilhelm Stekel,* ed. Emil A. Gutheil. New York: Liveright.

Sterba, Editha & Sterba, Richard (1954), *Beethoven and His Nephew.* New York: Pantheon.

Sterba, Richard (1940), "Aggression in the rescue fantasy." *Psychoanal. Quart.,* 9:505–508.

———— (1941), "The abuse of interpretation." *Psychiat.,* 4:9–12.

Storr, Anthony (1970), "Freudian Slips." London: *Sunday Times Review,* April 26.

Strachey, James (1955), Editor's introduction (Breuer and Freud, 1893–1895). *Standard Edition,* 2: ix–xxx. London: Hogarth Press, 1955.

———— (1957), Editor's note (Freud, 1917a). *Standard Edition,* 14:239–242. London: Hogarth Press.

——— (1959), Editor's introduction (Freud, 1926). *Standard Edition*, 20:77–86. London: Hogarth Press.

Stricker, Solomon (1894), Über das medicinische Unterrichtswesen." *Wiener klin. Wochenschr.*, 7:86–88, 105–108, 143–145, 161–163, 198–200.

Swoboda, Hermann (1904), *Die Periode des menschlichen Organismus in ihrer psychologischen und biologischen Bedeutung*. Leipzig/Vienna: Deuticke.

——— (1906), *Die gemeinnützige Forschung und der eigennützige Forscher*. Vienna/Leipzig: Braunmüller.

Taft, Jessie (1958), *Otto Rank*. New York: Julian Press.

Tausk, Viktor (1912), "On masturbation." *The Psychoanalytic Study of the Child*, 6:61–79, 1951. New York: International Universities Press.

——— (1913a), "Compensation as a means of discounting the motive of repression." *Internat. J. Psycho-Anal.*, 1924, 5:130–140.

——— (1913b), "Zur Psychologie der Kindersexualität." *Internat. Zeitschr. ärztl. Psychoanal.*, 1:444–458.

——— (1914a), "Ein Zahlentraum." *Internat. Zeitschr. ärztl. Psychoanal.*, 2:39–41.

——— (1914b), Review of: *Psychoanalyse der Philosophie und psychoanalytische Philosophie*. *Jahrb. Psychoanal. N. F.*, 6:405–412.

——— (1915), "On the psychology of the alcoholic occupational delirium." *Psychoanal. Quart.*, 38:406–431, 1969.

——— (1916a), "On the psychology of deserters." *Psychoanal. Quart.*, 38:354–381, 1969.

——— (1916b). "Diagnostic considerations concerning the symptomatology of the so-called war psychoses." *Psychoanal. Quart.*, 38:382–405, 1969.

——— (1916c), "Bemerkungen zu Abrahams Aufsatz Über Ejaculatio praecox." *Internat. Zeitschr. ärztl. Psychoanal.*, 4:315–327.

——— (1917), "Zur Psychopathologie des Alltagsleben." *Internat. Zeitschr. ärztl. Psychoanal.*, 4:156–158.

——— (1919), "On the origin of the 'influencing machine' in schizophrenia." *Psychoanal. Quart.*, 2:519–556, 1933; *Psychoanal. Reader*, 1948, 1:52–85.

——— (1934), "Ibsen the druggist." *Psychoanal. Quart.*, 3:137–141. Original in *Almanach der Psychoanalyse*, Vienna: *Internationaler Psychoanalytischer Verlag*, 1934, pp. 161–166.

Toch, Josef (1970), "Freud, Kraus and Feuchtwanger." *Jerusalem Post*, July 22.

van den Haag, Ernest (1965), Introduction to *Psychopathia Sexualis* by Dr. Richard von Krafft-Ebing. New York: G. P. Putnam's Sons, pp. 7–19.

van Dovski, Lee (1959), *Genie und Eros*. Frankfurt/Main & Hamburg: Fischer-Bücherei.

van Ophuijsen, J. H. W. (1920), "On the origin of the feeling of persecution." *Internat. J. Psycho-Anal.*, 1:233–239.

Waelder, Robert (1928), "Sigmund Freud: Hemmung, Symptom und Angst; under Referate." In: *Internat. Zeitschr. Psychoanal.*, 14:416–423.

———— (1929), Review of *Hemmung Symptom und Angst*, by Sigmund Freud. *Internat. J. Psycho-Anal.*, 10:103–111.

———— (1951), "The structure of paranoid ideas. A critical survey of various theories." *Internat. J. Psycho-Anal.*, 32:167–177.

———— (1956), "Freud and history of science." *J. Amer. Psychoanal. Assn.*, 4:602–613.

———— (1963), "Historical fiction." *J. Amer. Psychoanal. Assn.*, 11:628–651.

Wagner-Jauregg, Julius (1950), *Lebenserinnerungen*, ed. L. Schönbauer & M. Santoch. Vienna: Springer Verlag.

Weininger, Otto (1903), *Sex and Character*. New York: Putnam, 1908.

———— (1904), *Über die letzten Dinge*. Vienna & Leipzig: Braumüller (3rd ed.), 1912.

———— (1912), *Taschenbuch und Briefe an einem Freund*, ed. Hans Gerber. Leipzig & Vienna: Tal & Co. Verlag.

Weiss, Edoardo (1970), *Sigmund Freud as a Consultant. Recollections of a Pioneer in Psychoanalysis*. New York: Intercontinental Medical Book Corp.

Whitman, Roy M. (1970), Book review of *Brother Animal: The Story of Freud and Tausk*, by Paul Roazen. *Comprehensive Psychiat.* 11:385–386.

Winterstein, Alfred R. F. (1913), "Psychoanalytischen Anmerkungen zur Geschichte der Philosophie." *Imago*, 2:175–237.

Wittels, Fritz. (1923), *Sigmund Freud. His Personality, His Teaching and His School*. New York: Dodd Mead, 1924.

———— (1933), "Revision of a biography." *Psychoanal. Rev.*, 20:361–374.

Zweig, Stefan (1931), *Mental Healers: Franz Anton Mesmer, Mary Baker Eddy, Sigmund Freud*. New York: Viking Press.

NAME INDEX

SUBJECT INDEX

DUE DATE

GL/Rec	DEC 1 0 1994		
	201-6503		Printed in USA